Drawn & Engraved by John Sartain, Phila

THE SCOUT.

U. S. Grant

THE CAMP,

THE

BATTLE FIELD,

AND THE

HOSPITAL;

OR,

LIGHTS AND SHADOWS

OF THE

GREAT REBELLION.

INCLUDING ADVENTURES OF SPIES AND SCOUTS, THRILLING INCIDENTS, DARING EXPLOITS, HEROIC DEEDS, WONDERFUL ESCAPES, SANITARY AND HOSPITAL SCENES, PRISON EXPERIENCES, ETC., ETC.

BY DR. L. P. BROCKETT,

AUTHOR OF "OUR GREAT CAPTAINS," "PHILANTHROPIC RESULTS OF THE WAR," "LIFE OF ABRAHAM LINCOLN," "HISTORY OF THE CIVIL WAR IN THE UNITED STATES," ETC., ETC.

Splendidly Illustrated with over 100 Fine Portraits and Beautiful Engravings.

NATIONAL PUBLISHING COMPANY,

PHILADELPHIA, PA.; BOSTON, MASS.; CINCINNATI, OHIO; CHICAGO, ILL.; ST. LOUIS, MO.; RICHMOND, VA.; AND ATLANTA, GA.

S. A. GEORGE,
STEREOTYPER, ELECTROTYPER AND PRINTER,
124 N. SEVENTH STREET, PHILADELPHIA.

TO

THE SOLDIERS AND SAILORS

OF THE

VOLUNTEER AND REGULAR SERVICE OF THE UNITED STATES,

TO THE NOBLE WOMEN,

WHO, IN THE CAMP, ON THE BATTLEFIELD,

AND IN THE HOSPITAL,

HAVE

MINISTERED TO THE SICK, THE WOUNDED AND THE DYING,

AND

TO THE WIVES, MOTHERS, AND SISTERS,

WHO HAVE

GIVEN UP THEIR HUSBANDS, SONS AND BROTHERS

FREELY TO

PRESERVE THE NATION'S LIFE,

THIS BOOK IS RESPECTFULLY DEDICATED.

PREFACE.

THIS book, friendly reader, was not created; like Topsy, "it growed." The author or compiler, whichever term you may choose to give him, had for four years past been a not uninterested observer of the great struggle, which it had been his duty elsewhere to chronicle. In his researches into the causes and events of the war, its fearful battles, its alternations of light and shadow, its changes of policy, and its final and glorious triumphs, he had had abundant occasion to notice those personal achievements, those noble sacrifices, and that fearless devotion to the national cause which have so greatly distinguished this conflict. In the pages of a history of the war, such narratives and incidents could find no place; yet it seemed unjust to the great souls who had laid every thing upon their country's altar, without a murmur or a sigh, that their glorious sacrifices should not be held in grateful remembrance; and it was from the desire to do some justice to their memory, that at an early day the writer commenced, at first for his own private reading merely, the collection of narratives and incidents of personal adventure and sacrifice in the war. Some of these were found in print, in books, periodicals, and newspapers; others were preserved in the annals or reports of charitable institutions, like the Sanitary and Christian Commissions; a few had found record from a poet's pen, and a considerable number, though matters of oral tradition, had never appeared in print but were gleaned from the narrations of the parties themselves, or their friends. The garnering of these was a work of great delight to the writer, and as time passed on he felt desirous that others should share the pleasure he had enjoyed, in the perusal of the heroic deeds of his countrymen and country-women; and so the book grew into such form and symmetry as it now possesses. In the hands of the American public he leaves it, with the conviction that they will be lenient to any faults they may observe in it, and will appreciate his honest and pains-taking endeavor to present to them a record of some of the personal adventures and incidents of the war.

J. P B.

Brooklyn, N. Y., May, 1866.

THIS work will be beautifully illustrated with groups of the following Naval and Military Heroes, distinguished civilians, prominent Rebel Generals; and will contain an elegant full-page steel portrait of Lieutenant-General Grant, besides numerous fine engravings of battle-scenes, etc.

LIST OF ILLUSTRATIONS.

PORTRAITS.

BATTLE SCENES, ETC.

CONTENTS.

PART I.

NARRATIVES OF SPIES, SCOUTS, AND DETECTIVES.

PART II.

DARING ENTERPRISES OF OFFICERS AND MEN.

PART III.

INCIDENTS OF ARMY LIFE IN CAMP, FIELD, AND HOSPITAL.

PART IV.

DEEDS OF HEROIC COURAGE AND SELF-SACRIFICE.

PART I.

NARRATIVES OF SPIES, SCOUTS, AND DETECTIVES.

MOORE AND BLUE,

THE KANSAS SCOUTS.

THE border ruffian warfare, which had been waged for several years in Kansas and Western Missouri, before the rebellion, was admirably calculated to train up numbers of daring, adventurous spirits, to whom life would be altogether too tame, unless there were dangers to face, foes to outwit, and hazards to run. Among these, few have led lives of more extraordinary danger and lawless adventure, and at the same time made interesting by a more firm and enduring friendship, than the two young scouts whose history we sketch from the annals of the Army of the Cumberland.

In 1856, two young men—Frank M. Blue, formerly of Michigan, but now from Illinois, and Henry W. Moore, of Brooklyn, N. Y., met in Leavenworth City, Kansas, whither they had come for the purpose of preempting land in that territory. Taking a fancy for each other, they set out for the interior in company. At Ossawatamie they met John Brown, joined him in scouting after border ruffians, and participated in the fight at Hickory Point, where Brown, his son, and twenty-seven men, routed forty of them strongly posted in a blacksmith's shop, by backing up against it a load of hay, and burning them out. Leaving Brown, they next went to Jennison's camp at Mound City, which was made in such a shape as to resemble a group of hay-stacks. While here, they, in company with eight others, crossed the Missouri river, surprised the town of Rushville, capturing thirty border ruffians and a number of the citizens, broke their guns, and carried away their horses, money, watches, etc. Afterward they joined the Utah Expedition, under General A. S. Johnston, and with it went through to Salt Lake City. Leaving there on their own responsibility, the fame of the Mexican silver mines attracted them to Peubla, where they remained four months, in company with a mixed crowd of miners, Indians, and Mexican peons. Having accumulated a considerable amount of silver, the spirit of adventure led them to Santa Fe, where, some of the party getting themselves into a difficulty, a hasty flight northward became necessary. Procuring a Mexican boro (jackass), and loading him with a few crackers and their personal effects, they set out for Fort Union, one hundred miles distant. Here they procured a mule, and crossed over to Bent's Fort, where they joined the Kiowa Expedition, under Major Sedgwick. Returning from this, they proceeded to Camp Floyd, and thence across Kiowa Pass to Pike's Peak, where they "jumped" a claim, and went to mining. Here they spent the summer, and in the fall hired to Joe Doyle, a Mexican trader and ranchero, to go down the Waifoma river and oversee his peons and take charge of his herds. Remaining all winter on his ranch, they went again next spring to Leavenworth, and hired as riders to the California Overland Express Company, in which business they remained until the outbreak of the rebellion.

With the prospect of active service, they could not stand idly by and see others engaged, and accordingly recruited ten men, with whom they joined Captain William Cleaveland's independent company for the defence of the Kansas border. Their first exploit was a dash into De Kalb, Missouri, where they captured twelve or fourteen prisoners and forty horses and mules. A large party, however, pursued them, overtook and captured them at Atkinson's ferry, carried them to St. Joseph, and lodged them in jail. The good people of St. Joseph were very anxious to have them tried and sent to the penitentiary at once; but there was no court in session, and the only recourse was to lock them up in the jail, where they did not remain long. The guard was made drunk with drugged whiskey, the negro cook was bribed with a twenty dollar gold piece to steal the keys from the jailer, the door was unlocked at midnight, and the whole party walked out just ten days after they had been incarcerated. One John Seelover, a friend, had a skiff near at hand to cross them over the river, and a conveyance on the other side to take them to Atchison the same night. The next night, nothing daunted by their recent jail experience, the same party crossed in a flat boat to Missouri, captured from the rebel farmers horses enough to mount themselves, and returned again, after giving the people thereabouts a good scare. The evening following, a negro came to their headquarters at Pardee, eight miles from Atchison, and said that his rebel master, John Wells by name, and living twelve miles south of St. Joseph, was to leave the next morning for Price's army with two wagon loads of goods and a coffin full of arms. The company started over immediately, the negro acting as guide. The rebel was found, and so were the goods, consisting of bacon, flour, sugar, coffee, tobacco, whiskey, powder, and lead, but no arms. Demand was made for the latter, but the prisoner denied having any. A lariat was then thrown over his neck, and drawn tight for a few minutes, when he disclosed their place of concealment—a newly-made grave, with head and footboard—in which were found twenty stands of arms of all kinds, and a box of pistols, all of which were taken to Fort Leavenworth, and turned over to the United States Government.

Many other expeditions were made, until Cleaveland and his band were known and feared all over that country. On one of these, it was ascertained that Major Hart, of Price's army, was at his home, fifteen miles from Weston, with ten men. The company immediately set forth to capture them, a woman—Mrs. Chandler—acting as guide. The Major, his men, and the stock on his farm were taken and carried to Geary City, Kansas, where the stock was just put away and twelve men left as a guard over the prisoners, when forty Missourians rode up and demanded their surrender. Chandler, who stood in the porch, said they would never surrender—when he was shot dead, eleven bullets being found in his body. His wife and the remainder fired from the house, and picked them off so fast, that they were compelled to retire to Fort Leavenworth, eight miles distant, whence they brought up a company of the

First Missouri Cavalry, under Captain Fuller, to their assistance, and finally succeeded in capturing the little garrison. They were taken to the fort, and, no one appearing against them, were speedily released by Major Prince, of the U. S. Regulars, commanding the post. Not long after this, Moore, Blue, William Tuff, of Baltimore, and Cleaveland, dashed into Kansas City, and levied a contribution of some thirty-three hundred dollars in coin upon two secession bankers who had rebel flags flying at their windows. They were pursued, but made their escape, divided the money equally, and all four went to Chicago to spend it, which they did most liberally; and in June, 1861, returned to Leavenworth.

Here Moore and Blue, who had become fast friends, separated; the latter going into Missouri on several jay-hawking expeditions, and the former acting as guide to General Sturgis, and participating in the battles of Dug Spring and Wilson Creek. Moore relates many interesting adventures which befell him while thus engaged, of which, one is here given as an illustration of his shrewdness and foresight. Having been sent by General Lyon to ascertain about certain guerillas that were lurking about the country, he dressed himself in butternut uniform, and set out. Thinking, however, that he might be captured on the trip, he determined to avail himself of a trick he had somewhere read of; which was, to take a large minie ball, cut the top off, hollow it out, and then take the other part and make of it a screw to fit on again, thus forming a kind of little box. He then took a piece of parchment paper, and writing on it, in a peculiar hand, a commission in the secret service of the Confederate army, and signing to it the name of General

Price, enclosed it in the bullet, screwed it up, and started on again. He had gone but a little way when, sure enough, he fell into the hands of Sy Gordon's guerilla band, who proposed hanging him at once. Gordon told him he had orders to hang all such suspicious characters as he was, and that he should do it. Moore replied that he had very little to say, but he wished he would do him the favor to take that bullet to General Price after he had hung him. Gordon seemed much amused at so trifling a request, and said to his prisoner that he must be either crazy or a fool. When informed that there was more about the bullet than he had any idea of, he insisted that he should be shown what it was; but Moore refused, saying that he was sworn to say nothing about it. Gordon was nonplussed for a while, but, examining the bullet very closely, soon saw the trick, unscrewed the top, and took out and read the contents. Turning to Moore, he told him he was "all right," and furnished him with a better horse than he then had, on which he at once started back. On arriving at camp, he related his adventure, whereupon a body of cavalry was sent out in pursuit, and the next day succeeded in capturing a number of the band.

Late in the fall, Moore and Blue again met in Leavenworth, and both went toward Springfield as guides and spies for Lane and Sturgis's commands. On Christmas day, both were sent by General Steele into Price's camp, whither they went, and returned on January 3d, 1862. Four miles from Warsaw, they found Christmas was being celebrated by a ball, at which many rebel officers were present. In company with some rebel teamsters, they devised a plan to scare these officers off, and secure to themselves the field and the girls, by rushing up to the house and shouting, at the top of their voices, "The Feds are coming! the Feds are coming!" The plan worked admirably: the officers rushed away in hot haste—one even falling into the well—and our plotters were left in full possession of the premises. Coming back to Sedalia, they were engaged by Colonel Weir as guides. Going ahead one day to select a camping ground, they came to a house where was a man very hospitably inclined, asking them to stop, put up their horses and feed them with corn, of which he had plenty. Representing that they had been pressed into the service, but were in heart with the rebels, their entertainer grew confidential, and told them something about himself—that he acted as a spy, carried despatches wrapped in a cigar, etc. The information thus obtained from him, contributed to the capture, by General Pope, at Blackwater, of thirteen hundred rebels, with all their equipments. They accompanied General Pope on his expedition to Warrensburg, where he captured Colonel Parke's rebel force; and then returned to Kansas, where they jayhawked for a month or two. Going again to Missouri, they learned that Quantrell's guerilla band was in the vicinity of Independence. With eleven comrades, they went there, captured the town, quartered themselves in the court house, and badly frightened the people, who thought, of course, that they were only the advance-guard of a larger body behind. Quantrell soon came into the place with forty-five men, and demanded their surrender. This was refused, and a skirmish commenced, the occupants of the court house firing out of the doors and windows, and finally succeeded in dispersing the besiegers, who went off for reinforcements. The thirteen now thought it best to retire, which they did, skirmishing for one and a half miles to a stone fence, when the guerillas mounted. The jayhawkers now ensconced themselves behind the fence. Holding their position until dusk, they then scattered, having killed five and wounded seven of the guerillas. Pursuit was made by the latter; but the darkness enabled them to escape, and they soon put an effectual end to it by cutting the telegraph wire, and stretching it across the road from fence to fence.

The twain now joined Generals Curtis and Sigel as couriers, and made several dangerous trips between the army and Rolla, carrying despatches each way, on one of which Blue was taken prisoner and held as such for six weeks. Both accompanied General Curtis in his terrible march through Arkansas to Helena, and met with many stirring adventures by the way. One day while they were riding in company with Newton Blue, a brother of Frank and also a scout, they came suddenly upon five rebels in a lane, with whom they stopped and talked for some time, representing themselves as Southern men. The rebels soon heard a bugle behind them, however, and, suspecting all was not right, made a charge upon our scouts, who killed three of them and captured their horses, the remaining two falling into the hands of the Federal advance. At Helena they engaged in buying cotton for the speculators, and in one of their excursions were captured by the guerillas. Pretending to be rebels, they joined a portion of Jeff Thompson's gang, and, remaining with them eleven days, obtained much information concerning him. Having had enough of

HANCOCK
BALDY SMITH
WRIGHT
MEADE
HEINTZLEMAN
SICKLES
WARREN
VAN INGEN-SNYDER

guerilla life, they planned an escape, in this wise. An old negro, of whom they knew, was just going into Helena with a load of cotton for sale. By him they sent word to General Steele of an arrangement which had been made to rob him on his return of the proceeds of the cotton. The message was carried and delivered faithfully, and on his way back the negro was robbed, as proposed, of his eleven hundred dollars in greenbacks, which were found hidden away in his boots; but just as the thirty-one guerillas were dividing the spoils, the second battalion of the first Missouri Cavalry came up and captured the whole party, all of whom were subsequently sent to St. Louis as prisoners.

From Helena Moore and Blue next went to Columbia, and then to Corinth, where they detected and arrested two counterfeiters, making a great haul of counterfeit St. Louis city treasury warrants and gold dollars, both of which were well executed. Accompanying Colonel Truesdail's police force to Louisville, they there played the rebel, and hunted out Palmer and Estes, who burned the ammunition steamers at Columbus and were afterward sent to Camp Chase. With our army they came on to Nashville, and afterward ran as mail messengers—a very dangerous service. Getting on the track of a band of guerillas between Bowling Green and Nashville, they piloted a cavalry force to the neighborhood, and captured a considerable number, who were brought to Nashville and were properly dealt with. They next made a successful spy trip to Murfreesboro, going by way of Lavergne and crossing at Sanders' Ferry. Dr. Goodwin, of the rebel army, whom they had fallen in with on the way, vouched for them, and they passed the pickets into the town readily enough. Once in, they made the circuit of the town and camps, obtaining all the information they could, and then began to think of getting back. It was arranged that Moore should go to Chattanooga for further observation, while Blue would return to Nashville and report what they had already seen and heard. With this understanding, both went at once to the provost-marshal's office for passes. At that time Captain Williams was provost-marshal, whom they found somewhat crabbed and chary of words. Making known their wants, they were saluted in this manner:—

"Want a pass to Chattanooga, do you? Lots of people in that fix. What d'ye want to go there for?"

"We want to join Jack Jones's cavalry company," replied Moore, at a venture, who had heard of such a company.

"If that's all you want, you needn't go to Chattanooga for it. Jones and his company are here now."

This was a new and not pleasing phase of affairs; and, to add to their difficulty, Captain Brenton called Jones in at once, and told him here were two men who wished to join his company, and he'd better have them sworn in right away. Fairly caught in their own trap, there was no escape, and, trusting the future to good luck, they yielded to their fate, and were sworn in. Three days afterward, they with three others were detailed to duty on the second picket line, and determined to take advantage of this opportunity and make their escape. Some distance from their station was a house where whiskey could be obtained at exorbitant prices; and Moore and Blue proposed to their companions that if they would go and get the whiskey they would pay for it, and guard the post during their absence. This was agreed to; and the whiskey seekers were hardly out of sight when our two scouts rode off in hot haste to the outer pickets, two guards being on duty in the road, the remainder of the pickets being near by at their fire, and their horses tied close at hand. They were accosted by the guard with the usual—

"Halt! who comes there?"

"Friends, with the countersign!" was the answer.

"Dismount; advance, one, and give the countersign," was now the order.

Our scouts had foreseen this, and planned accordingly. Hence, they rode up briskly to the pickets; and while they pulled and tugged upon the bridle reins to hold in their fiery steeds, the spurs upon their heels were doing equally good service in urging the animals forward, and they could not be stopped until abreast of the pickets and nearly touching their opposing muskets. Moore then leaned forward, without dismounting, as if to give the password, and suddenly jerked to one side the bayonet and loaded gun of the nearest guard, while with his other hand he shot him dead with his pistol, suddenly drawn from his holster. The ball penetrated the forehead, the guard falling over backward, his mouth wide opened. Blue at the same time drew a pistol and shot the other guard dead in his tracks, and away they flew down the road, and were speedily lost in the darkness and distance. The rest of the rebel pickets did not pursue them, but our scouts could hear them shout after them long and loudly, "Oh, you —— infernal Yankees!" etc., etc. The scouts soon took to the woods, travelling all night in the direction of Nashville, and meeting with no further adventure until soon after sunrise, when one of them espied a moving object in their front, at a considerable distance. A second glance revealed it to be a "butternut," with gun in hand, who at that instant glided behind a tree and took deliberate aim at them. Our scouts, who were also in butternut, were not taken aback. Keeping on at an easy horse walk, and apparently noticing no one, one of them begins to sing, in a brisk, cheery voice, a verse of the "Dixie" song, ending—

"In a Southern land I'll take my stand,
And live and die in Dixie," etc.

As they neared the butternut, he was observed to lower his gun and emerge from behind the tree. When abreast, he accosted the twain:—

"Halloo, boys! which way?"

"All right!—taking a little scout this morning," was the answer.

The "butternut," who was a rebel scout or guerilla, was now near them, unsuspecting, and inclined to be inquisitive and sociable, his gun over his shoulder. But our men were in haste, and had a vivid remembrance of that previous moment when he had drawn a bead on them, in such a cold-blooded manner, from behind the tree. One of them draws his revolver as quick as thought and shoots him dead; and again they ride forward briskly for a while, and eventually reach the Federal lines near Nashville in safety, but through dangers to be feared upon every hand, from behind each tree, or rock, or bush—as they were traversing debatable land, between two great contending armies, and known to be swarming with scouts, spies, and troops, and especially rebel guerillas or "partisan rangers."

Acting as secret policemen and detectives, they now assisted in developing several important cases, a full mention of which would fill many pages of this work. Occasionally they varied their daily routine by acting as guides to cavalry expeditions, in which they rendered efficient service. One of their adventures in Nashville is worth relating.

After the battle of Stone River large numbers of rebel prisoners were sent to the city and allowed their parole, whereupon the wealthy secessionists of the place seized every opportunity to feed, clothe, and encourage them. One day, as Moore and Blue were walking down High street in the dress of Confederate prisoners, they were invited into an elegant residence and were kindly entertained by Miss Hamilton, one of the reigning belles of Nashville. Conversation naturally ensued concerning the relative merits and demerits of the North and South, in the course of which Miss Hamilton said she had done every thing in her power to aid the Southern cause. She had sent letters of encouragement, she said, and also a Southern flag, through the lines. She told them of an old Irishwoman who was in the habit of carrying out goods in a market wagon which had a false bottom. She said, too, that Governor Andy Johnson once had her brought before him and gave her a severe lecturing, but she soon talked him over, and persuaded him into giving her a pass to go two miles out of the city to see her aunt, and that when once beyond the lines she went to the rebel army at Murfreesboro. She further said that a Mrs. Montgomery, who lived two miles out on the Franklin pike, had taken out more goods than anybody else in Nashville. When she went to Murfreesboro she took out with her letters, and had given to Southern soldiers coming into Nashville large quantities of clothing, and finally demonstrated her good will by presenting Moore with a fine pair of pants and other clothing and a pair of new boots. In return for these acts of kindness, Colonel Truesdail sent her the following letter of thanks:—

"OFFICE CHIEF ARMY POLICE, *January* 10, 1863.

"MISS HAMILTON, HIGH STREET:—

"Dear Miss:—Please accept my grateful acknowledgment for your kindness—during the arrival of a large number of Confederate prisoners in the city from the battle of Stone River, and their stay here—in calling into your beautiful residence one of my secret police, and for the kind and benevolent treatment you extended to him. Also for the new suit of clothes and the cavalry boots given him, the valuable information of your labors in the Confederate cause furnished to him, and the knowledge afforded me of your persevering energy as a spy and smuggler. I shall endeavor to profit by it, and may have occasion to send another officer to you.

"Respectfully,

"WILLIAM TRUESDAIL,

"*Chief Army Police.*"

After this they accompanied a cavalry police expedition for the purpose of capturing Captains Young and Scruggs—the leaders of a band of guerillas on White's Creek, who were a terror to the whole country. They were at the house of an old man named McNeil, which was surrounded and a demand made for Young and Scruggs. There being some sixty troops to back the demand, the old man did not dare to deny their presence, and, without deigning any reply, turned at once, went into the house, and bolted the door. This slight barrier was speedily broken down, and the crowd rushed in. Search was made everywhere—down-stairs and up, under beds, in chimneys, and under the floor; but neither Young nor Scruggs was found. As a last resort, they went to the girl's bedroom; and there—in bed between two full-grown young women—the valiant Young was found snugly hidden away. He was unceremoniously dragged out, and Scruggs, in the meanwhile, having been found in a hay-loft, both were taken to Nashville, and thrown into the penitentiary at that place, awaiting their trial.

After their return to Nashville, Moore and Blue were constantly engaged for a number of months in the investigation of numerous minor cases of smuggling and fraud, and succeeded in making Nashville too hot a place for the swarms of rebel emissaries who had so long made it their headquarters.

At the outbreak of the war, in 1861, a Southern merchant wrote to a large firm in New York, requesting a list of the names of those who supported and sympathized with the "movement against the South." The New Yorker replied by sending, through Adams & Co.'s Express, a copy of the "City Directory!"

A NAMELESS SPY.

General Garfield relates, in the annals of the Army of the Cumberland, a thrilling and interesting narrative of a nameless Union spy (nameless, because, at that time to have given his real name, would have brought down upon him and his family the bitter vengeance of the influential rebels of Kentucky and Tennessee), who, as he states, went into and came out from Bragg's army at Murfreesboro three times during the week of battles at Stone river—who even dined at the table of Bragg and of his other generals—who brought us correct information as to the force and position of the rebel army, and of the boasts of its head officers. This spy was the first to assure us positively that Bragg would fight at Stone river, telling us of that general's boast, that "he would whip Rosecrans back to Nashville if it cost ten thousand men." For the four days' service thus rendered by our spy he was paid five thousand dollars by order of our general, and the author saw the money passed to him.

In 1862 there lived in the State of Kentucky a Union man, with his wife and children. He was a friend of the Union, and an anti-slavery man upon principle. After the rebellion broke out, and when the "Southern heart" had become fired, this man, living in a strong pro-slavery region, and surrounded by opulent slaveholders—his own family connections and those of his wife being also wealthy and bitter secessionists—very prudently held his peace, feeling his utter inability to stem the tide of the rebellion in his section. This reticence, together with his known Southern birth and relations, enabled him to pass unsuspected, and almost unobserved, at a time when Breckinridge, Marshall, Preston, and Buckner, and other ardent politicians of Kentucky chose the rebellion as their portion, and endeavored to carry with them the State amidst a blaze of excitement. Thus, without tacit admissions or any direct action upon his part, the gentleman of whom we write was classed by the people of his section as a secessionist.

Circumstances occurred during that year by which this person was brought into contact with a Federal commander in Kentucky, General Nelson. Their meeting and acquaintance was accidental. Mutual Union sentiments begat personal sympathy and friendship. Nelson wished a certain service performed in the rebel territory and he persuaded the citizen to undertake it—which the latter finally did as a matter of duty, we are assured, rather than of gain, for he made no charge for the service after its speedy and successful performance. Soon after, a similar work was necessary; and again was the citizen importuned, and he again consented, but did not consider himself as a professional spy.

During this or a similar trip, and while at Chattanooga, our man heard of the sudden death of General Nelson. He was now at a loss what to do. Finally he determined to return and report his business to Major-General Rosecrans, who had assumed command of the Federal army. Thus resolved, he proceeded to finish his mission. After ascertaining the position of military affairs at Chattanooga, he came to Murfreesboro, where Bragg's army was then collecting. Staying here several days, he was urged by his Southern army friends to act as their spy in Kentucky. The better to conceal his own feelings and position, he consented to do so, and he left General Bragg's headquarters to go to that State by way of Nashville, feigning important business, and from thence to go to his home, passing by and through Rosecrans' army as it lay stretched out between Nashville and Louisville.

The nameless man now makes his way to the Federal headquarters, seeks a private interview with General Rosecrans, and states his case fully as we have just related. Here was something remarkable, surely—a spy in the confidence of the commanders of two great opposing armies! Our general took much pains to satisfy himself of the honesty and soundness of the stranger. He was pleased with the man's candid manner, and his story bore an air of consistency and truth. Yet, he was a Southerner, surrounded by rebellious influences, and enjoyed Bragg's confidence; and what guarantee could be given that he was a Union man at heart? None; and General Rosecrans, in great perplexity, held council with his Chief of Police, and requested the latter to "dig up" the case to its very root. This was done; but in what manner we need not specially state. Satisfied that it would do to trust the spy, to a certain extent at least, he was now sent on his way to perform his mission for Bragg. At all events, that scheming general so supposed when our man's report was made at the rebel headquarters a few days afterward. His information was very acceptable to Bragg; but we strongly question its value to rebeldom, as the spy reported only what he was told by that old fox Colonel Truesdail.

Perhaps the reader will inquire, how can we answer for the report thus made to Bragg? it may have been more true and valuable than we supposed. Well, there is force in the query. We are fallen upon strange times, when honesty, virtue, and patriotism are at heavy discount in rebeldom, and the Indian's idea of the uncertainty of white men is by no means a myth. However, we were then quite confident of the worthlessness of the report of our spy to Bragg, because *he had nothing else* to tell him. For five days did our spy keep himself locked in a private room in the police building at Nashville. His meals were carried to him by a trusty servant. His door was "shadowed" constantly by our best detectives, and so were his steps if he ventured upon the street for a few moments after dark. It was cold and bleak winter weather, and he toasted himself before his comfortable fire, read books and papers, and conferred often with the Chief of Police and his assistant, affording them, strangers as they were to that region of country, a fund of valuable information respecting the rebels of Kentucky and Tennessee. He was a man of fine address and good intellectual attainments. When our man concluded it was about time for his return to Bragg's army, he was politely escorted by our mounted police to a proper point beyond our lines, and by a route where he would see nothing of our forces. The reader will now appreciate the grounds of our confidence, we doubt not, in the worthlessness of at least one of General Braxton Bragg's spy reports.

In due time this nameless gentleman again enters our lines, and is escorted in by our pickets to the general commanding, to whom he reports in person concerning all that is transpiring in Bragg's army at Murfreesboro, and then he resumes his pleasant private quarters at the army police building. How little could the rebel General Zollicoffer have thought, or have imagined as the wildest dream, while building his elegant house in High street, Nashville, that its gorgeous rooms should ever be devoted to such purposes! After a brief stay, another trip was made by our man to Bragg's headquarters, we using the same precautions as previously. In fact, our spy desired and even demanded, such attention at the hands of the Chief of Police. Said he—

"I am a stranger to you all. I can give you no guarantee whatever of my good faith. It is alike due to you and to myself that I be allowed no opportunities for deceiving you."

The report he carried to Bragg on his second trip delighted the latter. His officers talked with our man freely, and after staying at Murfreesboro two or three days, and riding and walking all about in the most innocent and unconcerned manner, he was again sent back to Nashville to "fool that slow Dutchman, Rosecrans," as one of the rebel officers remarked. Of the importance of the report now brought to the "slow Dutchman" we need not state further than that it contributed its due weight to a decision fraught with tremendous consequences to the army and to the country. Marching orders were soon after issued for the advance of the Army of the Cumberland upon Murfreesboro.

Now commenced a period of excessive labor and peril for the nameless spy. General Rosecrans and Bragg each wanted instant and constant information as the armies approached. The minutiæ of this man's work for four or five days we need not stop to relate: it is easily imagined. Within that time he entered the rebel lines and returned three times. He gave the outline of Bragg's line of battle, a close estimate of his force, an accurate account of his artillery and his earthworks, the movements of the rebel wagon and railroad trains, etc., etc. He was very earnest in assuring Rosecrans that Bragg intended to give severe battle with superior numbers.

This information proved true in all essentials, and its value to the country was inestimable. We had other spies piercing the rebel lines at this time, but they did not enjoy the facilities possessed by the nameless one. Almost with anguish did he exclaim against himself, in the presence of the author, for the severe manner in which he was deceiving the rebel general and involving the lives of his thousands of brave but deluded followers.

After the first great battle the work of such a spy is ended, or, rather, it ceases when the shock of arms comes on. Thenceforth the armies are moved upon the instant, as circumstances may require. Our man, who, during the four days, had been almost incessantly in the saddle, or with his ears and eyes painfully observant while in the camps, took leave of our army upon the battle field, and retired to a place of rest.

One incident occurred, during his last visit to Bragg, which is worthy of mention. That general took alarm in consequence of his report, and at once started a special messenger to General John H. Morgan—who was then absent with his cavalry in Kentucky to destroy Rosecrans' railroad communications (in which Morgan succeeded)—to return instantly with his command by forced marches to Murfreesboro. That same night our man reported this fact to the Federal commander, described the messenger and what route he would take, etc. The information was telegraphed at once to Nashville, Gallatin, and Bowling Green, and a force was sent from each of those posts to intercept the messenger. They failed to apprehend him—which, however, proved of no consequence, as the battles of Stone River were fought, and Bragg was on his retreat from Murfreesboro by the time Morgan could have received the orders.

Our spy was a brave man: yet, during the last three days of his service he was most sensible of its peril. To pass between hostile lines in the lone hours of the night—for he did not wait for daylight—to be halted by guerillas and scouts and pickets, with guns aimed at him, and, finally, to meet and satisfy the anxious, keen eyed, heart searching rebel officers as well as our own, was a mental as well as physical demand that could not long be sustained. While proceeding upon his last expedition, the author met the nameless one upon a by-road. We halted our horses, drew near, and conversed a few seconds in private, while our attendants and companions moved on. He was greatly exhausted and soiled in appearance—his clothing having been rained upon and splashed by muddy water, caused by hard riding, and which had dried upon him. He said he was about to try it once more, and, though he had been so often and so successfully, yet he feared detection and its sure result, the bullet or the halter. He had been unable, amid the hurry and excitement, to make some final disposition of his affairs. He gave us a last message to send to his wife and children in case it became necessary; and he also desired a promise—most freely given

—that we would attend to the settlement of his account with General Rosecrans for services recently rendered. Thus concluding, he wrung our hand most earnestly, and, putting spurs to his fresh and spirited animal, dashed off upon his mission. Twenty hours afterward we were relieved of our anxious forebodings by his safe and successful return. We have stated the price paid him for his labors: it was well earned, and to our cause was a most profitable investment.

THE PRAYER OF THE WICKED.—During the month of December last, and for many weeks previous, a severe drought prevailed in Tennessee. The Cumberland river was fordable in many places, the smaller streams nearly dry, and in sundry localities water for stock very scarce. During its continuance, a Union man at Shelbyville, while in attendance upon the Methodist church at that place, heard a prayer offered from the pulpit by the officiating minister, in which occured a sentence somewhat as follows:—

"O Lord, as a nation free and independent, look down upon us in mercy and loving-kindness, and hold us within the hollow of thy hand amidst all our desolation and sorrow. Let the rays of heaven's light smile upon our fields, and the dews of beneficent mercy be shed upon our valleys. Let the rain descend to beautify and fructify the earth and to swell the rivers of waters; but, O Lord, do not raise the Cumberland sufficient to bring upon us the damnable Yankee gunboats!"

CORPORAL PIKE, SCOUT AND RANGER.

WHETHER we consider the length of time during which he was employed, or the variety and hazardous character of the service in which he was engaged, we think no one of the scouts and spies employed by the commanders of the Union armies has ever passed through a greater number of startling and perilous adventures than Corporal James Pike, of the Fourth Ohio Cavalry. He has published a narrative of his services, which is replete with interest. We cannot follow him in any except the most remarkable of these, for want of space. A native of Leesburg, Ohio, and a printer by profession, he possessed in a large degree that love of adventure which is so often a characteristic of Western men. He gives us no clue to his age; but he must have been not more than five or six and twenty years old, when, in the winter of 1858–9, he had come to the determination, after working at his trade for some time at Jefferson City, to migrate to Kansas, where the border ruffian war was then raging, in search of adventures. Having been turned aside from this intention by the solicitation of a Texan adventurer, he went to Texas; and very soon joined a company of Rangers, and for nearly two years was engaged in warfare with the Camanches and other of the savage Indian tribes in Northern Texas. After numerous hair-breadth escapes, and terrible suffering in the ill advised expedition against the Camanche Indians, prosecuted under Colonel Johnston, he returned to Waco, Texas, and found the community there, as elsewhere, all alive with excitement in regard to Mr. Lincoln's election. Avowing himself a Union man, he was soon obliged to fly; though not until he had recorded himself as against the iniquitous ordinance of Secession. Great numbers of Union men were murdered at this time in Texas, simply for the avowal of Union sentiments; and Pike, desirous of doing his country some service against the bloodthirsty secessionists, escaped from the State into Arkansas; and when he fell in with rebels, represented himself as the nephew of Albert Pike, a rebel general then in the western part of the Indian Territory. More than once he found himself in situations from whence escape seemed impossible; but his ready wit, before long, enabled him to find some way of evading the picket lines of the enemy: and passing through Memphis and Nashville—meeting his father at the latter place—he made his way to Portsmouth, Ohio, by midsummer of 1861; and soon after enlisted, first in Fremont's body-guard, and subsequently in the Fourth Ohio Cavalry. After spending two months in acquiring a knowledge of cavalry drill, Corporal Pike and the rest of his company were mustered into the U. S. service at Camp Dennison, on the 20th of November, 1861; and early in the spring moved to Louisville, where they were assigned to General O. M. Mitchel's division, and soon marched toward Bowling Green. General Mitchel was too shrewd a judge of character not to discern quickly Pike's qualifications for the secret service; and before he had been under him a week, he sent him, with some twenty comrades, on a scout toward Green River, Ky. On his return, he found General Mitchel's division before Bowling Green, and with another soldier, crossed the Big Barren river on a raft, with a coil of rope, to facilitate the construction of a pontoon bridge. The army being safely in Bowling Green, Corporal Pike explored the adjacent region, and arrested the guerillas, who, in the guise of Union soldiers, were plundering, burning, and destroying private and public property. In one of these expeditions, he was told of two of these marauders named Robinson and Keaton, about sixteen miles distant, who were constantly committing depredations. He started alone to arrest them, but before proceeding far met two men, and soon after a third, whom he knew to be guerillas and secessionists; but whom he addressed as law-abiding citizens, telling them whom he was going to arrest, and insisted upon their coming with him and giving him assistance. They at first endeavored to excuse themselves, but as they were personally hostile to Robinson and Keaton, they finally consented to go with him, and he arrested the culprits, while they guarded and took charge of them. The Union people of the vicinity, not aware of the real character of Robinson and Keaton, and believing that this was a movement of the secessionists, followed in some force to Bowling Green, to demand their release; but by hard riding Pike reached there first, and delivered up, not only the two marauders, but the three guerillas he had compelled to aid him in capturing them; and when the Union party, who had come on to demand their release, arrived at the provost-marshal's, it was found that there were three more bushwhackers in their ranks, who were also arrested and sent to jail.

General Mitchel next sent him to ascertain the location and strength of Morgan's band, then just beginning to make some disturbance in Middle Tennessee. He succeeded in having an interview with Morgan, passing himself off as a Texan ranger; ascertained the strength of his command, and after narrowly escaping capture two or three times, succeeded in reaching the Union lines near Nashville.

General Mitchell, who was one of the most active and energetic of commanders, now determined to explore the roads and bridges leading to Shelbyville, preparatory to a movement upon that town, and sent Corporal Pike to perform that service—one of great difficulty and danger, inasmuch as it was remote from the Union lines, and all the roads were picketed by the Texan Rangers and Morgan's battalion. But danger only added new zest to any enterprise, and he undertook it cheerfully. His encounters on this expedition were many and startling, but when meeting the rebels in considerable numbers, he passed himself off as Captain Bonham, of the First Louisiana Cavalry, just escaped from the Union lines; and told his story so plausibly that it met with perfect credence. If there were but one or two, he trusted to his pistols and the speed of his good horse; and on one occasion, meeting at night a part of Morgan's battalion, the audacious fellow professed to be on picket duty, and demanded the countersign; but finding them ignorant of it, compelled them to file past, and when they were nearly across a rickety bridge in the vicinity, he put spurs to his horse and rode in an opposite direction.

On the 8th of April, 1862, General Mitchell sent Pike to Decatur, Alabama, to get information as to the state of the country, and destroy the railroad bridge at that point if possible. Some of his adventures on this expedition were so characteristic of the shrewdness and audacity of the man that we cannot do better than to give them in his own words.

"Near to the town of Fayetteville, Lincoln county, Tennessee, night overtook me, and I left the road for a short distance and slept in the woods. This was Saturday night, and Sunday morning I rode into town. The citizens were astonished to see a single man, dressed in full Yankee costume—blue jacket, blue blouse, and blue pants—and armed with the well known Yankee accoutrements, venture among them. They gathered about me in a great crowd, and seemed to regard it as the freak of a madman, but on approaching me at the hotel, they found me entirely rational, cool, and of decent deportment, and they at once changed their minds, and took me for one of their own men in disguise. Seeing it was my best plan to encourage this belief, I ordered my breakfast, went to the stable to see my horse fed, and then returned to my room at the hotel. There were about three hundred men gathered on the sidewalk to ascertain what the strange arrival meant, and to hear the news; and they were watching me with eager interest. I felt that I was playing a delicate game, with my neck in a halter. If they had only known my true character, they would but too gladly have hanged me to the nearest tree. They asked me my name, which I told them; next my regiment, and with a swaggering air, I said:

"'The Fourth Ohio Cavalry.'

"'What is your colonel's name?' said one.

"'Colonel John Kennett,' I answered, slowly, and with a dubious look.

"'What is your captain's name?' inquired another.

"'Captain O. P. Robie,' I told him.

"'Where is your command?' asked one who appeared to be a man of consequence.

"'At Shelbyville.'

"'Well,' he continued, 'if your command is there, what are you doing here by yourself?'

"'Why, sir,' I responded, 'if you want to know, I came to demand the surrender of this town.'

"'Well, well,' said the man; 'that is too good. One man to take a town like this,' and they enjoyed the joke hugely.

"They now began to look exceedingly wise; and I heard the whisper pass from mouth to mouth, that I was one of Morgan's men. This declaration I heard again and again, as I passed through the crowd. Soon after, a gentleman stepped up to me and requested to examine my gun, which I handed to him after removing the cap; but I at the same time drew out my pistol, cocked it, and held it in my hand till my piece was returned to me. After a brief survey of the gun, it was delivered over to me with trembling hand, when I restored the cap and put up my pistol.

"At this moment I was called to breakfast, and walked into the dining-room and sat down to the table, keeping an eye on every thing at once. I seated myself beside a man of good appearance, who had on a handsome uniform and the three stars of a rebel colonel. Slinging my carbine across my knees, with the hammer up, ready for instant use, I loosed my pistols, in the scabbard on one side, and a vicious bowie knife on the other, after which I began to appease my appetite on the good things before me, watching the colonel closely. He looked at me three different times, and then rising abruptly from the table, darted out into the crowd, and I saw no more of him. A few minutes after, I heard the people on the sidewalk raise a loud laugh at the expense of some one.

"After eating a meal—the first since I had left camp—I went out into the crowd again, and called for the mayor, saying I wanted him to surrender the town. Again the bystanders raised a laugh, and called for some one to go for the mayor, as he was not present. They then began to joke me about our gunboats, saying the Yankees would never fight unless backed by them. I told them that General Mitchel had dry land gunboats, with steel soles and spring runners, and that he had used them with great effect at Bowling Green. One of the men said:

"'If you're a Yankee, show us a Yankee trick, and we will believe you.'

"'Gentlemen,' said I, 'I will do my best to show you one, before I leave this neck of timber.'

"'Where are you going?' said one.

"'Down the country,' I replied.

"'Look here, now,' one of the fellows pursued, 'you may as well own up and tell us where the captain is.'

"'What captain?' I asked.

"'Why Captain Morgan, to be sure.'

"'Gentlemen,' said I, slowly, 'you have waked up the wrong passenger. I belong to the Fourth Ohio Cavalry;' and again the laugh rung out at my preposterous assertion.

In obedience to directions, my horse was brought out, and it was a favorable time to leave, as they were all in a good humor, and I consequently mounted and took the road to Huntsville at a gallop. Just as I passed the crowd one fellow sung out:

"'Hold on there, you haven't shown us that Yankee trick yet.'

"'There's plenty of time,' said I, turning in my saddle to watch their movements, 'before I leave this section of the country.'

"About five miles from Fayetteville is a very noted highland called Wells' Hill, and on the top of it there is a fork in the road, the left going directly south to Huntsville, and the right to Athens and Decatur. On reaching this road, I was in the act of turning into it, when I looked across on still another road, called the Meridian road, and discovered a train of wagons coming slowly up the hill. I watched it till I saw there was no guard near, and then riding around till I met the first wagon, I caused it to be drawn close along against the fence, and there stopped; then the next two to be drawn close alongside, thus making an effectual barricade against any force which was approaching from that direction. Next I seized the wagon master, who was some distance in the rear of the train, and shoved him and the drivers up into the fence corner, making one of them turn the mules loose from the wagons. The loads were covered with corn blades and other forage, so one could not see them, but the drivers told me that the wagons were loaded with bacon.

"After arranging things to my satisfaction, I produced a bunch of matches, and fired the fodder on the top of each of the wagcr.s, which were of the old-fashioned curved bodies, Conestoga pattern, each of which had on it four thousand pounds of bacon.

"The guns of the party all happened to be in the wagons, and none of them had any side arms, except the wagon master, who had something under his coat that looked like a pistol; and as he wore a belt, it is very probable he had one; and some of the citizens, I know had, for I saw three or four of them; but I was ready to shoot before they could recover from their surprise, so that it would have been foolhardy for them to resist, as I would certainly have killed the first man who made a motion to draw a weapon. I made no attempt to take their side arms, as I did not want to lose my advantage over them for an instant. There were three good guns burned up in the wagons, one a double barrelled shot gun, and two old muskets.

"When the flames shot up, several citizens came to the scene of action, but I thrust them into the fence corner, along with the wagon master and teamsters. As soon as the wagons were so far destroyed that they began to fall down, and I saw that it would be impossible to save any thing of the wreck, I made the drivers mount the mules, and the wagon master his horse, and taking them on the road to Fayetteville, I told them that I was going to count one hundred; and that if, by that time, they were not out of sight, I would shoot the last one of them within range. I then began to count; 'one,' 'two,' 'three,' etc., very deliberately, while they put spurs to their steeds, and in a brief time they were beyond my ken, over the hills, toward Fayetteville, to give the inhabitants an account of my Yankee trick.

"Wheeling my horse I put out once more for Decatur,

but at the same time inquiring my way to Athens, as if I intended to go there. As I passed the burning wagons again, I told the citizens standing around, that if they did not leave instanter, I would shoot the last one of them, and they scattered like blackbirds.

"About ten miles farther down the road, I heard the deep, sonorous tones of a preacher, belaboring a sinful congregation. He was evidently a devout believer in a terrible and endless punishment for the wicked, for he was holding out to his audience the fearful picture of a lost sinner in hell; making a comparison between his condition and that of Dives, who, he asserted, was once in a similar state of sinfulness while on earth, and who eventually brought up in hell, and from whence he expressed a strong desire to visit Abraham in his new abode; adding that the wishes of the unfortunate Dives could not be complied with for some geographical cause —something in the topography of the country—a gulf in the way, I believe. Over this subject he grew eloquent, and had probably got about to his 'thirdly,' and the congregation were almost breathless with attention, when it occurred to me that there might be soldiers in the church, and I had better look after them; otherwise they might give me some trouble. Riding up to the door, I made my horse enter about half way, so that I could see every man in the house. As his feet struck the floor of the church, with a loud, banging sound, the people were astonished to see a soldier, under arms, riding boldly in among them. Turning to the preacher, I inquired if there were any southern soldiers in the house. The clergyman was standing with his hand raised, as he was about to enforce some point he had made, being the very picture of earnest honesty, looking as if he believed every word that he had said. When he saw me, his hand dropped, and he seemed as badly frightened as if the identical devil he had so vividly described had appeared before him. He was almost overpowered with fright, and supporting himself by the rough pulpit, he glanced at the back door, and then faltered out: 'Not now, I believe, sir.' I saw that there had been rebel soldiers there, and that they had escaped in the direction of his glance; I instantly pulled my horse back, and spurred to the corner of the log church, just in time to see four men disappear in the brush across a field which lay back of the building. They were too far off for me to shoot at, and not desiring to disturb the worship further than the strictest military necessity demanded, I rode on, after desiring the clergyman to pray for the President of the United States. The rebel papers had an account of the affair, but they lied when they stated that I tried to make the preacher take a drink of whiskey; for I hadn't a drop to bless myself with.

"Pretty soon I met two soldiers riding leisurely along to church. I halted them, demanded their names, regiments, and companies, and informed them that they were prisoners of war; that I was a federal soldier, but that there was no way for me to dispose of them so far from our lines except one; I was sorry it was so—but I must shoot them. They begged I would spare their lives, and pledged their honor that they would go with me in good faith, if I would not kill them. I pretended to be in a deep study for a few moments, and then told them if they would take the oath of allegiance to the

United States I would let them go; and to this they agreed eagerly.

"Holding up my right hand, and removing my cap, they imitated my example, uncovered their heads, raised their hands, and with a solemn look, that would well become a court room, waited for me to administer 'the oath.' I had joked them far enough, however, and not wishing to be guilty of blasphemy by administering an obligation I had no authority to require of them, I told them that I would rely upon their honor, but they must do nothing toward pursuing me, or giving information concerning my whereabouts; and I then told them to 'go in peace.'

"The next man I met was an old citizen, riding a very spirited horse, and dressed in a suit of butternut-colored homespun. Tall, thin featured, and gaunt, he was the very picture of a secesh planter. I stopped him, and inquired the way to Camargo; he pointed to the road he had just left, and told me to follow that. I now told him I was a confederate officer, and that I had orders from General Beauregard to gather up all the stragglers I could find, and bring them forthwith to Corinth; that we were expecting a great battle there with our 'detestable foe,' the Yankees, and that it was absolutely necessary for every one to be at his post.

"'You will,' said I, 'do me a favor and your country good service by giving me the names of all soldiers who are at home without leave in your neighborhood.'

"'Certainly, sir,' he replied; 'I will do so with pleasure; and if I had time,' he added, 'I would go with you, and help to find them.'

"I then drew out a note-book, and wrote down each

name he gave me, with the company and regiment of each man, together with his residence; and then asked him to refer me to some responsible citizens, who would give assistance if necessary. He gave me the names of half a dozen, who, he said, would not only assist me, but would give the names of other delinquents.

"He now prepared to ask me a few questions, and preface them with the statement that he was the 'Chief Justice, of Lincoln county, and that he was on his way to Fayetteville to open court on Monday morning.

"'Are there many cases to be disposed of?' I asked.

"'Yes, a good many,' he said.

"'What is their nature generally?' was my next inquiry.

"'Why, they are mostly political,' said he.

"I was at no loss to know what the phrase meant; the accused were Union men, who, true to their principles, had refused to yield to the demands of the secessionists, but chose persecution rather than dishonor. I then concluded to have a little fun out of the old fellow, and render the persecuted loyalists what assistance I could. But as I did not desire to kill him in cold blood, I concluded to frighten him a little by way of punishment. Pointing to the dense column of smoke that was rising from the burning bacon, I said, roughly:

"'Look there, old man.'

"'Why, what in the name of God does that mean?' inquired he, raising his eyes in utter astonishment.

"'Why, sir,' I responded, 'it means that I am a United States soldier, and I have just burned a rebel train up there, and am now about to dispose of the Chief Justice of Lincoln county'—at the same moment raising the hammer of my gun, and drawing a bead on him.

"'Great God! don't kill me, sir,' he piteously pleaded; 'don't kill me.'

"'Look here, old man,' said I, savagely, 'if I let you live, do you think you will trouble Union men in this county again?'

"'O, no, no, I will not.'

"'Won't bring 'em to trial?' I asked.

"'No, indeed, I will not,' he solemnly asserted; 'I have been compelled to enforce the law,' he then began in extenuation, when I interrupted him with,

"'Don't talk to me about enforcing the laws, you old reprobate, or I will kill you in your tracks. Now, see here,' I continued, 'I will give you a chance for your life. This is a level road, and a straight one; now, I will count one hundred and fifty, and if you are not out of sight in that time, I shall kill you, just as sure as God made little apples.'

"I gave the word, and began to count, and he darted off, like an arrow, and was soon lost to my view in a cloud of dust.

"Again taking the Athens road, I pushed on rapidly for some time till I passed several houses, and then, reaching a shallow creek, leading into the woods, I turned down it, so that the place where I left the road could not be found. I traveled up by-ways till near sunset, when I met with an old man, who had just crossed the Athens road, and he told me that he had seen twelve of Young's Tennessee Cavalry and fifteen mounted citizens after a man 'who had been raising a disturbance up the country.' He said that I answered the description exactly, and that he believed I was the man.

"'You had better hide somewhere till after dark,' he advised me; 'for they are alarming the whole country wherever they go.'

"I saw that he was a Union man, so that I told him that if I kept on riding they could better see and hear me, and perhaps it would give them a chance to bushwhack me. I then told him I wanted to find a sequestered spot, where I could leave my horse, and have him taken care of till I could get him again; and he told me of a very good Union man, who lived down in the woods, away from any public road, and advised me to leave my horse there; and he gave me such directions as would enable me to find the place, which I reached in safety.

"Leaving my horse, I took to the woods on foot, making direct for Decatur, taking the sun for my guide. The second night overtook me in the woods very near Madison depot, on the railroad between Huntsville and Decatur. I had tried to travel in the night, but was overtaken by a terrible storm, and the darkness was so great that I could not find my way. Being very tired, I slept soundly, with no other bed than the ground, and no cover but my rubber Talma."

Soaked with the rain and famished with hunger, he made his way, in the early morning, toward the railroad and followed it till about ten o'clock, when near Minerville he found the residence of a Union man, and obtained a meal, his host and himself being mutually suspicious of each other and both acting a part. Here he met some rebel cavalry soldiers, and passing himself off as a Texan ranger ascertained what were the defences of the railroad bridge he was sent to inspect. After they were gone, he pursued his journey, seeking the opportunity of reaching and firing the bridge, but falling in with the camp of the (rebel) Second Tennessee Cavalry, and though their suspicions were not aroused as to his character, they insisted on fraternizing with him to such an extent that he had great difficulty in shaking them off, and was finally obliged to use threats, which, while they had the effect of driving his pertinacious friends away, rendered his own escape a matter of necessity. In attempting this, he got into a swamp, and endeavored to find his way through it to the river, and stealing a boat float down under the bridge and fire it. Failing in this, and knowing that there was no time to be lost, he turned his course and moved northward across the country to find the Union army. Travelling all day and until late at night, he was at length startled by the deep-mouthed baying, first, of a single bloodhound, and then soon after of several, and realized at once that the pursuers with their bloodhounds were on his track. Turning into a dense body of timber near by, he soon found a stream of water about waist deep, into which he plunged, and having crossed and broken their trail by so doing, he plunged into another swamp, where he kept on for an hour, the water being still nearly to his waist. Finding at length a pile of new rails rising a little above the water he clambered upon them and was soon asleep, though he could yet hear the distant baying of the hounds. In the morning, benumbed, and almost perishing with cold and hunger, he again waded the swamp for half an hour, till he came to the rear of a plantation, and attracting the attention of an aged negro, who, on finding that he was a Yankee soldier, brought him food, procured him a guide, and cheered him on his way. After some farther adventures, in which he confiscated a fine rebel horse and buggy and brought the driver, a stalwart negro, into the Union lines, he reached General Mitchel's headquarters at Huntsville, Alabama. Immediately on his return, he was sent with despatches to General Buell, at Corinth. Though very weary from his previous adventures, he set out immediately, and riding a powerful, thoroughbred horse at the top of his speed to Fayetteville, thirty-six miles distant, which he made in three hours, he procured another horse there, and continued his journey at the same rapid rate, but near Columbia, he was so much exhausted that he fell from his horse insensible, and lay an hour, unconscious, on the ground, but recovering his senses, he mounted his horse again and delivered his despatches at Columbia, from whence General Negley telegraphed them to General Buell. On his return, a negro hailed him and informed him that his master and eight other men were in ambush a little farther on, at a small mill, and intended to kill him. Thanking the negro for the information, he rode rapidly to the mill, and as the miller ran in when he saw him coming, he called him out and charged him with his murderous intention. He, at first denied it, but being told that it was of no use, and that if he did not own up the whole affair he (Pike) would bring a party of cavalry from Columbia and burn the mill, his house and barn, and carry off all his property, he finally confessed who were his confederates and what had been their plans. Taking down their names, and lecturing the old man severely, Corporal Pike rode away. He soon overtook a comrade from his own regiment, and feeling ill, stopped with his friend and another Union soldier at the house of a citizen, near Meridian, to pass the night. Here an attempt was made during the night to assassinate him, but being awake and seeing one of the assassins raise and aim his gun at him through the window, he fired his pistol, and wounded the assassin, probably mortally. His comrades carried him off, and Pike was not again disturbed. The next morning he reached Huntsville.

General Mitchel immediately sent him to ascertain the rebel force at Bridgeport, Tennessee. He reached the vicinity without any notable adventure, ascertained the number and position of the rebel troops, made his report and sent it by a Union officer who had escorted him nearly to Bridgeport, told the officer he would remain in the mountains till the Union army came to take Bridgeport. Here, after some adventure, escaping once from the rebel pickets only by shooting the sergeant, and running the gauntlet of the fire of the squad; he was taken prisoner, partly in consequence of his own carelessness. He was taken first to Bridgeport, and thence to Chattanooga, where he was confined in the jail, where were, at that time, in the dungeon twenty-one men from the Second, the Twenty-first, and the Thirty-third Ohio regiments, whose adventures are related elsewhere in this work.* After considerable suffering here, Corporal Pike was removed to Knoxville to another jail, where he was confined in an iron cage. Here he was told that he was

---

* See "The Great Railroad Chase." Part II.

to be tried as a spy and would undoubtedly be hung. From Knoxville, he was sent to Mobile, and eight days later, removed to Tuscaloosa, and thence to Montgomery, Alabama, where he was taken very sick with pneumonia and typhoid fever, and was treated with great inhumanity, all medicine being refused him, and he being left for twelve days lying upon the deck of the boat, without a bed and with nothing but corn bread and spoiled old salt junk for food. From Montgomery he was sent to Macon, Georgia. Here, weak as he was, he attempted to escape, but was recaptured six days later, being run down with bloodhounds. About the 1st of October, 1862, he was sent with numerous other prisoners by way of Savannah, Augusta, Columbia, Raleigh, Petersburg, and Richmond, for exchange. They all suffered fearfully on the route, and many died. On the 18th of October, they were exchanged, and poor Pike, reduced to a skeleton, and almost in a dying state, was taken to the Cliffburn hospital at Washington. Here, for some months, he lay almost hopelessly ill, but in March, 1863, had recovered sufficiently to join his regiment.

Here he was soon again at his old work. Riding out one day some distance beyond the lines with a lieutenant of his company, they met an old negro preacher, who told them that there was a large body of rebel soldiers not far off. Corporal Pike requested the lieutenant to return to Murfreesboro while he went to see where the rebels were. After some scouting he discovered them, about one hundred and fifty in number, at the foot of a considerable hill; his position being above them, and two of their men, one mounted and the other on foot, being near him, he approached and ordered them to halt, and as they fled repeated the order and fired, mortally wounding the mounted one, and then reloading, fired at the one on foot, whom he also wounded severely, and then in a loud voice called out "*Forward the Fourth! FORWARD THE FOURTH OHIO!*" Hearing the name of that regiment, which was a terror to the rebels in all that region, the whole rebel troop took to their horses and fled at the top of their speed (abandoning, as he afterward learned, a large forage train) toward Auburn, seven miles distant. After seeing them well started Pike rode off toward Murfreesboro. Stopping at a house which they had passed, he told the woman to tell them, when they returned, that there was but one man in the attacking party, and that he said he had flogged one hundred and fifty of them and could do it again.

He next explored the rebel position at Woodbury, Tennessee, dodging and frightening the rebel pickets by some sharp practice, and on his return accompanied General Stanley in his raid on the rebel camps near Middleton, Tennessee, and while acting as aide to Colonel (acting Brigadier-General) Long, had some very narrow escapes, being at one time for a considerable period under the steady and continuous fire of a squad of rebel soldiers.

Starting soon after on a scouting expedition in the vicinity of Harpeth Shoals, he found himself among a band of guerillas, with whom he passed himself off as a Texan ranger, and learned from one of them the purposes of the rebel officers, and especially their intention of arresting and sending South a Union lady, the wife of a brave Union officer, then in that vicinity. Professing an intention of going to the rebel camp, he ascertained the truth of the information he had received, and then riding to the house of the imperiled Union lady, he informed her of her danger, caught her a horse, and accompanied her to Nashville, avoiding by means of by-roads the rebel pickets.

The forward movement of Rosecrans' army on Chattanooga had now commenced, and Corporal Pike was sent by General Stanley as a scout to search for some steamboats on the Hiawassee. While on this expedition he passed through the region where he was captured the year before, and after frightening relatives of the man who had betrayed him, he went up to the summit of Cumberland mountain, and near Cowan, in a narrow and crooked pass of the mountain, discovered that the rebels were blockading the gap, with the intention of cutting off and destroying any Union troops who might pass that way. They had felled some timber, but had not put much of it in position. There were about twenty rebel soldiers, who were guarding the gap and directing a force of fifty or more negroes who were felling the trees. Finding his position a safe one, Pike determined to put a stop to this proceeding, and accordingly fired at the evident leader of the movement, and the bullet striking his horse he was thrown and severely injured, and the whole band of rebels were thrown into confusion; firing again, Pike ordered an imaginary comrade tc run back and tell the regiment to hurry up, and then turning sent another shot whizzing among them, while he ordered a pretended body of skirmishers to come down from the opposite ridge and close in with the rebels, accompanying this order with such gestures

THE LEAP FOR LIFE.

as to lead the rebels, who could see him, to believe that he was pointing them out to his friends. Firing again, he shouted "hurrah, boys, we'll surround them!" and the rebels fled in the greatest terror, the negroes shuffling along after them. As soon as they were gone he crossed the pass to the opposite ridge, and followed the top of the ridge the remainder of that day and night, and till nine o'clock the following morning, when he was startled by hearing the sound of horses' feet behind him, stopping a moment and listening, he ascertained that there were about a dozen of them. He attempted to elude their observation by running out upon a spur which branched off from the main mountain, but the timber was open and they caught sight of him and immediately pursued. The mountain was steep, but they gained upon him, and although at first he seemed likely to escape, he soon came to the top of a cliff about three hundred feet high; turning to the right a few hundred yards, he again found a place where he could descend for some distance, but was then stopped by another cliff, which projected out like a shelf. Below the right-hand end of this cliff, a huge hickory tree was growing, and its shaggy top just reared itself above the shelf on which he stood, the trunk being about eight feet from the edge of the cliff. There was no time to lose, for already he could hear his pursuers clattering over the rocks above him; so running to the edge of the cliff and looking over the giddy height, he slung his rifle across his back and leaping out headforemost, with all his strength, succeeded in grasping the body of the tree with his arms and holding, although the weight of his accoutrements almost jerked him off. Sliding rapidly down the tree he landed on another bench of the mountain, from which, though with torn clothing and his hands, arms, and breast bleeding profusely from wounds received from the rough bark of the tree, he made his way down into the bottom of a deep ravine, and neither saw nor heard any thing more of his pursuers. Following the ravine to the base of the mountain he was an involuntary witness to the patriotic devotion of a loyal Tennessee family, the husband and father of which had been obliged to conceal himself for months to escape the rebel conscription, and his devoted wife had brought him food until such time as he could join the Union army.

Continuing his search for the steamboats, he came upon the home of "Bob White," on Walden Ridge. White was a thorough Unionist and the leader of a body of thirty to sixty Union Tennesseans, bush wackers, who were the terror of the rebel cavalry in that region. He was welcomed by White's family and remained with them one night, though the rebel cavalry came to the house in search of him, and White's men also called him up, fearing he might be a spy. After stirring up the rebels at one or two points, and again finding shelter for two or three nights among the persecuted East Tennessee Unionists, attending one of their religious meetings where every man was armed, and the services were conducted, like those of the Covenanters three hundred years ago, after night and in the concealment of the forest, lest their enemies should come upon them.

In the battle of Chickamauga, as well as in the marches and skirmishes which preceded it, Corporal Pike was actively employed as a scout, and was much of the time in imminent peril, while he rendered excellent service to the Union army. Leaving the Union army at Chattanooga, he next set out with General Crook's cavalry in pursuit of Wheeler's rebel cavalry, which had been attempting to break up the Union lines of communication with Nashville, where he had his share in some of the most desperate cavalry fighting of the war, being on two occasions the target of the enemy's rifles, and once of their artillery. Having arrived at Brownsboro, General Crook sent him with an important despatch from General Grant to General Sherman, whose location was not definitely known, though he was supposed to be not far from Corinth. The journey was a perilous one and the chances of success, to say the least, small; but the brave fellow did not hesitate for a moment, and taking a canoe at Whitesburg, opposite Huntsville, he descended the Tennessee river for more than a hundred miles, every mile of which was picketed by the enemy, ran the perilous rapids of the Muscle Shoals, forty miles in length, alone, and after being pursued and fired at by the rebels repeatedly landed near Tuscumbia, where he found Union troops, and was sent by special train to Iuka, where General Sherman was, but immediately on delivering the despatch he sunk down exhausted and fainting from intense fatigue. General Sherman, who is ever chary of his praise, so fully appreciated the daring and skill of this achievement, that he gave the corporal a testimonial in which he spoke of him in the highest terms. Returning to Chattanooga, he took part in the great battles of November 23–25.

In a subsequent scouting expedition at the beginning of 1864, they found that a certain rebel, Colonel W. C.

Walker, who had commanded a brigade at Cumberland Gap, had returned to his home in Cherokee county, N. C., with plenary conscripting powers, and was endeavoring to force every Union man in the region into the rebel army, committing, at the same time, great outrages on the families of the Unionists. Pike and his companions resolved to take this villain prisoner and convey him to Chattanooga. Pike's party consisted of ten scouts and a few citizens, and on New Year's night they went to Walker's house, surrounded it, and called on him to surrender. He demanded who they were, and being told that they were Yankee soldiers, and that if he gave himself up he should be treated like a gentleman, and be regarded as a prisoner of war, he refused with an oath; and Pike then informed him that resistance would be useless, that his house was surrounded, and that they would take him, dead or alive. He answered, "I will surrender when I please." Pike and his scouts, knowing that he had a body-guard constantly about him, now resolved to storm the house, and broke in the doors, front and rear. Walker retreated to an inner room, and still refused to surrender, making a stand with the evident intention of selling his life as dearly as possible. The doors of this room also having been broken in, Pike aimed at him with his pistol, again demanding his surrender; but he raised his Sharp's carbine to shoot Pike. Seeing, however, that the latter had the advantage of him, he replied, after a moment's hesitation, "Yes, boys, I'll surrender," and partly turned to lay his carbine on the bed, when his wife caught Pike's arm, and with a sudden jerk destroyed his aim. Walker now wheeled instantly, caught up his gun, and again raised it to shoot Pike, but delayed for an instant, his daughter being between them, and Pike called to his men to shoot, as he saw Walker was determined to kill him, and Jack Cook, of the 37th Indiana, fired, and killed him instantly. By this time, Walker's body-guard were heard in another part of the house, and the daring scouts instantly attacked and captured them, without firing a shot, and took them all but two to Charleston, Tenn. After some months spent in scouting, and the destruction of rebel property, under the direction of General Custer, Colonel Miller, and General Logan, Pike and a brother scout, Charles A. Gray, were sent by direction of General Thomas to Augusta, Ga., to endeavor to destroy the great bridge over the Savannah river, and, if possible, also the immense powder-mill which supplied most of the powder for the rebel armies. Having obtained their outfit at Nashville, they set out on their perilous undertaking, going by way of Chattanooga and Rocky Faced Ridge. The great campaigns of Sherman and Grant had now commenced, and it was of the greatest importance to prevent the two rebel generals Johnston and Lee from sending troops or supplies to each other. The destruction of the railroad bridge at Augusta would materially derange their communications, and once destroyed, it could not be repaired for months. Having taken part in the battle of Rocky Faced Ridge, the two scouts proceeded thence to the Charleston turnpike, and thence went on foot, over the region which Pike had traversed the preceding winter, and where Colonel Walker had been killed, and found the rebels still in terror over that event; scaled the Blue Ridge on the 20th of May, and descending its eastern slope, came to the head waters of the Tallulah river, remarkable for its numerous cataracts. They followed this stream to its junction with the Chattooga, the two forming the Tugalo, one of the two affluents of the Savannah river. Procuring a canoe, they floated down this stream, which had numerous rapids, and thence entered the Savannah, which above Augusta is a very rapid and rocky stream. They reached Hamburg, opposite Augusta, on the 3d of June, 1864, and concealed themselves where they could overlook both cities; but to their surprise and annoyance, they found that there were great numbers of Union prisoners there (twelve or fifteen hundred), on their way to Andersonville, and a large body of rebel troops guarding them, and that it would be utterly impossible for them to make any effort to accomplish their object, and nearly so to make their escape. The latter was all they could attempt, and during the night they got off and attempted to retrace their steps. They stole a couple of horses and rode them rapidly till morning, but were then overtaken and compelled to give up the horses, though their real character and objects were not suspected. Starting off, then, on foot, they made the best of their way toward the northwest, but two hours later they heard the baying of the bloodhounds, and knew that they were pursued. They made every effort to break the trail, passing through swamps and streams, doubling in their tracks, etc., etc., but all to no purpose.

The pack of hounds was thirty-six in number, and just after nightfall their loud baying showed that they were close upon them; and in the midst of a dense thicket, the two men were compelled to stand at bay

UNION SOLDIERS PURSUED BY BLOODHOUNDS.

and fight with the savage brutes, and the equally savage men who had used the dogs to hunt them down. On came the hounds through the thick undergrowth, making the deep forest echo with their savage baying, until, with a sudden bound, the leading dog was upon the fugitives, his eyes glaring, and his mouth foaming. For an instant he paused, as he saw them through the gloom, and the next he made a spring directly at Gray's face. He was large and snow-white, and this made him the better target, and as he sprang Pike turned upon him and fired, and he fell dead in an instant But at that moment the whole pack rushed upon them, and they could only distinguish them by their glaring eyes in the darkness, but they aimed at those, and killed one more and wounded four others, with nine shots, when the men came up, forcing their horses through the brush, cursing and swearing like madmen. When they had approached within about a hundred yards, the two scouts ordered them to halt, saying, that if they did not stop, they would fire on them.

"Who are you?" demanded one of the men.

"Yankee soldiers," answered Pike.

"What are you doing in our country?"

"We are here by order of our general."

"How many are there of you?"

"Two."

"Are you up a tree?"

"No! we are not the sort of men to take to trees!"

Then moving toward them, Pike said: "There are but two of us, but we are well armed, and can do you a great deal of damage if you drive us to it. We know that you have a strong force after us, for we have seen you two or three times to-day; we know that resistance on our part would only result in useless bloodshed; still it is our privilege to sell our lives at as dear a price as we can make you pay; but we don't want to hurt you, nor do we want you to hurt us; and therefore, if you will agree to treat us as prisoners of war, we will surrender without a fight, because we see that one would be useless."

"You will soon be made to surrender on our terms," replied the rebels.

"Then approach us at your peril," answered Pike, "for we shall shoot as long as we can crook a finger."

Resolute as this reply was, they were in fact helpless; their ammunition exhausted, and the four or five charges in their pistols had all been tried on the dogs, but had failed to go off from the foulness of the weapons.

While this parley had been going on, another large party had come up, and the two were disputing among themselves. Presently they hailed the two scouts pleasantly, "Halloo, Yank." "Halloo yourself," was the answer. "If you will surrender, we will treat you as prisoners of war, and there shall not one hair of your head be touched," said the commander of the party. "All right," answered the scouts, "on these conditions, and no others, you can have our arms. Let two men come over and take our weapons," they asked. . The rebels consented, but demanded that they should fire them in the air first. The scouts could not do this, because the attempt would show how helpless they were, but they objected on the ground that it evinced a lack of confidence in their honor. The rebel commander then ordered them to stand still and they would come to them. They did so, and when completely surrounded, gave up their arms, Gray joking with them freely. No sooner were the arms delivered, than a part of the rebels changed their manner, and began to abuse them, a man by the name of Chamberlain, a renegade from Massachusetts, who it seemed owned the bloodhounds, swearing that if they had shot one of the dogs he would kill them. They now set out on their return toward Augusta, or rather toward Edgefield, S. C., and stopped at the house of a Mr. Serles, who treated them kindly, and endeavored to pacify the drunken crowd who were taking them along, as did his wife; but his two daughters went among the gang, and begged them to hang the two Yankees. "Don't let them live, men! don't let them live!" they said, and by their urgency they had soon "fired the Southern heart" up nearly to the point of murder. Mr. Serles exerted himself to the utmost, however, to quiet them, and they finally were allowed their supper, and moved off to the house of Lieut. Col. Talbot, one of their captors. Here they were allowed an hour or two sleep, and on awakening in the morning, found that the party who had captured them had all left, and that they were in the hands of a party of drunken militia, who did not regard themselves as bound in any respect by the stipulations of their captors. These brutes roused them up, tied them very securely, and then marched them to the woods near by, and made preparations to hang them. They began with Pike, and having their rope ready, asked him if he had any confession to make?

"No," was his reply "I have nothing to confess to you"

"Do you desire to pray?" they asked.

"No," was his reply again. "I am ready to die, and don't fear death."

"Have you nothing to say?" they asked, astonished at his coolness.

"Yes," he replied, "I have something to say that may interest you."

"Out with it then," said one.

He then told them very coolly that they were United States soldiers, acting in the discharge of their duties, and that they, as citizens, had no right to interrupt them; that the general under whose orders they (the scouts) were acting would retaliate promptly if a hair of their heads were injured, and their sons in the Confederate army might be the men on whom the retaliation would fall. He told them farther, that he and Gray belonged to different regiments, and that if they were hung, their regiments, which were sure to come thither, would burn every dollar's worth of property they possessed, and hang every man concerned in the transaction. "If," he continued, "you are prepared to abide these consequences, I am."

The ringleaders now withdrew for a short time, for consultation, leaving the two scouts under a guard. After a little they returned, took them back to Talbot's house, and untied them, and Mrs. Talbot gave them a bountiful breakfast. Talbot himself was a villain; he had attempted the preceding night to murder them, after giving his pledge that not a hair of their heads should be touched, and had only failed because his gun would not go off. He and Chamberlain now promised to take them to Edgefield, and as they had been forewarned that a crowd had assembled on the lower road to murder them, they asked to be taken by the upper route, and their captors finally consented. Arriving at Edgefield, the provost-marshal, who desired to have them murdered by a mob, refused to receive them from the militia, but a rebel lieutenant who was there, overruled him and ordered them to be put in the jail, subject to the orders of the military authorities at Augusta. Here, they were examined very closely, and questioned carefully, separately; but as they had buried all their bridge-burning fixtures before leaving Hamburg, and had agreed upon the statements they were to make, there was no such thing as entangling them. On the 9th of June, they were taken to Augusta. Here, they were confined on the smallest possible allowance of food, for fifty-seven days, when they were removed under a strong guard to Charleston, where they were put in the tower of the jail and kept five months under fire from the Union batteries. Vigorous efforts were made to procure their exchange, by the highest officers of the Union army, but in vain. When General Sherman's march through the Carolinas compelled the evacuation of Charleston, they were removed to Columbia, and when that was threatened, they were sent to Winnsboro on foot, with the intention of taking them to Salisbury, North Carolina, but on the way both escaped, Gray getting away first, and Pike the next night, February 18th, 1865, and after wandering about for two days, the latter found his way into the Union lines, where Gray had preceded him.

He was most cordially received and fitted out in connection with Kilpatrick's command, and when General

Sherman reached Cheraw, was sent to carry despatches to Wilmington which was then occupied by the Union troops under Generals Schofield and Terry. The journey was a perilous one, as he descended Cape Fear river from the mouth of Rockfish creek, a distance of more than a hundred miles, in an open boat; and the whole shore of the river was lined with rebel troops. Having reached Wilmington in safety and delivered his despatches, he was immediately requested to carry despatches also to Newbern and Kinston, where he found General Schofield. Three hours after the delivery of these, General Schofield entrusted him with a despatch for General Sherman which he wished taken across the country. He started immediately, and after a long and somewhat dangerous tramp (for he could only go on foot in safety), he reached the general near Faison's depot. After the battle of Bentonville he applied for and received his discharge, having been in the service seven months over the time for which he had enlisted, and on the 1st of April, 1865, was mustered out at Columbus. It would be hard, we think, to find in the history of any war, an instance of a scout or spy who had encountered more dangers, hardships, and risks, or surmounted them more gallantly than Corporal James Pike.

A FEMALE SCOUT AND SPY.

During the war, a very considerable number of women nave entered the secret service of the commanders of the Union armies, and perhaps quite as many, or more, have been employed by the rebel generals in obtaining

ROSECRANZ.
SLOCUM.
HOWARD
SHERMAN.
ROBT. McCOOK
McCLERNAND
LOGAN.
J.W.ORR N.Y.

information of the situation and purposes of the Union troops. The adventures of many of these, for obvious reasons, have not as yet been made public, and some of them may perhaps never be recorded. Among them have been a number of actresses, whose profession has given them extraordinary facilities for this service, and whose intense loyalty has caused them to run fearful risks to render it service. Of some of these we shall have occasion to speak by-and-by. One of the most adroit and successful of these was not an actress, nor a native of the United States. Miss S. E. E. Edmonds, better known, perhaps, as "The Nurse and Spy," is a native of the province of New Brunswick, and having an earnest desire to acquire a superior education, with a view to becoming a foreign missionary, and possessing besides an energetic and independent disposition, came to the United States, we believe, in 1859 or 1860, and for a time acted as a canvasser for some books published in Hartford, Conn. When the war broke out, she at once resolved to devote herself to the work of nursing the sick and wounded soldiers in the hospitals, and went to Washington for that purpose. After spending eight or nine months in this duty, she learned that one of the spies in General McClellan's service had been captured by the rebels in Richmond, and executed, and that it was necessary that his place should be filled. Miss Edmonds was daring and resolute, capable of enduring an extraordinary amount of fatigue, an accomplished equestrienne, and a capital shot, and possessed of quick and ready perceptions, and great intelligence, while her powers of impersonation were unrivalled. She applied for the position, and was accepted after a very thorough examination. Her first disguise was that of a negro boy. Passing safely through the Union lines, and past the rebel pickets, she entered the suburbs of Yorktown, and met with some negroes who were carrying out supplies to the pickets. Mingling with these, the pretended contraband soon attracted the attention of a young rebel officer, who demanded, "Who do you belong to, and why are you not at work?" "I doesn't b'long to nobody, massa; I'se free, and allers was; I'se gwyne to Richmond to work," was the reply. The officer, apparently astonished that a free negro should aver his freedom, ordered him immediately set to work wheeling gravel up a parapet about eight feet high, for strengthening the works, and ordered that he should receive twenty lashes if he did not do his work well. The work was very severe, even for a strong and robust man, and though the negroes comprising the gang helped what they could, yet before night the hands of the pseudo-contraband were blistered from the wrists to the tips of the fingers, and she was completely exhausted. After resting a little, however, she made an inspection of the fortifications, sketched them, ascertained the number, size, and position of the guns, carefully concealing her notes between the soles of her contraband shoes. Securing the services of a young negro to take her place the next day on the parapet, she entered upon the easier service of carrying water to a brigade stationed near the rebel headquarters. Here she obtained some important information in regard to the numbers and intentions of the rebels, and detected a rebel spy, who, under the guise of a peddler, had often visited the Union headquarters, and who had caused the death of one of

McClellan's staff officers, a friend of Miss Edmunds. At night, going out to the picket lines, the pretended contraband was entrusted with a fine rifle, and put upon picket duty. Availing herself of the opportunity, she now escaped to the Union lines, bringing her rifle as a trophy, and soon after reported at headquarters. Her next expedition was under the guise of an old Irish woman, engaged in peddling cakes, etc., among the rebel soldiers. This was soon after McClellan had reached the banks of the Chickahominy. Losing her way in the Chickahominy swamps, she suffered from a violent attack of fever and ague, and for two days lay in the swamp without food or shelter, her stock of food having been spoiled in crossing the Chickahominy. On the third day she was roused by heavy firing, and crawling in the direction whence it proceeded, came soon to an opening and a small frame house, which had been deserted by its inhabitants, but in which she found a dying rebel officer. She ransacked the house for articles of food, and succeeded in finding a little meal and some tea, and soon prepared a tolerable meal for the dying soldier, who had been some days without food, and also something to stay her own hunger. Being unable, from exhaustion, to go upon her mission, and finding that the poor man had but a few hours to live, she cared for him as tenderly as she could, and before he died, he gave her his watch and papers, with directions to deliver them to Major McKee, of General Ewell's staff, and expressed his gratitude to her for her kindness.

After his death, she rested for a short time, and then gathering from the house what supplies she could, to make up an outfit for her assumed character, she wended her way to the rebel camp, five or six miles distant, and having ascertained what she could of the position and intentions of the rebels, and the location of the batteries they had concealed along the route of the approach of the Union army, she sought Major McKee, but was obliged to wait till five P. M. before she could see him. He was very much affected at the intelligence of Captain Hall's death, and offered to reward her, but she would accept no reward. He then requested her to guide a detachment of his men to the place where the captain had died. As she was really unable to walk that distance, at her request he furnished her with a horse to ride. The lone house was on debatable ground, and there was reason to fear that the Union troops might fall upon them while engaged in this humane work; but they reached the place in safety and found the body, and the commander of the detachment requesting her to ride down the road and see if there were any Yankees in sight, she complied with his request very willingly, and became so much interested in her search that she did not draw rein till she arrived in the Union camp, when she reported her discoveries, and prevented the army from falling into the traps set for them. The horse thus taken from the enemy, though spirited, proved a vicious brute, and with its teeth and heels came near costing her her life. At the battle of Fair Oaks, she acted as orderly to General Kearny, and twice swam the Chickahominy to hurry forward reinforcements for the sorely pressed Union troops. In the retreat across the Peninsula, she was again repeatedly under fire, while serving as orderly or on detached duty with the wounded; and under the assumed name of Frank Thompson took part in most of the battles of that famous retreat. During the last few days of Pope's campaign, she was sent three times into the enemy's camp, and under different disguises; once as a negress; and again, in other characters, she penetrated to their headquarters, and brought away, not only information of their intended movements, but valuable orders and papers.

After the battle of Antietam, when following Lee back to the Rapidan, while on detached service, a body of cavalry with whom Miss Edmonds was travelling, were attacked by guerillas and her horse killed under her, and she herself seriously injured and robbed. Union troops soon came up, however, and defeated the guerillas and restored her money. In the battle of Fredericksburg, under her assumed name of Frank Thompson, she acted as aid-de-camp to General Hancock, and was under fire during the whole period. After General Hooker took command of the Army of the Potomac, she went to the Western army, overtaking at Louisville the Ninth Army Corps, to which she had been for some time attached.

Here she was not long in resuming her former vocation as a spy, and having aided in the capture of some rebel prisoners, she donned the butternut garb, and as a Kentuckian, sympathizing with the rebels, wandered into their camp, but was presently pounced upon by a rebel cavalry captain and conscripted into service; but having to go into action before taking the oath, the conscript managed to get upon the Union side, and wounded severely, though not mortally, the rebel captain who had attempted to secure her services. As the duty of a spy after this was likely to be extra hazardous, the commanding general detailed Miss Edmonds to detective duty in Louisville, and with great skill and tact she managed to detect and secure the capture of several rebel spies then in the city. She next visited Vicksburg, and after serving some time in the hospitals there as a nurse, was compelled by broken health to leave the army for a time.

THE IRISH SENTINEL.—A son of the Green Isle, a new member of Colonel Gillem's Middle Tennessee regiment, while stationed at Nashville recently, was detailed on guard duty on a prominent street of that city. It was his first experience at guard-mounting, and he strutted along his beat apparently with a full appreciation of the dignity and importance of his position. As a citizen approached, he shouted—

"Halt! Who comes there?"

"A citizen," was the response.

"Advance, citizen, and give the countersign."

"I haven't the countersign; and, if I had, the demand for it at this time and place is something very strange and unusual," rejoined the citizen.

"An', by the howly Moses, ye don't pass this way at all till ye say Bunker Hill," was Pat's reply.

The citizen, appreciating the "situation," advanced and cautiously whispered in his ear the necessary words.

"Right! Pass on." And the wide awake sentinel resumed his beat.

ADVENTURES OF HARRY NEWCOMER.

A SCOUT AND SPY IN THE ARMY OF THE CUMBERLAND.

AMONG the many spies and detectives employed by the commanders of the Union armies, in procuring information concerning the condition, purposes, and position of the enemy, or the evil deeds of rebel sympathizers, none perhaps, has passed through more interesting adventures, than he whose name appears at the head of this sketch. We have compiled from the police record of the "Annals of the Army of the Cumberland," the following history of some of his adventures and escapes.

Harry Newcomer is a native of Pennsylvania, and was born in Lancaster county, in March, 1829. He was born and brought up in a hotel, and was employed as a bar tender in his boyhood. At the age of fourteen, his mother died, and his father broke up housekeeping, and soon afterward he was apprenticed to a miller in Ohio. After serving out his time, he continued for some years in the business, until his brother-in-law was elected sheriff of Ashland county, Ohio, when he was appointed one of his deputies. In 1857, he removed to Cleveland, and was employed by United States Marshal Jabez Fitch, as a detective officer. He retained this situation for about three years, and was successful in ferreting out and bringing to punishment a number of noted cases of crime, especially of counterfeiters. At that time the authorities had ascertained that a large business was done in the manufacture and sale of counterfeit money in Geauga county, Ohio, but all attempts to obtain any positive evidence to fasten the guilt upon the suspected parties had failed. Newcomer had already acquired a high reputation as a shrewd and successful detective, and it was determined tc set him at work upon the case. He was instructed to make the acquaintance of an old blacksmith, named Jesse Bowen, who cultivated also a small farm in the vicinity of Burton Square in that county. Bowen was notoriously a lawless, bad man, and had been for many years engaged in all manner of frauds and crimes, but had managed to escape detection and punishment. He was now seventy-eight years of age, a friendless, unsocial old villain, whose house was shunned by all who cared for their reputation or candor. Newcomer introduced himself to him as William H. Hall, an extensive manufacturer and dealer in counterfeit money. He had with him, as evidence of his belonging to the fraternity, considerable amounts of counterfeit bills on various banks, with which he had been abundantly supplied. After two or three interviews, by that sort of fascination with which he is so eminently endowed, he succeeded in winning completely the old man's confidence, and learned from him the names of all those who were connected with the gang of counterfeiters. He did more than this. Won by the apparent cordiality of Newcomer, who assisted him on his little farm, he unearthed his machinery and engaged with him in the manufacture of bogus coin, gave him the pass-word, and introduced him to all the members of the gang, with whom he was presently on the best of terms. In an excess of communicativeness, Bowen one day called young Newcomer into an orcnard and revealed to him, in confidence, that he and his brother had, in early life, murdered their brother-in-law, in Vermont, and that they had only been saved from the gallows, by a man being found who bore a remarkably strong resemblance to the murdered man, and who was induced to swear that he was the man supposed to be killed. This was the celebrated Corbin case so often referred to, in criminal trials.

Having finally implicated the entire gang of counterfeiters, and acquired a thorough knowledge of their haunts and residences, Newcomer plead that urgent business called him away, and repairing to Cleveland, reported progress to the United States Marshal, and officers were sent, and the whole number arrested, tried, convicted, and sent to the penitentiary.

In 1860, he removed to Pittsburg, Pennsylvania, where he was soon employed in the detection and arrest of a noted counterfeiter, named Charles Coventry, a man of gigantic strength, and the terror of the whole region. This was accomplished with his usual adroitness, and the desperate villain trapped, tried, convicted, and sent to prison for five years. In about a year, he had succeeded in detecting and bringing to justice sixty-eight criminals, counterfeiters, burglars, horse thieves, and villains of all sort. In 1861, his extraordinary success having excited the jealousy of the other detectives of Pittsburg, he removed to Chicago, but finding no employment which suited him, he enlisted as a non-commissioned officer in the Eleventh Indiana Battery. With this battery he served throughout Buell's campaign to Nashville and Shiloh, to Corinth and Huntsville, Alabama, when the old love of adventure coming upon him, he began to act as a scout on his own account, reporting, when any thing of interest came to his knowledge, to

Colonel, afterward General Harker, of the Sixty-fifth Ohio Volunteers, who then commanded the brigade to which he was attached. The colonel, pleased with his skill and adroitness, gave him passes and encouraged him to continue to make these scouting expeditions as he had opportunity.

Frequently he would go down to the Tennessee river in sight of the rebel pickets; and one night he concluded to cross the river and get a nearer view of them. Striking the stream at a point three miles from Stevenson, he built a raft of rails and paddled himself across. Crawling up the bank through the bush, he came close upon the pickets, seven in number, without being observed. After watching their movements awhile, and finding nothing of particular interest, he returned safely as he went. Soon afterward, a negro told him of an island in the Tennessee river, some ten miles below Stevenson, on which a company of guerilla cavalry were in the habit of rendezvousing every night. This opened a large field of operations for our scout, and he determined to visit the island forthwith. One afternooon, borrowing a suit of butternut from a negro at Stevenson, he set forth in that direction. The butternut clothes were carried under his saddle until he was fairly outside of our lines, when he exchanged his own for them and went on in the character of a genuine native. Reaching the river opposite the island after dark, he again constructed a raft of rails, fastening them together this time with grape-vines, and shoved across the narrow channel to the island, landing in a dense canebrake. Carefully feeling his way through this, he came soon to a corn-crib, around which twenty-five or thirty horses were feeding. It was now ten o'clock, and quite dark, but clear and starlight. Examining the crib, the entrance was discovered about half-way up, and our adventurer at once clambered up and put his head and shoulders through. Careful listening revealed the presence of sleepers within. Putting his hand down to see how far it was to them, it came in contact with the body of a man. Wishing to know in what direction he was lying, he felt along carefully and came upon a pistol in his belt. Working at this, he soon drew it out, and, finding it a good Colt's revolver, put it into his pocket and got down again. Exploring around, he came to a corn patch and a cabin near by, in which there seemed, from the noise within, to be a family or two of negroes. Crossing to the south or rebel side of the island, he found that the stream was much narrower there than on the other side, and that close to the shore a number of boats and scows, in which the band crossed and recrossed, were tied. It was now time to think about getting home, and he circled around the crib and cabin to reach the place where he had left his raft. When he came in sight of it, there was also to be seen a human form standing by the water's edge and apparently regarding the raft with no little astonishment. In the uncertain light, it was impossible to tell whether it was man or woman, white or black; and there was nothing to do but wait until it disappeared. Crouching down amid the canes, he soon saw it turn and begin to climb the bank directly toward him; as a precautionary measure he took out the pistol and cocked it, though he could not see or feel whether it was loaded or not. The person proved to be a negro, and passed by, unconscious of the presence of any one so near, soliloquizing to himself thus:—"Mighty quare boat dat ar; 'spec's some of Masser John's work." This danger having passed, our self-appointed spy descended, and re-embarked on his raft. Lest any one should see him, he lay flat upon it, paddling with extended arms, the whole presenting very much the appearance of a floating mass of drift wood. By the time he reached the opposite shore his butternut suit was pretty thoroughly soaked, but without stopping to dry it, he mounted his horse, which he found straying about the woods, rode on to Stevenson, and reported to Colonel Harker. An expedition for the capture of this band—afterward ascertained to be Captain Rountree's company—was just about starting, when orders were received to evacuate the place and fall back to Nashville with the remainder of Buell's army.

The battery went no farther backward than Nashville, remaining there during the famous investment of the city and until the Army of the Cumberland again reached it. Meanwhile, Newcomer was occasionally employed by General Negley as a detective; but most of the time was spent with his command. Early in December the police and scout system was fully organized and in successful operation. Our former scout, thinking that he could serve the Government to better advantage in the business with which he was so familiar, made application to Colonel Truesdail for employment as a scout and spy. The colonel, pleased with his appearance and conversation, at once made an engagement with him, and procured his detail for that special service. Having previously made the acquaintance of one Cale Harrison, a livery-stable-keeper, he now called on him, and, ex-

HALLECK.
CASEY.
FRANKIIN.
SCOTT.
SHIELDS.
BUELL
DIX

hibiting a forged certificate of discharge, told him that he was on his way to the rebel army. Harrison, of course, was highly pleased to hear it, and gave him some valuable hints and information for his guidance in the matter. There was, he said, a man living on the Charlotte pike, by the name of Spence, whose son was an aide-de-camp on the staff of General Polk, and who would undoubtedly assist him in getting south and give him a letter of introduction to his son. In this event the road would be clear, and no difficulty need be apprehended in making the trip.

Thus directed, he set forth from Nashville on a scout south, with saddle-bags well filled with fine-tooth combs, needles, pins, thread, etc., and carrying two fine navy revolvers. Going directly to Spence's, he introduced himself, said he had called by recommendation of Harrison, made known his business, and asked for a letter to his son, on General Polk's staff. Spence received him cordially, but would not furnish him with the desired letter. He referred him, however, to J. Wesley Ratcliffe, living about one mile from Franklin, on the Lewisburg pike, as a person likely to render him very material assistance. This Ratcliffe was a rebel agent for the purchase of stock and commissary stores, and was well known throughout the whole country. Pushing on, he accordingly called at Ratcliffe's, and made his acquaintance. When informed of his plans and purposes and shown the goods, Ratcliffe was much pleased, and soon became very friendly, advising him to go to Shelbyville, where such articles were greatly needed and could easily be disposed of. Newcomer accordingly started for Shelbyville, and for some time met with no incidents on the way. Between Caney Springs and Rover, however, he fell in with a band of rebel cavalry belonging to General Buford's command, who, on being made acquainted with his business, advised him not to go to Shelbyville, as considerable trouble might be experienced there. Their bushy shocks of hair suggesting that they were combless, he offered his stock for sale, chatting meanwhile with them about matters and things in general and in that vicinity in particular. Combs which cost two dollars per dozen he sold for two dollars each, and other articles in proportion, and, by the time his trading was finished, had ascertained that General Buford was stationed at Rover to guard a large mill full of flour and meal—the size of his command, the number and calibre of his guns, and other items of importance, and also what generals and troops were at Shelbyville. The cavalrymen now wished him to go back to Nashville and bring them some pistols on his return. This he agreed to do, and, having obtained all the information he cared for at this time, turned his horse about and once more set his face toward Nashville. The two pistols which he had carried with him he had not shown, and still had them in his possession—which circumstance was the cause of a slight adventure on the way home. He had proceeded but a little way when he met with a small squad of cavalry, who halted him, as usual, and demanded his name, business, and where he was going. These questions satisfactorily answered, he was next asked if he had any pistols about him. He replied that he had two, and was forthwith ordered by a rough-looking Texan to produce them, which was hardly done before they were coolly appropriated by his interrogator. Remonstrance was followed by abuse and threats of violence; and it was only by the intervention of the other parties that the matter was compromised by the sale of the pistols at fifty dollars each, and our traveller allowed to go on his way rejoicing. Without interruption headquarters were reached, and a report of operations duly made.

Remaining two days at Nashville, he started again, with three pistols and the balance of the old stock of goods. The first night was spent at Ratcliffe's, and the next day both went to Murfreesboro in a buggy. Ratcliffe had business to transact with the provost-marshal, and a number of the generals and inferior officers to see, and Newcomer was taken round and introduced to all, as a co-laborer in the cause of the South. During his four days' stay, he was all over the town, through several of the camps, in many of the houses, drank whiskey with General Frank Cheatham, went to a grand party at the court house, and made love to a dozen or more young ladies of secession proclivities—aided in all this by a perfect self-possession, an easy, graceful manner, and a winning face. In addition to pleasure seeking and love making, he also drove a thriving business in the sale of pistols and other contraband goods, and, with pockets filled with money and head stored with information, returned with Ratcliffe to his house, and thence to Nashville—having first made an arrangement with the former to accompany him to Shelbyville the next day. Arriving at Nashville after dark, he remained there until morning, and then made preparations and started for a third trip.

With a pair or two of cotton cards, a lot of pistol caps,

and some smaller knick-knacks, as passports to favor, he set forth once more to join Ratcliffe; but having been unavoidably delayed in starting, he found him already gone. Nothing was now to be done but to boldly push ahead in the hope of overtaking him on the road, or meeting him at Shelbyville. With the exception of Ratcliffe, not a soul there knew him. Trusting to good fortune, he travelled on, and reached Shelbyville in due season without trouble. The usual questions were asked him by guards and pickets, to all of which he replied that he lived in Davidson county, was going to visit some friends in the 44th Tennessee regiment, and had, moreover, a small stock of contraband goods for sale. These answers proving satisfactory, he was passed through and reached the town early in the forenoon. Most of the day he spent in riding about, looking into quartermasters' and commissary depots, inquiring the names of officers, the number of troops, commanders, etc., until he had ascertained all that he wished. By this time night was drawing near, and it was high time to think about getting out of town; for should he remain after dark, he was certain to be arrested. Ratcliffe was nowhere to be seen, and on inquiry he was told that he had gone to Atlanta, Georgia, on the train, and that nobody knew when he would be back. Here was a desperate state of affairs. Get out of town he must, and to get out he must have a pass. It was easy enough to come in, but very difficult to get out. Nobody knew him; and, in fact, for once in his life, he was at a loss what to do. While thus troubled, he met some citizens of Davidson county who had been over the river to the camps of Cheatham and McCown's divisions, and were

FOSTER
SYKES
TERRY
McCLELLAN.
GILMORE
WALLACE
GARFIELD
SCHOFIELD
J.W. Orr N.Y.

now on their way to the provost-marshal to procure return passes. Misery loves company, and with a long face he told them his trouble—dressing it up with a considerable amount of fiction to suit the occasion. By way of adding earnestness to his entreaty and to open a sure path to their sympathies, he bought a bottle of whiskey and invited them all to drink with him. The liquor warmed their hearts as well as stomachs; and while hobnobbing together he asked them if they wouldn't vouch for him to the provost-marshal, and thus enable him to procure a pass. Being now in a condition to love the world and everybody in it, they promised to do so, and in due season all went for passes. His seven newly-made friends found no difficulty in their suit, their names being all written on a single pass; but our scout was left unnoticed. The attention of the provost-marshal was called to him, when that functionary asked if any of them was personally acquainted with him. Though rebels, they would not lie; possibly they thought it was not necessary; and answered, "No," but they would vouch for him. But that would not do. His situation now was worse than ever. He not only had no pass, but had not the slightest chance of getting one. The whiskey investment had proved a losing speculation; and he knew not where to turn for relief. The loungers about the office began to eye him suspiciously, and even the dogs seemed disposed to growl and snap at him as having no business there. The place was getting too hot for safety; and his only hope of escape was to hurry out and lose himself in the crowd.

His new friends were still outside, waiting for him; and with them a long consultation was held as to what had better be done about getting away, as every moment added to his already serious danger. Finally, one of the party suggested that he should go with them anyhow—that the pickets would not be likely to notice that his name was not in the pass, there being so many already on it. In default of any thing better, this proposition was agreed to, and all set out together. Newcomer, however, was still far from easy about the matter, and was fearful that the plan would not work. As they were journeying along, he proposed to the one who had the pass that he should be allowed to write his own name on the pass with a pencil, and if any objection should be made to it they might say that he belonged to the party but did not come in until the pass was made out, and that the provost marshal, to save writing a new one, had inserted the name in pencil-mark. This was assented to and done. The amended pass carried them safely through, and the last cloud of anxiety was lifted from his troubled mind.

Some twelve or fifteen miles having been passed over pleasantly, Newcomer purposely lagged behind and allowed the others to get far ahead, when he turned off and struck across to the Lewisburg and Franklin pike. Travelling on this about ten miles, he stopped for the night, with five of Wheeler's cavalry, at the house of a man who had a son in Forrest's command. Starting the next morning betimes, he reached Ratcliffe's the same evening, but found he had not yet reached home. Stopping a few moments, he passed on through Franklin toward Nashville. He had gone some seven miles, and was near Brentwood, when he saw four cavalrymen riding furiously down a lane just ahead of him. They and our hero reached its entrance at the same moment. The leader of the squad—who proved to be Captain Harris, a scout of John Morgan's, and who, as well as his three men, was very drunk—roughly halted him, and riding up, pistol in hand, shouted:

"Who are you? and where do you live?"

"My name is Newcomer, and I live six miles from Nashville, near Brent Spence's," was the ready, respectful reply.

Spence was well known to all, and no further troub was apprehended; but the drunken captain was not so easily satisfied. He soon asked:

"Where have you been? and what in the —— are you doing here?"

"I have been to Shelbyville to see Spence's son, and I took along some contraband goods to sell."

"You can go back to Franklin with me, sir!"

Protestation was unavailing; and without more ado he turned about and all started toward Franklin. On the way Harris asked if he had any arms with him, and on being told that he had two fine revolvers and some cartridges, ordered him to give them up, which was done. With a savage leer he then said:

"I know all about you. You're a —— Yankee spy. You have been going backward and forward here so much that the citizens of Franklin have suspected you for a long time, and have reported you. I am satisfied that you are a Yankee spy; and I am going to hang you, —— you. Bragg has ordered me never to bring in spies, but to shoot or hang them like dogs on the spot; and I am going to make a beginning with you, now, this very night."

"If you do that," was the reply, "you'll take the life of a good and true man. I can show by J. W. Ratcliffe that I am a true Southerner, that I have done much good for the cause—very likely much more than you have—and that I am doing good every day I live."

"Captain," said one of the men, "it may be that he *is* an important man to our cause; and you had better see Ratcliffe and inquire into his case,"

Harris studied a moment, and finally concluded to go with the prisoner to Ratcliffe's and confer about the matter—at the same time assuring him that it was of no use, for he should certainly hang him anyhow. At Franklin all stopped to drink, and Harris and his men became beastly drunk. Reeling into their saddles, they were once more on their way to Ratcliffe's, but had gone only a short distance, when Harris wheeled his horse and hiccoughed out—

"Boys, there's no use in fooling. I am satisfied this fellow's a —— Yankee spy; and here's just as good a place as we can find to hang him. Take the halter off that horse's neck and bring it here."

It was indeed a fitting place in which to do foul murder. Not a house was to be seen; and the road wound through one of those cedar thickets so dense that even in mid-day it was almost dark within them. It was now night, and the sombre shade even more gloomy than ever, as Harris jumped from his horse, and, taking the halter, made a noose of it, and, fitting it around the neck of the unlucky scout, drew it up uncomfortably tight, until, in fact, it was just about strangling him.

Now or never was the time to expostulate and entreat. In a moment it might be too late; and then farewell home, friends, and all the joys of life! It is not hard to die in peace, surrounded by weeping friends, or even to meet the dread king in the shock and excitement of battle; but to hang like a dog!—the idea is sickening, appalling; and it is no sign of cowardice to shrink from it. One more effort, then, for life, even if it be to supplicate for mercy from a drunken rebel.

"Captain," said he, with great feeling, "it is wrong to take a man's life on so slight a suspicion. It is a vast responsibility to take upon one's self; and you may do something for which you will be sorry by-and-by, in your calmer moments, and for which you may be even punished when it comes to the knowledge of General Bragg."

To which came the rough and heartless answer, "I know my business, and I don't want any advice from a —— Yankee spy. When I do, I'll let you know. Come along," shouted he, seizing the rope and dragging his victim toward a tree. "I know my duty, and am going to do it, too. Come on, men, and let's swing up this —— rascally spy."

They refused to come to his assistance, however, saying that they were as ready as he to do their duty, but they wanted to be a little better satisfied about the matter. It was only half a mile to Ratcliffe's, and it would be a very easy thing to go and see what he said about it. Harris would not listen a moment, and again ordered them to come and help him, which they dared not longer refuse.

The case now appeared hopeless. Death stared him in the face, and life, with all its memories and pleasures, seemed passing dreamily away. Looking into the cedars hanging heavy with darkness, they seemed the entrance to the valley of the shadow of death, beyond which lay the infinite and mysterious future. On the verge of the grave life was yet sweet—yet worth striving for; and, as a last effort, the unfortunate man went up to Harris, placed his hand on his shoulder, and asked him if he would promise, on the word and honor of a gentleman, that he would go to General Bragg and give him a true statement of the affair, narrating every circumstance as it actually occurred. Then, turning to the men, he asked them if they would do it, provided the captain did not. Less hardened than the captain, they feelingly answered that they would; and the earnestness with which they replied was proof enough that they would make good their words. This set the captain to thinking. He evidently didn't like the idea of Bragg's hearing about it, and, after some moments' reflection, concluded to go to Ratcliffe's and see what he would say. The rope was removed, and they resumed their journey—the captain still swearing it would do no good, as nothing could save him, for he was bound to hang him that very night.

Life still hung on a thread, however. In the afternoon, when Newcomer had been there, Ratcliffe had not returned, and if he were not now at home, nothing would prevent Harris from carrying out his threat, which he seemed determined to execute. That half mile was the longest ride Newcomer ever took. No lights were to be seen; but it was near midnight, and it might be that all were abed. Harris left the prisoner at the gate, in charge of the other three, and went up to the house. He knocked on the window, and Newcomer thought it was the thumping of his own heart. Fortunately Ratcliffe was at home, and came hurriedly to the door, without stopping to dress. The two conversed in a low tone for some time, when Ratcliffe was heard to exclaim, "I'll be —— if you do!" and instantly started down toward the gate. Coming up to the prisoner, and throwing one arm around his neck, while he took his hand in his, he said to him—

"Great God! Harry, how fortunate that I am at home!"

After they had talked awhile together, Harris came up again, and called Ratcliffe to one side, where they had another protracted conversation, in a low, whispering tone. While they were thus engaged, a large owl on a tree near by began hooting, and was speedily answered by another some distance up the road. The three men mounted their horses at once and galloped to the road, shouting at the top of their voices—

"Captain, we're surrounded! This is a trap. Don't you hear the signals?"

The captain stepped to the road, listened a moment, and then, with a volley of oaths, ordered them back for a "pack of —— fools, to be scared at an owl." Still quaking with fear, which did not entirely leave them until they were fairly away from the place, they resumed their places, the owls hooting lustily all the while.

Harris and Ratcliffe continued their conversation for a few minutes, when the former came towards Newcomer with a pistol and some papers in each hand, saying, as he gave them to him:

"I release you and restore your property on the word of Quartermaster Ratcliffe. He assures me that you are one of the most important men in the south, and a secret agent of the Confederacy. I am very sorry that this thing has occurred, and will make any amends in my power. If you desire, I will go with you to the Charlotte pike as an escort, or will do you any favor you may ask."

"No," said Ratcliffe; "he must come in and stay all night with me. I can't let him go on to-night."

While standing at the gate, during this conversation, our released prisoner sold his pistols to the cavalrymen for Tennessee money. Just at this moment, too, a squad of cavalry belonging to Starns's command came by. One of them—to whom Newcomer had sold a pistol some weeks before—recognized him at once, and shook hands with him very cordially. He corroborated Ratcliffe's statement, saying that Newcomer was on very important business for the South, which was rendered still more so by the fight having begun at Stewart's creek. A short time was passed in general conversation, when all left except Newcomer, who hitched his horse to the porch and went in with Ratcliffe. When sufficient time had elapsed for them to be well out of the way, Newcomer said his business was of too much importance to brook delay, and he must be off at once. Ratcliffe said if he must go he could not urge him to stay. "I will go with you to your horse," said he; "meanwhile take this to keep you from further trouble. If anybody stops you again, just show them this, and you will be passed at once."

So saying, he took from his pocket a large government envelope—of which he had an abundance—and wrote on it:

"*All Right.*

"J. W. RATCLIFFE."

Armed with this, he started again, and reached the pickets of the Fifth Kentucky Cavalry, who brought him into the city. It was nearly three o'clock in the morning when he arrived at the police office; but the colonel was still up, and immediately telegraphed his report to headquarters.

The next day, nothing daunted, he set out again, and went, as usual, first to Ratcliffe's, where he remained all night—thence the next morning travelled, by way of Hart's crossroads and Caney Springs, to Murfreesboro, reaching that place on the Saturday evening closing the week of battles at Stone river. Riding about the town, he observed that nearly every house in it was a hospital. Every thing was confusion and excitement. Immense crowds of straggling soldiers and citizens were gathered about the court house and depot. Commissary and quartermaster stores, artillery, ammunition, and camp equipage, were being loaded on the cars, and trains were starting as fast as loaded. An evacuation was evidently on hand, and that right speedily; and he determined to leave as soon as possible. The only trouble was how to get out. After wandering around some time, seeking an opportunity, he came across a train of small wagons, with which the neighboring farmers had come to take home their wounded sons and brothers. Quick to embrace opportunities, he saw that now was his chance to escape. Dismounting from his horse, he led him by the bridle, and walked demurely behind one of these wagons, as though it was in his charge. Clad in butternut, and in every outward appearance resembling the others accompanying it, the deceit was not discovered, and he safely passed all the pickets. It was now nearly two o'clock in the morning, and he rode rapidly on, in a cold, driving rain, until fairly benumbed. Some nine miles out, he came to a deserted school-house, which he unceremoniously entered, leading his horse in after him. Within, a large fireplace and an abundance of desks suggested the idea of a fire, and a huge blaze roaring and crackling on the hearth soon demonstrated its practicability. The next step was to wring the water out of his well-soaked garments, and partially dry them. Both horse and man enjoyed themselves here until near daybreak, when he mounted again and rode on to Ratcliffe's, reaching there about three o'clock Sunday afternoon. Here he remained awhile to converse with his friend, refresh the inner man, and care for his horse—neither having eaten a mouthful since the morning before. Ratcliffe was rejoiced to see him, and wished him to remain longer; but he pushed ahead, and reached Nashville late that evening, well nigh worn-out with hunger, fatigue, and want of sleep. His report was immediately telegraphed to General Rosecrans; but he had been so long in making his way back that the general did not receive it until he had himself entered Murfreesboro.

Late the next night he started again, with a single pistol, and a small stock of needles, pins, and thread. On Monday evening he reached Ratcliffe's, and, staying but two hours, rode on two miles farther, to the house of one M. H. Perryear, with whom he remained all night. Thence he travelled, by way of Hart's crossroads, toward Caney Springs, but before reaching the latter place fell in with some of Wheeler's cavalry, with whom he rode along, friendly and companionably enough. Some of them were old acquaintances, and very confidential. They were, they said, just on their way to burn a lot of Federal wagons at Lavergne and Triune, and, deeming him a good fellow well met, invited him to go with them. Thinking that there might be some chance to save the wagons, he declined the invitation, urging the pressing nature and importance of his mission as an excuse. It was soon found, however, that every avenue of escape northward was guarded, and the whole country filled with the cavalry, of whom there were, in all, about three thousand. There was nothing to do, then, but to leave the wagons to their fate and push on, which he did, and, arriving at Caney Springs, remained there over night. The next morning the cavalry began to loiter back from their marauding expedition, in squads of from fifteen to a hundred or more, and from them he learned the complete success of the enterprise. Making the acquaintance of a lieutenant, he was told that they were going at once to Harpeth Shoals, to burn a fleet of boats which was then on its way to Nashville. This determined him to abandon the idea of going to Shelbyville, and he accompanied a detachment back as far as Hart's crossroads, where they went on picket-duty at a meeting-house by the road. Bidding them good-day, he started on alone toward Ratcliffe's. Stopping at Perryear's, he was told that Forrest was in Franklin, that the roads were all guarded, and that there was a picket just at Ratcliffe's gate. Perryear then gave him an open letter of introduction, recommending him to all officers and soldiers of the Confederate army as a true and loyal Southern man, engaged in business of the highest importance to the Government. With this he again set out, and, as he had been told, found a picket at Ratcliffe's gate. Requesting to be admitted, he was asked if he was a soldier, and, on answering negatively, was passed in without hesitation. Ratcliffe corroborated Perryear's statement, saying, furthermore, that Forrest was very strict, and that it would be much better for him to remain there until they had all gone down the river.

"But," added he, "if you must go, I'll go with yon as far as Franklin and help you through."

The town was found to be full of cavalry, who were conscripting every man whom they could lay hands on. Ratcliffe introduced his companion to Will Forrest—a brother of the general, and captain of his body-guard. The captain was profuse of oaths and compliments, and, withal, so very friendly that Newcomer at once told him his story and business, all of which was indorsed by Ratcliffe. More oaths and compliments followed. The captain was glad to know so important a man, and, by way of business, asked him if he had any pistols to sell.

"No," was the reply; "I have nothing but a single navy revolver, which I carry for my own defence, and which I wouldn't like to part with. But I am just going to Nashville for more goods, and, fearing trouble in getting away, I thought I would come and see about it."

"Oh, I guess there will be none," said the captain. "The general wants to know something about Nashville, and will be very apt to send you there to get the information for him. Come; let's go and see about it."

The two set forth, and found the general, surrounded by the usual crowd, at his hotel. Calling him to one side, the captain pointed out his new friend, and, explaining who and what he was, concluded by remarking that he wished to go to Nashville for goods, and would bring him any information he desired. The general, not just then in the best of humor, swore very roundly that he knew as much about Nashville as he wanted to—it was men he wanted—and concluded by ordering the captain to conscript his friend into either his own or some other company. Turning on his heel, he walked briskly away, leaving his brother to his anger and our would-be rebel spy to his disappointment. The captain fumed with great, sulphurous oaths, and consoled Newcomer thus wise:

"He's a —— fool, if he is my brother. You are the last man I'll ever bring to him to be insulted. But you sha'n't be conscripted. Come with me, and I'll help you through. You can go with my company, but not as a soldier, and I will send you to Nashville myself. My company always has the advance, and there'll be plenty of chances."

Making a virtue of necessity, this proposition was gladly accepted, and all started on the march. By this time Wheeler had come up and taken the lead, Forrest following in the centre, and Starns bringing up the rear. About eight miles from Franklin the whole command encamped for the night, and our hero slept under the same blanket with Captain Forrest and his lieutenant, —a Texan ranger named Scott, whose chief amusement seemed to consist in lassoing dogs while on the march, and listening to their yelping as they were pitilessly dragged along behind him. Toward midnight, one of their spies—a Northern man, named Sharp, and formerly in the plough business at Nashville—came in from the Cumberland river. Captain Forrest introduced Newcomer to him as a man after his own heart—"true as steel, and as sharp as they make 'em." The two spies became intimate at once, and Sharp belied his name by making a confidant of his new acquaintance. He had formerly been in Memphis, and acted as a spy for the cotton-burners. More recently he had been employed with Forrest; and now he had just come from Harpeth Shoals, where he had learned all about the fleet coming up the river, and to-morrow he was to guide the expedition down to a place where they could easily be captured and burned. Early next morning the march was resumed, and at the crossing of the Hardin pike General Forrest and staff were found waiting for them. Upon coming up, the captain was ordered to take his company down the Hardin pike, go on picket there, and remain until eleven o'clock; when, if nothing was to be seen, he was to rejoin the expedition. These instructions were promptly carried out—a good position being taken on a hill some eight miles from Nashville, from which could be had a view of the whole country for many miles in every direction. About ten o'clock the captain came to Newcomer and said he was going to send him to Nashville himself; at the same time giving him a list of such articles as he wished, consisting principally of gray cloth, staff-buttons, etc.

As may be imagined, no time was lost in starting, and

still less in getting into Nashville, where he arrived in due season to save the fleet. A force was at once sent out on the Hillsboro pike to cut off the retreat of the rebels, and another on the Charlotte pike to attack them directly. The latter force succeeded in striking their rear-guard, and threw them into confusion, when they hastily fled across the Harpeth river, which was at the time very high. Our forces, being principally infantry, could not cross in pursuit, but the troops on the Hillsboro pike succeeded in killing, wounding, and capturing considerable numbers of them. They were thoroughly scattered, however, and the fleet was saved—which was the main object of the expedition.

General Rosecrans had now been in Murfreesboro several days, and Colonel Truesdail immediately on his arrival sent the scout to that place. Here he made a full report, and, having received instructions for another trip, returned to Nashville the next day to make ready for it. The only item of interest on this trip was that at Eagleville he met Wheeler's command, by many of whom, and by the general himself, he was well and favorably known. Here Wheeler employed him as a secret agent, and gave him a permanent pass, which he still retains. Borrowing from one of his officers one hundred dollars in Tennessee money, the general gave it to him, and instructed him to buy with it certain articles which he mentioned—among which were gray cloth and staff buttons, always in demand for uniforms. Stopping at Ratcliffe's on his return, he showed him the pass, and related the circumstances of getting it, at which the former was highly gratified—"as," said he, "you'll have no more trouble now, Harry."

At Nashville, he succeeded, of course with the permission of the Union authorities, in filling General Wheeler's order, and charged with such information as General Mitchell and Colonel Truesdail saw fit to impart, he took another trip to the rebel lines. Wheeler was at this time at Franklin, quartered in the court house. The goods and information were delivered, much to the gratification of the rebel general, who forthwith instructed him to return to Nashville for more information and late Northern papers. He was by this time so well known, and so highly esteemed by the rebels, that the cashier of the Franklin branch of the Planter's bank of Tennessee, entrusted to him the accounts and valuable papers of the branch bank to carry to the parent institution at Nashville. This duty he performed faithfully. On his way, he stopped at the house of one Prior Smith, a violent rebel, and extensive negro dealer. He was cordially received by Smith, who tried to interest him in the business of running off negro children from Nashville, to be sold south. Newcomer declined entering upon it; but Smith insisted, and gave him a letter of introduction to his "right bower," in Nashville, who proved to be a Dr. Hudson, a man of wealth, who professed to be a Union man, but had long been considered suspicious. The Chief of Police, Colonel Truesdail, desired him now to spend some time in Nashville in developing the case of Dr. Hudson, but he deemed it necessary first, to return to Wheeler, and received permission to do so. At Franklin, he found that Wheeler had gone on to Shelbyville, and stopping with his friend Ratcliffe, the two wrote out the information he had received, and sealed it up with the papers in large (rebel) government envel-

KILPATRICK.
MERRITT
BUFORD
SHERIDAN.
AVERILL.
TORBERT
CUSTER
VAN INGEN & SNYDER

opes, and forwarded by carrier to Wheeler. Having spent the night with Ratcliffe, he returned the next morning, and immediately entered upon the work of following up the Hudson case. Delivering Prior Smith's letter of introduction, he very soon gained the full confidence of Dr. Hudson and his wife, and found them ready to do any thing to further and aid the rebel cause. Dr. Hudson was very wealthy, and possessed an elegant residence in Nashville, with every comfort and convenience to be desired, extensive iron-works near Harpeth Shoals, and a tract of three thousand acres, attached together, with a large amount of other property. He had taken the oath of allegiance, and furnished milk to several of the hospitals as a cover for his plans for furnishing arms, ammunition, medicines, equipments, etc., to the rebel armies; aided rebel prisoners to escape, kidnapped negroes, and sold them south; aided and stimulated the burning of Union warehouses, transports, etc., etc. In all these iniquitous transactions his wife assisted to the best of her ability, and the two were in communication with all the principal rebels in Louisville and south of the Union lines. In all these operations, Newcomer soon succeeded in making him commit himself before other detectives, whom he had introduced as officers of Ashby's cavalry, paroled rebel prisoners, Wheeler's spies, etc., etc., and when the proof was complete, caused the arrest of Dr. and Mrs. Hudson, and several of their accomplices. On examination, there were found at his house large quantities of contraband goods, including numerous pistols (revolvers), muskets, rifles, bullets, and shot, domestic and woollen goods, morphine and quinine, of the latter, ninety-nine ounces. After imprisonment and trial, the Dr. and his wife were sent south beyond the lines, and their property confiscated.

Newcomer was subsequently employed in ferreting out other cases of a similar character, of which there were great numbers in Louisville and Nashville. In one of these he detected one Trainer, a wagon master in the Union army, and his wife, who were engaged in rendering all possible aid and comfort to the rebels, by smuggling supplies, and placing the trains of the Union army in dangerous positions, and caused their arrest, as well as that of several of their accomplices. From these adroit smugglers was taken about five thousand five hundred dollars' worth of quinine, morphine, and opium, and in consequence of the discoveries made, two drug stores, a wholesale and a retail store, were seized with their contents, to the value of about seventy-five thousand dollars more.

Through his efforts, and those of other detectives in the employ of the army police, the extensive smuggling which had been carried on by rebel emissaries in Nashville and Louisville was rendered so dangerous that most of it was abandoned.

PAULINE CUSHMAN,

THE CELEBRATED UNION SPY AND SCOUT OF THE ARMY OF THE CUMBERLAND.

Among the wild and dashing exploits which have signalized the recent war—rivalling in heroic and dramatic interest the most famous achievements of the earlier days of chivalry—few are more striking or picturesque than the simple narrative of facts which we are about to relate.

Miss Pauline Cushman, or "Major" Cushman, as she is, by right, most generally called, was born in the city of New Orleans, on the 10th day of June, 1833, her father being a Spaniard, a native of Madrid, and a prosperous merchant of the Crescent city, and her mother a French woman of excellent social position and attainments. In course of time, her father met with losses which followed one another in rapid succession, and unable to stay the tide of adversity, after a brave but unavailing struggle, he abandoned his enterprises in New Orleans, and removed with his family to Grand Rapids, Michigan. This town was at that time little more than a frontier settlement, and opening an establishment for the purposes of trade with the neighboring Indians, he soon found himself in active and successful business. Pauline, meanwhile, the only girl in a family of six brothers, had arrived at the age of ten years, and was growing in beauty and intelligence. The circumstances which surrounded her domestic life, however, somewhat clouded the joy of the young girl's earlier years. Her father's rigid nature and strong passions ill matched with her mother's gentle and retiring temperament, and she was therefore sometimes compelled to witness scenes of domestic discord, which made home far less desirable than it should have been. Fortunately, however, her natural inclinations led her mostly to indulge in out-door sports, and she was thus enabled to disperse in the sun shine of forgetfulness the oppressive gloom which too frequently clouded their little home circle. And, more than that, amid the plains, the varied scenes of frontier life, and the wild companions that surrounded her in her new western home, she insensibly laid the foundation of that physical strength and beauty, and that courageous spirit, which has since distinguished her every action. In her father's store, little Pauline became acquainted with the most noted "braves" of the neighboring Indian tribes, and by her kindly attentions to their wants, and her many innocent, childish ways, completely gained their confidence and good-will, as was manifested by the poetic appellation, "Laughing Breeze," which they bestowed upon her. As time passed, she grew up as straight as an arrow, and beautiful as a prairie rose. None could use the rifle more dexterously than she; none could excel her—whether coursing the broad plains, mounted on the back of a half-tamed steed, without saddle or bridle, or stemming the fierce mountain currents in her light canoe—while few among the dusky natives of the region could wing an arrow with greater certainty than this pale-faced maiden. But gradually civilization in his westward march reached and revolutionized the frontier town where she dwelt. And with the novelties and luxuries, the inventions and improvements, which came from the far eastern cities—from New York, Philadelphia, etc.—came also wonderful reports of the fascinations and delights of life to be found there. Exaggerated by distance, and by her own bright imagination, which pictured all things *couleur de rose*, these glowing descriptions awakened in Pauline's breast the most intense desire to see and participate in their realities. And, ere long, we find her in New York, waiting for an opportunity to take her first step in the *real* life of which, on the far off prairies, she had so often dreamed. The opportunity was nearer than she thought, for soon she fell in with Mr. Thomas Placide, manager of the New Orleans "Varieties," who, struck by her handsome face and figure, at once proposed that she should enter into an engagement with him, and appear at his theatre. She accepted the proposition, and, in due time, made her *debut* upon the boards of the "Varieties," inspiring in the hearts of the impressible people of New Orleans an admiration which partook of the nature of a *furor*. Gifted with rare natural gifts of mind and body, she soon became widely known as one of the first of American actresses. It was not, however, until the spring of March, 1863, that Miss Cushman exchanged the *role* of the actress for the *real acting* of a noble and patriot woman, risking her life in solemn and terrible earnestness for her country's good.

She was, at that time, playing at Mozart Hall, or "Wood's Theatre," in Louisville, Ky., then the headquarters of the rebel sympathizers of the southwest; and, although under Union rule, these gentry had become so emboldened, from long continued success, as to almost set the Federal authorities at defiance. At the house where Miss Cushman boarded, she was unavoidably thrown into the company of many of these disloya persons; and among her acquaintances she numbered two paroled rebel officers, Colonel Spear, and Captain J. H. Blincoe, whom, apart from all political considerations, she had admitted to a certain degree of friendship. She was at that time acting the part of Plutella, in the "Seven Sisters," and every one who has seen this widely popular play, will remember that Plutella has to assume, during the course of the piece, many characters—at one time a dashing Zouave officer, at another, a fine gentleman of fashion, and in this last character is supposed to drink wine with a friend. One afternoon, while receiving a call from these two rebel officers, and talking over the play, they suddenly proposed to her to "drink a Southern toast in the evening, and see what effect it will have upon the audience." In surprise, she exclaimed, "But I should be locked up in jail, if I were to attempt any thing of that kind." They, however, scouted the idea, and finally offered her three hundred dollars in greenbacks, if she would do it. Stifling her indignation at the base proposal, she pretended to assent, and asked merely for a little time to think it over. The gentlemen left to prepare matters for the expected surprise; but no sooner were they fairly out of sight, than with cheeks burning and eyes flashing, the actress proceeded to the office of Colonel Moore, the United States Provost-Marshal, with whom she had a slight acquaintance, and to whom she related the whole affair. He quietly and kindly heard her story, and then, thanking her for her confidence, coolly advised her to carry out the programme of her rebel advisers, and drink the toast, as proposed, at the theatre that evening. Her amazement at this may be better imagined than described; but the colonel finally overcame her scruples, giving her to understand that she could render her country a true service by following his advice, and promising that he would himself be present at the theatre. "Fear not," he said; "it is for a deeper reason than you think, that I beg you to do this thing. Good may come of it, to your country, that you know not of." To the view of her duty, as thus presented, she patriotically yielded her assent, and returned to her lodgings to prepare for the new *role* which she was to act, and to get ready foı the momentous event of the evening. It was enough for her to know that good to her country was to flow from her apparently treasonable act, and that some design, of which she was yet unconscious, was concealed beneath it. The afternoon was well improved by her rebel friends in publishing abroad in the "secesh" circles of the city, that something rich was to come off that evening at the theatre. It seemed to our heroine that the afternoon would never wear away; and yet, as the hour approached, her heart beat fast at the thought that the momentous moment was hastening on. At last the hour arrived for her to set out to the theatre. No sooner had she stepped within the building, than she saw that it was literally packed. Not even standing room was to be had for love or money. Every rebel sympathizer in town had heard of it, and all were there. The time approached for the play to begin. The musicians in the orchestra tuned their big fiddles in their usual mysterious manner. Ushers began to call out the numbers of seats, and to slam the doors in their wonted style. The "call-boy" flew here and there, and at last, in obedience to the prompter's bell, the curtain began to rise, discovering Mr. Pluto at breakfast, within the shades of Hades. There was, however, a veritable Pluto to burst upon them, that they wot not of. This was coming. In the meantime, the jokes and mirth of the "Seven Sisters" were more than ordinarily relished. It may have been that those in the secret were so delighted at the prospect of seeing the Federal authorities thus wantonly insulted, that they greeted every thing with rapture, and that this became contagious among the good Union people of the house, who of course, were ignorant of the joke. At length the critical moment arrived, and advancing in her theatrical costume to the foot lights, our heroine, goblet in hand, gave, in a clear, ringing voice, the following toast:

"HERE'S TO JEFF. DAVIS AND THE SOUTHERN CONFEDERACY. MAY THE SOUTH ALWAYS MAINTAIN HER HONOR AND HER RIGHTS!"

Miss Cushman had prepared herself for a fearful outbreak of popular opinion, but for a moment even the hearts of the audience seemed to stop beating. Then, however, it burst forth, and such a scene followed as beggars description. The good Union portion of the audience had set, at first, spell-bound and horrified by the fearful treason thus outspoken, while the "secesh" were frozen with the audacity of the act, though conscious that it was to occur. But then came the mingled storm of applause and condemnation. Fierce and tumultuous it raged, until it seemed as though it would never stop. Nor was the scene behind the scenes less intense. The manager, rushing up to our heroine, demanded, in his most tragic tone, "what she meant by such conduct;" while the rest of the professional gentlemen and ladies avoided her as though she had suddenly been stricken with some fearfully contagious disease. The brave girl, however, had her cue, and boldly avowed that she "wasn't afraid of the whole Yankee crew, and would do it again." In short, she carried out her part so well, that no one doubted for a moment that she was a most virulent secessionist. Before she had left the theatre, the guards arrived to arrest her; but—out of respect to Mr. Wood, the proprietor of the theatre—they were deterred from actually executing their errand,

and it was arranged that she should report at headquarters at ten o'clock the next morning. There she was welcomed in the private office in the kindest manner, and earnestly thanked by Colonel Moore, and his superior, General Boyle, for the capital manner in which she had carried out the *pseudo*-treasonable plan. She was now enlightened as to the design of the United States officers, who informed her that she must enter the *secret service* of the government. They also advised her to moderate her "secesh" proclivities in *public*, as if she had received a severe reprimand from General Boyle; but, in *private*, to abuse the government, and say all the harm she could about it; by which means she would inspire confidence among the disaffected, and would be of incalculable use to the national cause. Promising a ready and strict compliance with these requests, she returned to her lodgings, where she found a note awaiting her from the management of the theatre, discharging her from her engagement there.

Thrown afresh, as it were, upon the world, Miss Cushman now found herself in a most peculiar and embarrassing position. Shunned by her former friends as bearing the brand of disloyalty—slighted—jeered at—flung by the force of her own act upon the sympathies and companionship of a cowardly crew of rebel sympathizers, from whose treason her very nature revolted, her situation was one of peculiar hardship and disagreeableness. She was sustained, however, by the thought that she was sacrificing her own prospects and feelings for her country's good. The work before her was full of danger, excitement, and importance. Louisville, at this time, was undermined by disloyal sentiments and treasonable plots. Every expedient that human and disloyal ingenuity could devise to annoy and harass the loyal Union people of that section, or to cripple the power and operations of the government, was resorted to with malignant delight—even by wealthy and well known citizens of Louisville. Many of these plots Miss Cushman was the means of bringing to light and to punishment; and, in so doing, had to assume various disguises, mingling with every class of people, from the cut-throats of the low groggeries to the best circles of "secesh" society. Her most dangerous service, however, was scouting in search of guerillas, to accomplish which, she was frequently compelled to don male attire and to remain in the saddle all night; and many and varied were the strange adventures which she met with. But her coolness, her energy, and patriotism carried her successfully through these experiences, and God's special providence seemed always to be with her. The most important service, however, which she rendered her country while in Louisville, was the detection of her landlady in the act of mixing up poison in the coffee of a number of sick and wounded Union soldiers, who had been quartered upon her. She managed to play the "sympathizer" until she had gained a full knowledge of the plan, and then secretly informed the United States authorities, by whom the poor soldiers were removed in time from the fate which awaited them, and the fiend-woman was treated to her deserved punishment.

At another time, personating the somewhat notorious George N. Sanders, purporting to have just returned from Europe with highly important despatches, concerning the recognition of the Confederacy, etc., and also a certain Captain Denver, *alias* Conklin, Miss Cushman most successfully "gammoned" some of the leading secessionists of Louisville, especially a Mrs. Ford, and placed a very effectual embargo on a large amount of quinine, morphine, and other medicines, which were in transit to the rebel army.

In course of time, Mr. J. R. Allen, of the new theatre of Nashville, Tenn., arrived at Louisville, engaged in looking up a good company of actors, and meeting with Mr. Wood of the Louisville theatre, was recommended to secure Miss Cushman. "She is a good looking woman, and an accomplished actress, but she will talk 'secesh.' If you can only keep her out of the provost-marshal's hands, you will make a good thing, for she will be popular at once," said Mr. Wood. So the proposition was made to Pauline, and, after advising with the military authorities, under whose guidance she was acting, she determined to accept it. Of course, in order to maintain her assumed part, the authorities had to refuse her a "pass," and her only way, therefore, to get out of Louisville, was to "run the blockade." Proceeding, at the appointed time, to the cars, she got a "secesh" gentleman, going to Nashville, to attend to her trunk; then she requested leave of the guard, at the door of the car, to speak to a friend inside, "only for one minute." Her woman's face prevailed, he let her pass, and she took pains to stay within the car. When the officer of the guard came around to inspect the passes, she had a "made up story" all ready, at the same time showing her order from Mr. Allen to report herself immediately at his theatre. He hesitated, but her pleasing face and a few womanly tears carried the point, and our heroine was soon on her way to Nashville, at that time the base of operations of the glorious Army of the Southwest.

On her arrival at Nashville, she met with a warm reception from "Secessia," who were brimful of congratulations at her escape from the Federal power at Louisville, and of exultation at her having got away from that place without even securing a "pass" or taking the oath of allegiance. In her character of actress she soon became exceedingly popular, but her stay at the theatre was a short one; for, on her return from rehearsal one day, she found a summons from Colonel Truesdail, the chief of the army police of Nashville. On entering his office, she was received by him politely but distantly, as due to a stranger; but, no sooner had he dismissed his clerks, than his whole manner changed to one of cordiality. After complimenting her for her previous important services to the country, he informed her that he had selected her for a duty that would not only require the greatest discretion, constancy, and quickness of perception which she could command, but which was one of extraordinary peril—an undertaking which might end in glory, or in an ignominious death by the bullet, or *by the rope!* At these words she involuntarily shrank back, but yet she answered in a firm tone:

"Colonel Truesdail, hundreds, aye, thousands of our noble soldiers, each one of greater service to our country than my poor self, have gladly given up their lives in her cause. Should I hesitate to do as much? No; I will do all that a woman *should* do, and all that a man *dare* do, for my country and the Union!"

Charmed with the noble heroism which breathed in these words, the colonel proceeded to reveal the service for which she was to be detailed, and to give her the necessary instructions. The duty which was required of her, was to secretly visit the rebel General Bragg's headquarters, an enterprise at that time of the greatest importance, and one upon which the whole fate of the Union cause seemed to depend. First, she was to be sent out of the lines, in company with many other rebel women who were being sent South, in obedience to a late order of General Mitchell. To this very natural reason, she added another, *i. e.*, that she had a brother, A. A. Cushman, who was a colonel somewhere in the rebel army, and a professed anxiety to find him afforded a very clever *ostensible* reason for her travelling from headquarters to headquarters, and from place to place through the South. She was then instructed to make no confidants; not to talk *too much;* to make the same answers to all parties, and never to deviate from the story, when once framed. The search for her brother was to be the free and confessed object of her travels, and under this pretence she was to visit the rebel armies at Columbia, Shelbyville, Wartrace, Tullahoma, and Manchester. She was to make no direct inquiries of officers or others concerning the strength of the Confederate forces, movements, supplies, etc., but, in accepting the offers to ride and other attentions which her personal attractions would probably secure her from officers, she was to keep her eyes open, and note every thing of importance which she might see. In the hospitals, she was to make such observations as she could, concerning the medical and hospital supplies, the number of sick and wounded soldiers, etc. But she was especially advised not, on any account, to make any memorandum or tracings of any kind; only keeping a brief memoranda of the houses at which she stopped, amount of bill, and date, which being so customary as not to excite suspicion, would yet serve to refresh the memory on certain points. The Oath of Fidelity to the United States was then solemnly administered to Miss Cushman; the gallant colonel presented to her a handsome "six-shooter," and on a glorious May morning, under the pretended surveillance of an officer, she was conveyed beyond the lines as a disloyal woman. Arrived at a point some three miles distant from Nashville, out of sight of any human habitation, the carriage stopped, and Miss Cushman found awaiting her a fine bay horse, fully caparisoned, which she mounted, and bidding farewell to her military escort, she galloped gayly down the Hardin pike, followed by the good wishes of the few who knew her real character and purpose.

The close of her first day's journey brought her to the Big Harpeth river, the bridge across which had been so injured by the rebels that it was impossible for any one to cross it, and in following a side path which seemed to lead to a ford, Miss Cushman came upon a nice looking dwelling house, where she stopped to inquire about the road. From the inmates she found that it would be impossible to cross at present, at least without help; and accordingly, the sympathies of the woman of the house having been fully enlisted by the story of the cruel treatment received by Miss Cushman from the Federal authorities of Nashville, she was allowed to spend the night there. In the morning, her host, Milam by name, who carried on a considerable business in smuggling goods and supplies out of Nashville for the benefit of his rebel friends across the river, purchased her horse and equipments, giving her confederate funds therefore and hired her a buggy and driver under whose care she set forth in the direction of Columbia. Through dreary woods and terrible roads and a drenching rain they pursued their way, finally arriving at her destination; where she was, fortunately for her strength, compelled to wait, for three days, the re-opening of the railroad to Shelbyville, which had been destroyed by the Union troops. While here, she met with much sympathy from the rebels, to whom she appeared in the character of an abused woman, seeking for her brother, an officer in the army; and she also had to pass the scrutiny of more experienced judges—officers, and others high in official rank. But she bore the test, and in turn made the most suspicious her most useful tools. Columbia proved a rich field to our heroine, who made many friends and accumulated much valuable acquaintance while there. Soon she went to Shelbyville, from whence she found, much to her annoyance, that Bragg had removed his headquarters—and where she could not ascertain. But, ever alive to any opportunity that offered of doing good to her country, she acquired some valuable information which more than compensated her for the frustration of her original object in visiting Shelbyville. It chanced that she learned that at the same hotel table where she dined there sat a young officer of engineers, who was engaged in drawing important plans for the rebel government. She immediately conceived the plan of obtaining these plans, at whatever risk to herself, and to get back to the Federal lines, which she thought could be easily effected, and in time to be of the utmost service to her country. As an excuse for wishing to return to the Federal lines, she would represent that having been hurriedly sent out of Nashville by the Federal officers, she had been compelled to leave all her theatrical wardrobe behind her in her flight, and now she was desirous of recovering it, so that she might be able to accept some engagement at some of the theatres throughout the country, and earn enough money to enable her to pursue her journey in search of her brother. Luckily, as if to further her plans, about this time, she received the offer of an engagement from the manager of the Richmond theatre, which of course tallied exactly with her scheme. Her next move was to get acquainted with the young engineer officer, which was soon effected by a letter of safeguard given her by one of her Shelbyville friends, Major Boone; and soon, with her pretty woman's ways, she had won his entire confidence so completely, that he even offered to give her letters of introduction to General Bragg. Calling upon him at his office, she was warmly welcomed, and finally excusing himself whilst he retired to an adjoining room to write the promised letters of introduction, Miss Cushman found herself alone in the room with the much coveted plans and drawings. In the few moments which elapsed during his absence from the room, she contrived to slip the plans into her bosom, and when he returned, she received from him the letters and left him as unsuspecting and as pleasant as ever—unconscious of his loss. Shortly after she left Shelbyville on her way to

Mc PHERSON.
WADSWORTH
KEARNEY.
SEDGEWICK.
REYNOLDS.
SUMNER.
LYON.
RENO.
BIRNEY.
O M MITCHELL.

Nashville; and, during a short halt, at a place called Wartrace, she undertook a scouting enterprise with the view of communicating valuable information to some of the roving bands of Union cavalry, who were almost daily engaged in skirmishing with the rebel cavalry. In carrying out this plan, her first requisite was, of course, a man's suit of clothes, and to get these she now set her wits to work. At the same hotel where she was stopping was a young man of about seventeen years of age, whose clothes she thought would just fit her, but how to get them was the question. With only the knowledge that he slept in the upper story of the house, but provokingly ignorant of which room he occupied, she resolved to "scout" around in the dark, and, "hit or miss," make a desperate attempt to secure the clothes.

So after a series of adventures in the dark, which succeeded only in arousing nearly all the inmates of the several rooms on the corridor, our discomfited heroine, beating a hasty retreat from the discovery which now seemed inevitable, desperately tried the handle of a small door near at hand. To her great joy it yielded, and slipping hastily in, she found herself in a low, poorly-furnished chamber—in which lay sleeping the very man whose clothes she had been seeking. Luckily, the uproar in the hall had not awakened him, and waiting till all was quiet again, she grabbed the clothes and sped silently to her own room. Hastily dressing herself in the stolen suit, she crept softly down-stairs, past the sleeping negro boy in the hall, out to the stables, and there she speedily saddled one of the best horses which she could find, and pushed her way out of the town.

Into the woods she rode, and finally, when some three miles out of Wartrace, came suddenly upon a guerilla encampment, and was busily engaged in playing the eavesdropper to their camp-fire conversation when she unluckily stepped upon a brittle branch which snapped under her feet. Instantly they took the alarm, and she scarcely had time to mount her horse before they were in full chase after her. Gradually they gained upon her, when suddenly she found herself approaching, at full speed, a precipitous rock, at the foot of which meandered a small stream. It was impossible to check the headlong speed of her horse, and her pursuers were close upon her; so, shutting her eyes, and striking the spurs deep into the animals flanks, she plunged down the mountain side. Her pursuers did not dare to follow, but standing at the top of the bluff, contented themselves with winging their pistol bullets after her. Suddenly, just as she hoped that she was fairly escaped, one of her pursuers discovered a bridle path, and the chase recommenced. Pushing hastily into the woods which lined the creek, she endeavored to regain the road to Wartrace, for she was now threatened with two dilemmas; if daylight overtook her before she could get back to the hotel, her theft of the clothes and horse would be discovered; and if taken by her pursuers she would inevitably be taken to Wartrace, it being the nearest town. On she rode, at full speed, until she found herself gaining upon the rebel riders, and suddenly came upon a wounded Union cavalryman, scarce able to sit upon his horse, from the effects of a wound received while scouting, a few hours before. She at first mistook him for a "reb," but ascertaining the truth, a plan of escape flashed through her brain, and she quickly revealed to him her sex and name, and asked his aid. The brave fellow had heard of the "Woman scout of the Cumberland," and, faint and wounded as he was, gladly and bravely offered to carry out her plan at the risk of his life. Firing her pistol into the air, she instructed the soldier to say to the pursuing party, who would inevitably be drawn thither by the report, that he had been met and shot by a "reb." She told him that he could not expect, from his wounds, to escape capture, and advised him to stir himself around so as to make his wound bleed afresh. He obeyed, and let himself fall off his horse, while Miss Cushman gave the animal a sharp blow which sent him flying down the road. When the rebel horsemen galloped up to the spot, they found the soldier lying at the foot of a tree, bleeding freely, and in a state of unconsciousness from his sudden fall, while over him bent our heroine, pistol in hand. To their surprised and hurried query who she was, she promptly replied: "I am a farmer's son, over near Wartrace, and I surrender to you; but I have shot your best fellow, here, and only wish I had shot more of ye." To their astonished looks and questions as to what he meant, she replied in the same bitter vein; "I mean just what I say. I am only sorry that I didn't kill more of you darned Yankees, that comes down yhere and runs all our niggers off!" Completely misled by her skilful acting, the rebels now saw that the boy had mistaken them for Yankees; and on questioning the Yankee soldier, who was gradually recovering from his faintness, the brave fellow, true to instructions, designated the "farmer's boy," as the one who had shot him, "because he was a Yankee." It now became evident to the "rebs" that each party had mistaken the other for "Yanks;" but for further precaution, Pauline was ordered to accompany them, and the wounded soldier was placed on a horse, and the party took up their march to Wartrace. This was a programme not at all agreeable to her, and as they rode along through the darkness of the forest, she conceived the idea of creating a "scare," hoping to avail herself of the confusion to get off and make her escape to Wartrace before daylight should make it too late to escape detection as a thief. So as they were passing through a narrow gorge of the road, thickly overshadowed by tall forest trees, —a nice place for an ambush—she managed to fall behind the party and become hidden by a bend in the road. Then taking out her revolver, she fired five shots in rapid succession. As she expected, her rebel companions were startled. Supposing themselves ambushed by Federal cavalry, fear lent a thousand terrors to their minds, and their imaginations gave new echoes to the reports of the pistol. Away they went, pell-mell, and laughing heartily at the success of her "scare," Miss Cushman rapidly galloped to Wartrace, where she luckily succeeded in comfortably housing her steed and in returning the borrowed clothes, without detection—and, in due time, answered the summons of the breakfast bell, as rosy and fresh-faced, and as innocent in look and manner, as if the night had been spent comfortably in her bed.

After several stirring adventures at Tullahoma, where she made a short stay, she returned to Columbia, where she remained awhile, engaged in picking up all the information which it was possible to secure. Here, too, she met her friends (and lovers too, if truth were spoken),

Major Boone, and Captain P. A. Blackman, rebel quartermaster, the latter of whom urged her to adopt man's apparel and join the Confederate army, with the promise of a position as his aide-de-camp, and the rank of lieutenant. This flattering proposition was accepted—the enamored captain forthwith ordered a complete rebel officer's uniform, and it was agreed that so soon as she should return from her proposed trip to Nashville, she should accompany him as *aide*. Meanwhile, she was not slow to accept every invitation from him to ride over the neighboring country, thereby gaining that complete knowledge of camps, fortifications, and the paraphernalia of war, which was deemed essential to the new officer. It may here be noticed that Miss Cushman now departed from the strict instructions which she had received from her military superiors, not to make drawings, plans, etc., of fortifications; and at Shelbyville and Tullahoma she made careful and accurate drawings, which she concealed between the inner and outer soles of her boot. This dereliction of duty, though intended for the best, proved the ultimate cause of the troubles and miseries which afterward befell her. On her return to the house at the crossing of the Big Harpeth river, in company with the same man who had brought her over before, he induced her to cross the bridge on foot, saying that the ford was impassable, owing to late rains. She did so, and instead of following by another ford, he incontinently disappeared, leaving her with but a small moiety of her baggage, some distance from her destination, and the night rapidly approaching. Indeed it was quite dark when she reached Milam's house, where she had spent the night and sold her horse before going to Columbia.

Mrs. Milam, who had before been so cordial, was now evidently suspicious, and our heroine's comfort was not increased by her interview with the husband on the following morning. He informed her that her trunks which she had left at Nashville, had been seized by Colonel Truesdail, whereupon she made a great show of pretended indignation, declaring that she would go to Nashville, "if she had to walk all the way," and get them back; and offering to buy back her horse. Unfortunately, her host, who had made her a confidant of his treasonable plans and acts when she was his guest on the occasion of her going to Columbia, as he thought, permanently, was suspicious of her sudden return, and by no means inclined to injure his own prospects, by helping her to return to Nashville, where, if false to her assumed character, he knew she would "post" the authorities concerning him. He therefore communicated with the nearest rebel scout post, and ere long she was placed under arrest, and transferred to Anderson's Mill, where she was disarmed and examined by the officer in charge. Finding that she had no "pass," she was held as a prisoner of war, until her case could be reported to and acted upon by General Bragg. Moreover, she was not allowed to return to the house at Big Harpeth where she had left a satchel containing her rebel uniform and several articles of pressing use and value. Fortunately she had come across her horse on the road to Anderson's Mill, at the house of one De Moss, and claiming him at once, had taken possession of him, and as night closed in, she found herself again on the road, still a prisoner. About noon the next day, her guide stopped with her for refreshment at the house of a well-known physician, and while there, a large body of Confederate cavalry passed, under command of the famous General Morgan. His attention being called to Miss Cushman, he detailed her guard to another special duty, and took her under his own care and watch, and she enjoyed his gallant attentions until they reached Hillsboro, where she was handed over to another scout to be taken to General Forrest's headquarters.

During the long ride which ensued she concocted another nice little scheme for escape. Knowing that General Rosecrans was much dreaded by the rebels in that part of the country, who hardly knew where they might next expect an attack from him, she knew that if she could raise the cry, "Old Rosy is coming," a general "skedaddle" would ensue, *instanter*. She felt sure, also, that she was not regarded as a very important political prisoner, and would probably be dropped immediately by her guards, in order to effect their own escape. Her horse, she noticed, stood still saddled in a small outhouse, and the storm which raged with much fury, was favorable to her project. Watching her opportunity, therefore, she made friends with an aged negro man about the place, and gave him a ten dollar greenback if he would, at a proper time of night, run up the road a piece, and then back again, shouting as loud as he could, "the Yankees are coming!" The old negro entered heartily into the plan, and carried it out successfully. At the darkest hour of the stormy night, the whole "negro quarters" poured into the house where the guards and their prisoner were sleeping, and "the Yanks! the Yanks am a-coming!" resounded from a dozen thoroughly frightened throats. *Sauve qui peut,* was the word, the rebels fled incontinently, and our heroine, flinging herself upon her horse, sped away on the road to Franklin. She had provided herself, somehow, with a pistol belonging to a wounded rebel soldier in a house where she had stopped; and pushing her way fearlessly along she reached and passed, with peculiar adroitness, five rebel pickets, but was finally foiled and obliged to turn back before the unswervable honesty of the last picket on the road, who would not allow her to pass him without the proper document. At a house near the road, where death had bereaved the family of an infant child, the tired girl found a refuge and shelter from storm and fatigue.

She was awakened from her sound slumbers the next morning by the unwelcome appearance of four of the rebel scouts from whom she had escaped the night before, and who had tracked her all the way from Hillsboro. Although she pretended to be glad to see them and explained her separation from them as the result of her fears of the "Yanks," they were neither gulled nor mollified, but gruffly ordered her to accompany them back, without even taking the breakfast which her kind hostess pressed upon them. And soon she was in the saddle, and proceeding on her journey, under the care of her scouts, who evinced more than usual watchfulness over her. She was first taken to General Morgan, who received her with his wonted courteousness, and he accompanied her to General Forrest's headquarters. That celebrated chief, after a trying examination, sent her, under guard, to General Bragg. On arriving at Shelbyville, she was shown at once to the general's headquarters, which were in the heart of the camp. On entering she was met by a small sized man, with small, dark gray eyes, iron gray hair and whiskers, and bronzed face. This was General Bragg. His manner was stern, but gentlemanly, and after glancing over the papers handed to him by her guide, he began:

"Of what country are you a native, Miss Cushman?" he asked, waving her to a chair with his hand.

"I am an American, sir; but of French and Spanish parentage," she answered.

"And you were born where?" he asked.

"In the city of New Orleans."

"Hum!" ejaculated the general, doubtingly. "How comes it, then, that—that your pronunciation has the Yankee twang?"

"It comes, probably, from the fact that I am, professionally, an actress," she answered promptly, "and as I am in the habit of playing Yankee characters very frequently, it may be that I've caught the "twang" by it, and show it in my ordinary conversation, as well as on the stage."

"Hum!" growled the general again. "But what brought you down South?"

"I was not *brought*, sir; I was *sent*," answered Pauline, proudly.

"By whom, may I ask, Miss Cushman?"

"By the Federal Colonel, Truesdail."

"And *why* were you *sent?*" inquired Bragg, with a sly look of incredulity.

"Because I gave warm utterance to my Southern feelings, and refused to take their oath of allegiance," replied our heroine, pretending to shed tears, "and a pretty way I'm paid for it, too!'

"Why wouldn't you take the oath?" persisted Bragg, apparently untouched by her youth and beauty in tears.

"I had declared that I wouldn't take it, and I meant to stick to my word!" replied Pauline, stoutly.

The general studied the expression of her countenance for a moment, and then continued.

"What was the main charge that the Federals made against you?"

"I had publicly drank to the success of the South and our Confederacy. It was on the stage of the Louisville theatre, and I did it at the request of two paroled Confederate officers, who, if they were now here, would tell you the same thing," and our heroine related the whole occurence of the toast, etc.

"Well, what happened then?" remarked the general.

"I was at once discharged from the theatre, and went to Nashville, where I got a fresh engagement, only to be sent away in turn; for Colonel Truesdail, the chief of the Federal army police, getting wind of my Southern sentiments, and hearing of my drinking the toast wishing success to the South, immediately ordered me to leave the Federal jurisdiction, and wouldn't even allow me to take my trunk or theatrical wardrobe with me."

The perfect coherence of her story, and her apparently calm and truthful manner was not without its effect upon the general, who after a brief pause, during which he carefully scrutinized her, resumed in a more kindly tone:

"Miss Cushman, this statement of yours *may* be all correct, but still I should like to have you give some *positive proof* of your loyalty to our cause; for, as it stands, I must say it appears, at best, very doubtful."

"General," replied Pauline, pointedly, "I have been seized and brought hither to meet charges laid against me, I presume; but assuredly not to *investigate and decide my own case.* You cannot be expected to believe *my* statement; therefore, all I can say is, to produce your charges and the evidence, and when the examination is over, I think that my loyalty to the South will shine with as bright and steady a lustre as does your own. After that, if you still doubt me, or if one suspicion still lingers in your mind, give me a place near you in battle, and you will see that Pauline Cushman will fight as bravely and faithfully as any man in your army."

Half amused, and half convinced by this speech, the old soldier continued his searching examination, striving in every way to entrap and confuse her, and to elicit from her all the information which he could concerning the plans, movements, and operations of the Federal commanders. She, on the contrary, assumed an innocent appearance of ignorance on these points, although careful to speak the truth in whatever she did say. It was a keen contest of wit, and finally the general terminated the interview by saying, "As for yourself, Miss Cushman, I have to tell you plainly, that there are very serious charges against you, and I must give you into the custody of our provost-marshal-general, Colonel McKinstry, who is, however, a very just and humane man, and who will treat you kindly. Your subsequent fate will depend entirely upon the result of our investigation."

"Colonel McKinstry is, then, precisely the man I desire to see; for through him will the proofs of my guiltlessness of these charges appear," rejoined Miss Cushman, boldly, "and if they *are* proved false, how then, general?"

"You will be acquitted with honor," replied he.

"How, though, if I am found guilty?"

"You know the penalty inflicted upon convicted spies. If found guilty, YOU WILL BE HANGED," replied the general, dryly.

Leaving Bragg, she was taken before Colonel McKinstry and there subjected to another strict examination, in which she was interrogated concerning the manner in which she became possessed of the Confederate uniform found among her effects when captured. To this she answered frankly, although, to her annoyance, it caused the instant issue of an order for the arrest of the gallant captain who had procured it for her. But, finally, the colonel produced from his desk the plans, maps, and documents which she had abstracted from the rebel engineer's table at Columbus, together with the sketches and memoranda that she had made, of various fortifications at Tullahoma, Shelbyville, Spring Hill, etc. Staggered almost to faintness by the sight of these tell-tale documents which she had placed in the soles of her gaiters, and which had been purloined from her satchel, left in the hurried flight from Hillsboro, she yet assumed a light demeanor and admitted that she made the sketches. She stoutly asserted, however, with a laugh, that they were mere fancy sketches, "gotten up with the idea of stuffing the Yankees when she should find herself among them, so that she should be permitted to recover her theatrical wardrobe." The colonel, although surprised at her consummate and audacious acting, was too old a bird to be caught in that way, and remanded her to custody. She was taken to the house of a Mr. Morgan, near Duck river, where she was carefully guarded in a room fitted up as a dungeon, with barred windows and doubly fastened doors. Hers was now a truly distressing and apparently hopeless case. Under the long protracted suspense as to her ultimate fate, added to the great privations and fatigues which she had previously gone through, she fell seriously ill; and the discomforts of her situation—sick and helpless, surrounded by foes and strangers—can hardly be described by tongue or pen. Long, weary days she lay thus, at the very verge of death—the court-martial which had been appointed to investigate her case had not yet been able to agree upon a verdict, and imagination added its horrors to the dread reality of her situation. Ten days thus passed, with the dread of death in its most ignominious form, hanging, like the sword of Damocles, ever above her head. Finally, Captain Pedden brought to her the unwelcome news which he tenderly broke to her, that she had been found GUILTY and that she was condemned TO BE HANGED AS A SPY.

The situation of our heroine, mental and physical, was now deplorable in the extreme. Condemned to death upon the gallows, surrounded by foes, with her fate unknown, even to her friends, hers was indeed a position to shake the hearts of the strongest and firmest. Yet there *was* a small ray of hope that illumined the darkness of this dismal prospect, and that was that, as she was still confined to her bed by the deepest physical prostration, the rebels would scarcely drag her from there to the gallows; and there was a *slight* chance that, during the brief respite thus afforded, some change of the military situation *might* yet afford relief to her. She well knew that Shelbyville, where she then was, was the objective point of the Union army of the Southwest, and they might reach there in time to save her from her horrid fate. Yet the chances which were thus suggested, were too slight to encourage our heroine, who had made up her mind heroically to meet her fate; and she met her fearful situation with an angelic courage and sweetness which won the love of the few friends whom she had drawn to her during her imprisonment.

Slowly and surely the Union army advanced on its glorious career, and soon Miss Cushman's guards and the Confederate army generally, began to show evident signs of evacuating Shelbyville. Finally it was decided by a council of war to retreat, and what a thrill of mingled hope and joy ran through Miss Cushman's veins as her friends announced to her that she would have to be left behind, as she was too weak to be moved. Before leaving the town, however, she was removed to a more comfortable house, and left in the hands of an excellent physician, who was Union at heart. At length it was rumored that a large body of Federals was just outside the town: then followed the battle of Shelbyville, and ere long the streets of that town echoed to the tread of the Union army and the peal of its bugles. It was a moment of supremest joy and ecstacy to the wan and feeble girl, who felt new life surging through every vein, and springing from her bed, she staggered to the open window, despite the remonstrances of her kind hostess. As the blessed certainty came upon her, that the Union flag once more waved over the town, and that she was *safe*, the fictitious strength which excitement had lent her gave way to weakness, and she sank to the floor, overcome by joy and happiness. Ere the close of that happy day, Generals Granger and Mitchell called upon her and expressed the liveliest interest in her situation; the brave soldiers heard of the noble woman whom they had thus opportunely saved from a terrible death, and, on every hand, she received the most tender and convincing tokens of the general esteem in which she was held.

At eleven o'clock the next morning, in the general's own ambulance, well stocked with all the comforts and necessaries which the generosity and courtesy of her new friends could suggest, she left Shelbyville *en route* to Murfreesboro. There a day and a night's rest enabled her to take the cars to Nashville; and under the care of an officer of General Granger's staff, who had himself done her the honor of attending her thus far, she began her return journey to that city. On her arrival there, she was waited upon by the most distinguished generals of the army, and by others less prominent—all of whom, however, were united in treating her with a delicate and even affectionate courtesy, which left her no comfort to be desired but the boon of absolute health. As a deserved and appropriate acknowledgment of the great services which this brave girl had rendered the Union cause, she was, through the efforts of Generals Granger and Garfield, honored with the commission and rank of a major of cavalry, with full and special permission to wear the equipment and insignia of her new rank. The ladies of Nashville, hearing of her promotion, and deeply sensible of the honor thus conferred upon one of their own sex, prepared a costly riding-habit, trimmed in military style, with dainty shoulder-straps, and presented the dress to the gallant major with all the customary honors.

Amusing Instance of Rebel Desertion.—After the recent advance of our army upon Bragg at Tullahoma, and his retreat, the Pioneer Brigade pushed on to Elk river to repair a bridge. While one of its men, a private, was bathing in the river, five of Bragg's soldiers, guns in hand, came to the bank and took aim at the swimmer, one of them shouting:

"Come in here, you —— Yank, out of the wet!"

The Federal was quite sure that he was "done for," and at once obeyed the order. After dressing himself, he was thus accosted:

"You surrender, our prisoner, do you?"

"Yes; of course I do."

"That's kind. Now we'll surrender to you!" And the five stacked arms before him, their spokesman adding—

"We've done with 'em, and have said to old Bragg, 'good-by!' Secesh is played out. Now you surround us and take us into your camp."

This was done accordingly, and is but one of hundreds of instances of wholesale desertion coming to the knowledge of our officers during two months—July and August—in Lower Tennessee.

KELLER OR KILLDARE,

ONE OF THE SCOUTS OF THE ARMY OF THE CUMBERLAND.

KELLER, or as he was usually called in the Army of the Cumberland, Killdare, was of German, and perhaps Jewish extraction, and during the first eighteen months of the war had been concerned with Besthoff, and three Jews by the names of Friedenburg, in smuggling goods into rebeldom, but being arrested in connection with them, it appeared that he had not been as guilty as the others, and that what he had done had been rather to support his family than from a desire to aid the rebels. He was therefore released, and being offered an appointment as scout in the Union service, he accepted it and was of great service to the Union cause.

In March 1863, he left Nashville on horseback, with a small stock of goods, not exceeding one hundred dollars in value, with the intention of making his way into and through a certain portion of the Confederacy. Swimming his horse across Harpeth creek, and crossing with his goods in a canoe, he journeyed on, and passed the night at a house about six miles beyond Columbia, having previously fallen in with some of Forrest's men going to Columbia. The next morning he started for Shelbyville, where he arrived in due season. The occurrences there and in the subsequent portions of the trip are best related in his own words:

"When I arrived, I could find stabling but no feed for my horse. I put the animal in the kitchen of a house, and gave a boy five dollars to get me a half bushel of corn, there being none in the town. I sold the little stock of goods to the firm of James Carr & Co., of Nashville, who gave me eight hundred dollars for the lot, and then went to visit General Frank Cheatham, General Maney, and General Bates, whom I saw at the house where I stopped. At the headquarters of General Cheatham, Colonel A—— arrived from the front, and stated in my presence that the whole Federal line had fallen back; and I further understood from the generals present and Colonel A—— that there would be no fight at Shelbyville. They said that probably there would be some skirmishing by the Federals, but that the battle would be fought at Tullahoma, and they had not more than one corps at Shelbyville, which was under General Polk.

"Forage and provisions for man and beast it is utterly impossible to obtain in the vicinity of Shelbyville. The forage trains go as far as Lewisport, in Giles county, and the forage is then shipped to Tullahoma, and even farther back, for safe keeping—as far as Bridgeport. Confederate money is two for one of Georgia; Tennessee, two and one half for one.

"I next went to Tullahoma; and there I met on the cars a major on Bragg's staff, and scraped an acquaintance through the introduction of a Nashville gentleman. When we arrived within a few miles of Tullahoma, he made a short statement to me, called me to the platform, and pointed out the rifle-pits and breastworks, which extended on each side of the railroad about a mile, in not quite a right angle. The whole force of Bragg's army is composed of fifty-five thousand men, well disciplined; twenty thousand of them are cavalry. When I left Tullahoma, I could not buy meat nor bread.

When I arrived at Chattanooga, I gave a nigger one dollar for a drink of whiskey, one dollar for a small cake, and fifty cents for two eggs, which I took for subsistence, and started for Atlanta. I met, going thitherward, a good many acquaintances on the trains. When I arrived at Atlanta, I found a perfect panic in money matters. Georgia money was at seventy-five cents premium, and going up; gold, four and five dollars for one. I remained at Atlanta three days. Full one half of those I met were from Nashville; they were glad to see me.

"I commenced my return to Tullahoma with a captain from Nashville, who also showed me the rifle-pits, as I before stated. I made my way on to Shelbyville, and then I got a pass from the provost-marshal—a Major Hawkins—to Columbia, where I arrived on Sunday morning. There I found Forrest and his command had crossed Duck river on their way to Franklin. As I started from the Nelson hotel to the provost-marshal's office, I was arrested on the square as a straggling soldier; but I proved myself the contrary, and started without a pass to Williamsport. There some fool asked me if I had a pass. I told him 'yes,' and showed him the pass I had from Shelbyville to Columbia and the documents I had in my possession, which he could not read. I gave the ferryman a five dollar piece to take me across the river, and he vouched for my pass—when I safely arrived at the Federal pickets."

About a month after this, Killdare made another, and his last trip, the full report of which is subjoined. It will be seen that he was watched and several times arrested. Though he finally escaped, his usefulness as a spy was totally destroyed, his name, appearance, and business having been betrayed to the enemy. He has consequently retired from the business. On his return, he made the following report:

"I left the city of Nashville on Tuesday, the 14th instant, to go South, taking with me a few goods to peddle. I passed down the Charlotte pike, and travelled two miles up the Richland creek, then crossed over to the Hardin pike, following that road to Harpeth creek, and crossed below De Morse's mill. At the mill I met —— De Morse, who said to me, 'Killdare, do you make another trip?' I replied, 'I do not know.' De Morse then said, 'if you get below the meeting-house you are saved,' and smiled. I proceeded on my way until I came to a blacksmith shop on the pike, at which a gentleman by the name of Marlin came out and asked if I had heard any thing of Sanford being killed on the evening of the 13th instant. I told Marlin I did not know any thing about it, and proceeded on to South Harper to Squire Allison's, which is seventeen miles from Nashville. I then fed my mules, stopped about one hour, and proceeded across South Harper toward Williamsport.

"About one mile the other side of South Harper, two rebel scouts came galloping up, and asked me what I had for sale. I told them needles, pins, and playing-cards. They then inquired, 'have you any papers to go South?' I replied I had, and showed them some recommendations. They asked me to get down from my carryall, as they wanted to talk with me. This I did; and they then asked:

"'Have you any pistols?'

"'No,' I replied.

"Stepping back a few paces, and each drawing a pistol, one of them said, 'you —— scoundrel, you are our prisoner; you are a Yankee spy, and you carry letters from the South, and at the dead hour of night you carry these letters to Truesdail's office. We lost a very valuable man on Monday while attempting to arrest you at your house; his name was Sanford, and he was a great deal thought of by General Van Dorn. So now we've got you, —— you, turn your wagon round and go back.'

"We turned and went to Squire Allison's again, at which place I met Dr. Morton, from Nashville, whom I requested to assist in getting me released. Dr. Morton spoke to the men, who, in reply, said, 'we have orders to arrest him as a spy, for carrying letters to Truesdail's headquarters.' They then turned back to South Harper creek, and took me up the creek about one mile, where we met about eight more of these scouts and Col onel McNairy, of Nashville, who was riding along in a buggy. The lieutenant in command of the squad wrote a despatch to Van Dorn, and gave it to one of the men, by the name of Thompson, who had me in custody, and we then proceeded up the creek to Spring Hill, toward the headquarters of General Van Dorn. About six miles up the creek, Thompson learned I had some whiskey, which I gave him, and of which he drank until he got pretty well intoxicated. In the neighborhood of Ivy we stopped until about six o'clock in the evening. About one mile from Ivy the wheel of my carryall broke. A neighbor came to us with an axe and put a pole under the axletree, and we proceeded on our way. We had gone but a few hundred yards when the wagon turned over; we righted it, and Thompson took a carpet-sack full of goods, filled his pockets, and then told me 'to go to ——: he would not take me to headquarters.' Changing his mind, however, he said he *would*, as he had orders so to do, and showed me the despatch written by Lieutenant Johnston to General Van Dorn. It read as follows:

"'I have succeeded in capturing Mr. Killdare. Archy Cheatham, of Nashville, says Killdare is not loyal to the Confederacy. The Federals have mounted five hundred light infantry. Sanford's being killed is confirmed. (Signed)

"'LIEUT. JOHNSTON.'

"Thompson, being very drunk, left me, taking the goods he stole. Two citizens came up shortly and told me to turn round, and stop all night at Isaac Ivy's, 1st District, Williamson county. There we took the remainder of the goods into the house. At three o'clock in the morning a negro woman came and knocked at the door.

"Mr. Ivy says, 'what do you want?'

"'A soldier is down at the creek, and wants to know where his prisoner is,' was the reply.

"'What has he done with the goods he took from that man?'

"'He has left them at our house, and has just started up the creek as I came up.'

"'That will do. Go on.'

"I was awake, and tried to make my escape, asking Mr. Ivy if he had a couple of saddles to loan me. He said he had; and I borrowed from him seven dollars, as Thompson took all my money (fifty dollars in Georgia currency.) He (Ivy) then told me the route I should take—going a few miles toward Franklin, and then turn toward my home in Nashville. Taking Ivy's advice, we proceeded on our way toward Franklin. About eight miles from Franklin, four guerillas came up to me and fired two pistols. 'Halt!' said they; 'you want to make your way to the Yankees. We have a notion to kill you, any way.'

"They then ordered me to turn, which I did,—two going behind whipping the mules, and hooting and hallooing at a great rate. We then turned back to Ivy's. When we got there, I said:

"Where is Thompson, my guard, who told me to go on?'

"'He was here early this morning, and has gone up the hill hunting you, after borrowing my shot gun,' was the answer.

"Some conversation ensued between the parties, when Ivy wrote a note to General Van Dorn and gave it to Thompson. Ivy then gave us our equipage, and we went toward Spring Hill On the way we met, on

Carter's Creek pike, a camp of four hundred Texan rangers. We arrived at Spring Hill at sundown of the day following. At Van Dorn's headquarters I asked for an interview with the general, which was not allowed, but was ordered to Columbia to prison until further orders.

"On Friday evening, a Nashville soldier who stood sentinel let me out, and said: 'you have no business here.' I made my way toward Shelbyville; crossed over Duck creek; made my way to the Louisburg and Franklin pike, and started toward Franklin. Before we got to the pickets we took to the woods, and thus got round the pickets. A farmer reported having seen me to the guard, and I was taken again toward Van Dorn's headquarters, six miles distant. I had gone about one mile, when I fell in with Colonel Lewis's command, and was turned over to an orderly sergeant with whom I was acquainted and by whom I was taken to the headquarters of Colonel Lewis. There I was discharged from arrest, and was told by the colonel what route I should take in order to avoid the scouts. I then started toward Columbia, and thence toward Hillsboro. At Hillsboro I met a friend by the name of Parkham, who guided me within five miles of Franklin, where I arrived at daylight this morning. On Friday last Colonel Forrest passed through Columbia with his force (three thousand strong), and six pieces of artillery, to Decatur, Alabama. One regiment went to Florence. The whole force under Van Dorn at Spring Hill does not exceed four thousand; and they are poorly clothed. I understand that the force was moving toward Tennessee river, in order to intercept forces that were being sent out by General Grant.

"SAM. KILLDARE."

This Archy Cheatham, who it appears had informed upon Killdare, was a government contractor, and professed to be loyal. The manner in which he obtained his information was in this wise.

One day a genteel, well-dressed young man came to the police office and inquired for Judge Brien, an employee of the office. The two, it seems, were old acquaintances, and for some time maintained a friendly conversation in the presence of Colonel Truesdail. The visitor, whose name was Stewart, having taken his leave, Brien remarked to the Colonel:

"There is a young man who can do us a great deal of good."

"Do you know him?" said the colonel.

"Very well. He talks right."

The result was that Stewart and Colonel Truesdail soon afterward had a private conversation in reference to the matter. Stewart stated that he lived about two miles from the city upon his plantation, that he was intimate with many prominent secessionists, was regarded as a good Southern man, and could go anywhere within the lines of the Confederacy. The colonel replied that he was in want of just such a man, and that he could be the means of accomplishing great good. It was an office, however, of vast responsibility, and, if he should be employed, he would be required to take a very stringent and solemn oath, which was read to him. To all this Stewart assented, and took the oath, only stipulating that he should never be mentioned as having any connection with the police office. He was consequently employed, and told to go to work at once.

For a time all seemed well enough. One or two minor cases of smuggling were developed by him. He subsequently reported that he had become acquainted with the cashier of the Planters' Bank, and a Mrs. Bradford, who lived five miles from the city, and made herself very busy in carrying letters, in which she was aided by Cantrell, the cashier. He was also in the habit of meeting large numbers of secessionists, among whom was Archy Cheatham. He also was a member of a club or association which met every Saturday, to devise ways and means for aiding the rebellion, and at which Mrs. Bradford and Cantrell were constant attendants. One day he reported that Mrs. Bradford was just going to carry out what was ostensibly a barrel of flour, but really a barrel of contraband goods covered over with flour at each end. And so it went on from week to week. Somebody was just going to do something, but never did it, or was never detected; and, despite the many fair promises of Stewart, the results of his labors were not deemed satisfactory.

On the night that Killdare came in from his last trip, Stewart was at the office. Something was evidently wrong, and Stewart soon left. To some natural inquiries of the colonel, Killdare answered, excitedly:

"Somebody has nearly ruined me, colonel!"

"How is that, and who can it be?"

"Well, I am sure that it is a man by the name of Stewart and Archy Cheatham who have done the mischief. Cheatham has been out in the country some fourteen miles, and there he met Lieutenant Johnston, whom he told that I was disloyal to the Confederacy, and one of your spies. The result was that I was arrested, and came near—altogether too near hanging for comfort. Johnson telegraphed to Van Dorn that he had caught me, but I got away; and to make a long story short, I have been arrested and have escaped three times."

This opened the colonel's eyes somewhat, and inquiries were at once set on foot, which disclosed the fact that Stewart was a rebel of the deepest dye, and had been "playing off" all the time. It was found that he had not only informed Cheatham of Killdare's business and position, but had himself been out in the country some fourteen miles, and had told the neighbors that Killdare had gone south in Truesdail's employ. He told the same thing to two guerillas whom he met, and even taunted Killdare's children by saying that he knew where their father had gone. The colonel, for once, had been thoroughly deceived by appearances; but it was the first and last time. After a month or six weeks' search, Stewart was found and committed to the penitentiary; and before he leaves that institution it is by no means improbable that he will have ample time and opportunity to conclude that his operations, though sharp and skilful, were not of the most profitable character.

A Fighting Parson.—Colonel Granville Moody, of the Seventy-fourth Ohio, is a famous Methodist preacher from Cincinnati. He is something over fifty, six feet and two or three inches, of imposing presence, with a fine, genial face and prodigious vocal range. The reverend colonel, who proved himself a fighting parson of the first water, was hit four times at the battle of Murfreesboro, and will carry the marks of battle when he goes back to the altar. His benevolence justifies his military flock in the indulgence of sly humor at his expense; but he never permits them to disturb his equanimity. Several battle anecdotes of him are well authenticated. Not long ago, General Negley merrily accused him of using heterodox expletives in the ardor of conflict.

"Is it a fact, colonel," inquired the general, "that you told the boys to 'give 'em hell'?"

"How?" replied the colonel, reproachfully: "that's some more of the boys' mischief. I told them to give the rebels 'Hail Columbia;' and they have perverted my language."

The parson, however, had a sly twinkle in the corner of his eye, which left his hearers in considerable doubt.

Our Western circuit preachers are known as stentors. Where others are emphatic, they roar in the fervor of exhortation, especially when they come in with their huge "Amen." This fact must be borne in mind to appreciate the story. The colonel's mind was saturated with piety and fight. He had already had one bout with the rebels, and given them "Hail Columbia." They were renewing the attack. The colonel braced himself for the shock. Seeing his line in fine order, he thought he would exhort them briefly. The rebels were coming swiftly. Glancing first at the foe, then at the lads, he said, quietly, "Now, my boys, fight for your country and your God," and, raising his voice to thunder-tones, he exclaimed, in the same breath, "AIM LOW!" Says one of his gallant fellows, "I thought for an instant it was a frenzied ejaculation from the profoundest depths of the 'Amen corner.'" Any day now you may hear the lads of the Seventy-fourth roaring, "Fight for your country and your God—aim low!"

A DARING SCOUT AND SPY.

Among the Union men and officers in our armies, none have been more earnest in their patriotism, or more ready to do and dare every thing for the Union cause, than some of the citizens and natives of Southern States. To be a Union man in the Southern Atlantic or Gulf States, meant, unless the man's social position was of the very highest, to be a martyr; to be robbed, persecuted, stripped of all the comforts of life, deprived of a home, and often to be conscripted, imprisoned, shot, hung, or to suffer a thousand deaths in the tortures and indignities inflicted on his helpless family. Yet, with all this before them, many Southern men dared to be true to their allegiance to the National Government, and to enter its service. As was to be expected, these men proved the most serviceable and fearless of the Union scouts and spies. Their familiarity with the country was of great service to them, and the remembrance of the wrongs they had endured fired them with an energy and zeal, and a desire to punish the foe, which rendered them invaluable. Among the men of this class who have rendered most efficient service to the national cause, was a young Georgian, born of Scotch parents, near Augusta, Georgia, in the year 1832. His real name was concealed, in consequence of the peril which would have accrued to his relatives, had it been known; but he was known to some extent in the Union army as John Morford. A blacksmith by trade, he early engaged in railroad work, and at the opening of the war was master mechanic upon one of the Southern railroads.

He was a decided Union man, and made no secret of his opinions, and was in consequence discharged from his situation, and not allowed employment upon any other railroad. Morgan's cavalry was also sent to his farm, and stripped it; and when he applied to the guerilla leader for pay for the property thus taken, he was told he should have it if he would only prove his loyalty to the South. As he would not do this, Morgan cursed and abused him, threatened to have him shot, and finally sent him under arrest to one Major Peyton. The major endeavored, but without any success, to convince him that the cause of the South was right; but Morford proving firm to his Union sentiments, he began to threaten him, declaring that he should be hung within two weeks. Morford coolly replied that he was sorry for that, as he should have preferred to live a little longer, but if it must be so, he couldn't help it. Finding him unterrified, Peyton cooled down, and finally told him that if he would give a bond of one thousand dollars, as security for his good behavior, and take the oath of allegiance to the Southern Confederacy, he would release him and protect his property. After some hesitation—no other plan of escape occurring to him—Morford assented, and took the required oath, upon the back of which Peyton wrote, "If you violate this, I will hang you."

With this safeguard, Morford returned to his farm and lived a quiet life. Buying a span of horses, he devoted himself to the cultivation of his land, seeing as few persons as he could, and talking with none. His house had previously been the headquarters of the Union men, but was now deserted by them; and its owner endeavored to live up to the letter of the obligation he had taken. For a short time all went well enough; but one day a squad of cavalry came with a special written order from Major Peyton to take his two horses, which they did. This was too much for human nature; and Morford, perceiving that no faith could be placed in the assurances of those in command, determined to be revenged upon them and their cause. His house again became a secret rendezvous for Unionists; and by trusty agents he managed to send regular and valuable information to General Buell—then in command in Tennessee. At length, however, in May, 1862, he was betrayed by one in whom he had placed confidence, and arrested upon the charge of sending information to General Crittenden, at Battle Creek. He indignantly denied the charge, and declared that he could easily prove himself innocent if released for that purpose. After three days' confinement, this was assented to; and Morford, knowing full well that he could not do what he had promised, made a hasty retreat and fled to the mountains, whence, some days afterward, he emerged, and went to McMinnville, at which place General Nelson was then in command.

Here he remained until the rebel force left that vicinity, when he again went home, and lived undisturbed upon his farm until Bragg returned with his army. The presence in the neighborhood of so many officers cognizant of his former arrest and escape rendered flight a second time necessary. He now went to the camp of General Donelson, with whom he had some acquaintance, and soon became very friendly there—acting the while in the double capacity of beef contractor for the rebel army, and spy for General Crittenden. Leaving General Donelson after some months' stay, although earnestly requested to remain longer, Morford next found his way to Nashville, where he made numerous expeditions as a spy for General Negley. Buell was at Louisville, and Nashville was then the Federal outpost. Morford travelled about very readily upon passes given him by General Donelson, making several trips to Murfreesboro, and one to Cumberland Gap.

Upon his return from the latter, he was arrested near Lebanon, Tennessee, about one o'clock at night, by a party of four soldiers upon picket duty at that point. Halting him, the following conversation occurred:

"Where do you live?"

"Near Stewart's Ferry, between here and Nashville."

"Where have you been, and what for?"

"Up to see my brother, to get from him some jeans cloth and socks for another brother in the Confederate army."

"How does it happen you are not in the army yourself? That looks rather suspicious."

"Oh, I live too near the Federal lines to be conscripted."

"Well, we'll have to send you to Murfreesboro. I reckon you're all right; but those are our orders, and we can't go behind them."

To this Morford readily consented, saying he had no objection; and the party sat down by the fire and talked in a friendly manner for some time. Morford soon remembered that he had a bottle of brandy with him, and generously treated the crowd. Further conversation was followed by a second drink, and soon by a third. One of the party now proposed to exchange his Rosinantish mare for a fine horse which Morford rode. The latter was not inclined to trade; but objection was useless, and he finally yielded, receiving seventy-five dollars in Confederate money and the mare. The trade pleased the soldier, and a present of a pair of socks still further enhanced his pleasure. His companions were also similarly favored, and testified their appreciation of the gift by endeavoring to purchase the balance of Morford's stock. He would not sell, however, as he wished to send them to his brother at Richmond, by a person who had given public notice that he was soon going there. A fourth drink made all supremely happy; at which juncture their prisoner asked permission to go to a friend's house, only a quarter of a mile off, and stay uutil morning, when he would go with them to Murfreesboro. His friend of the horse-trade, now very mellow, thought he need not go to Murfreesboro at all, and said he would see what the others said about it. Finally it was concluded that he was "right," and might; whereupon he mounted the skeleton mare and rode rejoicingly into Nashville.

On his next trip southward he was arrested by Colonel John T. Morgan, just as he came out of the Federal lines, and, as his only resort, joined Forrest's command, and was furnished with a horse and gun. The next day Forrest made a speech to his men, and told them that they were now going to capture Nashville. The column immediately began its march, and Morford, by some means, managed to have himself placed in the advance. Two miles below Lavergne a halt for the night was made; but Morford's horse was unruly, and could not be stopped, carrying its rider ahead and out of sight. It is needless to say that this obstinacy was not overcome until Nashville was reached, nor that, when Forrest came the next day, General Negley was amply prepared for him.

At this time Nashville was invested. Buell was known to be advancing toward the city, but no scouts had been able to go to or come from him. A handsome reward was offered to any one who would carry a despatch safely through to Bowling Green, and Morford undertook to do it. Putting the document under the lining of his boot, he started for Gallatin, where he arrived safely.

For some hours he sauntered around the place, lounged in and out of bar rooms, made friends with the rebel soldiers, and toward evening purchased a small bag of corn meal, a bottle of whiskey, a pound or two of salt, and some smaller articles, which he threw across his shoulder and started up the Louisville road, with hat on one side, hair in admirable disorder, and, apparently, gloriously drunk. The pickets jested at and made sport of him, but permitted him to pass. The meal, etc., was carried six miles, when he suddenly became sober, dropped it, and hastened on to Bowling Green, and there met General Rosecrans, who had just arrived. His information was very valuable.. Here he remained until the army came up and passed on, and then set out on his return on foot, as he had come. He supposed that our forces had gone by way of Gallatin, but when near that place learned that it was still in possession of the rebels, and so stopped for the night in a shanty between Morgan's pickets, on the north side, and Woolford's (Union), on the south side. During the night the two had a fight, which finally centered around the shanty, and resulted in driving Morford to the woods. In two or three hours he came back for his clothes, and found that the contending parties had disappeared, and that the railroad tunnels had been filled with wood and fired. Hastily gathering his effects together, he made his way to Tyree Springs, and thence to Nashville.

For a short time he acted as a detective of the army police at Nashville, assuming the character of a rebel soldier, and living in the families of prominent secessionists. In this work he was very successful; but it had too little of danger and adventure, and he returned again to scouting, making several trips southward, sometimes without trouble, but once or twice being arrested and escaping as best he could. In these expeditions he visited McMinnville, Murfreesboro, Altamont, on the Cumberland mountains, Bridgeport, Chattanooga, and other places of smaller note. He travelled usually in the guise of a smuggler, actually obtaining orders for goods from prominent rebels, and sometimes the money in advance, filling them in Nashville, and delivering the articles upon his next trip. Just before the battle of Stone river, he received a large order to be filled for the rebel hospitals; went to Nashville, procured the medicine, and returned to McMinnville, where he delivered some of it. Thence he travelled to Bradyville, and thence to Murfreesboro, arriving there just as the battle began. Presenting some of the surgeons with a supply of morphine, he assisted them in attending the wounded for a day or two, and then went to a hospital tent in the woods near the railroad, where he also remained one day and part of another. The fight was now getting hot, and, fearful that somebody would recognize him, he left Murfreesboro on Friday, and went to McMinnville.

He had been there but little more than an hour, having barely time to put up his horse and step into a house near by to see some wounded men, when two soldiers arrived in search of him. Their description of him was perfect; but he escaped by being out of sight—the friend with whom he was supposed to be, declaring, though closely questioned, that he had not seen and knew nothing of him. In a few minutes pickets were thrown out around the town, and it was two days before he could get away. Obtaining a pass to Chattanooga at last, only through the influence of a lady acquaintance, with it he passed the guards; but when once out of sight, turned off from the Chattanooga road and made his way safely to Nashville.

General Rosecrans was now in possession of Murfreesboro, and thither Morford proceeded with some smuggler's goods, with a view to another trip. The necessary permission was readily obtained, and he set out for Woodbury. Leaving his wagon outside the rebel lines, he proceeded on foot to McMinnville, arriving there on the 19th of January 1863, and finding General John H. Morgan, to whom he represented himself as a former resident in the vicinity of Woodbury; his family, however, had moved away, and he would like permission to take his wagon and bring away the household goods. This was granted, and the wagon brought to McMinnville, whence Morford went to Chattanooga, representing himself along the road as a fugitive from the Yankees. Near Chattanooga he began selling his goods to Unionists and rebels alike, at enormous prices, and soon closed them out at a profit of from four hundred to five hund ed dollars. At Chattanooga he remained a few days, obtained all the information he could, and returned to Murfreesboro without trouble.

His next and last trip is the most interesting and daring of all his adventures. Making a few days' stay in Murfreesboro, he went to McMinnville, and remained there several days, during which time he burned Hickory Creek bridge, and sent a report of it to General Rosecrans. This he managed with so much secrecy and skill as to escape all suspicion of complicity in the work, mingling freely with the citizens and talking the matter over in all its phases. From McMinnville Morford proceeded to Chattanooga, and remained there nearly a week, when he learned that three of our scouts were imprisoned in the Hamilton county jail, at Harrison, Tennessee, and were to be shot on the first Friday in May. Determined to attempt their rescue, he sent a Union man to the town to ascertain who was jailer, what the number of the guards, how they were placed, and inquire into the condition of things in general about the jail. Upon receipt of his report, Morford gathered about him nine Union men, on the night of Tuesday, April 21, 1863, and started for Harrison. Before reaching the place, however, they heard rumors that the guard had been greatly strengthened; and, fearful that it would prove too powerful for them, the party retreated to the mountains on the north side of the Tennessee river, where they remained concealed until Thursday night. On Wednesday night the same man who had previously gone to the town was again sent to reconnoitre the position. Thursday morning he returned and said that the story of a strong guard was all false: there were but two in addition to the jailer

Morford's party was now reduced to six, including himself; but he resolved to make the attempt that night. Late in the afternoon all went down to the river and loitered around until dark, when they procured boats and crossed to the opposite bank. Taking the Chattanooga and Harrison road, they entered the town, looked around at leisure, saw no soldiers nor any thing unusual, and proceeded toward the jail. Approaching quite near, they threw themselves upon the ground and surveyed the premises carefully. The jail was surrounded by a high board fence, in which were two gates. Morford's plan of operations was quickly arranged. Making a prisoner of one of his own men, he entered the enclosure, posting a sentinel at each gate. Once inside, a light was visible in the jail, and Morford marched confidently up to the door and rapped. The jailer thrust his head out of a window and asked what was wanted. He was told, "Here is a prisoner to put in the jail." Apparently satisfied, the jailer soon opened the door and admitted the twain into the entry. In a moment, however, he became alarmed, and hastily exclaiming, "Hold on!" stepped out.

For ten minutes Morford waited patiently for his return, supposing, of course, that he could not escape from the yard, both gates being guarded. Not making his appearance, it was found that the pickets had allowed him to pass them. This rather alarming fact made haste necessary, and Morford, returning to the jail, said he must put his prisoner in immediately, and demanded the keys forthwith. The women declared in positive terms that they hadn't them, and did not know where they were. One of the guards was discovered in bed and told to get the keys. Proving rather noisy and saucy, he was reminded that he might get his head taken off if he were not quiet—which intimation effectually silenced him. Morford again demanded the keys, and the women, somewhat frightened, gave him the key to the outside door. Unlocking it, and lighting up the place with candles, he found himself in a room around the sides of which was ranged a line of wrought-iron cages. In one of these were five persons, four white and one negro. Carrying out the character he had assumed of a rebel soldier in charge of a prisoner, Morford talked harshly enough to the caged men, and threatened to hang them at once, at which they were very naturally alarmed, and began to beg for mercy. For a third time the keys to the inner room, in which the scouts were, were demanded, and a third time the women denied having them. An axe was then ordered to be brought, but there was none about the place: so said they. Morford saw that they were trifling with him, and determined to stop it. Snatching one of the jailer's boys standing near by the collar, and drawing his sabre, he told him he would cut his head off if he did not bring him an axe in two minutes. This had the desired effect, and the axe was forthcoming.

Morford now began cutting away at the lock, when he was startled by hearing the word "halt!" at the gate. Of his five men two were at the gates, two were inside as a guard, and one was holding the light. Ready for a fight he went out to see what was the matter. The sentinel reporting that he had halted an armed man outside, Morford walked out to him and demanded:

"What are you doing here with that gun?"

"Miss Laura said you were breaking down the jail, and I want to see McAllister, the jailer. Where is he?" was the reply.

"Well, suppose I am breaking down the jail: what are you going to do about it?"

"I am going to stop it if I can."

"What's your name?"

"Lowry Johnson."

By this time Morford had grasped the muzzle of the gun, and told him to let go. Instead of complying, Johnson tried to pull it away; but a blow upon the neck from Morford's sabre soon made him drop it. Morford now began to search him for other weapons, but before he had concluded the operation Johnson broke away, leaving a part of his clothing in Morford's hands. The latter drew his revolver and pursued, firing five shots at him, sometimes at a distance of only six or eight paces. A cry, as of pain, showed that he was struck, but he managed to reach the hotel (kept by his brother), and, bursting in the door, which was fastened, escaped into the house. Morford followed, but too late. Johnson's brother now came out and rang the bell in front, which gathered a crowd about the door; but Morford, not at all daunted, told them that if they wanted to guard the jail they had better be about it quick, as he was going to burn it and the town in the bargain. This so frightened them that no further demonstration was made, and Morford returned to the jail unmolested. There he and his men made so much shouting and hurrahing as to frighten the people of the town beyond measure; and many lights from upper story windows were extinguished, and the streets were deserted.

A half hour's work was necessary to break off the outside lock—a splendid burglar-proof one. Morford now discovered that the door was double, and that the inner one was made still more secure by being barred with three heavy log chains. These were cut in two with the axe; but the strong lock of the door still remained. He again demanded the key, and told the women if it was not produced he would murder the whole of them. The rebel guard, Lew. Luttrell by name, was still in bed. Rising up, he said that the key was not there. Morford now ordered Luttrell to get out of bed, in a tone so authoritative that that individual deemed it advisable to comply. Scarcely was he out, however, before Morford struck at him with his sabre; but he was too far off, and the blow fell upon one of the children, drawing some blood. This frightened the women, and, concluding that he was about to put his threat in execution and would murder them surely enough, they produced the key without further words. No time was lost in unlocking the door and releasing the inmates of the room. Procuring their clothes for them, and arming one with Johnson's gun, the whole party left the jail and hurried toward the river. Among the released prisoners was a rebel with a wooden leg, the original having been shot off at Manassas. He persisted in accompanying the others, and was only induced to go back by the intimation that "dead men tell no tales."

Crossing the river in the boats, they were moved to another place at some distance, to preclude the possibility of being tracked and followed. All now hid themselves among the mountains, and the same Union man was again sent to Harrison, this time to see how severely

Johnson was wounded. He returned in a day or two, and reported that he had a severe sabre cut on the shoulder, a bullet through the muscle of his right arm, and two slight wounds in one of his hands. Morford and his men remained in the mountains until all search for the prisoners was over, then went to the Cumberland mountains, where they remained one day and a portion of another, and then proceeded in the direction of McMinnville. Hiding themselves in the woods near this place during the day, seeing but not seen, they travelled that night to within eleven miles of Woodbury, when they struck across the road from McMinnville to Woodbury. Near Logan's Plains they were fired on by a body of rebel cavalry, but, though some forty shots were fired, no one of the ten was harmed, Morford having one bullet hole in his coat. The cavalry, however, pursued them across the barrens, surrounded them, and supposed themselves sure of their game: but Morford and his companions scattered and hid away, not one being captured or found. Night coming on, the cavalry gave up the chase, and went on to Woodbury, where they threw out pickets, not doubting that they would pick up the objects of their search during the night. Morford, however, was informed of this fact by a citizen, and, in consequence, lay concealed all the next day, making his way safely to Murfreesboro, with all of his company, the day after.

General Palmer and the Hog.—Early one morning in 1862, while at Farmington, near Corinth, Mississippi, as Brigadier- (now Major-) General Palmer was riding along his lines to inspect some breastworks that had been thrown up during the previous night, he came suddenly upon some of the boys of Company I, Twenty-seventh Illinois Volunteers, who had just shot a two-hundred-pound hog, and were engaged in the interesting process of skinning it. The soldiers were startled; their chief looked astonished and sorrowful.

"Ah! a body—a corpse. Some poor fellow gone to his last home. Well, he must be buried with military honors. Sergeant, call the officer of the guard."

The officer was speedily at hand, and received orders to have a grave dug and the body buried forthwith. The grave was soon prepared, and then the company were mustered. Pall-bearers placed the body of the dead upon a stretcher. The order was given to march, and, with reversed arms and funeral tread, the solemn procession of sixty men followed the body to the grave. Not a word passed nor a muscle of the face stirred while the last rites of sepulture were being performed. The ceremony over, the general and his staff waved their *adieux*, and were soon lost in the distance.

The philosophy of the soldier is usually equal to the emergency. He has read and pondered. He now painfully realizes that flesh is as grass, and that life is but a shadow. But he thinks of the *resurrection*, and his gloom passes away. So with the philosophic boys of Company I, Twenty-seventh Illinois. Ere their general was fairly seated at his own breakfast-table, there was a raising of the dead, and savory pork steaks were frying in many a camp pan.

SCOUTING IN EAST TENNESSEE.

EDMUND KIRKE (Mr. J. R Gilmore), who has explored extensively the regions desolated by the war, thus narrates one of the adventures of a Union East Tennessean, who had been acting as a scout for General Rosecrans, in his little volume "Down in Tennessee:"

I was dreaming of home, and of certain flaxen-haired juveniles who are accustomed to call me "Mister Papa," when a heavy hand was laid on my shoulder, and a gruff voice said:

"Doan't want ter 'sturb yer, stranger, but thar haint nary nother sittin'-place in the whole kear."

I drew in my extremities, and he seated himself before me. He was a spare, muscular man of about forty, a little above the medium height, with thick, sandy hair and beard, and a full, clear, gray eye. There was nothing about him to attract particular attention except his clothing, but that was so out of all keeping with the place and the occasion, that I opened my eyes to their fullest extent, and scanned him from head to foot. He wore the gray uniform of a secession officer, and in the breast of his coat, right over his heart, was a round hole, scorched at the edges, and darkly stained with blood! Over his shoulder was slung a large army revolver, and at his side, in a leathern sheath, hung a weapon that seemed a sort of cross between a bowie-knife and a butcher's cleaver. On his head, surmounted by a black plume, was a moose-colored slouched hat, and falling from beneath it, and tied under his chin, was a white cotton handkerchief stiffly saturated with blood! Nine motley-clad natives, all heavily armed, had entered with him and taken the vacant seats around me, and at first view I was inclined to believe that in my sleep the train had gone over to the enemy and left me in the hands of the Philistines. I was, however, quickly reassured, for, looking about, I discovered the Union guard and my fellow-travellers all in their previous places, and as unconcerned as if no unusual thing had happened. Still, it seemed singular that no officer had the new-comer in charge; and more singular that any one in the uniform he wore should be allowed to carry arms so freely about him. After awhile, having gleaned all the knowledge of him that my eyes could obtain, I said in a pleasant tone:

"Well, my friend, you appear to take things rather coolly."

"Oh, yes, sir! I orter. I've been mighty hard put, but I reckon I'm good fur a nother pull now."

"Where are you from?"

"Fentress county, nigh onter Jimtown (Jamestown). I'm scoutin' it fur Burnside—runnin' boys inter camp; but these fellers wanted ter jine Cunnel Brownlow—the old parson's son—down ter Triune. We put plumb fur Nashville, but hed ter turn norard, case the brush down thar ar thick with rebs. They'd like ter a hed us."

"Oh, then you wear that uniform as a disguise on scouting expeditions?"

"No, sir; I never hed sech a rig on afore. I allers shows the true flag, an' thar haint no risk, 'case, ye see, the whole deestrict down thar ar Union folks, an' ary one on 'em would house'n *me* ef all Buckner's army wus at my heels. But this time they run me powerful close, an' I hed to show the secesh rags."

As he said this, he looked down on his clean, unworn suit of coarse gray with ineffable contempt.

"And how could you manage to live with such a hole there?" I asked, pointing to the bullet rent in his coat.

"Oh! I warn't inside of 'em just then, though I warrant me he war a likely feller thet war. I ortent ter a done hit—but I hed ter. This war he;" and taking from his side pocket a small miniature, he handed it to me.

It was a plain circlet of gold, attached to a piece of blue ribbon. One side of the rim was slightly clipped, as if it had been grazed by the passing ball, and the upper portion of the ivory was darkly stained with blood; but enough of it was unobscured to show me the features of a young man, with dark, flowing hair, and a full, frank, manly face. With a feeling akin to horror I was handing the picture back to the scout, when, in low, stammering tones, he said to me:

"'Tother side, sir! Luk at 'tother side."

I turned it over, and saw the portrait of a young woman, scarcely more than seventeen. She had a clear, transparent skin, regular, oval features, full, swimming, black eyes, and what must have been dark, wavy, brown hair, but changed then to a deep auburn by the red stains that tinged the upper part of the picture. With intense loathing, I turned almost fiercely on the scout, and exclaimed: "And you killed that man?"

"Yes, sir, God forgiv me—I done hit. But I couldn't holp hit. He hed me down—he'd cut me thar," turning up his sleeve, and displaying a deep wound on his arm;

"an' thar!" removing the bandage, and showing a long gash back of his ear. "His arm wus riz ter strike agin —in another minhit he'd hev cluv my brain. I seed hit, sir, an' I fired! God forgiv me, I fired! I wouldn't a done hit ef I'd a knowed thet," and he looked down on the face of the sweet young girl, and the moisture came into his eyes: "I'd hev shot 'im somewhar but yere— somewhar but *yere!*" and laying his hand over the rent in his coat, he groaned as if he felt the wound. With that blood-stained miniature in my hand, and listening to the broken words of that ignorant scout, I realized the horrible barbarity of war.

After a pause of some minutes, he resumed the conversation.

"They killed one on our boys, sir."

"Did they! How was it?"

"Wal, sir, ye see they b'long round the Big Fork, in Scott county; and bein's I war down thar, an' they know'd I war a runnin' recruits over the mountins ter Burnside, they telled me they wanted me ter holp 'em git 'long with the young cunnel. They'd ruther a notion ter him—an' he *ar* a feller thet haint grow'd everywhar—'sides all the folks down thar swar by the old parson."

"Well, they ought to, for he's a trump," I remarked, good-humoredly, to set the native more at his ease.

"Ye kin bet high on thet; he haint nothin' else," he replied, leaning forward and regarding me with a pleased, kindly expression. "Every un down my way used ter take his paper; thet an' the Bible war all they ever seed, an' they reckoned one war 'bout so good as 'tother. Wall, the boys thort I could git 'em through—an' bein's it made no odds to me *whar* they jined, so long as they *did* jine, I 'greed ter du hit. We put out ten days, yisterday—twelve on 'em, an' me—an' struck plumb for Nashville. We lay close daytimes, 'case, though every hous'n ar Union, the kentry is swarmin' with Buckner's men, an' we know'd they'd let slide on us jest so soon as they could draw a bead. We got 'long right smart till we fotched the Roaring river, nigh onter Livingston. We'd 'quired, an' hedn't heerd uv ary rebs bein' round; so, foolhardy like, thet evenin' we tuk ter the road 'fore hit war clar dark. We hedn't gone more'n a mile till we come slap onter 'bout eighty secesh calvary. We skedaddled fur the timber, powerful sudden; but they war over the fence an' on us 'fore we got well under cover. 'Bout thirty on 'em slid thar nags, an' come at us in the brush. I seed twarn't no use runnin'; so I yelled out: 'Stand yer ground, boys, an' sell yer lives jest so high as ye kin!' Wall, we went at hit ter close quarters—hand ter hand, an' fut ter fut—an' ye'd better b'lieve thar war some tall fightin' thar fur 'bout ten minhits. Our boys fit like fien's—thet little chunk uv a feller thar," pointing to a slim, pale-faced youth, not more than seventeen, "laid out three on 'em. I'd done up two myself, when the cap'n come onter me—but, I've telled ye 'bout him;" and drawing a long breath, he put the miniature back in his pocket. After a short pause, he continued:

"When they seed the cap'n war done fur, they fell back a piece—them as war left on 'em—ter the edge uv the timber, an' hollered fur tuthers ter come on. Thet guv us time ter load up—we'd fit arter the fust fire wuth knives—an' we blazed inter 'em. Jest as we done hit, I heer'd some more calvary comin' up the road, an' I war jest tellin' the boys we'd hev ter make tracks, when the new fellers sprung the fence, an' come plumb at the secesh on a dead run. Thar warn't only thirty on 'em, yit the rebs didn't so much as make a stand, but skedaddled as ef old Rosey himself hed been arter 'em."

"And who were the new comers?"

"Some on Tinker Beaty's men. They'd heerd the firin' nigh two mile off, an' come up, suspicionin' how things wus."

"But, are there Union bands there? I thought East Tennessee was overrun with rebel troops."

"Wall, hit ar; but thar's a small chance uv Union goorillas in Fentress an' Overton county. They hide in the mountins, an' light down on the rebs, now an' then, like death on a sick parson. Thar is places in them deestricts thet a hundred men kin hold agin ten thousand They know 'em all, 'case they wus raised thar, an' they know every bridle path through the woods, so it's well nigh unpossible ter kotch 'em. I reckon thar's a hundred on 'em, all mounted, an' bein' as they haint no tents, nor wagins, nor camp fixin's, they git round mighty spry. Thar scouts is allers on the move, an' wharever thar's a showin', they pounce down on the rebs, cuttin' 'em ter pieces. Thet's the how they git powder an' provisions. They never trouble peaceable folk, an' haint no sort o' 'spense ter guverment; but they does a heap uv damage ter the secesh."

"Well, they did you a 'powerful' good turn."

"They did thet; but we lost one on our boys. He war only sixteen—brother ter thet feller thar," pointing to a young man sitting opposite. They hung his father, an' now—they's killed him," and he drew a deep sigh.

"Why did they hang his father?"

"Wall, ye see, they kunscripted him—he war over age, but they don't mind thet—an' he desarted, meanin' ter git ter the Union lines. They kotched him in the woods, an' hung him right up ter a tree."'

"Was only one of your men hurt?"

"Yes, two on 'em wus wounded too bad ter come wuth us. The calvary toted 'em off ter the mountins, an' I reckon they'll jine 'em when they gits round. But we left elevin uv the rebs dead on the ground."

"Did your men kill so many? The cavalry had a hand in that, I suppose?"

"Yes, they killed two—thet's all. They couldn't git at 'em, they run so. We done the rest."

"You must have fought like tigers. How many were wounded?"

"Nary one; what wan't dead the boys finished."

"You don't mean to say that your men killed the wounded *after the fight?*"

"I reckon they did—some four on 'em."

"My friend, that's nothing but murder. I had hoped the rebels did all of that work."

"Wall, they does—anuff on hit; an' I never could bring my mind ter think it war right or human: but I s'pose thet's case I never hed a father hung, or a sister ravig'd, or a old mother shot down in har bed. Them things, you knows, makes a difference."

"And have any of your men suffered in such ways?"

"In sech ways? Thar haint one on 'em but kin tell you things 'ud turn yer blood ter ice D'ye see thet feller thar?" pointing to a thin, sallow faced man, two seats in our rear. "Not two months gone, some twenty rebs come ter his house while he war layin' out in the woods, an' toted his wife—as young an' purty a 'oman as yer own sister—off 'bout a mile, an' thar tuk thar will uv her—all on 'em! She made out ter crawl home, but it killed har. He warn't wuth har when she died, an' hit wus well he warn't, fur he'd hev gone clean crazy ef he hed been. He's mor'n half thet now—crazy fur blood! An' kin ye blame him? Kin ye 'spect a man thet's hed sech things done ter him ter show quarter? 'Taint in natur' ter do hit. All these boys hes hed jest sich, an' things like hit; an' they go in ter kill or be kilt. They doan't ax no marcy, an' they doan't show none. Nigh twenty thousand on 'em is in Burnside's an' old Rosey's army, an' ye kin ax *them* if they doan't fight like devils. The iron has entered thar souls, sir. They feel they's doin' God sarvice—an' they is—when they does fur a secesh. An' when this war ar over—ef it ever ar over—thar'll be sech a reckonin' wuth the rebs uv East Tennesseee as creation never know'd on afore. Thar wont be one on 'em left this side uv hell!" This was said with a vehemence that startled me. His eyes actually blazed, and every line on his seamed face quivered with passion. To change the subject, I asked:

"And what did you do after the fight?"

"Not knowin' what moight happen, we swapped cloes with sech uv the rebs as hed gray 'uns, an' put North—plumb fur the mountins. Nigh onter Meigsville we come onter a Union man, who holped us ter cut some timber an' make a raft—fur we 'lowed the secesh would track us wuth houns, an' ter throw 'em off the scent we hed ter take ter the water. We got inter Obey's Fork, an' floated down ter the Cumberland; hidin' in the bushes in the daytime, an' floatin' at night. We got nigh onter Carthage, an' knowin' the river wan't safe no longer, we left hit an' struck 'cross fur the railroad. Thet kentry ar full uv rebs, but hevin' the secesh cloes on, we made out ter git 'nuff ter eat till we got yere."

BIBLE SMITH,

THE EAST TENNESSEE SCOUT AND SPY.

No troops in the Union service were more thoroughly patriotic than the Union men of East Tennessee. Mostly, of Scotch Irish stock, and often imbued with the most profound and earnest religious sentiment, they united the earnest puritanism of Cromwell's Ironsides to the skill, tact, and daring of the pioneers of the border. These qualities, added to their thorough knowledge of the country, and its inhabitants, and a sort of free masonry which prevailed among the hunted and persecuted Union men of the region made them invaluable as scouts and spies. Among them all none perhaps acquired more renown or accomplished more for the benefit of the Union armies of the Cumberland and the Ohio, in their great work of putting down the rebellion, than William Jehosaphat Smith, better known throughout East Tennessee as Bible Smith from his Scriptural middle name. Smith was one of the middle class of farmers of that mountain region; and had had very little education; his wife, who, as was often the case with the class to which she belonged, was of somewhat higher social position than her husband, and better educated, had taught him to read. He was a man of very strong affections, and was deeply attached to his wife, whom he regarded as almost a superior being. Next to her his most ardent love was bestowed on the flag of his country. For it and the cause it represented he would dare any thing and every thing. Mr. J. R. Gilmore ("Edmund Kirke") gives an admirable history of Smith's experiences in connection with the war and as a scout, from which we quote the following:

Seated after dinner on the piazza of the hospitable Southern lady, Bible told me his story.

He had been stripped of all his property, his wife and children had been driven from their home, his house had been burned to the ground, and he himself hunted through the woods like a wild beast, because he had remained true to what he called democratic principles—"free schools, free speech, free thought, and free a'r fur all o' GOD'S critters."

The world went well with him till the breaking out of the rebellion. That event found him the owner of fifteen likely negroes, a fine plantation of nine hundred and thirty acres, and a comfortable frame dwelling and out-buildings. His elder daughter had married a young farmer of the district, and his younger—little Sally, whom I remembered as a rosy-cheeked, meek-eyed, wee thing of only seven years—had grown up a woman.

In the spring of 1861, when there were no Union troops south of the Ohio, and the secession fever was raging furiously all over his county he organized one hundred and six of his neighbors into a company of Home Guards, and was elected their captain. They were pledged to resist all attacks on the person or property of any of their number, and met frequently in the woods in the vicinity of their homes. This organization secured Bible safety and free expression of opinion till long after Tennessee went out of the Union. In fact, he felt so secure that, in 1862—a year after the State seceded—under the protection of his band of Home Guards, he inaugurated and carried through a celebration of the fourth of July at Richmond, Tennessee, under the very guns of a rebel regiment then forming in the town.

An act of so much temerity naturally attracted the attention of the Confederate authorities, and not long afterward he was roused from his bed one morning, before daybreak, by three hundred armed men, who told him that he was a prisoner, and that all his property was confiscated to the Government. They at once enforced the "confiscation act;" "and this," he said, taking from his wallet a piece of soiled paper, "ar' whot I hed ter 'tribute ter the dingnation consarn. It'r Sally's own handwrite, an' I knows ye loikes har, so ye kin hev it, fur it'll nuver be uv no manner uv account ter me."

The schedule is now before me, and I copy it *verbatim:* "14 men and wimmin" (Jake eluded the soldiers and escaped to the woods), "1600 barrils corn, 130 sheeps, 700 bushls wheat, 440 barley, 100 rye, 27 mules, 5 cow-brutes, 105 head hogs, 17 horses and mars, and all they cud tote beside."

"Wall, they tied me hand an' fut," he continued; "an' toted me off ter the Military Commission sittin' ter Chattanooga. I know'd whot thet meant—a short prayer, a long rope, an' a break-down danced on the top o' nothin'. Better men nur me hed gone thet way ter the Kingdom—sevin on 'em wuthin a month—but I detarmined I wouldn't go ef I could holp it; not thet I 'jected ter the journey, only ter goin' afore uv Sally. Ye sees, I hedn't been nigh so good a man as I'd orter be, an' I reckoned Sally—who, ye knows, ar the best 'ooman thet uver lived—I reckoned she, ef she got thar a leetle afore o' me, could sort o' put in a good word wuth the LORD, an' git Him ter shot His eyes ter a heap o' my doin's; an' sides, I should, I know'd, feel a mighty strange loike up thar without har. Wall, I detarmined not ter go, so thet night, as we war camped out on the ground, I slid the coil, stole a nag, an' moseyed off. Howsumuver, I hedn't got more'n a hun'red rods, 'fore the durned Secesh yered me, an' the bullets fell round me thicker'n tar in January. They hit the hoss, winged me a trifle, an' in less nur ten minnits, hed me tighter'n uver. They swore a streak uv blue brimstun', an' said they'd string me up ter onst, but I telled 'em they wouldn't, 'case I know'd I war a gwine ter live ter holp do thet ar' same turn fur Jeff. Davis. Wall, I s'pose my impudence hed suthin' ter do wuth it, fur they didn't hang me—ye mought know thet, Mr. ———, fur, ye sees, I hes a good neck fur stretchin' yit.

"Wall we got ter Chattanooga jest arter noon. The Commission they hed too many on hand thet day ter 'tend ter my case, an' the jail wus chock-heapin', so they put me inter a tent under guard uv a hull Georgy regiment. Things luck'd 'mazin' squally, an' much as I detarmined ter be a man, my heart went clean down inter my boots whenuver I thort uv Sally. I nuver felt so, afore or sence, fur then I hedn't got used ter luckin' at the gallus uvery day.

"Wall, *I* didn't know whot ter do, but thinkin' the Lord did, I kneeled down an' prayed right smart. I telled Him I hedn't no face ter meet Him afore I'd a done suthin' fur the kentry, an' thet Sally's heart would be clean broke ef I went afore har, but, howsumuver, I said, He know'd best, an' ef it war His will, I hed jest nothin' ter say agin it. Thet's all I said, but I said it over an' over, a heap o' times, an it war right dark when I got off uv my knees. The Lord yered me, thet's sartin, 'case I hedn't mor'n got up fore a dirty grey-back, drunker'n a member uv Congress, staggered inter the tent. I recken he thort he war ter home, fur he drapped down onter the ground an' went ter sleep, wuthout so much as axin' ef I was willin'.

"Then it come inter my head, all ter onst, whot ter do. Ye sees, the critters hed tied me hand an' fut, an' teddered me wuth a coil ter one o' the tent stakes, so I couldn't move only jest so fur; but the Lord He made the drunken feller lop down jest inside uv reachin'. Wall, when I war shore he war dead asleep, I rolled over thar, drawed out the bowie-knife in his belt wuth my teeth, an' sawed off my wristlets in no time. Ye kin reckon it didn't take long ter undo the 'tother coils, an' to 'propriate his weapons, tie 'im hand an' fut loike I war, strip off his coat, put mine onter 'im, swap hats, an' pull the one I guv him down onter his eyes loike as ef he never wanted to see the sun agin. When I'd a done thet, I stopped ter breathe, an' luckin' up I seed a light a comin'. I 'spicioned it war ter 'xamine arter me, so I slunk down inter a corne• o' the tent, jest aside the door. They wus a leftenant, an' three privits, makin' the rounds, an' the light showed me nigh onter a army uv sentinels all about thar. Thet warn't no way encouragin', but sez I ter myself: 'Bible,' sez I, 'be cool an' outdacious, an' ye'll git out o' this, yit;' so, when the leftenant luck'd in, an' sayin': 'All right,' put out agin, I riz up, an' jined the fellers as wus a follerin' on him. I kept in the shadder, an' they, supposin' I war one on 'em, tuck no kind uv notice uv me. We'd luck'd arter three or four pore prisoners loike I war, when I thort I'd better be a moseyin', so I drapped ahind, an' arter a while dodged out beyont the second line o' pickets. I'd got nigh onter a patch uv woods half a mile off, when all ter onst a feller sprung up frum a clump uv bushes, yelled, 'Halt,' an' pinted his musket stret at me. I mought hev eended 'im, but I reckoned others wus nigh, an' sides, I nuver takes humin life ef I kin holp it; so I sez ter 'im; 'Why, Lord bless me, cumrad', I didn't seed ye.' 'I s'pose ye didn't. Whot is ye doin' yere?' sez he. 'Only pursuin' a jug o' blue ruin I'se out thar hid under a log,' sez I. 'Ye knows it'r agin rule to tote it inside, but a feller must licker.' 'Wall, licker up ter-morrer,' sez he. 'We's got 'ticklar orders ter let no 'un out ter-night. 'Blast the orders,' sez I. 'Ye'd loike a swig yerself.' 'Wall, I would,' sez he. 'Wull you go snacks?' 'Yas,' sez I; 'an' guv ye chock-heapin measure, for I *must* hev some o' thet afore mornin'.'

"Thet brung him, an' I piked off for the ruin. (It warn't thar, ye knows—I nuver totch the dingnation stuff.) Ye'd better b'lieve the grass didn't grow under my feet when o ɪst I got inter the woods. I plumbed my coorse by the stars, an' made ten right smart miles in no time. Then it come inter my head thet I'd a forgot all about the Lord, so I kneeled down right thar, an' thanked Him. I telled Him I seed His hand jest so plain as ef it war daytime, an' thet, as shore as my name war Bible, I'd foller His lead in futur'—an' I'se tried ter, uver sense.

"I'd got to be right well tuckered out by thet time—the 'citement, ye see, hed holt me up, but I'd no sooner gone to prayin' fore my knees guv out all ter onst—so, I put fur a piece uv timber, lay down under a tree, an' went ter sleep. I must hev slept mighty sound, fur, long 'bout mornin', some'un hed ter shuck me awful hard, an' turn me clar over, 'fore it woked me. I got up. 'Twar nigh so light as day, though 'twarn't sun-up. Yit I luck'd all around an' didn't see a soul! Now, what d'ye s'pose it war that woked me?"

"Your own imagination, I reckon. You were dreaming, and in your dream you thought some one shook you," I replied.

"No; 'twarn't thet. I nuver dreams. It war the LORD! An' He done it 'case I'd prayed ter' im. I'se nuver gone ter sleep, or woke up, sense, wuthout prayin' ter HIM, an' though I'se been in a heap uv wuss fixes nur thet, He's got me out uv all on 'em, jest 'case I does pray ter Him."

I did not dispute him. Who that reads the New Testament as Bible reads it—like a little child—*can* dispute him. In a moment he went on with his story

"Wall, I luck'd all round, an' seed nuthin', but I *yered*—not a mile off—the hounds a bayin' away loike a young thundergust. They wus arter me, an' thet wus the why the GOOD LORD woked me. I luck'd at the 'volver I'd stole from the sodger, seed it war all right, an' then clumb a tree. 'Bout so quick as it takes ter tell it, the hounds—two 'maizin' fine critters, wuth a hun'red an' fifty apiece—wus on me. I run my eye 'long the pistol-barr'l, an' let drive. It tuck jest two shots ter kill 'em. I know'd the Secesh wus a follerin' the dogs, so ye'd better b'lieve I made purty tall racin' time till I got ter the eend uv the timber.

"Just at night I run agin some darkies, who guv me suthin ter eat, an' nothin' more happen'd 'fore the next night, when I come in sight o' home. I got ter the edge uv the woods, on the hill jest ahind uv my barn, 'bout a hour by sun; but I darn't go down, fur, ye knows, the house stood in a clarin', an' some uv the varmints mought be a watchin' fur me. I lay thar till it war thick dark, an' then I crept ter the r'ar door. I listened; an' whot d'ye 'spose I yered? Sally a prayin'—an' prayin' fur *me*, so 'arnest an' so tender loike, thet I sct down on the door step, an' cried loike a child—I did."

Here the rough, strong man bent down his head and wept again. The moisture filled my own eyes as he continued:

"She telled the Lord how much I war ter har; how she'd a loved me uver sense she'd a fust seed me; how 'fore har father, or mother, or even the chillen, she loved me; how she'd tried ter make me love Him; how she know'd thet, way down in my heart, I did love Him, though I didn't say so, 'case men doan't speak out 'bout sech things loike wimmin does. An' she telled Him how she hed tried ter do His will; tried ter be one on His raal chillen; an' she telled Him He hed promised not ter lay onter His chillen no more'n they could b'ar, an' *she* couldn't b'ar ter hev me hung up as ef I war a traitor: thet she could part wuth me if it war best; thet she could see me die, an' not weep a tear, ef I could only die loike a man, wuth a musket in my hand, a doin' suthin' for my kentry. Then she prayed Him ter send me back ter har fur jest one day, so she mought ax me once more ter love Him—an' she know'd I would love Him ef she axed me agin—an' she said ef He'd only do thet, she'd—much as she loved me—she'd send me away, an' guv me all up ter Him an' the kentry fur uver!

"I couldn't stand no more, so I opened the door, drapped onter my knees, tuck har inter my arms, lay my head on har shoulder, an' sobbed out: 'The Lord hes yered ye, Sally! I wull love Him! I wull be worthy of sech love as y's guv'n me, Sally!'"

He paused for a moment, and covered his face with his hands. When he spoke again there was a softness and tenderness in his tone that I never heard in the voice of but one other man.

"Sense thet minnit this yerth hes been another yerth ter me; an' though I'se lost uverythin'; though I hes no home; though night arter night I sleeps out in the cold an' the wet, a scoutin'; though my wife an' chillen is scattered; though nigh uvery day I'se in danger uv the gallus; though I'se been roped ter a tree ter die loike a dog; though a thousand bullets hes yelled death in my yeres; though I'se seed my only boy shot down afore my vury eyes, an' I not able ter speak ter him, ter guv him a mossel uv comfort, or ter yere his last word, I'se hed suthin allers yere (laying his hand on his heart) thet hes holt me up, an' made me luck death in the face as of I loved it An ef ye hain't got thet, Mr. ——, no matter whot else ye's got, no matter whot money, or larnin', or friends, ye's pore—porer nur I ar!"

I made no reply, and after a short silence he resumed his story.

"Jake—that war my boy—ye remember him, ye hed him on yer knee—he war eighteen an' a man grow'd then: wall, Jake an' me made up our minds ter pike fur the Union lines ter onst. Sally war all night a cookin' fur us, an' we a gittin' the arms an' fixin's a ready—we hed lots o' them b'longin' ter the Guards, hid away in a panel uv the wall—an' the next day, meanin' ter start jest arter sunset, we laid down fur some sleepin'. Nigh onter dark, Black Jake, who war a watchin', come rushin' inter the house, sayin the secesh wus a comin'. Thar wus only twenty on 'em, he said, an' one wus drunk an' didn't count fur nuthin', so, we detarmined ter meet 'em. We tuck our stands nigh the door, each on us men—Black Jake, the boy, an' me—wuth a Derringer in his pocket, two 'volvers in his belt, an' a Bowie-knife in the breast uv his waistcoat, an' the wimmin wuth a 'volver in each hand, an' waited fur 'em. Half a dozen on em went round ter the r'ar, an' the rest come at the front door, yellin' out:

"'We doan't want ter 'sturb ye, Miss Smith (they's chivurly, ye knows), but we reckons yer husban' ar yere, an' we must sarch the house. We hes orders ter take him.'

"I opened the door stret off, an' steppin' down onter the piazzer—Black Jake an' the boy ter my back, an' the wimmin' ter the winder—I sez ter 'em:

"'Wall, I'se yere. Take me ef ye kin!'

"They wus fourteen on 'em thar, uvery man wuth a musket, but they darn't lift a leg! They wus cowards. It'r nuthin but a good cause, Mr. ——, thet guvs a man courage—makes him luck death in the face as ef he loved it.

"Wall, they begun ter parley. 'We doan't want ter shed no blood,' said the leftenant. 'but we's orders ter take ye, Mister Smith, an' ye'd better go wuth us, peaceable loike.'

"'I shan't go wuth ye peaceable loike, nur no other how,' sez I; 'fur ye's a pack o' howlin thieves an' traitors as no decent man 'ud be seed in company uv. Ye disgraces the green yerth ye walks on, an' ef ye doan't git off uv my sheer uv it in less nur no time, I'll send ye —though it'r agin my principles ter take humin life—whar ye'll git yer desarts, sartin.'

"Then the leftenant he begun ter parley agin, but I pinted my 'volver at him, an' telled him he'd better be a moseyin' sudden. Sayin' he'd 'port ter his cunnel, he done it.

"We know'd a hun'red on 'em 'ud be thar in no time, so, soon as they wus out o' sight, the boy an' me, leavin' Black Jake ter luck arter the wimmin, struck a stret line fur the timber. We hedn't got mor'n four mile—ter the top uv the tall summit ter the ra'r uv Richmond—afore, luckin' back, we seed my house an' barns all a blazin'! The Heaven-defyin' villuns hed come back—shot Jake down in cold blood, druv my wife an' darter out o' doors, an' burnt all I hed ter the ground! We seed the fire, but not knowin whot else hed happin'd, an' not bein' able ter do nothin', we piked or inter the woods.

"We traviled all thet night through the timber, an' jest at sundown uv the next day come ter a clarin'. We wus mighty tired, but 'twouldn't do ter sleep thar, fur the trees wus nigh a rod asunder; so we luck'd round, an' on t'other side uv the road, not half a mile off, seed 'bout a acre uv laurel bush—ye knows whot them is, some on 'em so thick a dog karn't git through 'em. Jake war tireder nur I war, an' he said ter me, 'Dad,' sez he: 'let us git under kiver ter onst. I feels loike I couldn't stand up no longer.' It wus foolhardy loike, fur the sun warn't clar down, but I couldn't b'ar ter see the boy so, an', agin my judgment, we went down the road ter the laurels. We lay thar till mornin', an' slep' so sound thet I reckon ef forty yerthquakes hed shuck the yerth, they wouldn't hev woked us. Soon as sun-up, Jake riz, an' went ter the edge uv the thicket ter rekonnoitter. He hedn't stood thar five minutes—right in plain sight, an' not more'n two hun'red rods frum me—afore I yered a shot, an' seed the pore boy throw up his arms, an' fall ter the ground. In less nur no time fifty Secesh wus on him. I war springin' up ter go ter him, when suthin' tuck me by the shoulder, helt me back, an' said ter me: 'Ye karn't do nothin' fur him. Leave 'im ter the Lord. Save yerself fur the kentry.' It went agin natur,' but it 'peared the LORD'S voice, so I crouched down agin 'mong the bushes. I nuver know'd whot it war thet saved me till nigh a y'ar arterwuds. Then I tuck thet leftenant pris'ner—I could hev shot him, but I guv him his life ter repent in, an' he done it: he's a decent man now, b'longin' ter Cunnel Johnson's rigiment. Wall, I tuck him, an' he said ter me: "I wus aside uv thet pore boy when he war dyin'. He turned his eyes onter me jest as he war goin', an' he said: 'Ye karn't kotch him. He's out o' the bush! Ha! ha!' He said thet, and died. Ter save me, died wuth a lie on his lips! Does ye b'lieve the LORD laid that agin him, Mr. ——?"

"No, no! I am sure not. It was a noble action."

"It 'pears so ter me, but it war loike the boy. He war allers furgettin' himself, an' thinkin' uv other folk. He war all—all the pride uv my life—him an' Sally—but it pleased the LORD ter tuck him afore me—but only fur a time—only fur a time—'fore long I shill hev him agin—agin—up thar—up thar!"

His emotion choked his utterance for awhile. When he resumed, he said:

"At the eend uv a fortn't, trav'lin' by night an' sleepin' by day, an' livin' on the darkies when my fixin's guv out, I got inter the Union lines 'bove Nashville."

"And what became of your wife and daughter?" I asked.

"Lettle Sally went ter har sister. My wife walked eighty miles ter har father's. He's one on yer quality folk, an' a durned old secesh, but he's got humin natur' in him, an' Sally's safe thar. I'se seed har twice ter his house. The old 'un he's know'd on't, but he hain't nuver said a word."

Bible's scouting adventures would fill a volume, and read more like a romance of the middle ages than a matter-of-fact history of the present time. On one occasion, when about five miles outside of our lines, he came, late at night, upon a party of rebel officers, making merry at the house of a wealthy secessionist Riding coolly up to the mounted orderly on guard before the door-way, he pinioned his arms, thrust a handkerchief into his mouth, and led him quietly out of hearing Then bidding him dismount, and tying him to a tree, he removed the impromptu gag, and levelling a revolver at his head, said to him :

"Now, tell me, ye rebel villun, whot whiskey-kags wus ye a watchin' thar ? Speak truth, or I'll guv ye free passage ter a hot kentry."

"Nine ossifers," said the trembling rebel ; a cunnel, two majors, a sargeon, two cap'ns, an' the rest leftenants."

"Whar's thar weapons ?"

"Thar swords is in the hall-way. None on 'em hain't pistols 'cept the sargeon—he mought hev a 'volver."

"What nigs is they round ?"

"Nary one, I reckon, more'n a old man thar (pointing to the kitchen building) an' the gals in the house."

"Wall, I'll let ye go fur this, ef ye's telled the truth. Ef ye hain't, ye'd better be a sayin' yer prayers ter onst, fur the Lord wont yere ye on the t'other side uv Jurdan."

Fastening his horse in "the timber," and creeping up to the house, he then reconnoitered the kitchen premises. The old man—a stout, stalwart negro of about fifty—sat dozing in the corner, and his wife, a young mulatto woman, was cooking wild-fowl over the fire. Opening the door, and placing his finger on his lips to enjoin silence, Bible beckoned to the woman. She came to him, and looking her full in the eye for a moment, he said to her : "I kin trust ye. Wud ye 'an yer old 'un loike ter git out o' the claws uv these durned secesh ?"

"Yas, yas, massa," she replied, "we wud. We's Union! We'd loike ter git 'way, massa!"

Then awakening her husband, Bible said to him: "Uncle, wud yer risk yer life fur yer freedom?"

"Ef dar's a chance, massa, a right smart chance. Dis dark'y tinks a heap ob his life, he does, massa. It 'm 'bout all him got."

"Yas, yas, I know; but ye shill hev freedom. I'll see ye ter the Free States, ef ye'll holp tuck them secesh ossifers."

"Holp tuck dem, massa! Why, dar's a dozen on 'em; dey'd chaw ye up in no time," exclaimed the astonished African.

"No, thar hain't a dozen on 'em; thar's only nine; but—ye's a coward," replied the scout.

"No, I hain't no coward, massa; but I loikes a chance, massa, a right smart chance."

Bible soon convinced the negro that he would have a "right smart chance," and he consented to make the hazardous strike for his freedom. Entering the house, he returned in a few moments to the scout, confirming the sentinel's report: the weapons were reposing quietly in the hall, near the doorway, and the officers, very much the worse for liquor, were carousing with his master in the dining-room.

Selecting three of the best horses from the stables, Bible directed the yellow woman to lead them into the road, and to bring his own from where it was fastened in the woods. Then, with his sooty ally, the scout entered the mansion. Removing the arms from the hall, he walked boldly into the dining-room. "Gentlemen," he said, pointing his pistols—one in each hand—at the rebel officers, "ye is my pris'ners. Surrender yer shootin' irons, or ye's dade men."

"Who are you?" exclaimed one of them, as they all sprang to their feet.

"Cunnel Smith, uv the Fust Tennessee Nigger Regiment—one old black man an' a yaller 'ooman," coolly replied the scout.

"Go to ——," shouted the surgeon, quickly drawing his revolver, and discharging it directly at Bible's face. The ball grazed his head, cut off a lock of hair just above his ear, and lodged in the wall at his back. The report was still sounding through the apartment, when the surgeon uttered a wild cry, sprang a few feet in the air, and fell lifeless to the floor! The negro had shot him.

"Come, gentlemen, none o' thet," said Bible, as coolly as if nothing had happened, "guv me the shootin' iron, an' surrender, or we'll sot the rest on ye ter his wuck—rakin' coals fur the devil's funnace—in less nur a minnit."

Without more hesitation the rebel colonel handed the scout the fallen man's pistol, and then all, followed by the scout and the negro, marched quietly out of the front door. The mulatto woman, holding the horses, was standing in the highway.

"Hitch the nags, my purty gal," said the scout, "an' git a coil. An' ye, gentlemen, sot down, an' say nothin' —'cept it mought be yer prayers; but them, I reckon, ye hain't larned yit."

The negress soon returned with the rope, and while Bible and her husband covered them with their revolvers, she tied the arms of the prostrate chivalry. When this was done, the scout affixed a long rope to the waist of

THE FIRST TENNESSEE CAVALRY ESCORTING REBEL PRISONERS.

the officer on either flank of the column, and, taking one in his own hand, and giving the other to the negro, cried out:

"Sogers uv the Fust Tennessee! Mount!"

The regiment bounded into the saddle, and in that plight—the planter and the eight captive officers marching on before, the self-appointed "cunnel" and his chief officer bringing up the rear, and the rest of his command—the yellow woman—*a-straddle* of a horse between them, they entered the Union lines.

On another occasion, hunted down by several companies of rebel cavalry, Bible took refuge in a grove of laurel bushes. Among the bushes was a hollow tree in which he had once or twice slept on previous expeditions. It had been overthrown by a tornado, and the soil still clung, in huge boulders, to its upturned roots. Creeping into this tree, he closed the small opening with earth, and boring a hole through the trunk with his Bowie-knife to admit air, and give him a look-out on his pursuers, he lay there without food for three days and nights. The rebels saw him enter the grove, and at once surrounded it, so that escape was impossible. A party then beat the bushes, and after examining every square yard of the ground, came and sat upon the hollow tree. Listening, he heard them recount some of his exploits, and assert very positively, that he had sold himself to that notorious dealer in human chattels—the devil—who, they thought, had given him power to make himself invisible at will. "An' bein' thet's so, cumrades," very logically remarked one of the number, "doan't it nat'rally foller thet the devil ar' on the Union side, an' moughtent we 'bout so wall guv it up fur a dade beat 'ter onst!"

When the rebel army retreated from Murfreesboro, its advance column came suddenly upon the scout as he was eating his breakfast in an "oak opening" near the highway. There was no chance of escape or concealment, for the "opening" was covered with immense trees standing fifteen and twenty feet apart, with only a short grass growing between them. Bible was disguised in an immense mass of red hair and beard, and wore a tattered suit of the coarse homespun of the district. Knowing he would certainly be discovered, he assumed a vacant, rustic look, and, rising from the ground, gazed stupidly at the soldiery.

"I say, green one, what are you doing thar?" shouted the officer at the head of the column.

"I'se loss my cow-brutes, cunnel," replied the scout; "two right loikely heffers; 'un on 'em speckle all over, 'cept the tail, an' thet white'n yer face. Ye hain't seed 'em no whar 'long the road, nohow, hes ye?"

"No, I hain't seed 'em, no whar, nohow," rejoined the officer. "Come, step into the ranks; we need just such fellows as you are. Why the devil haven't they conscripted you before. Step into the ranks, I say," he repeated, as Bible, not seeming to comprehend his meaning, remained standing in his previous position. The second command having no more effect on him than the first, the officer directed a couple of soldiers to take Bible between them, and to fall in at the rear of the column. It was not till he was fairly in the road that the scout seemed to awaken to the reality of his condition.

'Why, why, ye hain't a gwine to tuck me 'long o' ye!" he exclaimed, frantically appealing to the "cunnel." "Ye hain't a gwine ter tuck me 'long o' ye! Ye karn't mean thet!"

"We do mean that, and you just keep quiet, or, like St. Paul, you'll fight against the pricks," said the officer, alluding perhaps to the bayonets which the two soldiers had unslung and were holding ready to apply to Bible's flanks.

"Why, ye karn't mean thet! ye karn't mean thet, cunnel!" again piteously cried the scout, "Wh—wh—whot'll become on the old 'ooman—whot'll become on the cow-brutes?"

"D—n the old woman and the cow-brutes," shouted the officer, riding forward and leaving the new recruit to his fate. And thus Bible marched to the Tullahoma, and thus he enlisted in the second regiment of Alabama Infantry.

He remained a fortnight at Tullahoma, and while there obtained a correct idea of the number and disposition of the enemies' forces, and brought away with him, in his head, an accurate map of the rebel fortifications. Desertions being frequent, the picket lines had been doubled, and when he was ready to leave, it had become next to impossible to penetrate them. But he was equal to the emergency, and hit upon a bold expedient which proved successful.

Restrictions had been laid by the commanding general on the importation of whiskey, and the use of that article, which is a sort of necessity to the Southern "native," had been prohibited within the lines of the army—except on the eve of battle Then the cold water generals, themselves, dealt it out—mixed with gunpowder—to every man in the ranks. The regulations concerning it were rigidly enforced in all the divisions except Hardee's. That general—to whose corps Bible belonged—who has, notoriously, a weakness for "spirits" and negro women, winked at the indulgence of his men in those luxuries, when it did not interfere with their strict observance of "Hardee's Tactics."

Knowing his proclivities, Bible, one evening just after sunset, took a tin "jug" under his arm, and sauntered past the general's tent.

"I say," shouted Hardee, catching sight of the long form of the scout, "where are you going with that big canteen?"

"Ter git some bust-head, giniral. Ye knows we karn't live wuthout thet," replied Bible, with affected simplicity.

"Perhaps you karn't: don't you know it's against regulations. I'll string you up, and give you fifty."

"Oh, no! ye woan't do thet, I knows, giniral, fur ye's a feller feelin' for we pore sogers," said Bible. "We karn't livė wuthout a leetle ruin; wuthout a leetle, nohow, giniral!"

"Where do you expect to get it?" asked the general.

"Ter Squire Pursley's," said the scout, naming a planter living a few miles outside of the lines. "He's got some on the tallest old rye ye uver seed. I knows him. An' he's the biggest brandy, too, an' the purtiest nigger gal (rolling his tongue in his mouth and smacking his lips) thar is anywhar round. She's whiter'n ye is, giniral, an' the snuggest piece uv house furnitur' as uver wus grow'd."

"And how do you expect to pass the pickets?" asked the standard authority on "Tactics."

"I reckon' this wull brung 'em," answered Bible, tapping his canteen significantly.

"Well, it wont," replied the general, laughing; "but I'll give you something that will. And here, take this canteen and get me some of that 'big brandy,' and tell the squire I'll be over there one of these days."

The general gave Bible a pass, another canteen, and five dollars of Confederate scrip, to effectually "raise the spirits;" and then the scout, saying, "Ye kin reckon on gittin' sich brandy, giniral, as wull sot ye up so high ye'll nuver come down agin," walked leisurely out of the rebel lines.

Once, while scouting near McMinnville, Bible was captured by a small party of Forrest's cavalry. One of the Confederates knew him, and he was told he must die. Throwing a rope over the limb of a tree, they adjusted it about his neck, and the rebel officer, taking out his watch, said to him: "You can have five minutes to say your prayers."

"I thanks ye, cap'n," said Bible; "fur thet shows ye's got a spark uv humin feelin' in ye; an' ef ye'll jest pile a lettle light 'ood on ter thet spark, it mought be it 'ud blaze up an' make ye a better man nur ye is, or kin be, whiles ye's a fightin' agin' yer kentry. As ter prayin', cap'n, I doan't need no time fur thet; fur I'se allers a prayin', not wuth words—but silent, deep, down yere" —placing his hand on his heart—"whar I'se allers a sayin' 'OUR FATHER!' *Our* FATHER, cap'n; *your'n* as wull as mine! An' doan't ye 'spose He's luckin down on ye now sorry, grieved ter His vury heart thet ye,

His chile, thet His own SON died a wus death nur this fur, should be a doin' whot ye is?—not a hangin' uv me; I hain't no complaint ter make o' thet, fur it'r His wull, or ye wouldn't be a doin' on it—but sorry thet ye's lifted yer hand agin' yer kentry, agin truth, an' right, an' the vury liberty ye talks so much about. Prayin'! I'se allers a prayin', cap'n; allers been a prayin' uver sense Sally said ter me: 'Pray, Bible, fur it'r the only way ye kin come nigh ter Him: it'r the only way ye kin know, fur shore, thet ye's His raal chile.' An' I does know I'se his chile, 'case I loves ter pray; an' I'll pray fur ye, cap'n—ye needs it more nur me. It woan't do ye no hurt, an' it mought do ye some good, fur the LORD promises ter yere His chillen, an' He has yered *me*, over an' over agin."

The five minutes had elapsed, but the Confederate officer still stood with his watch in his hand. At last, turning suddenly away, he said to his men:

"Take off the rope! Take him to the general. *He* may do what he likes with him. I'll be d—d if *I'll* hang him."

Before they reached Forrest's headquarters at McMinnville, they were set upon by a squad of Union cavalry, who rescued the prisoner, captured a half dozen of the privates, and gave the captain a mortal wound in the side. Bible laid him upon the grass, and, taking his head tenderly in his lap, prayed for him. As the captain turned his eyes to take a last look at the setting sun, he placed the scout's hand against his heart, and saying: "I'm going now—I feel at peace—I owe it to you—GOD bless you for it, may GOD forever bless you," he uttered a low moan and died.

While the rebel forces lay encamped around Chattanooga, Bible made them a professional visit. For twc days, from the top of Lookout Mountain, he looked down on their fortifications. With the works fully mapped in his mind, so that, in his rude way, he could sketch them upon paper, he started, just at nightfall of a murky, stormy day, to make his way northward. Arriving at the house of a pretended friend, he took supper, and retired to sleep in a small room on the ground floor. It was not far from eleven o' clock, and raining and blowing violently, when a light rap came at his window. He got up—he always slept in his clothes, with his arms about him—and applying his ear to the glass, heard a low voice say:

"Ye is betrayed. Come out ter onst. They'll be yere in a hour."

He lifted the sash, and, springing lightly into the yard, saw—as well as the night would permit—a young octoroon woman standing unprotected in the storm, thinly clad, and drenched from head to foot. Leading him out into the darkness, she said to him:

"This man's son war at master's house not a hour back. He's telled on ye ter git the reward! They's 'spectin' the cavalry uvery minnit. Hark! I yere's 'em now!"

While she yet spoke he heard the heavy tramp of horsemen along the highway. Placing her hand in his, the woman fled hurriedly to the woods. When they had gone about a mile, she paused, and said to him:

"I karn't go no furder. I must git home or they 'll 'spect suthin'. When they find ye's gone, the cavalry 'll make fur the landin'. Ye must go up the river, an' 'bout two mile frum yere ye'll find a yawl. It'r chained, but ye kin break thet. Doan't cross over—a hull regiment is 'camped on t'other side—put up the river so fur as ye kin."

With a mutual "God bless ye," they parted. Bible made his way to the river, and narrowly inspected its banks, but no boat was to be seen! He had spent two hours in the search, when he came to a bend in the stream which gave him an uninterrupted view of it for miles below. All along the river the air was alive with torches hurrying to and fro. He knew his pursuers would soon be upon him, and ejaculating a short prayer, in which he reminded the LORD that the information he carried in his head was of "no oncommon vallu, orter be got ter the giniral ter onst, an' wouldn't be uv no yerthly use" if he were hanged just then, he crept down to the water. Entangled in the underbrush just above him was a large log, the estray property of some up-country sawyer. Dropping himself into the water, he made his way to the log, and, laying down on it at full length, paddled out into the river. When he had reached the middle of the stream, he let himself drift down with the current, and in a short time was among his pursuers. A thousand torches blazing on either bank lit up the narrow river with a lurid glare, and made the smallest object on its surface distinctly visible. Knowing that if he kept his position he would certainly be seen, Bible rolled off into the water, turned over on his back, and, keeping one hand upon the log, floated along beside it. When he came opposite to the landing, he heard one cavalryman say to another:

"See! thar's a log; moughtent the durned critter be on thet?"

"No," replied the other; "thar's nothin' on it. Yer eyes is no better 'n moles."

"Wall, I'll guv it a shot, anyhow," rejoined the first, and fired his carbine. The bullet glanced from the log, and struck the water a few feet from the scout. The one shot attracted others, and for a few minutes the balls fell thickly around him, but he escaped unhurt! The God to whom he had prayed shielded him, and brought him safely out of the hands of his enemies. In six days, after unparalleled hardships, he reached the Union lines.

A few days before I left Murfreesboro, Bible started on another trip into the enemies' lines to establish a chain of spy stations up to Bragg's headquarters. He succeeded in the perilous enterprise, and, when I last heard of him, was pursuing his usual avocation, doing really more service to the country than many a star-shouldered gentleman who is talked of now in the newspapers, and may be read of centuries hence in history.

If I have outlined his character distinctly, the reader has perceived that he is brave, simple-hearted, outspoken, hospitable, enterprising, industrious, loyal to liberty, earnest in his convictions—though ignorantly confounding names with things—a good husband and father, with a quiet humor which flavors character as Worcester sauce flavors a good dinner, a practical wisdom which "trusts in the Lord, but keeps its powder dry," some talent for bragging, and that intensity of nature and disposition to magnify every thing (illustrated in his stories and conversation) which leads the Southerner to do nothing by halves, to throw his whole soul into whatever he undertakes, to be, like Jeremiah's figs, "if good, very good: if bad, not fit to feed the pigs." Though morally and intellectually superior to the mass of "poor Southern whites," he is still a good representative of the class. They nearly all possess the same traits that he does, and differ from him only in degree, not in kind. That is saying little against them, for one might travel a whole summer's day in our Northern cities, and not meet many men who, in all that makes true manhood, are his equals.

THREE SOLDIERS CAPTURED BY A BOY WITH A COFFEE-POT.—An amusing instance of the value of a ready wit and presence of mind occurred during the advance of the Second Corps of Federal troops, near Hatcher's Run. A young lad in the Fourteenth Connecticut regiment, going with a coffee-pot to get water from the stream, suddenly found himself surrounded by three of the enemy.

With all the fierceness of voice the little fellow could muster, he commanded them to throw down their arms and surrender. Supposing that the brave youth had companions near to enforce his command, they complied, when he seized one of their muskets and marched them into camp in great triumph. This story was related in his camp as the capture of three Johnnies with a coffee-pot.

THE GREAT RAILROAD RAID.

PART II.

DARING ENTERPRISES OF OFFICERS AND MEN.

THE GREAT RAILROAD CHASE.

THE most remarkable and thrilling railroad adventure that ever occurred on the American continent, was that which happened to the twenty-two members of an expedition sent out by the Union General O. M. Mitchel, to destroy the communication on the Georgia State Railroad, between Atlanta and Chattanooga. The expedition itself, in the daring of its conception, possessed the wildness of a romance, and which, had it been successful, would have suddenly and completely changed the whole aspect of the war in the South and Southwest. It was as sublime in the results aimed at, as it was daring in execution; for it would have given full possession of all East Tennessee to the Union forces, which, moving then on Lynchburg, would have had the valley of Virginia at their mercy, and could have attacked Stonewall Jackson in the rear. In addition to this advantage, they would have held the railroad to Charlottesville and Orange Court House, as well as the Southside railroad leading to Petersburg and Richmond; and thus, by uniting with McClellan's army, could have attacked the rebel General Joe Johnston's army, front and flank, driven him from Virginia, and flanked Beauregard.

This admirable *coup d'etat*, the sagacity and importance of which challenged even the warmest admiration of the Confederates themselves, as being "the deepest laid scheme, and on the grandest scale, that ever emanated from the brains of any number of Yankees combined," was planned and set on foot in April, 1862, by Mr. J. J. Andrews, a citizen of Kentucky, who had been previously engaged in the secret service of the United States Government. The plan of operations which he proposed was to reach a point on the State road, where they could seize a locomotive and train of cars, and then dash back in the direction of Chattanooga, cutting the telegraph wires and burning the bridges behind them as they went, until they reached their own lines. The party consisted of twenty-four men, who, with the exception of its leader, Mr. Andrews, and another citizen of Kentucky, William Campbell by name—who volunteered as substitute for a soldier—were selected from different companies of the Second, Twenty-first, and Twenty-third Ohio regiments, with particular reference to their known courage and discretion. These brave men were informed that the movement was to be a secret one, and doubtless comprehended something of its perils; but Mr. Andrews and one other alone seem to have known any thing of its precise direction and object. They all, however, cheerfully and voluntarily engaged in it; and before starting, Andrews divided among them seven hundred dollars of Confederate scrip, informed them that they were now venturing upon important and dangerous duty, and threatened to shoot on the spot the first man that got drunk or flinched in the least. They then made their way through the lines in parties of two and three, in citizens' dress, and carrying only side arms, to Chattanooga, the point of rendezvous agreed upon, where twenty-two out of the twenty-four arrived safely. Here they took passage, without attracting attention, for Marietta, which place they reached at twelve o'clock on the night of the 11th of April. The next morning, before daylight, they took the cars and went back on the same road to a place called Big Shanty, a regular stopping-place for refreshments, and where, within forty or fifty yards of the road, some twenty thousand Confederate troops were encamped, it being a general rendezvous for recruits and the organization of regiments. The train upon which the conspirators were, contained, also, a number of soldiers, as well as citizens, together with a quantity of provisions, and an iron safe containing a large amount of Confederate money, designed for the payment of the rebel troops at Corinth, Mississippi. Here, for the first time, they knew the nature of their duty, which was to destroy the track and bridges from Big Shanty, to and beyond Chattanooga, or as far as Bridgeport, Tennessee. This section of the road is built over innumerable creeks and rivers; and as General Mitchel had already cut off all communication from Corinth, by holding Huntsville, Alabama, the destruction of bridges which they were expected to effect, would have completely prevented rebel reinforcements and commissary stores from reaching Virginia, Tennessee, and Georgia.

At Big Shanty, therefore, the train stopped for breakfast, and passengers, conductor, engineer, and "hands," all went into the saloon, and were soon engaged in enjoying their matutinal meal. The conspirators were prompt to seize the golden moment of opportunity now offered to them. Leaving the cars, they quietly and naturally grouped together in squads of three and four, taking station with apparent carelessness on each side of the train, Andrews stationing himself at the coupling pin of the third car. A number of their party were engineers, and thoroughly understood the business in hand. One of these engineers was at his post, and found every thing right. All hands then quickly mounted the cars, although the guard was within three feet of them; the word was given, Andrews drew the coupling pin and cried, "All right!" The engineer opened the valve and put on all steam, and the train, now consisting of three box cars and the engine, moved quietly but swiftly off—leaving rebel conductor, engineer, passengers, spectators, and the soldiers in the camp near by, all lost in amazement, and dumbfounded at the strange, startling, and daring act. And now commenced the most exciting railroad race and chase, which it has ever fallen to the pen of historian to describe. They soon lost sight of the lights at Big Shanty station, and at the first curve the train was stopped just long enough to allow one of the party to climb the telegraph pole and cut the wires. Starting again, they pushed along—making stops here and there to tear up the track, and taking with them on the cars a few of the rails thus removed. But unforseen difficulty now began to meet them. According to the schedule of the road, of which Mr. Andrews had possessed himself, they should have met but a single train on that day, whereas they met three, two of which were engaged on extraordinary service, and they were compelled to switch off and let them pass. At the first station where this happened, the engineer of the road made his appearance, and was about to step on the engine, when Andrews told him he could not come on board, as this was an extra train running through to Corinth, and that his party were engaged to run it, and in support of his assertion the iron safe was shown. This apparently satisfied the engineer, and after taking in wood and water, the train again started. A second time they were compelled to switch off, and in order to get the switch-keys, Andrews, who knew the road well, went into the station and took them from the office. This caused considerable excitement, which he partly quieted by stating that the train contained gunpowder for Beauregard, at Corinth. About an hour was lost in waiting to allow these trains to pass, which, of course, enabled their pursuers to press closely after them. But they pushed on as rapidly as possible, removing rails, throwing out obstructions along the track, and cutting the telegraph lines from time to time—attaining, when in motion, a speed of sixty miles per hour—but they could not regain the time which they had lost. Reaching a bridge about twenty miles south of Dalton, Georgia, they set fire to one of their cars, piled on wood, and left it on the bridge, to which they thus hoped to set fire.

Now, let us return to the rebel engineer, conductor, and passengers, thus unceremoniously left at Big Shanty, by the amazing and sudden disappearance of the engine and part of the train. The party who had thus stolen the march upon them, had evidently done so at that time and place, with the presumption that pursuit could not be made by an engine short of Kingston, some thirty miles above Big Shanty; and that, by cutting the telegraph wires as they proceeded, they should gain at least three or four hours' start of any pursuit which could be made. This was a legitimate and reasonable conclusion, and but for the energy and quick judgment of Mr. Fuller, the conductor, and Mr. Cain, the engineer of the stolen train, and of Mr. Anthony Murphy, foreman of the Wood Department of the State road, who accidentally happened on the train that morning, the plans of Mr. Andrews and his party would have resulted as originally contemplated, and with crushing disaster to the rebel cause.

But these three determined men, without a moment's delay, put out after the flying train *on foot*, amidst shouts of laughter from the crowd, who, though lost in amazement at the unexpected and daring act, could not repress their merriment at seeing three men starting on foot after a train which had just whirled away from before their eyes, under the highest power of steam. But Messrs. Fuller, Cain, and Murphy, nowise daunted by the disparity of motive power, put on all their speed and ran along the track for three miles, until they came up with some track raisers who had a small truck car, which is shoved along by men so employed on railroads, on which to carry their tools. Truck and men were at once "impressed," and they took it by turns of two at a time to run behind the truek and push it along all up-grades and level portions of the road, and let it drive at will on all the down-grades. Reaching the spot where the runaways had cut the telegraph wires and torn up the track, they found themselves suddenly tumbled out, pell-mell, truck and men, upon the side of the road. Finding, however, that "nobody was hurt on our side," the plucky "rebs" put the truck again on the track, left some hands to repair the road, and with all the power of determined will and muscle, they pushed on to Etowah station, some thirty miles above. Here, the first thing that met their sight was the "Yonah," an old coal engine, one of the first ever used on the State road, standing already "fired up."

This venerable locomotive was immediately turned upon the track, and like an old racer at the tap of the drum, pricked up her ears and made fine time to Kingston. There they found themselves but twenty minutes behind the runaway train; and leaving the "Yonah" to blow off, they mounted the engine of the Rine Branch road, which was ready fired up, and waiting for the arrival of the passenger train nearly due. Here a number of persons volunteered for the chase, taking such arms as they could lay their hands on at the moment, and with the fresh engine they started for Adamsville. But a little before reaching that place they found the train at a standstill, in consequence of the destruction of a portion of the road by the Yankee runaways. This was vexatious, but it did not discourage Fuller and Murphy, who left the engine and once more put out *on foot*, alone. After two miles running, they met the down freight train from Adamsville—reversed and ran it backward to that place, switched off the cars on a side track, and with the engine made fine time to Calhoun, where they met the regular down passenger train. Here they made a momentary halt, took on board a number of well armed volunteers, a company of track hands to repair the track as they went along, and a telegraph operator, and continued the chase. A short distance above Calhoun they saw, for the first time, the runaway train ahead of them. The "Yanks," supposing themselves now well out of danger, were quietly oiling the engine, taking up track, etc., but finding themselves discovered, they mounted and sped away, throwing out upon the track, as they fled, the heavy cross-ties with which they had provided themselves; which was done by breaking out the end of the hindmost box car, and pitching them out. The rails which they had last taken up they now carried off with them, but their rebel pursuers, on coming to where the rails were torn up, stopped, tore up the rails behind them and laid them down, without fastening, before the engine, which ran over them cautiously but safely; and then carefully throwing off from the track the cross-ties which had been thrown there to impede their progress, pushed on after the fugitives. Now the race became terrible in its intensity. "Nip and tuck" the two trains swept with fearful speed past Resaca, Tilton, and on through Dalton, where the rebel train stopped to put off the telegraph operator, with instructions to telegraph to Chattanooga to have them stopped there, in case he should fail to overhaul them. On and on, fast and still faster the rebel train pressed with hot speed, sometimes in sight, as much to prevent their cutting the wires before the message could be sent, as to catch them. The daring Yankees indeed stopped just opposite, and very near to the encampment of a rebel regiment, and cut the wires, but the operator who had been dropped at Dalton had *put the message through about two minutes before.* They also again tore up the track, cut down a telegraph pole, and placed the two ends of it under the cross-ties, and the middle over the rail on the track. Their pursuers, however, got over this impediment in the same manner they did before—taking up rails behind and laying them down before. Once over this, they shot through the great tunnel at Tunnel Hill, *only five minutes behind* the adventurous "Feds," who, finding themselves closely pressed, uncoupled two of the box-cars from their engine, hoping to impede the progress of their pursuers. Quick-witted Fuller, however, hastily coupled them to the front of his engine, and pushed them ahead of him to the first turn-out, where he switched them off out of his way, and dashed ahead. As they passed Ringgold, the runaways began to show signs of "giving out." They were out of wood, water, and oil; their rapid running and inattention to the engine had melted all the brass from its journals; and they had no time for repair, so rapid was the pursuit. Nearer and nearer panted the iron steed behind them, until, when it was within four hundred yards of them, seeing that their only safety was in flight, they jumped from the engine, scattering in the thicket, each for himself. And now their troubles commenced. The whole country immediately swarmed with armed pursuers. Unacquainted with the country, they lost their way, were hunted down by mounted men and bloodhounds, and finally were all captured. Their plan had failed from causes which reflected neither upon the genius by which it was planned, nor upon the intrepidity and discretion of those engaged in it, but from a combination of unforeseen circumstances. It was a plan which the rebels themselves declared to have been "entirely practicable on almost any day for the last year," but they did not expect to meet two "extraordinary" or special trains on the road; they did not expect that any men would be so apparently foolhardy as to attempt their pursuit *on foot;* and they did not expect that their pursuers would find any such "God-send" as the old coal engine, "Yonah," standing on the track, ready fired up. Their calculations on every other point were admitted by their enemies, and those best acquainted with the road and its arrangements, to have been "dead certainties," which would have met with perfect success.

It might have been hoped that the signal bravery of such an exploit would have commanded the respect of their captors, and mitigated in some degree the resentment which such an attempt excited. But it was not so.

The twenty-two captives, when secured, were thrust into the negro jail at Chattanooga. There they occupied a single room, half under ground, and but thirteen feet square, so that there was not space enough for them all to lie down together, and a part of them were, in consequence, obliged to sleep sitting and leaning against the walls. The only entrance to this vile room was through a trap door in the ceiling, through which, twice a day, their scanty meals were lowered in a bucket; and they had no other light or ventilation than that which came through two small, triple grated windows. They were covered with swarming vermin, and the oppressiveness of the heat obliged them to strip themselves entirely naked. Added to this, they were all handcuffed, and fastened to each other in companies of twos and threes, by trail chains, secured with padlocks around their necks. Their food, doled out to them twice a day, consisted of a little flour moistened with water, and baked in the form of bread, together with spoiled pickled beef. And, as their pockets had been rifled of whatever money they contained at the time of their capture, they were utterly without the means to procure any better supplies from outside. Shortly after their capture, Jacob Parrot, an orphan boy, aged twenty years, belonging to the Thirty-third Regiment of Ohio Volunteers, was taken by a Confederate officer and four soldiers, who stripped him, bent him over a stone, and while two pistols were held to his head, a lieutenant in rebel uniform inflicted, with a raw hide, over a hundred lashes on his bare back. This was done in the presence of an infuriated crowd, who clamored for his death, and actually brought a rope with which to hang him. The object of this prolonged scourging was to force from him (the youngest of the the party) a confession as to the objects of the expedition and the names of his comrades, especially that of the engineer who had run the train. Three times, in the course of this horrible flogging, it was suspended, and young Parrot was asked if he would confess; but, steadily and firmly, with unswerving fidelity to the trusts of friendship and the inspirations of patriotism, he refused all disclosures, and it was not until his tormenters were weary of their cruel labor, that they abandoned the attempt.

While thus imprisoned at Chattanooga, their leader, Mr. Andrews, was tried, condemned, and executed as a spy, at Atlanta, on the 7th of June. The remainder, although strong and healthy when they entered this prison, at the end of three weeks, when they were required to leave it, were so exhausted by their confinement and treatment, as scarcely to be able to walk. Finally, twelve of their number were transferred to the prison at Knoxville, Tenn., and there seven of them were tried by court-martial as spies. Their trial, of course, was summary, and although permitted to be present, they were not allowed to hear either the argument of their own counsel or of the judge-advocate. Their counsel, however, afterward visited them in prison, and read to them his argument, which was, in substance, that the fact of their being dressed in citizens' clothes was no more than what had been authorized in similar cases by the Confederate Government itself; that the object of the expedition was a purely military one, and as such lawful, according to the rules of war; and that not having lingered about or visited any of the camps, obtaining or seeking information, they could not rightly be considered as spies. This just and unanswerable presentation of the case, appears to have produced a favorable impression, and the whole party soon after were removed to Atlanta, Ga., under the impression that those who had been tried had been acquitted. But, on the 18th of June, after their arrival at Atlanta, their prison door was opened, and, without warning, the death-sentence was read to the seven who had been tried at Knoxville, and who, little dreaming of their hapless fate, were even then engaged in whiling away the time by playing *euchre*. No time for preparation was allowed —they were bid to say farewell to their comrades, and "be quick about it"—then were tied, carried out, and hung. One of their number, too ill to walk, was pinioned like the rest, and dragged off in this condition to the scaffold; while two, whose weight broke the ropes which suspended them, were denied another hour's respite for prayer. One of their number, Alfred Wilson, of the Twenty-first Ohio, did not hesitate, while standing under the gallows, to make a brief, manly, and patriotic address to the scowling mob who surrounded him.

The remaining prisoners, now reduced to fourteen, were kept closely confined under special guard, in the Atlanta jail, until October, when, overhearing a conversation among their guards, they became convinced that they were to be hung, as their companions had been. This led them to devise a way of escape, which they carried out on the evening of the next day, by seizing the jailor when he opened the door to carry away the bucket in which their supper had been brought. Seizing and disarming the guards, eight of the fugitives were soon beyond pursuit. Of these, six, after long and painful wanderings, succeeded in reaching the Union lines. Of the other two, nothing has ever been heard. The remaining six of the fourteen were recaptured and confined in the barracks until December, when they were removed to Richmond, where they were confined in Castle Thunder. There they shivered through the winter, without fire, thinly clad, and with but two small blankets, which they had saved with their clothes, to cover the whole party. So they remained until the early part of March, 1863, when they were exchanged; and thus, at the end of eleven months, terminated their pitiless sufferings and persecutions in the South—persecutions begun and continued amid indignities and sufferings on their part, and atrocities on the part of their captors, which illustrate, more fully than pen or words can ever express, the diabolical spirit of the rebellion, against which they and thousands of our brave Union soldiers have fought and suffered in every part of the South.

The railroad lines along the border were the scenes of some startling adventures and narrow escapes, during the war. The following, very graphically told by a former engineer, has the merit also of truthfulness:

THE WRONG SIDE OF THE CURVE.

AN EX-ENGINEER'S STORY.

"Among the many incidents that during the late rebellion were connected with that great national artery, the Baltimore and Ohio Railway, is one that I will relate.

"In the fall of 1861, having been detained by business in the town of Cumberland, Maryland, I was at last about to start for Wheeling, when I learned by a despatch that the road was occupied below Harper's Ferry by a force of rebels, and therefore no train would pass.

"This proved to be true in reference to ordinary trains, but a 'special,' with which was the Hon. Mr. Pierpont, and a few other notabilities, had passed before the rebels cut the track, and was therefore approaching. On inquiry, I found that the engineer of the coming train had been one of my old chums, ere I had discarded engine-driving for more profitable business. My friend Joe M—— was a cool, bold, skilful engineer, and as generous as reckless of danger.

OBSTRUCTING THE TRAIN.

"As I expected, I no sooner saw him and stated my wish to go up the road, than he swore that, special or no special, I should ride with him, if for nothing but to see the "fast time" his engine, "Wildfire," would make.

"As we dashed rapidly along and were passing through Black Oak Bottom, a couple of ill-looking fellows in citizen's dress fired at the engineer, but doing no damage, merely provoked a laugh of derision from him for their want of marksmanship. On arriving at Oakland, Maryland, we were disagreeably surprised by receiving a telegram, informing us that a party of rebels were making extraordinary haste to reach the railway at a point many miles ahead of us. Also they seemed to know who the special contained, and would therefore use all endeavors to capture or kill us.

"There was but one car behind the engine, and in it was briefly discussed the question of go or stay, while Joe was having the tender refilled with wood and water.

"Mr. Pierpont's business was too urgent to admit of any possible delay; two or three others concluded to risk the trip, and I—well, if it's not too egotistical to say so—I had run risks on railways too often to back out because there was danger ahead, while the rest concluded to stay and trust to luck for the opportunity of getting away.

"Just as we were about to start, the fireman making a misstep on the 'running board,' fell and struck the ground with such force as to break his arm. Joe hurriedly picked the poor fellow up, but time was precious just then, so leaving him to the care of the gentlemen who had accompanied us, he started directly toward me, asking me to come and 'run' for him, as, having no fireman, he would have more than he could do. I told him, however, to consider me his fireman for the rest of the trip, as he was best acquainted with the road; so without any more ado, I doffed my coat, we jumped on, and away we went, past hamlets, through wildernesses of stunted bushes, up grade and down hill, at a speed rarely equalled. Our light train made firing an easy task for me, and I had frequent leisure to scan the beautiful ranges of the Alleghanies along which we skirted. Joe was sitting, as was usual with him, with his left hand on the throttle lever, and his body half out of the side window of the 'cab,' that he might the better scan the track ahead.

"A few miles south of the famous Cheat river bridge, is a deep mountain gorge, with precipitous, rocky sides.

"It is shaped like an hour-glass, wide at each end, but tapering each way toward the middle. The track runs for quite a distance along one side of the gorge, makes a very abrupt turn to cross the chasm, a very deep one, in a straight line, and then, still curving inwardly, follows the gorge in a line nearly parallel with the track on the opposite side, for three fourths of a mile.

"We were pitching along with that peculiar rocking, bounding motion, so different from the jar of ordinary fast speed. As we swept to the top of a grade, around the side of a hill that commanded a view of the gorge—Joe and I both on the lookout—we saw, at a moment's glance, enough to make us concentrate our thinking faculties, and act in a hurry, whatever was best to be done.

"There, on the straight track, just at the near edge of the gorge, a lot of men, in gray uniform, were hastily piling up some old ties, logs, etc., while at the point where the curve was sharpest—before reaching the gorge—were several more, tugging furiously at a rail, one end of which seemed to baffle them, as they pulled it outward. We were within a mile of them when we discovered them, and as each noticed them, the shout came simultaneously from both of us, 'The wrong side of the curve!' The ignorant fools were pulling out the inside rail, instead of the outside. In the latter case, nothing could have saved us from running off the track, and probably into the gorge. Our single brakesman, seeing the danger—I suppose from habit—was commencing to tighten the brake, but at a look from Joe I signalled 'off brakes,' Joe, meanwhile, opening the throttle to its widest extent, as we dashed down the grade at a positively frightful velocity.

"As we neared them, a party of them huddled together near the track. I seized a large stick of wood, intending, if possible, to hurt 'somebody.' We were going altogether too swift to fear their taking aim at us; and for that matter, I suppose they considered our destruction such a certainty that firing at us would be needless. I was poising the big stick of wood, guessing at the rate of speed—I've had some practice throwing parcels from trains in motion—when Joe suddenly pulled the whistle-rope. The hoarse shriek seemed to startle them for an instant; they huddled closer together, and I tossed the stick outward and downward. I had barely time to see it crash through the group with the force of a thunderbolt, when, with a jarring plunge, the wheels on one side struck the naked ties. That part of the trouble we had feared but little, as the impetus of the engine was almost sure to make it mount the track again. On the track again, but a few rods ahead of us, was the formidable barricade, and beyond that the yawning chasm. Joe was standing up now, with eyes blazing, still holding the throttle wide open, as he braced himself for the shock. I had grasped the brake rod of the tender the instant I threw the piece of wood. Crash—my hold didn't avail me, as I was pitched head over heels against the fire-box, and laid flat on my back on the footboard or floor of the engine.

"Joe was as suddenly jerked half around, his back striking the little door in front of where he had stood, breaking the door and shivering the glass to atoms. But we were through; how, we couldn't tell, except that we were still on the track, and thundering over the gorge. Joe's spirits rose with the occasion. Extricating himself almost as suddenly as he had been deposited in the little glass door, he jerked a tin flask from his pocket, sprung on top of the tender, and from thence to the roof of the cab. Steadying himself for a moment, with his face toward the rebels, he shouted, 'good-by,' made them a low bow, and took a drink, perfectly regardless of the white puffs of smoke, as one after another discharged their pieces at him; as he afterward explained, 'the engine made too much noise for him to hear the bullets, and they didn't seem to be hitting anybody.'

"After having, in spite of sore bones, performed a jig, which he had extemporized for that occasion for the express edification of the 'rebs,' Joe descended from his perch and deliberately shutting off steam, stopped.

"We were still in sight of them, though at a tolerably safe distance, and now saw a group of them standing near several men who had been wounded, perhaps some killed, by that 'irrepressible' stick of wood.

"Our damages were a few bruises each, but no serious hurts. Our engine suffered the loss of the pilot, or cow-catcher, and head light; the front of the smoke-box was stove in, besides sundry dents and bruises on the brass casings of the cylinders; but for running purposes was absolutely uninjured. The rebels having piled the logs squarely across the top of the track, the point of the cow-catcher had gone under them, and though broken by the shock, had raised them sufficiently to keep them from under the wheels, while the engine dashed them right and left into the gorge.

"The rebels, seeing us stop, started in pursuit; but as we found nothing serious to impede our further progress, and, as in their case, 'distance lent enchantment to the view,' we were off again in high spirits, and without further adventure worth recounting, arrived safely at our destination.

"Poor Joe, after being shot at so often as to have acquired a sovereign contempt for rebel bullets, was shot dead about a year ago, while running a government engine near Chattanooga."

ZAGONYI'S CHARGE.

THE charge of Fremont's Body-Guard and the Prairie Scouts of Major Frank White, upon the rebel garrison in Springfield, Missouri, under the leadership of Major Charles Zagonyi, is justly regarded as one of the most daring and gallant achievements of the war.

Charles Zagonyi was a Hungarian refugee who, like so many of his countrymen, had fled to this country after the suppression of the revolution in his native country by the iron hand of the Russian Czar. His daring character brought the young officer to the notice of the invincible General Bem, by whom he was placed in command of a troop of picked cavalry for extraordinary service. His story, after that hour, up to the date of his capture by the enemy, was one of unparalleled daring. His last act was to charge upon a heavy artillery force. Over one half of his men were killed and the rest made prisoners, but not until after the enemy had suffered terribly. He was then confined in an Austrian dungeon, and finally released, at the end of two years, to go into exile in America.

Fremont drew around him a large number of such refugees from European tyranny, and found in them men of great value, in all departments of the service. Zagonyi enlisted three hundred carefully chosen men, who, as a "Body-Guard," served as pioneers and scouts in Fremont's advance. The exploit at Springfield was only one of many similar services for which they were designated by Fremont; but, the suspension of his command in Missouri broke up the Guard, and Zagonyi withdrew from the service until his leader should again be given a command.

The Guard was mounted, and was armed with German sabres and revolvers—the first company only having carbines. The horses were all bay in color, and were chosen with special reference to speed and endurance.

The expedition to Springfield was planned, as it afterward appeared, upon false information. Instead of Springfield being held by a small force, it was in possession of twelve hundred infantry and four hundred cavalry. Major Frank White had been ordered by General Sigel to make a reconnoissance toward Springfield—the Union army then being at Camp Haskell, south of the Pomme de Terre river, thirty-four miles from Warsaw and fifty-one from Springfield. The major had just come in with his dashing "Prairie Scouts," one hundred and fifty-four strong, from their gallant dash into Lexington; and the order to strike out for the reconnoissance found them jaded from over service. The major, however, put out, and was far on his way when, on the 24th (of October), he was joined by Zagonyi, who assumed command of the expedition, by order of Fremont. Zagonyi had with him one half of his Guard, provided with only one ration. The march to Springfield was to be forced, in order that the enemy should be surprised and the place secured before rebel reinforcements could reach it. The combined Scouts and Guard marched all Thursday (October 24th) night; briefly rested Friday morning, then pushed on and were before Springfield at three P. M. on the 25th—the fifty-one miles having been accomplished in eighteen hours.

Eight miles from Springfield five mounted rebels were

caught; a sixth escaped and gave the alarm to the forces in the town, whose strength, Zagonyi learned from a Union farmer, was fully two thousand strong. Nothing was left but a retreat or bold dash. Zagonyi did not hesitate. His men responded to his own spirit fully, and were eager for the adventure, let it result as it would. Major White was so ill from overwork that, at Zagonyi's entreaty, he remained at a farm-house for a brief rest. The Union farmer offered to pilot the Body-Guard around to the Mount Vernon approach on the West—thus hoping to effect a surprise in that direction, as the enemy was, doubtless, aligned to receive the assault on the Boliver road, on the North. Of this detour White knew nothing, and after his rest he pushed on with his guard of five men and a lieutenant, to overtake his troops. He travelled up to the very outskirts of the town, and yet did not come up to his men. Supposing them in possession of the place, he kept on and soon found himself in a rebel camp—a prisoner. He was immediately surrounded by a crew of savages, who at once resolved to have his life. Captain Wroton, a rebel officer, only saved the Federal officer and his men from murder by swearing to protect them with his life. The blood thirsty wretches were only kept at bay by the constant presence of Wroton.

The particulars of the charge are given by Major Dorsheimer in his admirable papers on Fremont's Campaign, in the *Atlantic Monthly:*

The foe were advised of the intended attack. When Major White was brought into their camp, they were preparing to defend their position. As appears from the confession of prisoners, they had twenty-two hundred men, of whom four hundred were cavalry, the rest being infantry, armed with shot guns, American rifles, and revolvers. Twelve hundred of their foot were posted along the edge of the wood upon the crest of the hill. The cavalry was stationed upon the extreme left, on top of a spur of the hill, and in front of a patch of timber. Sharpshooters were concealed behind the trees close to the fence alongside the lane, and a small number in some underbrush near the foot of the hill. Another detachment guarded their train, holding possession of the county fair ground, which was surrounded by a high board fence.

This position was unassailable by cavalry from the road, the only point of attack being down the lane on the right; and the enemy were so disposed as to command this approach perfectly. The lane was a blind one, being closed, after passing the brook, by fences and ploughed land: it was in fact a *cul-de-sac*. If the infantry should stand, nothing could save the rash assailants. There are horsemen sufficient to sweep the little band before them as helplessly as the withered forest-leaves in the grasp of the autumn winds; there are deadly marksmen lying behind the trees upon the heights and lurking in the long grass upon the lowlands; while a long line of foot stand upon the summit of the slope, who, only stepping a few paces back into the forest, may defy the boldest riders. Yet, down this narrow lane, leading into the very jaws of death, came the three hundred.

On the prairie, at the edge of the woodland in which he knew his wily foe lay hidden, Zagonyi halted his command. He spurred along the line. With eager glance he scanned each horse and rider. To his officers he gave the simple order, "Follow me! do as I do!" and then, drawing up in front of his men, with a voice tremulous and shrill with emotion, he spoke:

"Fellow-soldiers, comrades, brothers! This is your first battle. For our three hundred, the enemy are two thousand. If any of you are sick, or tired by the long march, or if any think that the number is too great, now is the time to turn back." He paused—no one was sick or tired. "We must not retreat. Our honor, the honor of our general and our country, tell us to go on. I will lead you. We have been called holiday soldiers for the pavements of St. Louis; to day we will show that we are soldiers for the battle. Your watchword shall be—'*The Union and Fremont!*' Draw sabre! By the right flank—quick trot—march!'

Bright swords flashed in the sunshine, a passionate shout burst from every lip, and with one accord, the trot passing into a gallop, the compact column swept on in its deadly purpose. Most of them were boys. A few weeks before they had left their homes. Those who were cool enough to note it say that ruddy cheeks grew pale, and fiery eyes were dimmed with tears. Who shall tell what thoughts, what visions of peaceful cottages nestling among the groves of Kentucky, or shining upon the banks of the Ohio and the Illinois—what sad recollections of tearful farewells, of tender, loving faces, filled their minds during those fearful moments of suspense? No word was spoken. With lips compressed, firmly clenching their sword-hilts, with quick tramp of hoofs and clang of steel, honor leading and glory awaiting them, the young soldiers flew forward, each brave rider and each straining steed members of one huge creature, enormous, terrible, irresistible.

> "'Twere worth ten years of peaceful life,
> One glance at their array."

They pass the fair ground. They are at the corner of the lane where the wood begins. It runs close to the fence on their left for a hundred yards, and beyond it they see white tents gleaming. They are half way past the forest, when, sharp and loud, a volley of musketry bursts upon the head of the column; horses stagger, riders reel and fall, but the troop presses forward undismayed. The farther corner of the wood is reached, and Zagonyi beholds the terrible array. Amazed, he involuntarily checks his horse. The rebels are not surprised. There to his left they stand crowning the height, foot and horse ready to engulph him, if he shall be rash enough to go on. The road he is following declines rapidly. There is but one thing to do —run the gauntlet, gain the cover of the hill, and charge up the steep. These thoughts pass quicker than they can be told. He waves his sabre over his head, and shouting, "Forward! follow me! quick trot! gallop!" he dashes headlong down the stony road. The first company, and most of the second follow. From the left a thousand muzzles belch forth a hissing flood of bullets; the poor fellows clutch wildly at the air and fall from their saddles, and maddened horses throw themselves against the fences. Their speed is not for an instant checked; farther down the hill they fly, like wasps driven by the leaden storm. Sharp volleys pour out of the underbrush at the left, clearing wide gaps through their ranks. They leap the brook, take down the fence, and draw up under shelter of the hill. Zagonyi looks around him, and to his horror sees that only a fourth of his men are with him. He cries, "They do not come—we are lost!" and frantically waves his sabre.

He has not long to wait. The delay of the rest of the Guard was not from hesitation. When Captain Foley reached the lower corner of the wood and saw the enemy's lines, he thought a flank attack might be advantageously made. He ordered some men to dismount and take down the fence. This was done under a severe fire. Several men fell, and he found the woods so dense that it could not be penetrated. Looking down the hill, he saw the flash of Zagonyi's sabre, and at once gave the order, "Forward!" At the same time, Lieutenant Kennedy, a stalwart Kentuckian, shouted, "Come on, boys! remember Old Kentucky!" and the third company of the Guard—fire on every side of them—from behind trees, from under the fences—with thundering strides and loud cheers—poured down the slope and rushed to the side of Zagonyi. They have lost seventy dead and wounded men, and the carcasses of horses are strewn along the lane. Kennedy is wounded in the arm, and lies upon the stones, his faithful charger standing motionless beside him. Lieutenant Goff received a wound in the thigh; he kept his seat, and cried out, "The devils have hit me, but I will give it to them yet!"

The remnant of the Guard are now in the field under the hill, and from the shape of the ground the rebel fire sweeps with the roar of a whirlwind over their heads. Here we will leave them for a moment, and trace the fortunes of the Prairie Scouts.

When Foley brought his troop to a halt, Captain Fairbanks, at the head of the first company of Scouts, was at the point where the first volley of musketry had been received. The narrow lane was crowded by a dense mass of struggling horses, and filled with the tumult of battle. Captain Fairbanks says, and he is corroborated by several of his men, who were near, that at this moment an officer of the Guard rode up to him and said, "They are flying; take your men down that lane and cut off their retreat"—pointing to the lane at the left. Captain Fairbanks was not able to identify the person who gave this order. It certainly did not come from Zagonyi, who was several hundred yards farther on. Captain Fairbanks executed the order, followed by the second company of Prairie Scouts, under Captain Kehoe. When this movement was made, Captain Naughton, with the Third Irish dragoons, had not reached the corner of the lane. He came up at a gallop, and was about to follow Fairbanks, when he saw a Guardsman, who pointed in the direction in which Zagonyi had gone. He took this for an order, and obeyed it. When he reached the gap in the fence, made by Foley, not seeing any thing of the Guard, he supposed they had passed through at that place, and gallantly attempted to follow. Thirteen men fell in a few minutes. He was shot in the arm and dismounted. Lieutenant Connolly spurred into the underbrush, and received two balls through the lungs and one in the left shoulder. The dragoons, at the outset not more than fifty strong, were broken, and, dispirited by the loss of their officers, retired. A sergeant rallied a few and brought them up to the gap again, and they were again driven back. Five of the boldest passed down the hill, joined Zagonyi, and were conspicuous for their valor during the rest of the day. Fairbanks and Kehoe, having gained the rear and left of the enemy's position, made two or three assaults upon detached parties of the foe, but did not join in the main attack.

I now return to the Guard. It is forming under the shelter of the hill. In front, with a gentle inclination, rises a grassy slope, broken by occasional tree-stumps. A line of fire upon the summit marks the position of the rebel infantry, and nearer and on the top of a lower eminence to the right stand their horse. Up to this time no Guardsman has struck a blow, but blue coats and bay horses lie thick along the bloody lane. Their time has come. Lieutenant Maythenyi with thirty men is ordered to attack the cavalry. With sabres flashing over their heads, the little band of heroes spring toward their tremendous foe. Right upon the centre they charge. The dense mass opens, the blue coats force their way in, and the whole rebel squadron scatter in disgraceful flight through the cornfields in the rear. The boys follow them sabering the fugitives. Days after, the enemy's horses lay thick among the uncut corn.

Zagonyi holds his main body until Maythenyi disappears in the cloud of rebel cavalry; then his voice rises through the air: "In open order—charge!" The line opens out to give play to their sword-arm. Steeds respond to the ardor of their riders, and quick as thought, with thrilling cheers, the noble hearts rush into the leaden torrent which pours down the incline. With unabated fire the gallant fellows press through. Their fierce onset is not even checked. The foe do not wait for them—they waver, break, and fly. The Guardsmen spur into the midst of the rout, and their fast-falling swords work a terrible revenge. Some of the boldest of the Southrons retreat into the woods, and continue a murderous fire from behind trees and thickets. Seven Guard horses fall upon a space not more than twenty feet square. As his steed sinks under him, one of the officers is caught around the shoulders by a grape-vine, and hangs dangling in the air until he is cut down by his friends.

The rebel foot are flying in furious haste from the field. Some take refuge in the fair ground, some hurry into the cornfields, but the greater part run along the edge of the wood, swarm over the fence into the road, and hasten to the village. The Guardsmen follow. Zagonyi leads them. Over the loudest roar of battle rings his clarion voice—"Come on, Old Kentuck! I'm with you!" And the flash of his sword-blade tells his men where to go. As he approaches a barn, a man steps from behind a door and lowers his rifle; but before it has reached a level, Zagonyi's sabre-point descends upon his head, and his life-blood leaps to the very top of the huge barn-door.

The conflict now raged through the village—in the public square, and along the streets. Up and down the Guards ride in squads of three or four, and wherever they see a group of the enemy, charge upon and scatter them. It is hand to hand. No one but has a share in the fray.

There was at least one soldier in the Southern ranks. A young officer, superbly mounted, charges alone upon a large body of the Guard. He passes through the line unscathed, killing one man. He wheels, charges back, and again breaks through, killing another man. A third time he rushes upon the Federal line, a score of sabre-points confront him, a cloud of bullets fly around him, but he pushes on until he reaches Zagonyi—he presses his pistol so close to the major's side, that he feels it, and draws convulsively back, the bullet passes through the front of Zagonyi's coat, who at the instant runs the daring rebel through the body; he falls, and the men, thinking their commander hurt, kill him with a dozen wounds.

"He was a brave man," said Zagonyi afterward, "and I did wish to make him prisoner."

Meanwhile it has grown dark. The foe have left the village, and the battle has ceased. The assembly is sounded, and the Guard gathers in the *Plaza*. Not more than eighty mounted men appear: the rest are killed, wounded, or unhorsed. At this time one of the most characteristic incidents of the affair took place.

Just before the charge, Zagonyi directed one of his buglers, a Frenchman, to sound a signal. The bugler did not seem to pay any attention to the order, but darted off with Lieutenant Maythenyi. A few moments afterward he was observed in another part of the field vigorously pursuing the flying infantry. His active form was always seen in the thickest of the fight. When the line was formed in the *Plaza*, Zagonyi noticed the bugler, and approaching him, said: "In the midst of battle you disobeyed my order. You are unworthy to be a member of the Guard. I dismiss you." The bugler showed his bugle to his indignant commander—the mouth-piece of the instrument was shot away. He said: "The mouth was shoot off. I could not bugle viz mon bugle, and so I bugle viz mon pistol and sabre." It is unnecessary to add, the brave Frenchman was not dismissed.

I must not forget to mention Sergeant Hunter, of the Kentucky company. His soldierly figure never failed to attract the eye in the ranks of the Guard. He had served in the regular cavalry, and the Body-Guard had profited greatly from his skill as a drill master. He lost three horses in the fight. As soon as one was killed, he caught another from the rebels: the third horse taken by him in this way he rode into St. Louis. The sergeant slew five men. "I wont speak of those I shot," said he—"another may have hit them; but those I touched with my sabre I am sure of, because I felt them."

At the beginning of the charge, he came to the extreme right, and took position next to Zagonyi, whom he followed closely through the battle. The major seeing him, said:

"Why are you here, Sergeant Hunter? Your place is with your company on the left."

"I kind o' wanted to be in the front," was the answer.

"What could I say to such a man?" exclaimed, Zagonyi, speaking of the matter afterward.

There was hardly a horse or rider among the survivors that did not bring away some mark of the fray. I saw one animal with no less than seven wounds—none of them serious. Scabbards were bent, clothes and caps pierced, pistols injured. I saw one pistol from which the sight had been cut as neatly as it could have been done by machinery. A piece of board a few inches long was cut from a fence on the field, in which there were thirty-one shot holes.

It was now nine o'clock. The wounded had been carried to the hospital. The dismounted troopers were placed in charge of them—in the double capacity of nurses and guards. Zagonyi expected the foe to return every minute. It seemed like madness to try and hold the town with his small force, exhausted by the long march and desperate fight. He therefore left Springfield, and retired before morning twenty-five miles on the Bolivar road.

Captain Fairbanks did not see his commander after leaving the column in the lane, at the commencement of the engagement. About dusk he repaired to the prairie, and remained there within a mile of the village until midnight, when he followed Zagonyi, rejoining him in the morning.

I will now return to Major White. During the conflict upon the hill, he was in the forest near the front of the rebel line. Here his horse was shot under him. Captain Wroton kept careful watch over him. When the flight began he hurried White away, and, accompanied by a squad of eleven men, took him ten miles into the country. They stopped at a farm-house for the night. White discovered that their host was a Union man. His parole having expired, he took advantage of the momentary absence of his captor to speak to the farmer, telling him who he was, and asking him to send for assistance. The countryman mounted his son upon his swiftest horse, and sent him for succor. The party lay down by the fire, White being placed in the midst. The rebels were soon asleep, but there was no sleep for the major. He listened anxiously for the footsteps of his rescuers. After long weary hours, he heard the tramp of horses. He arose, and walking on tiptoe, cautiously stepping over his sleeping guard, he reached the door and silently unfastened it. The Union men rushed into the room and took the astonished Wroton and his followers prisoners. At daybreak White rode into Springfield at the head of his captives and a motley band of Home Guards. He found the Federals still in possession of the place. As the officer of highest rank, he took command. His garrison consisted of twenty-four men. He stationed twenty-two of them as pickets in the outskirts of the village, and held the other two as a *reserve.* At noon the enemy sent a flag of truce, and asked permission to bury their dead. Major White received the flag with proper ceremony, but said that General Sigel was in command and the request would have to be referred to him. Sigel was then forty miles away. In a short time a written communication purporting to come from General Sigel arrived, saying that the rebels might send a party under certain restrictions to bury their dead: White drew in some of his pickets, stationed them about the field, and under their surveillance the Southern dead were buried.

The loss of the enemy, as reported by some of their working party, was one hundred and sixteen killed.

The number of wounded could not be ascertained. After the conflict had drifted away from the hill-side, some of the foe had returned to the field, taken away their wounded and robbed our dead. The loss of the Guard was fifty-three out of one hundred and forty-eight actually engaged, twelve men having been left by Zagonyi in charge of his train. The Prairie Scouts reported a loss of thirty-one out of one hundred and thirty: half of these belonged to the Irish Dragoons. In a neighboring field an Irishman was found stark and stiff, still clinging to the hilt of his sword, which was thrust through the body of a rebel who lay beside him. Within a few feet a second rebel lay shot through the head.

THE PASSAGE OF THE PORT HUDSON BATTERIES.

The rebels had blockaded the Mississippi from the beginning of the war with their batteries. In the progress of the war Farragut had captured the batteries below New Orleans, and above as far as Prophet's Island, just below Port Hudson, and Foote, Davis, and Porter had made a conquest of the batteries above Vicksburg, leaving only the Vicksburg, Warrenton, and Port Hudson batteries—a distance of two hundred and thirty-two miles by the river. Of these, the batteries at Port Hudson were, with the exception of those at Vicksburg, the most formidable on the river.

The bluff, rising forty feet above the level of the river, was covered with forts for a distance of nearly

PORTER
DUPONT
DAHLGREN
FARRAGUT
GOLDSBOROUGH
WINSLOW
FOOTE
CUSHING

four miles, constructed upon the most scientific principles of modern military art, and armed with the most approved and heaviest ordnance which England, seeking the ruin of the republic, could furnish the rebels. The river, just at the bend, suddenly narrows, and the current, striking upon the west bank, is thrown across, running with great velocity, and carrying the channel almost directly under the base of the precipitous cliffs. Any vessel attempting the passage would be compelled to run the gauntlet of a plunging fire from batteries which commanded the range for several miles above and below.

It was proposed, in order that the fleet might be able to co-operate with General Grant in the siege of Vicksburg, to attack Port Hudson, and, under the fire of the bombardment, to attempt to force a passage by several of our gunboats up the river.

To Rear-Admiral Farragut, already renowned for his naval victory at Forts St. Philip and Jackson, was assigned the work of attacking and passing this formidable river fortress. The fleet consisted of the flag-ship "Hartford," a fine sloop-of-war, carrying twenty-six guns; the "Richmond," a vessel of the same class and armament; the side-wheel steamship "Mississippi," with twenty-two eight and nine inch guns; the "Monongahela," a smaller steam sloop-of-war, with sixteen heavy guns; and the gunboats "Kineo," "Albatross," "Sachem," and "Genesee," each carrying three columbiads, and two rifled thirty-two pounders, together with six mortar boats, intended to assist in the bombardment, but not to attempt the passage of the batteries.

On the morning of the 14th of April, the squadron

having ascended the river from New Orleans, anchored off Prophet's Island, and the mortar boats took their position, and early in the afternoon commenced a vigorous bombardment of the rebel works. At half-past nine o'clock in the evening, a red light from the flag-ship signaled the ships and gunboats to weigh anchor. The "Hartford" led, the "Albatross" being lashed on her starboard side; the "Richmond" followed, having the "Genesee" lashed to her; next came the "Monongahela" and the "Kineo," while the "Mississippi" and the "Sachem" brought up the rear. The mortar boats, from their sheltered anchorage, were prepared to renew their bombardment with marked effect so soon as it should be necessary.

Signal lights were flashing along the rebel batteries, showing that they were awake to the movements of the Union squadron. Soon the gleam of a fire kindled by the rebels was seen, which blazed higher and more brilliant till its flashes illumined the whole river opposite the batteries with the light of day. This immense bonfire was directly in front of the most formidable of the fortifications, and every vessel ascending the stream would be compelled to pass in the full blaze of its light, exposed to the concentrated fire of the heaviest ordnance. Still it was hoped, notwithstanding the desperate nature of the enterprise, that a few at least of the vessels of the squadron would be able to effect a passage.

Silently in the darkness the boats steamed along, until a rebel field-piece, buried in the foliage of the shore, opened fire upon the "Hartford." The challenge thus given was promptly accepted, and a broadside volley was returned upon the unseen foe. The rebel batteries, protected by strong redoubts, extended, as we have mentioned, with small intervening spaces, a distance of nearly four miles, often rising in tier above tier on the ascending bluff. Battery after battery immediately opened its fire; the hill-sides seemed peopled with demons hurling their thunderbolts, while the earth trembled beneath the incessant and terrific explosions. And now the mortar boats uttered their awful roar, adding to the inconceivable sublimity of the scene. An eye-witness thus describes the appearance of the mammoth shells rising and descending in their majestic curve:

"Never shall I forget the sight that then met my astonished vision. Shooting upward, at an angle of forty-five degrees, with the rapidity of lightning, small globes of golden flame were seen sailing through the pure ether—not a steady, unfading flame, but coruscating like the fitful gleam of a fire-fly, now visible and anon invisible. Like a flying star of the sixth magnitude the terrible missile—a thirteen-inch shell—nears its zenith, up and still up, higher and higher. Its flight now becomes much slower, till, on reaching its utmost altitude, its centrifugal force becoming counteracted by the earth's attraction, it describes a parabolic curve, and down, down it comes, bursting, it may be, ere it reaches *terra firma*, but probably alighting in the rebel works ere it explodes, where it scatters death and destruction around."

The air was breathing gently from the east, and dense volumes of billowy smoke hung over the river, drifting slowly across in clouds which the eye could not penetrate, and adding greatly to the gloom and sublimity of the scene. It strains a ship too much to fire all the guns simultaneously. The broadsides were, consequently, generally discharged by commencing with the forward gun, and firing each one in its turn in the most rapid manner possible—as fast as the ticking of a clock. The effect of this bombardment, from ship and shore, as described by all who witnessed it, was grand and terrific in the extreme. From the innumerable batteries, very skilfully manned, shot and shell fell upon the ships like hail. Piercing the awful roar, which filled the air as with the voice of ten thousand thunders, was heard the demoniac shrieks of the shells, as if all the demons of the pit had broken loose, and were revelling in hideous rage through the darkness and the storm.

In the midst of this scene of terror, conflagration, and death, as the ships were struggling through the fire against the swift current of the Mississippi, there was heard from the deck of the "Richmond," coming up from the dark, rushing stream, the cry of a drowning man. "Help! oh, help!" The unhappy sufferer had evidently fallen from the "Hartford," which was in advance. In such an hour there could not be even an attempt made to rescue him. Again and again the agonizing cry pierced the air, the voice growing fainter and fainter as the victim floated away in the distance, until he sank beneath the turbid waves.

The whole arena of action, on the land and on the water, was soon enveloped in a sulphurous canopy of smoke, pierced incessantly by the vivid flashes of the guns. The vessels could no longer discern each other or the hostile batteries on the shore It became very difficult to know how to steer; and as in the impenetrable gloom the only object at which they could aim was the flash of the guns, the danger became imminent that they might fire into each other. This gave the rebels great advantage; for with their stationary guns trained upon the river, though they fired into dense darkness, they could hardly fire amiss. Occasionally a gust of wind would sweep away the smoke, slightly revealing the scene in the light of the great bonfire on the bluff. Again the black, stifling canopy would settle down, and all was Egyptian darkness.

At one time, just as the "Richmond" was prepared to pour a deadly fire into a supposed battery, whose flash the gunners had just perceived, Lieutenant Terry shouted out, "Hold on, you are firing into the 'Hartford!'" Another quarter of a minute and they would have been pouring a destructive broadside into the flagship which could scarcely have failed to sink her.

A shell from a rebel battery entered the starboard port of the "Richmond," and burst with a terrific explosion directly under the gun. One fragment splintered the gun-carriage. Another made a deep indentation in the gun itself. Two other fragments struck the unfortunate boatswain's mate, cutting off both legs at the knee, and one arm at the elbow. He soon died, with his last breath saying, "Don't give up the ship, lads!" The whole ship reeled under the concussion as if tossed by an earthquake.

The river at Port Hudson, as we have mentioned, makes a majestic curve. Rebel cannon were planted along the concave brow of the crescent-shaped bluffs of the eastern shore, while beneath the bluff, near the water's edge, there was another series of what were called water batteries lining the bank. As the ships entered this curve, following the channel which swept close to the eastern shore, they were, one after the other, exposed to the most terrible enfilading fire from all the batteries, following the line of the curve. This was the most desperate point of the conflict; for here it was almost literally fighting muzzle to muzzle. The rebels discharged an incessant cross-fire of grape and canister, to which the heroic squadron replied with double-shotted guns. Never did ships pass a more fiery ordeal.

Lieutenant-Commander Cummings, the executive officer of the "Richmond," was standing with his speaking-trumpet in his hand cheering the men, with Captain Alden by his side, when there was a simultaneous flash and roar, and a storm of shot came crashing through the bulwarks from a rebel battery, which they could almost touch with their ramrods. Both of the officers fell as if struck by lightning. The captain was simply knocked down by the windage, and escaped unharmed. The speaking-trumpet in Commander Cummings' hand was battered flat, and his left leg was torn off just below the knee.

As he fell heavily upon the deck, in his gushing blood, he exclaimed:

"Put a tourniquet on my leg, boys. Send my letters to my wife. Tell her that I fell in doing my duty!"

As they took him below, and into the surgeon's room, already filled with the wounded, he looked around upon the unfortunate group, and said:

"If there are any here hurt worse than I am let them be attended to first."

STONEWALL JACKSON.
BEAUREGARD.
LONGSTREET.
BRECKENRIDGE.
R. E. LEE.
A. P. HILL.
COL. MOSBY.
FITZ HUGH LEE.
EWELL.

His shattered limb was immediately amputated. Soon after, as he lay upon his couch, exhausted by the operation and faint from the loss of blood, he heard the noise of the escape of steam as a rebel shot penetrated the boiler. Inquiring the cause, and learning that the ship had become disabled, he exclaimed with fervor:

"I would willingly give my other leg if we could but pass those batteries!"

A few days after this Christian hero died of his wound.

Just above the batteries were several rebel gunboats. They did not venture into the melee, but anxiously watched the fight, until, apprehensive that some of our ships might pass, they put on all steam and ran up the river as fast as their web feet could carry them. But now denser and blacker grew the dark billows of smoke. It seemed impossible, if the steamers moved, to avoid running into each other or upon the shore. An officer of each ship placed himself at the prow, striving to penetrate the gloom. A line of men passed from him to the stern, along whom, even through the thunders of the battle, directions could be transmitted to the helmsman. Should any of the ships touch the ground beneath the fire of such batteries their destruction would be almost sure.

It was a little after eleven o'clock at night when the first shot had been fired. For an hour and a half the unequal conflict had raged. The flag-ship "Hartford" and the "Albatross" succeeded in forcing their way above the batteries, and in thus gaining the all-important object of their enterprise. The "Richmond" following, had just passed the principal batteries when a shot penetrated her steam-chest, so effectually disabling her for the hour that she dropped, almost helpless, down the stream. The "Genesee," which was alongside, unable to stem the rapid current of the river, with the massive "Richmond" in tow, bore her back to Prophet's Island. Just as the "Richmond" turned a torpedo exploded under her stern, throwing up the water mast-head high and causing the gallant ship to quiver in every timber.

The "Monongahela" and "Kineo" came next in line of battle. The commander of the "Monongahela," Captain M'Kinstry, was struck down early in the conflict. The command then devolved on a gallant young officer, Lieutenant Thomas. He manfully endeavored through all the storm of battle to follow the flag-ship. But in the dense smoke the pilot lost the channel. The ship grounded directly under the fire of one of the principal rebel batteries. For twenty-five minutes she remained in that perilous position, swept by shot and shell. Finally, through the efforts of her consort, the "Kineo," she was floated, and again heroically commenced steaming up the river. But her enginery soon became so disabled under the relentless fire, that the "Monongahela" was also compelled to drop down with the "Kineo" to the position of the mortar fleet. Her loss was six killed and twenty wounded.

In obedience to the order of Admiral Farragut, the magnificent ship "Mississippi" brought up the rear, with the gunboat "Sachem" as her ally, bound to her larboard side. She had reached the point directly opposite the town, and her officers were congratulating themselves that they had surmounted the greatest dangers, and that they would soon be above the batteries, when the ship, which had just then been put under rapid headway, grounded on the west bank of the river. It was an awful moment; for the guns of countless batteries were immediately concentrated upon her. Captain Smith, while, with his efficient engineer Rutherford he made the most strenuous exertions to get the ship afloat, ordered his gunners to keep up their fire with the utmost possible rapidity. In the short space of thirty-five minutes they fired two hundred and fifty shots. The principal battery of the foe was within five hundred yards of the crippled ship, and the majestic fabric was soon riddled through and through by the storm with which she was so pitilessly pelted. The dead and the wounded strewed the decks, and it was soon evident that the ship could not be saved.

Captain Smith prepared to destroy the ship, that it might not fall into the hands of the rebels, and to save the crew. Captain Caldwell, of the iron-clad "Essex," hastened to his rescue. Under as murderous a fire as mortals were ever exposed to, the sick and wounded were conveyed on board the ram. Combustibles were placed in the fore and after part of the ship, to which the torch was to be applied so soon as the crew had all escaped to the western shore. By some misunderstanding she was fired forward before the order was given. This caused a panic, as there were but three small boats by which they could escape. Some plunged into the river and were drowned. It is related, in evidence of the coolness of Captain Smith, that in the midst of this awful scene, while lighting his cigar with steel and flint, he remarked to Lieutenant Dewy:

"It is not likely that we shall escape, and we must make every preparation to secure the destruction of the ship."

After spiking nearly every gun with his own hands, and seeing that the survivors of his crew were fairly clear of the wreck, Captain Smith, accompanied by Lieutenant Dewey, Ensign Bachelder, and Engineer Tower, sadly took their leave, abandoning the proud fabric to the flames. Scarcely had they left, when two shells came crashing through the sides of the "Mississippi," overturning, scattering, and enkindling into flame some casks of turpentine. The ship was almost instantly enveloped in billows of fire. A yell of exultation rose from the rebels as they beheld the bursting forth of the flames. The ship, lightened by the removal of three hundred men, and by the consuming power of the fire, floated from the sand bar and commenced floating, bow on, down the river.

The scene presented was indeed magnificent. The whole fabric was enveloped in flame. Wreathing serpents of fire twined around the masts and ran up the shrouds. Drifting rapidly downward on the rapid current, the meteor, like a volcanic mountain in eruption, descended as regularly along the western banks of the stream as if steered by the most accomplished helmsman. As the ship turned round, in floating off, the guns of her port battery, which had not been discharged, faced the foe. As the fire reached them the noble frigate, with the stars and stripes still floating at her peak, opened a new bombardment of the rebel batteries. The shells began to explode, scattering through the air in all directions. The flaming vision arrested every eye, on the land and on the ships, until the floating mountain of fire drifted down and disappeared behind Prophet's Island. And now came the explosion of the magazine. There was a vivid flash, shooting upward to the sky in the form of an inverted cone. For a moment the whole horizon seemed ablaze with fiery missiles. Then came booming over the waves a peal of heaviest thunder. The very hills shook beneath the awful explosion. This was the dying cry of the "Mississippi" as she sank to her burial beneath the waves of the river from which she received her name.

Captain Caldwell, of the "Essex," who, as soon as he saw the "Mississippi," to be on fire, gallantly steamed to her aid, directly under the concentrated fire of the batteries, succeeded in picking up many who were struggling in the waves, and in rescuing others who had escaped to the shore. There were about three hundred men on board the "Mississippi" Of these sixty-five officers and men were either killed, wounded, or taken prisoners. Seventy, who escaped to the shore, wandered, for many miles, down the western banks of the stream, in constant danger of being taken captive, wading the bayous, and encountering fearful hardships, until they finally reached the ships below. Two ships, the "Hartford" and the "Albatross," succeeded in running the gauntlet.

RUNNING THE BATTERIES AT VICKSBURG.

The fate of the "Mississippi," in her attempt to pass the batteries at Port Hudson, might well have appalled the stoutest heart; but, in war, necessity is stronger than law—stronger than human suffering, or than any obstacle which may oppose its action. It was necessary for General Grant, while marching his troops overland on the west side of the Mississippi, toward the point from which he intended to cross and attack Vicksburg from the south and east, to have transports and gunboats below the Vicksburg and Warrenton batteries to bring supplies and ferry his troops across the Mississippi, as well as to attack the Warrenton batteries from below.

On consultation with Admiral Porter, that brave officer proposed to send down eight gunboats, three transports, and a number of barges and flat boats, laden with commissary supplies, past the batteries to New Carthage. These were all manned by volunteers, who were not deterred by the previous misfortunes of Farragut's squadron from undertaking this perilous expedition.

The former attempts at running the Vicksburg batteries had been made shortly before, or at daylight; this time a change was resolved upon. Eleven o'clock at night was appointed as the hour at which the boats should leave their rendezvous, which was near the mouth of the Yazoo river. To the anxious expectants of the coming events, the hours stole slowly by. As the appointed moment drew near, the decks of the various steamboats were crowded with watchful spectators.

A sort of apprehensive shudder ran through the collected gazers when it was announced that the first boat destined to pass the batteries was approaching. Sombre and silent it floated down, near the Louisiana shore; scarcely were its dark sides to be distinguished from the foliage lining the bank. Stealing slowly on, it passed the group of steamers, and at a point below took an oblique course, steering for the Mississippi side of the river; and, in the gloom, it was soon confounded with the dark shadow of the trees beyond.

Before this boat was lost sight of, another succeeded, and to that another, and another, until, before midnight, the whole had gained the Mississippi side of the river, and were swallowed up in the dim obscurity. With breathless interest their transit was watched by all of those on the boats of the fleet, whose position, a little above the entrance of the first canal, brought the rough heights of Vicksburg within their sphere of vision, though the town lay, for the present, buried in the darkness, except where now and then the twinkling of a starry light was seen.

As the boats, with lights out and fires carefully hidden, floated past, indistinct as the ghosts of Ossian in the mountain mists, it was curious to note the effect upon the spectators. Before they appeared, the hum of conversation was heard all around. All were busy with speculations as to the probabilities of success. The desponding prognosticated unmitigated disaster. The hopeful indulged in confident speculations. All were contented to endure some loss, provided a sufficiency arrived at the destined point to accomplish the object contemplated.

As the various boats came slowly into view, stole past with noiseless motion, then vanished into the recesses of the shadowy shore, each voice was hushed; only in subdued and smothered tones were persons, at intervals, heard to ask a question or venture an observation. It seemed as if each one felt that his silence was due to the impressive scene; as if an indiscreet utterance on his part might raise the vail of secrecy, so necessary to be preserved in the presence of a watchful foe.

A painful expectation weighed on every spirit. The boats must now be near the point opposite the beleaguered city. Will they be discovered at the first approach, or will a kindly fortune give them easy passage by? Suddenly a flame starts up! Another and another leaps into the darkness of the night! The enemy has seen the passing boats, and is sending across the river his death-dealing messengers. Rapid now dart the momentary fires; the iron rain of the remorseless cannon hurtles upon the dim and gliding boats. Dull upon the heavy air, scarce nerved by the night wind, which blows in a direction unfavorable for their hearing, reverberates the heavy thud of the cannon.

As the time passes, the batteries lower and still lower come into action. The gazers can trace the course of the fleet by new flames, that each moment startle the strained sight; and cannon, for miles along the hazy shore, are hurling their destructive missiles. A new accessory now adds its influence to the exciting scene. While the spectators had been engaged in watching the vivid flames leaping from cannon mouths and exploding shells, a gleam of light, first pale and soft, then red and lurid, and at last glaring and refulgent, stole up into the heavens above the opposing city. For the first time, the silence was broken by the gazing crowds upon the steamboats of the fleet. "Vicksburg is on fire!" was uttered in excited tones. But it was not so. Steady and with wonderful brilliancy, upon the hill on which the city stands, the fire assumed a circular outline on the upper edge, much like a third part of the full moon when, apparently magnified, it is rising above the horizon. The flame glowed brilliant and beautiful—no smoke was visible to dim its splendor. It was a beacon light, placed in a position to throw its beams along each arm of the bend of the river, the convex side of which is turned toward Vicksburg. So powerful was the light that, at the point where the steamboat fleet was moored, the shadow of a hand, held a foot from the boat's side, was distinctly thrown upon it. This beacon, with treacherous fidelity, showed to the foe the now fast disappearing boats; but, happily, it was fired too late. The sight of the boats appeared to add new rage to the enemy, who could not fail to count the cost to him of such a fleet joining Farragut's three gunboats already between Vicksburg and Port Hudson. The firing became more rapid. From the upper batteries to the last ones down at Warrenton, leaped flame on flame. The dull echo of the cannon, and the whirr and shriek of the flying shells, startled the midnight air. But now comes a roar which tells that the Union boys are awake and lively! The light that showed the boats to the enemy, revealed to the gunners on the gunboats the outlines of the batteries, and the roar which deafens the ear to every other sound is the peal of their heavy pieces. After an interval of maddest rage, the upper guns of the enemy almost cease their fire. It is evident that the boats have passed the first reached batteries—all of them that have escaped the deadly onset. That no large portion of them is missing, is apparent from the activity of the forts at Warrenton, and the answering thunders of the Union guns.

By this time the beacon light was burnt down, and

ceased to render its cruel aid. Just as the gathering darkness and the yet longer and larger intervals of silence gave intimation that the exciting scene was nearly over, another startling incident woke anew the emotions of the time. Midway between the extinct beacon in the city and the lower batteries at Warrenton, a new glow of light, soft as the dawn, but rapidly blushing into deeper intensity, climbed gently toward the sky. "They are lighting another beacon," shouted many voices; but again the speakers were mistaken. The light grew stronger every moment; it wanted the mellow, vivid, space-penetrating brilliancy of the beacon; above it rolled volumes of thick curling smoke; and more—the light, with slow and equal pace, was moving down the stream! There was no disguising the truth—one of our own boats was on fire. The white color of the smoke showed that among the fuel to the flame was cotton. The inference was plain; it was not a gunboat but a transport that was burning, for the latter, alone, were protected by bales of cotton. On floated the doomed vessel; her light doubtless exposed to the rebels' view the floating flat boats and barges; further firing, especially from the Warrenton batteries, was for a short time violently renewed.

The glow of the burning boat continued in sight until the beams of morning hid its glare. Before this, moreover, the solemn drama had reached its termination. The spectators reluctantly retired to their cabins, when nothing remained to engage the attention but the flaming wreck and scattering shots:

> "The distant and random gun,
> That the foe was sullenly firing."

It was not until noon of the next day (April 17, 1863) that the account of the fate of the expedition reached the Union camp at Young's Point. The eight gunboats reached their destination with but slight injuries or loss of life, only one man having been killed and two wounded. The transport Henry Clay was burned; but the other transports, flat boats, etc., made the passage in safety, and the crew of the Henry Clay reached the shore and joined some of the other boats. A few days later, Admiral Porter sent a second squadron of gunboats and transports down, but the transports in this expedition were seriously damaged.

THE CAVALRY FIGHT AT BRANDY STATION.

THIS action, one of the most brilliant in which our cavalry were engaged, and one of the first in which they won the reputation of being superior to the rebels in that arm of the service, in which they had especially plumed themselves, is thus graphically described by a participator in it:

"It was the prettiest cavalry fight that you ever saw," said the adjutant, stretching his legs, and lighting a fresh cigar.

"It was just my luck to lose it," I answered. "Here have I been lying, growling and grumbling, while you fellows have been distinguishing yourselves. It was miserable to be taken sick just when the army got in motion, and still worse not to hear a word of what was going on. I almost wished that we had been a *newspaper* regiment, so that I could learn something about our share in that day's work. Be a good fellow, and play reporter for my benefit. Freshen hawse, as the nautical novelists say, and begin."

"Well, we were lying at Warrenton Junction, making ourselves as comfortable as possible after the raid, when on the morning of the 8th of June, the whole division was ordered out in the very lightest marching order. That night we lay close to Kelly's Ford, in column of battalions, the men holding their horses as they slept, and no fires being lighted.

"At four o'clock on the morning of the 9th, we were again in motion, and got across the ford without interruption or discovery. Yorke, with the third squadron, was in advance, and as we moved, he managed so well that he bagged every picket on the road. Thus we had got almost upon the rebel camp before we were discovered. We rode right into Jones' Brigade, the First Jersey and First Pennsylvania charging together; and before they had recovered from the alarm we had a hundred and fifty prisoners. The rebels were then forming thick upon the hill-side by the station, and they had a battery playing upon us like fun. Martin's New York Battery on our side galloped into position, and began to answer them. Then Wyndham formed his whole brigade for a charge, except a squadron of the First Maryland, left to support the battery. Our boys went in splendidly, keeping well together, and making straight for the rebel battery on the hill behind the station. Wyndham himself rode on the right, and Broderick charged more toward the left, and with a yell we were on them. We were only two hundred and eighty strong, and in front of us was White's Battalion of five hundred. No matter for that. Wyndham and Broderick were leading, and they were not accustomed to count odds.

"As we dashed fiercely into them, sabre in hand, they broke like a wave on the bows of a ship, and over and through them we rode, sabreing as we went. We could not stop to take prisoners, for there in front of us was the Twelfth Virginia, six hundred men, riding down to support White. By Jove, sir, that was a charge! They came up splendidly, looking steadier than we did ourselves after the shock of the first charge. I do not know whether Wyndham was still with us, or if he had gone to another regiment; but there was Broderick, looking full of fight, his blue eyes in a blaze, and his sabre clenched, riding well in front. At them we went again, and some of them this time met us fairly. I saw Broderick's sabre go through a man, and the rebel gave a convulsive leap out of his saddle, falling senseless to the ground. It seemed but an instant before the rebels were scattered in every direction, trying now and then to rally in small parties, but never daring to await our approach.

"Now, there were the guns plain before us, the drivers yelling at their horses, and trying to limber up. We caught one gun before they could move it, and were dashing after the others, when I heard Broderick shouting in a stormy voice. I tell you, it was a startling sight. The fragments of White's Battalion had gathered together toward the left of the field, and were charging in our rear. The First Maryland was there, and Broderick was shouting at them in what their colonel considered a 'very ungentlemanly manner,' to move forward to the charge. At the same time two fresh regiments, the Eleventh Virginia, and another, were coming down on our front. Instead of dashing at White's men, the First Maryland wavered and broke, and then we were charged at the same time in front and rear. We had to let the guns go, and gather together as well as possible to cut ourselves out. Gallantly our fellows met the attack. We were broken, of course, by the mere weight of the attacking force, but, breaking them up too, the whole field was covered with small squads of fighting men. I saw Broderick ride in with a cheer, and open a way for the men. His horse went down in the melee; but little Wood, the bugler of Company G, sprang down, and gave him his animal, setting off himself to catch another. A rebel rode at the bugler, and succeeded in getting away his arms before help came. As Wood still went after a horse another fellow rode at him.

"The boy happened at that moment to see a carbine, where it had been dropped after firing. He picked up the empty weapon, aimed it at the horseman, made him dismount, give up his arms, and start for the rear Then he went in again. Lucas, Hobensack, Brooks, and Beekman, charged with twelve men into White's Battalion. Fighting hand to hand, they cut their way through, but left nine of the men on the ground behind them. Hughes was left almost alone in a crowd, but brought himself and the men with him safe through. Major Shelmire was seen last lying across the dead body of a rebel cavalryman None of us thought any thing

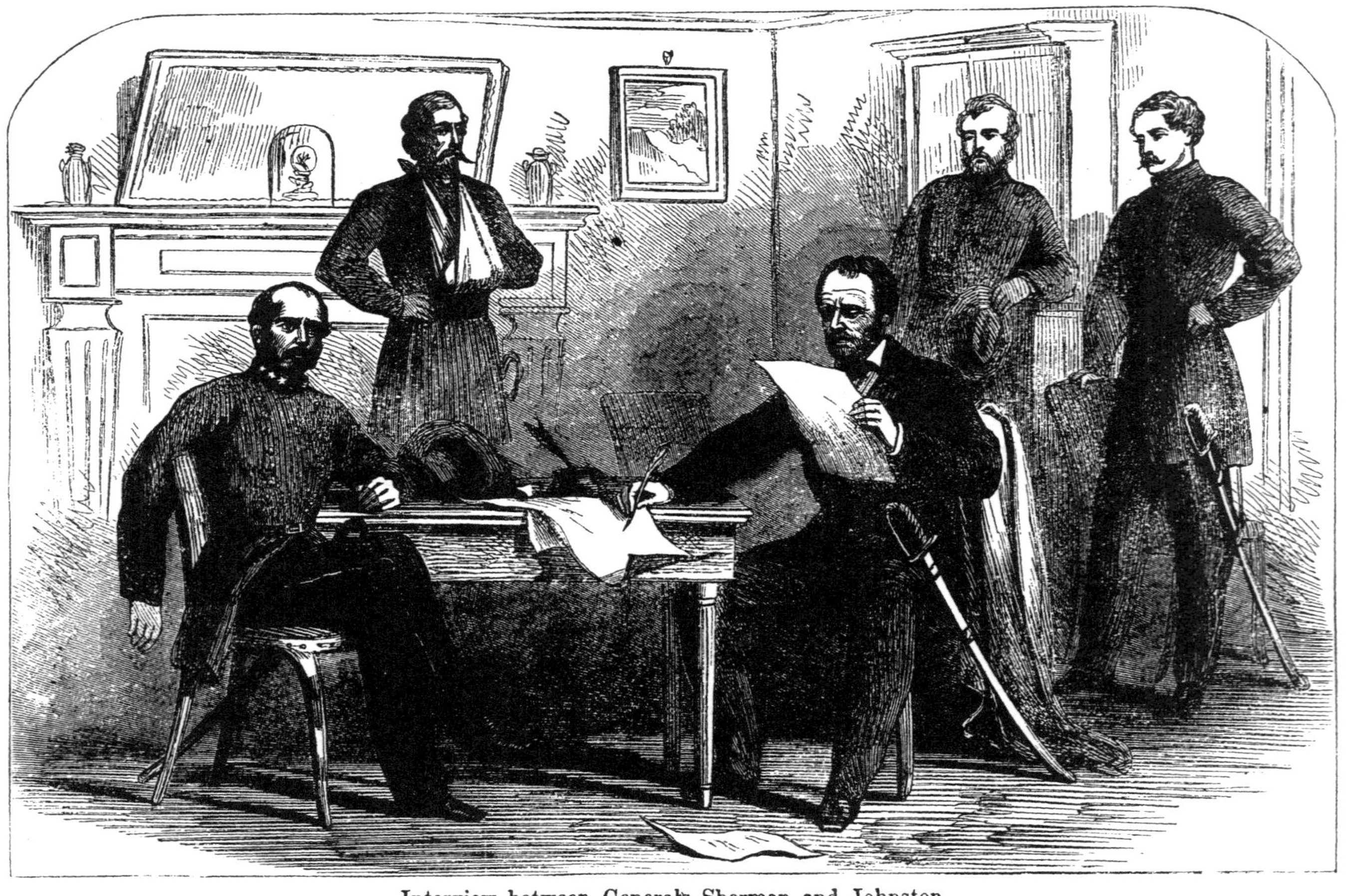

Interview between Generals Sherman and Johnston.

of two to one odds, as long as we had a chance to ride at them. It was only when we got so entangled that we had to fight hand to hand that their numbers told heavily. It was in such a place that I lost sight of Broderick. The troop horse that he was riding was not strong enough to ride through a knot of men, so that he had to fight them. He struck one so heavily that he was stunned by the blow, but his horse was still in the way; swerving to one side, he escaped a blow from another, and, warding off the thrust of a third, managed to take him with his point across the forehead; just as he did so, however, his sabre, getting tangled with the rebel's, was jerked from his hand.

"He always carried a pistol in his boot. Pulling that out, he fired into the crowd, and put spurs to his horse. The bullet hit a horse in front of him, which fell. His own charger rose at it, but stumbled, and as it did, Broderick himself fell, from a shot fired within arms' length of him and a sabre stroke upon his side.

"I saw all this as a man sees things at such times, and am not positive even that it all occurred as I thought I saw it; for I was in the midst of confusion, and only caught things around by passing glimpses. You see I was myself having as much as I could do. The crowd with whom Broderick was engaged was a little distance from me; and I had just wheeled to ride up to his help when two fellows put at me. The first one fired at me and missed. Before he could again cock his revolver I succeeded in closing with him. My sabre took him just in the neck, and must have cut the jugular. The blood gushed out in a black looking stream;

he gave a horrible yell, and fell over the side of his horse, which galloped away. Then I gathered up my reins, spurred my horse, and went at the other one. I was riding that old black horse that used to belong to the signal sergeant, and it was in fine condition. As I drove in the spurs it gave a leap high in the air. That plunge saved my life. The rebel had a steady aim at me; but the ball went through the black horse's brain. His feet never touched ground again. With a terrible convulsive contraction of all his muscles the black turned over in the air, and fell on his head and side stone dead, pitching me twenty feet. I lighted on my pistol, the butt forcing itself far into my side; my sabre sprung out of my hand, and I lay, with arms and legs all abroad, stretched out like a dead man. Everybody had something else to do than to attend to me, and there I lay where I had fallen.

"It seemed to me to have been an age before I began painfully to come to myself; but it could not have been many minutes. Every nerve was shaking; there was a terrible pain in my head, and a numbness through my side which was even worse. Fighting was still going on around me, and my first impulse was to get hold of my sword. I crawled to it and sank down as I grasped it once more. That was only for a moment; for a rebel soldier seeing me move, rode at me. The presence of danger roused me, and I managed to get to my horse, behind which I sank, resting my pistol on the saddle, and so contriving to get an aim. As soon as the man saw that, he turned off without attacking me. I was now able to stand and walk; so, holding my pistol in one hand and my sabre in the other, I made my way across the fields to where our battery was posted, scaring some with my pistol, and shooting others. Nobody managed to hit me through the whole fight. When I got up to the battery I found Wood there. He sang out to me to wait, and he would get me a horse. One of the men, who had just taken one, was going past, so Wood stopped him and got it for me.

"Just at that moment White's Battalion and some other troops came charging at the battery. The squadron of the First Maryland, who were supporting it, met the charge well as far as their numbers went; but were, of course, flanked on both sides by the heavy odds. All of our men who were free came swarming up the hill, and the cavalry were fighting over and around the guns. In spite of the confusion, and even while their comrades at the same piece were being sabred, the men at that battery kept to their duty. They did not even look up or around, but kept up their fire with unwavering steadiness. There was one rebel, on a splendid horse, who sabred three gunners while I was chasing him. He wheeled in and out, would dart away, and then come sweeping back and cut down another man in a manner that seemed almost supernatural. We at last succeeded in driving him away, but we could not catch or shoot him, and he got off without a scratch.

"In the meantime the fight was going on elsewhere. Kilpatrick's Brigade charged on our right. The Second New York did not behave as well as it has sometimes done since, and the loss of it weakened us a great deal. The Tenth New York, though, went in well, and the First Maine did splendidly, as it always does. In spite of their superior numbers (Stuart had a day or two before reviewed thirty thousand cavalry at Culpepper, according to the accounts of rebel officers), we beat them heavily, and would have routed them completely if Duffie's Brigade had come up. He, however, was engaged with two or three hundred men on the left; the aide-de-camp sent to him with orders was wounded and taken prisoner, and he is not the sort of man to find out the critical point in a fight of his own accord.

"So now, they bringing up still more reserves, and a whole division of theirs coming on the field, we began to fall back. We had used them up so severely that they could not press us very close, except in the neighborhood of where the Second New York charged. There some of our men had as much as they could do to get out, and the battery had to leave three of its guns. We formed in the woods between a quarter and half a mile of the field, another regiment moved back to cover the left of Buford, who was in retreat toward Beverly Ford. Hart and Wynkoop tried hard to cover the guns that were lost, but they had too few men, and so had to leave them. The rebels were terribly punished. By their own confession they lost three times as many as we did. In our regiment almost every soldier must have settled his man. Sergeant Craig, of Company K, I believe, killed three. Slate, of the same company, also went above the average. But we lost terribly. Sixty enlisted men of the First Jersey were killed, wounded, or missing. Colonel Wyndham was wounded, but kept his saddle; Lieutenant-Colonel Broderick and Major Shelmire were killed; Lieutenant Brooks was wounded; Captain Sawyer and Lieutenant Crocker were taken prisoners; and I, as you see, have had to come in at last and refit."

Capture of Lookout Mountain.

THE CAPTURE OF MISSION RIDGE.

THE campaign of Chattanooga, in October and November, 1863, was as brilliant as it was brief. It was not the continuous "pounding" of Vicksburg, the dogged and obstinate fighting, and the terrible slaughter of the battles in Virginia in the spring and summer of 1864; but in dash, in skilful surmounting of obstacles, in brilliant and heroic achievement, it was surpassed by no campaign of the war. Each of its five engagements had something of special merit to entitle it to lasting remembrance; the adroitly managed surprise by which the command of the river was won, and the toilsome sixty miles' travel of the supply trains over the worst roads in the world reduced to ten miles over a good road, and the subsequent sharp but successful battle of Wauhatchie, in which the gray-haired hero, Geary, showed himself as skilful as he was daring, indicated that the general in command at Chattanooga was fully master of the situation. The capture of Lookout mountain by General Hooker; the conflict "above the clouds," where the lurid light that flamed from Union and rebel cannon mimicked, with wonderful effect, the thunders of Heaven's own artillery, and where, with every struggle, the stars and stripes crept higher and higher toward that summit which overlooked so many battle fields, till the morning's light beheld them waving proudly from its highest point; the bold and rapid movement, by which, while marshalled, as the enemy supposed, for a dress parade, the Army of the Cumberland swept across the plain and captured Orchard Knob; that succession of fierce and persistent struggles in which Sherman wrestled for the capture of Tunnel Hill, and by which he drew to that point so large a portion of Bragg's troops; and last and most glorious of all that fiery ascent of Mission Ridge, in which that noble Fourth Corps marched and climbed for a long hour through a furnace of flame, and after struggling up an ascent so steep that to climb it unopposed would task the stoutest energies, swept their enemies from its summit, and over all that broad vista disclosed from its summit, saw only a flying and utterly routed foe. Many writers have attempted to describe, and with varying success, this brilliant feat of arms, but none have succeeded so admirably as Mr. B. F. Taylor, of the "Chicago Journal," himself an eye-witness of it. We give a portion of his description, which is as truthful as it is glowing:

The brief November afternoon was half gone; it was yet thundering on the left; along the centre all was still. At that very hour a fierce assault was made upon the enemy's left near Rossville, four miles down toward the old field of Chickamauga. They carried the Ridge; Mission Ridge seems everywhere—they strewed its summit with rebel dead; they *held* it. And thus the tips of the Federal army's wide-spread wings flapped grandly. But it had not swooped; the gray quarry yet perched upon Mission Ridge; the rebel army was terribly battered at the edges, but there full in our front it grimly waited, biding out its time. If the horns of the rebel crescent could not be doubled crushingly together, in a shapeless mass, possibly it might be sundered at its centre, and tumbled in fragments over the other side of Mission

Ridge. Sherman was halted upon the left; Hooker was holding hard in Chattanooga Valley; the Fourth Corps, that rounded out our centre, grew impatient of restraint; the day was waning; but little time remained to complete the commanding general's grand design; Gordon Granger's hour had come; his work was full before him.

And what a work that was to make a weak man falter and a brave man think! One and a half miles to traverse, with narrow fringes of woods, rough valleys, sweeps of open field, rocky acclivities, to the base of the ridge, and no foot in all the breadth withdrawn from rebel sight; no foot that could not be played upon by rebel cannon, like a piano's keys, under Thalberg's stormy fingers. The base attained, what then? A heavy rebel work, packed with the enemy, rimming it like a battlement. That work carried, and what then? A hill, struggling up out of the valley, four hundred feet, rained on by bullets, swept by shot and shell; another line of works, and then, up like a Gothic roof rough with rocks, a wreck with fallen trees, four hundred more; another ring of fire and iron, and then the crest, and then the enemy.

To dream of such a journey would be madness; to devise it a thing incredible; to *do* it a deed impossible. *But Grant was guilty of them all, and Granger was equal to the work.* The story of the battle of Mission Ridge is struck with immortality already; let the leader of the Fourth Corps bear it company.

That the centre yet lies along its silent line is still true; in five minutes it will be the wildest fiction. Let us take that little breath of grace for just one glance at the surroundings, since we shall have neither heart nor eyes for it again. Did ever battle have so vast a cloud of witnesses? The hive shaped hills have swarmed. Clustered like bees, blackening the housetops, lining the fortifications, over yonder *across* the theatre, in the seats with the Catilines, *everywhere*, are a hundred thousand beholders. Their souls are in their eyes. Not a murmur can you hear. It is the most solemn congregation that ever stood up in the presence of the God of battles. I think of Bunker Hill, as I stand here; of the thousands who witnessed the immortal struggle; and fancy there is a parallel. I think, too, that the chair of every man of them will stand vacant against the wall to-morrow, and that around the fireside they must give thanks without him if they can.

At half-past three, a group of generals, whose names will need no "Old Mortality" to chisel them anew, stood upon Orchard Knob. The hero of Vicksburg was there, calm, clear, persistent, far-seeing. Thomas, the sterling and steady; Meigs, Hunter, Granger, Reynolds. Clusters of humbler mortals were there, too, but it was any thing but a turbulent crowd; the voice naturally fell into a subdued tone, and even young faces took on the gravity of later years. *Generals Grant, Thomas, and Granger conferred, an order was given, and in an instant the Knob was cleared like a ship's deck for action.* At twenty minutes of four, Granger stood upon the parapet; the bugle swung idle at the bugler's side, the warbling fife and the grumbling drum unheard—there was to be *louder* talk—six guns, at intervals of two seconds, the signal to advance. Strong and steady his voice rang out: "Number one, fire! Number two, fire! Number three, fire!" it seemed to me the tolling of the clock of destiny—and when at "Number six, fire!" the roar throbbed out with the flash, you should have seen the dead line that had been lying behind the works all day, all night, all day again, come to resurrection in the twinkling of an eye—leap like a blade from its scabbard, and sweep with a two-mile stroke toward the ridge. From divisions to brigades, from brigades to regiments, the order ran. A minute, and the skirmishers deploy; a minute, and the first great drops begin to patter along the line; a minute, and the musketry is in full play, like the crackling whips of a hemlock fire; men go down, here and there, before your eyes; the wind lifts the smoke and drifts it away over the top of the ridge; every thing is too distinct; it is fairly *palpable;* you can touch it with your hand. The divisions of Wood and Sheridan are wading breast deep in the valley of death.

I never can tell you what it was like. They pushed out, leaving nothing behind them. There was no reservation in that battle. On moves the line of skirmishers, like a heavy frown, and after it, at quick time, the splendid columns. At right of us, and left of us, and front of us, you can see the bayonets glitter in the sun. You cannot persuade yourself that Bragg was wrong, a day or two ago, when, seeing Hooker moving in, he said, "Now we shall have a Potomac review;" that this is *not* the parade he prophesied; that it is of a truth the harvest of death to which they go down. And so through the fringe of woods went the line. Now, out into the open ground they burst at the double-quick. Shall I call it a Sabbath day's journey, or a long one and a half mile? To me, that watched, it seemed endless as eternity, and yet they made it in thirty minutes. The tempest that now broke upon their heads was terrible. The enemy's fire burst out of the rifle-pits from base to summit of Mission Ridge; five rebel batteries of Parrotts and Napoleons opened along the crest. Grape and canister and shot and shell sowed the ground with rugged iron, and garnished it with the wounded and the dead. But steady and strong our columns move on.

> "By heavens! It was a splendid sight to see,
> For one who had no friend, no brother there;"

but to all loyal hearts, alas! and thank God, those men were friend and brother, both in one.

And over their heads, as they went, Forts Wood and Negley struck straight out like mighty pugilists right and left, raining their iron blows upon the Ridge from base to crest; Forts Palmer and King took up the quarrel, and Moccasin Point cracked its fiery whips and lashed the rebel left till the wolf cowered in its corner with a growl. Bridges' Battery, from Orchard Knob below, thrust its ponderous fists in the face of the enemy, and planted blows at will. Our artillery was doing splendid service. It laid its shot and shell wherever it pleased. Had giants carried them by hand they could hardly have been more accurate. All along the mountain's side, in the rebel rifle-pits, on the crest, they fairly dotted the Ridge. General Granger leaped down, sighted a gun, and in a moment, right in front, a great volume of smoke, like "the cloud by day," lifted off the summit from among the rebel batteries, and hung motionless, kindling in the sun. The shot had struck a caisson, and that was its dying breath. In five minutes away floated another. A shell went crashing through a building in the cluster that marked Bragg's headquarters; a second killed the skeleton horses of a battery at his elbow, a third scattered a gray mass as if it had been a wasp's nest.

And all the while our lines were moving on; they had burned through the woods and swept over the rough and rolling ground like a prairie fire. Never halting, never faltering, they charged up to the first rifle-pits with a cheer, forked out the rebels with their bayonets, and lay there panting for breath. If the thunder of guns had been terrible, it was now growing sublime; it was like the footfall of God on the ledges of cloud. Our forts and batteries still thrust out their mighty arms across the valley; the rebel guns that lined the arc of the crest full in our front, opened like the fan of Lucifer, and converged their fire down upon Baird, and Wood, and Sheridan. It was rifles and musketry; it was grape and canister; it was shell and schrapnel. Mission Ridge was volcanic; a thousand torrents of red poured over its brink and rushed together to its base. And our men were there, halting for breath! And still the sublime diapason rolled on. Echoes that never waked before, roared out from height to height, and called from the far ranges of Waldron's Ridge to Lookout. As for Mission Ridge, it had jarred to such music before; it was the "sounding-board" of Chickamauga; it was *behind* us then; it frowns and flashes in our faces to-day; the old Army of the Cumberland was there; it breasted the storm till the storm was spent, and left the ground it held; the old Army of the Cumberland is *here!* It shall roll up the Ridge like a surge to its summit, and sweep triumphant down the other side. Believe me, that memory and hope may have made the heart of many a blue coat beat like a drum. "Beat," did I say? The feverish heat of the *battle* beats on; fifty-eight guns a minute, by the watch, is the rate of its terrible throbbing. That hill, if you climb it, will appal you. Furrowed like a summer-fallow, bullets as if an oak had shed them; trees clipped and shorn, leaf and limb, as with the knife of some heroic gardener pruning back for richer fruit. How you attain the summit, weary and breathless, I wait to hear; how *they* went up in the teeth of the storm no man can tell!

And all the while rebel prisoners have been streaming out from the rear of our lines like the tails of a cloud of kites. Captured and disarmed, they needed nobody to set them going. The fire of their own comrades was like spurs in a horse's flank, and amid the tempest of their own brewing they ran for dear life, until they dropped like quails into the Federal rifle-pits, and were safe. But our gallant legions are out in the storm; they have carried the works at the base of the Ridge; they have fallen like leaves in winter weather. Blow, dumb bugles!

Sound the recall! "Take the rifle-pits," was the order; and it is as empty of rebels as the tomb of the prophets. Shall they turn their backs to the blast? Shall they sit down under the eaves of that dripping iron? Or shall they climb to the cloud of death above them, and pluck out its lightnings as they would straws from a sheaf of wheat? But the order was not given. And now the arc of fire on the crest grows fiercer and longer. The reconnoissance of Monday had failed to develop the heavy metal of the enemy. The dull fringe of the hill kindles with the flash of great guns. I count the fleeces of white smoke that dot the Ridge, as battery after battery opens upon our line, until from the ends of the growing arc they sweep down upon it in mighty Xs of fire. I count till that devil's girdle numbers thirteen batteries, and my heart cries out, "Great God, when shall the end be!" There is a poem I learned in childhood, and so did you: it is Campbell's "Hohenlinden." One line I never knew the meaning of until I read it written along that hill! It has lighted up the whole poem for me with the glow of battle forever:

"And louder than the bolts of heaven,
Far flashed the red artillery."

At this moment, General Granger's aides are dashing out with an order; they radiate over the field, to left, right, and front; "Take the Ridge if you can"—"Take the Ridge if you can"—and so it went along the line. But the advance had already set forth without it. Stout-hearted Wood, the iron-gray veteran, is rallying on his men; stormy Turchin is delivering brave words in bad English; Sheridan—"little Phil"—you may easily look down upon him without climbing a tree, and see one of the most gallant leaders of the age if you do—is riding to and fro along the first line of rifle-pits, as calmly as a chess-player. An aide rides up with the order. "Avery, that flask," said the general. Quietly filling the pewter cup, Sheridan looks up at the battery that frowns above him, by Bragg's headquarters, shakes his cap amid that storm of every thing that kills, when you could hardly hold out your hand without catching a bullet in it, and with a "how are you?" tosses off the cup. The blue battle flag of the rebels fluttered a response to the cool salute, and the next instant the battery let fly its six guns, showering Sheridan with earth. Alluding to that compliment with any thing but a blank cartridge, the general said to me in his quiet way, "I thought it —— ungenerous!" The recording angel will drop a tear upon the word for the part he played that day. Wheeling toward the men, he cheered them to the charge, and made at the hill like a bold riding hunter; they were out of the rifle-pits, and into the tempest, and struggling up the steep, before you could get breath to tell it, and so they were throughout the inspired line.

And now you have before you one of the most startling episodes of the war; I cannot remember it in words; dictionaries are beggarly things. But I *may* tell you they did not storm that mountain as you would think. They dash out a little way, and then slacken; they creep up, hand over hand, loading and firing, and wavering and halting, from the first line of works to the second; they burst into a charge with a cheer, and go over it. Sheets of flame baptize them; plunging shot tear away comrades on left and right; it is no longer shoulder to shoulder; it is GOD for us all! Under tree trunks, among rocks, stumbling over the dead, struggling with the living, facing the steady fire of eight thousand infantry poured down upon their heads as if it were the old historic curse from heaven, they wrestle with the

HOOD
PRICE
KIRBY SMITH
A.S.JOHNSON.
JOS.E.JOHNSON
HARDEE
JNO.MORGAN.
FORREST.
BRAGG

Ridge. Ten, fifteen, twenty minutes go by like a reluctant century. The batteries roll like a drum; between the second and last lines of rebel works is the torrid zone of the battle; the hill sways up like a wall before them at an angle of forty-five degrees, but our brave mountaineers are clambering steadily on—up—upward still! You may think it strange, but I would not have recalled them if I could. They would have lifted you, as they did me, in full view of the heroic grandeur; they seemed to be spurning the dull earth under their feet, and going up to do Homeric battle with the greater gods.

And what do those men follow? If you look you shall see that the thirteen thousand are not a rushing herd of human creatures; that along the Gothic roof of the Ridge a row of inverted Vs is slowly moving up in line, a mighty lettering on the hill's broad side. At the angles of those Vs is something that glitters like a wing. Your heart gives a great bound when you think what it is—*the regimental flag*—and glancing along the front count fifteen of those colors that were borne at Pea Ridge, waved at Shiloh, glorified at Stone River, riddled at Chickamauga. Nobler than Cæsar's rent mantle are they all! And up move the banners, now fluttering like a wounded bird, now faltering, now sinking out of sight. Three times the flag of one regiment goes down. And you know why. Three dead color-sergeants lie just there, but the *flag* is immortal—thank God!—and up it comes again, and the Vs move on. At the left of Wood, three regiments of Baird—Turchin, the Russian thunderbolt, is there—hurl themselves against a bold point strong with rebel works; for a long quarter of an hour three flags are perched and motionless on a plateau under the frown of the hill. Will they linger forever? I give a look at the sun behind me; it is not more than a hand's breadth from the edge of the mountain; its level rays bridge the valley from Chattanooga to the Ridge with beams of gold; it shines in the rebel faces; it brings out the Federal blue; it touches up the flags. Oh, for the voice that could bid that sun stand still! I turn to the battle again: those three flags have taken flight! They are upward bound.

The race of the flags is growing every moment more terrible. There at the right, a strange thing catches the eye; one of the inverted Vs is turning right side up. The men struggling along the converging lines to overtake the flag have distanced it, and there the colors are, sinking down in the centre between the rising flanks. The line wavers like a great billow and up comes the banner again, as if heaved on a surge's shoulder. The iron sledges beat on. Hearts, loyal and brave, are on the anvil, all the way from base to summit of Mission Ridge, but those dreadful hammers never intermit. Swarms of bullets sweep the hill; you can count twenty-eight balls in one little tree. Things are growing desperate up aloft; the rebels tumble rocks upon the rising line; they light the fuses and roll shells down the steep; they load the guns with handfuls of cartridges in their haste; and as if there were powder in the word, they shout "Chickamauga!" down upon the mountaineers. But it would not all do, and just as the sun, weary of the scene, was sinking out of sight, with magnificent bursts all along the line, exactly as you have seen the crested seas leap up at the breakwater, the advance surged over the crest, and in a minute those flags fluttered along the fringe where fifty rebel guns were kenneled. GOD bless the flag! GOD save the Union!

What colors were first upon the mountain battlement I dare not try to say; bright honor itself may be proud to bear—nay, proud to follow the hindmost. Foot by foot they had fought up the steep, slippery with much blood; let them go to glory together. A minute and they were *all* there, fluttering along the ridge from left to right. The rebel hordes rolled off to the north, rolled off to the east, like the clouds of a worn out storm. Bragg, ten minutes before, was putting men back in the rifle-pits. His gallant gray was straining a nerve for him now, and the man rode on horseback into Dixie's bosom, who arrayed in some prophet's discarded mantle, foretold on Monday that the Yankees would leave Chattanooga in five days. They left in three, and by way of Mission Ridge, straight over the mountains as their forefathers went! As Sheridan rode up to the guns, the heels of Breckinridge's horse glittered in the last rays of sunshine. The crest was hardly "well off with the old love before it was on with the new."

But the scene on the narrow plateau can never be painted. As the blue coats surged over its edge, cheer on cheer rang like bells through the valley of the Chickamauga. Men flung themselves exhausted upon the ground. They laughed and wept, shook hands, embraced; turned round and did all four over again. It was as wild as a carnival. Granger was received with a shout. "Soldiers," he said, "you ought to be court-martialed, every man of you I ordered you to take the rifle-pits and you scaled the mountain!' but it was not Mars' horrid front exactly with which he said it, for his cheeks were wet with tears as honest as the blood that reddened all the route. Wood uttered words that rang like "Napoleon's," and Sheridan, the rowels at his horse's flanks, was ready for a dash down the Ridge with a "view halloo," for a fox hunt.

But you must not think this was all there was of the scene on the crest, for fight and frolic was strangely mingled. Not a rebel had dreamed a man of us all would live to reach the summit, and when a little wave of the Federal cheer rolled up and broke over the crest, they defiantly cried "Hurrah and be damned!" the next minute a Union regiment followed the voice, the rebels delivered their fire, and tumbled down in the rifle-pits, their faces distorted with fear. No sooner had the soldiers scrambled to the Ridge and straightened themselves, than up muskets and away they blazed. One of them, fairly beside himself between laughing and crying, seemed puzzled at which end of his piece he should load, and so abandoning the gun and the problem together, he made a catapult of himself and fell to hurling stones after the enemy. And he said, as he threw—well, you know our "army swore terribly in Flanders." Bayonets glinted and muskets rattled General Sheridan's horse was killed under him; Richard was not in his role, and so he leaped upon a rebel gun for want of another. Rebel artillerists are driven from their batteries at the edge of the sword and the point of the bayonet; two rebel guns are swung around upon their old masters. But there is nobody to load them. Light and heavy artillery do not belong to the winged kingdom. Two infantrymen claiming to be old artillerists, volunteer.

Battle of Chapin's Farm.

Granger turns captain of the guns, and—right about wheel!—in a moment they are growling after the flying enemy. I say "flying," but that is figurative. The many run like Spanish merinos, but the few fight like gray wolves at bay; they load and fire as they retreat; they are fairly scorched out of position.

A sharpshooter, fancying Granger to be worth the powder, coolly tries his hand at him. The general hears the *zip* of a ball at one ear, but doesn't mind it. In a minute away it sings at the other. He takes the hint, sweeps with his glass the direction whence the couple came, and brings up the marksman, just drawing a bead upon him again. At that instant a Federal argument persuades the cool hunter and down he goes. That long range gun of his was captured, weighed twenty-four pounds, was telescope-mounted, a sort of mongrel howitzer.

A colonel is slashing away with his sabre in a ring of rebels. Down goes his horse under him; they have him on the hip; one of them is taking deliberate aim, when up rushes a lieutenant, clasps a pistol to one ear and roars in at the other, "Who the h—l are you shooting at?" The fellow drops his piece, gasps out, "I surrender," and the next instant the gallant lieutenant falls sharply wounded. He is a "roll of honor" officer, straight up from the ranks, and he honors the roll.

A little German in Wood's Division is pierced like the lid of a pepper-box, but he is neither dead nor wounded. "See here," he says, rushing up to a comrade, "a pullet hit te preach of mine gun—a pullet in mine pocket-book—a pullet in mine coat tail—they shoots me tree, five time, and py dam I gives dem h—l yet!"

But I can render you no idea of the battle caldron that boiled on the plateau. An incident here and there I have given you, and you must fill out the picture for yourself. Dead rebels lay thick around Bragg's headquarters and along the Ridge. Scabbards, broken arms, artillery horses, wrecks of gun-carriages, and bloody garments, strewed the scene; and, tread lightly, oh! loyal-hearted, the boys in blue are lying there; no more the sounding charge, no more the brave, wild cheer, and never for them, sweet as the breath of the new-mown hay in the old home fields, "The Soldier's Return from the War." A little waif of a drummer-boy, somehow drifted up the mountain in the surge, lies there; his pale face upward, a blue spot on his breast. Muffle his drum for the poor child and his mother.

Our troops met one loyal welcome on the height. How the old Tennessean that gave it managed to get there nobody knows, but there he was, grasping a colonel's hand, and saying, while tears ran down his face: "God be thanked! I *knew* the Yankees would fight!" With the receding flight and swift pursuit the battle died away in murmurs, far down the valley of the Chickamauga; Sheridan was again in the saddle, and with his command spurring on after the enemy. Tall columns of smoke were rising at the left. The rebels were burning a train of stores a mile long. In the exploding rebel caissons we had "the cloud by day," and now we are having "the pillar of fire by night." The sun, the golden dish of the scales that balance day and night, had hardly gone down, when up, beyond Mission Ridge, rose the *silver* side, for that night it was full moon. The troubled day was done. *A Federal general sat in the seat of the man who, on the very Saturday before the battle, had sent a flag to the Federal lines with the words:*

"Humanity would dictate the removal of all non-combatants from Chattanooga, as I am about to shell the city!"

Sat there, and announced to the Fourth Corps the congratulations and thanks, just placed in his hands, from the commander of the department:

"BRAGG'S HEADQUARTERS, MISSION RIDGE, *November* 25, 1863.

"In conveying to you this distinguished recognition of your signal gallantry in carrying, through a terrible storm of iron, a mountain crowned with batteries and enriched with rifle-pits, I am constrained to express my own admiration of your noble conduct, and am proud to tell you that the veteran generals from other fields, who witnessed your heroic bearing, place your assault and triumph among the most brilliant achievements of the war. Thanks, soldiers! You have made, this day, a glorious page of history.

"GORDON GRANGER."

There was a species of poetic justice in it all, that would have made the prince of dramatists content. The ardor of the men had been quenchless: there had been three days of fitful fever, and after it, alas! a multitude had slept well. The work on the right, left, and centre cost us full four thousand killed and wounded. There is a tremble of the lip, but a flash of pride in the eye, as the soldier tells with how many he went in—how expressive that "went in!" Of a truth it was wading in deep waters—with how few we came out. I cannot try to swing the burden clear of any heart, by throwing into the scale upon the other side the dead weight of fifty-two pieces of captured artillery, ten thousand stand of arms, and heaps of dead rebels, or by driving upon a herd of seven thousand prisoners. Nothing of all this can lighten that burden a single ounce, but this thought may, and I dare to utter it: These three days' work brought Tennessee to resurrection; set the flag, that fairest blossom in all this flowery world, to blooming in its native soil once more.

That splendid march from the Federal line of battle to the crest, was made in one hour and five minutes, but it was a grander march toward the end of rebeldom; a glorious campaign of sixty-five minutes toward the white borders of peace. It made that fleeting November afternoon imperishable. Than the assault upon Mission Ridge, I know of nothing more gallant in the annals of the war. Let it rank foremost with the storming of Forts Scharnitz and Alma, that covered the French arms with undying fame.

Reader and writer must walk together down the heights another day; press that rugged earth with the first backward step a loyal foot has made upon it, and, as we linger, recall a few of the incidents that will render it historic and holy ground for coming time. Let the struggle be known as the Battle of Mission Ridge, and when, in calmer days, men make pilgrimage, and women smile again among the mountains of the Cumberland, they will need no guide. Rust will have eaten the guns; the graves of the heroes will have subsided like waves; weary of their troubling, the soldier and his leader will have lain down together; but there, embossed upon the globe, MISSION RIDGE will stand its fitting monument forever.

SHERIDAN AT MIDDLETOWN.

ONE of the most brilliant actions of the war—indeed, one of the most brilliant of any war of modern times—was that victory which the gallant Sheridan snatched from defeat and disaster at Middletown, Virginia, on the 19th of October, 1864. Three or four times in the military history of the last five hundred years, has an able and skilful commander succeeded in stemming the current of disaster, and turning a defeat into a victory; but it has usually been done either by bringing up reinforcements, and thus staying the progress of the exultant and careless foe, or by suffering a day to intervene between the defeat and the victory; at Marengo, it was the approach of reinforcements which enabled Dessaix to say to the first Napoleon: "We have lost one battle, but it is not too late to win another." At Shiloh, the reinforcements from Wallace's Division and Buell's Corps, and the intervention of the night, enabled Grant to recover, on the second day, all, and more than all, the losses of the first. At Stone River, the skill and genius of Rosecrans stayed the tide of disaster, and enabled the Army of the Cumberland, though suffering heavily, to maintain its position, and two days later to inflict upon the enemy a fearful punishment for his temerity. At Chickamauga, General Thomas maintained himself grandly in the face of a foe greatly superior to himself in numbers, and after one third of the army had been driven from the field, still held the rebels at bay; and, with the aid of Steedman's reinforcements, drove them back a little distance; but in none of these cases, except that at Marengo, was the army rallied from a defeat able at once to drive the foe in return, and, in that case, only by the aid of reinforcements.

In Sheridan's case, there were no reinforcements except himself; his army was defeated and routed; yet, at his cheering voice, and under the influence of his extraordinary personal magnetism, the flying, demoralized, and routed troops, turned back and hurled by his skilful hand upon the enemy, caused them in turn to fly with such precipitation as to leave cannon, arms, ammunition, every thing, behind them. Well did General Grant characterize the brave soldier who could do this as one of the greatest of generals.

With a brief description of the circumstances of the defeat, we will proceed to give the narrative of an eye-witness and participator in the subsequent victory Sheridan had, as those familiar with the history of the campaigns of the Army of the Shenandoah will recollect, repeatedly defeated Early during the previous month, driving him with heavy loss across and southward from the Opequan creek, on the 19th of September, and sending him "whirling" through Winchester; routing him at Fisher's Hill on the 22d of September, and sending his troops in rapid flight and disorder up the valley to Harrisonburg; had "fixed" the new cavalry general, Rosser, on the 8th of October, and repelled with heavy loss a covert attack made by Early from North mountain, on the 12th of October. Supposing that the rebel general had been sufficiently punished to be willing to remain quiet, General Sheridan made a flying visit to his out-stations along the newly repaired Manassas Gap Railroad, and thence to Washington, from whence he hastened back to his command, and, on the night of the 18th of October, reached Winchester.

But Early, restless and dissatisfied with the result of his previous encounters with the gallant cavalry general, was yet determined to try his fortune once more, and learning of his absence, and having received information, which he afterward found to his sorrow was false, that Sheridan had gone with the Sixth Corps to join the Army of the Potomac, he was emboldened to make another attack with, as he conceived, good hope of success. He had himself been reinforced meanwhile by a considerable body of troops (twelve thousand, it was said), a part of them without arms, but well drilled and ready for fight, if they could only procure weapons. With a daring which partook largely of rashness, he sent his troops into the gorge at the base of the Massanutten mountain, across the north fork of the Shenandoah, and skirted Crook's position for miles, passing for a considerable distance within four hundred yards of the Union pickets. Had his troops been detected in this march (and the chances of detection were almost a hundred to one), his army would have been ruined. The Union infantry would have cut his in two, and the Union cavalry would have prevented his retreat to Fisher's Hill. But his management of the advance was admirable. The canteens had been left in his camp, lest they should clatter against the shanks of the bayonets; the men crept noiselessly along in the darkness, and passed the dangerous points with complete success. Once, indeed, they were in danger of discovery. The rustling of the underbrush, and the muffled tramp of this large body of men, was heard by some of the outlying pickets, who reported it; but the approach of Early seemed so utterly improbable that no precautions were taken against a surprise. By dawn of day, Gordon's Rebel Division, closely followed by Ramseur, Pegram, Kershaw, and Wharton, had flanked Crook's Corps (Army of Western Virginia), and assaulted his camp before the men could form in line of battle. The Union army was ranged, in military phrase, *en echelon; i. e.*, in successive steps, the Army of Virginia, which was in front, extending also farthest south. Having flanked and rolled up this corps, the rebels, Gordon still heading, proceeded to flank the Nineteenth Corps, which occupied the next "step" of the *echelon*, and, after a short but determined struggle, drove that also northward. The Sixth Corps interposed a stronger obstacle to their progress, but that, too, was finally flanked, and all were compelled to retreat northward through Middletown toward Winchester. The first stragglers had by this time, about ten A. M., reached Winchester.

The camps, commissary supplies, and lines of earth works of the Union army, had fallen into the hands of the rebels, and they had captured twenty-four cannon and twelve hundred prisoners. The Union army was beaten, badly beaten, though not routed; they were retreating slowly and in good order, but still retreating toward Winchester.

How all this was changed by Sheridan's arrival, let Captain de Forest, himself a staff-officer and actor in the battle, tell:

At this time, at the close of this unfortunate struggle of five hours, we were joined by Sheridan, who had passed the night in Winchester, on his way back from Washington, and who must have heard of Early's attack about the time that its success became decisive. It was near ten o'clock when he came up the pike at a three-minute trot, swinging his cap and shouting to the stragglers: "Face the other way, boys. We are going back to our camps. We are going to lick them out of their boots!"

The wounded by the roadside raised their hoarse voices to shout; the great army of fugitives turned about at sight of him, and followed him back to the front; they followed him back to the slaughter as hounds follow their master. The moment he reached the army he ordered it to face about, form line, and advance to the position which it had last quitted. Then for two hours he rode along the front, studying the ground and encouraging the men. "Boys, if I had been here this never should have happened," he said, in his animated, earnest way. "I tell you it never should have happened. And now we are going back to our camps. We are going to get a twist on them. We are going to lick them out of their boots."

The Sixth Corps held the pike and its vicinity. On its right the Nineteenth Corps was formed in double line, under cover of a dense wood, the first division on the right, the second on the left. The rearmost line threw up a rude breastwork of stones, rails, and trees, covered by the advanced line standing to arms, and by a strong force of skirmishers stationed two hundred yards to the front, but still within the forest. For two hours all was silence, preparation, reorganization, and suspense. Then came a message from Sheridan to

Emory that the enemy in column were advancing against the Nineteenth Corps; and shortly afterward the column appeared among the lights and shadows of the autumnal woods, making for the centre of our second division. There was an awful rattle of musketry, which the forest re-echoed into a deep roar, and when the firing stopped and the smoke cleared away no enemy was visible. Emory immediately sent word to Sheridan that the attack had been repulsed.

"That's good, that's good!" Sheridan answered, gayly. "Thank God for that! Now then, tell General Emory if they attack him again to go after them, and to follow them up, and to sock it to them, and to give them the devil. We'll get the tightest twist on them yet that ever you saw. We'll have all those camps and cannon back again." All this, with the nervous animation characteristic of the man, the eager and confident smile, and the energetic gesture of the right hand down into the palm of the left at every repetition of the idea of attack.

At half-past three came more explicit orders. "The entire line will advance. The Nineteenth Corps will move in connection with the Sixth Corps. The right of the Nineteenth will swing toward the left so as to drive the enemy upon the pike."

One of our staff officers exclaimed, "By Jove, if we beat them now it will be magnificent!"

"And we are very likely to do it," said General Emory. "They will be so far from expecting us."

It must be understood that the enemy's left was now his strong point, being supported by successive wooded crests; while his right ran out to the pike across undulating open fields which presented no natural line of resistance. Sheridan's plan was to push them off the crests by a turning movement of our right, and then, when they were doubled up on the pike, sling his cavalry at them across the Middletown meadows. With a solemn tranquillity of demeanor our infantry rose from the position where it had been lying, and advanced through the forest into the open ground beyond. There was a silence of suspense; then came a screaming, crackling, humming rush of shell; then a prolonged roar of musketry, mingled with the long-drawn yell of our charge; then the artillery ceased, the musketry died into spattering bursts, and over all the yell rose triumphant. Every thing on the first line—the stone walls, the advanced crest, the tangled wood, the half finished breastworks—had been carried. The first body of rebel troops to break and fly was Gordon's Division, the same which had so perseveringly flanked us in the morning, and which was now flanked by our own first division of the Nineteenth Corps.

After this there was a lull in the assault, though not in the battle. The rebel artillery re-opened spitefully from a new position, and our musketry responded from the crest and wood which we had gained. Sheridan dashed along the front, re-organizing the line for a second charge, cheering the men with his confident smile and emphatic assurances of success, and giving his orders in person to brigade, division, and corps commanders. He took special pains with the direction of our first division, wheeling it in such a manner as to face square toward the pike, and form nearly a right angle to the enemy's front. Now came a second charge upon a

18

second line of stone walls, crests, and thickets, executed with as much enthusiasm and rapidity as if the army had just come into action. Remember that our gallant fellows had eaten nothing since the previous evening; that they had lost their canteens, and were tormented with thirst; that they had been fighting and manœuvring, frequently at double-quick, for nearly twelve hours; and that they were sadly diminished in numbers by the slaughter and confusion of the morning. Remember, too, that this lost battle was retrieved without a reinforcement. Only veterans, and only veterans of the best quality, disciplined, intelligent, and brave, could put forth such a supreme effort at the close of a long, bloody, and disastrous conflict. As one of Sheridan's staff officers followed up our first division, and watched the yelling, running, panting soldiers, not firing a shot, but simply dashing along with parched, open mouths, he said, "Those men are doing all that flesh and blood can."

"Your fellows on the right went in mighty pretty this afternoon," I heard Custer say that evening to Emory. "I had to sing out to my men, 'Are you going to let the infantry beat you?'"

Everybody now knows by reputation this brilliant officer, and can understand that we have a right to be proud of his praise.

The battle was over. Cavalry on the flanks, and infantry in the centre, we carried the second line with the same rush and with even greater ease than the first. Again Early's army was "whirling up the valley," in more hopeless confusion this time than after Winchester or Strasburg, no exertions of the rebel officers being sufficient to establish another line of resistance, or to check, even momentarily, the flow and spread of the panic. Colonel Love, of the One-hundred-and-sixteenth New York, dashed his horse into the broken ranks of the Second South Carolina, and captured its battle flag, escaping unhurt from the bullets of the color-guard. But the fighting soon swept far ahead of the tired infantry, which followed in perfect peace over the ground that during the morning it had stained with the blood of its retreat. Dead and wounded men, dead and wounded horses, dismounted guns, broken-down caissons, muskets with their stocks shivered and their barrels bent double by shot, splinters of shell, battered bullets, and blood over all, like a delirium of Lady Macbeth or the Chourineur, bore testimony to the desperate nature of the long, wide-spread conflict. The number of slaughtered horses was truly extraordinary, showing how largely the cavalry had been used, and how obstinately the artillery had been fought. I noticed that almost every dead soldier was covered by an overcoat or blanket, placed over him by some friend or perhaps brother. Of the wounded, a few lay quiet and silent; here and there one uttered wild, quavering cries expressive of intense agony or despair; others, and these the majority, groaned from time to time gently, and with a pitiful, patient courage. One man, whose light blue trowsers were clotted with that dull crimson so sickeningly common, and whose breath was short and voice hoarse, called feebly as we passed, "Hurrah for General Emory!"

"Are you badly hurt, my lad?" asked Emory, stopping his horse.

"My leg is broken by a rifle ball, general. I suppose I shall lose it. But I still feel—as if I could say—hurrah for General Emory. I fought under you—at Sabine Crossroads—and Pleasant Hill."

The general dismounted to give the sufferer a glass of whisky, and left a guard to see that he was put into an ambulance.

It was nearly dark when our corps reached its camps. No new arrangement of the line was attempted; in the twilight of evening the regiments filed into the same positions that they had quitted in the twilight of dawn; and the tired soldiers lay down to rest among dead comrades and dead enemies. They had lost every thing but what they bore on their backs or in their hands; their shelter-tents, knapsacks, canteens, and haversacks had been plundered by the rebels; and they slept that night, as they had fought that day, without food.

But there was no rest for the enemy or for our cavalry. All the way from our camps to Strasburg, a distance of four miles, the pike was strewn with the debris of a beaten army; and the scene in Strasburg itself was such a flood of confused flight and chase, such a chaos of wreck, and bedlam of panic, as no other defeat of the war can parallel. Guns, caissons, ammunition wagons, baggage wagons, and ambulances by the hundred, with dead or entangled and struggling horses, were jammed in the streets of the little town, impeding alike fugitives and pursuers. Our troopers dodged through the press as they best could, pistoling, sabreing, and taking prisoners. A private of the Fifth New York Cavalry riding up to a wagon, ordered the five rebels who were in it to surrender; and when they only lashed their horses into a wilder gallop he shot two with his revolver and brought in the three others. The usually gallant and elastic Southern infantry were so stupefied by fatigue and cowed by defeat that it seemed like a flock of animals, actually taking no notice of mounted men and officers from our army, who wandered into the wide confusion of its retreat. Lieutenant Gray, Company D, First Rhode Island Artillery, galloped up to a retreating battery and ordered it to face about. "I was told to go the rear as rapidly as possible," remonstrated the sergeant in command. "You don't seem to know who I am," answered Gray. "I am one of those d—d Yanks. Countermarch immediately!" The battery was countermarched, and Gray was leading it off alone, when a squadron of our cavalry came up and made the capture a certainty.

The victory was pushed, as Sheridan has pushed all his victories, to the utmost possible limit of success, the cavalry halting that night at Fisher's Hill, but starting again at dawn, and continuing the chase to Woodstock, sixteen miles from Middletown.

It was a gay evening at our headquarters, although we were worn out with fatigue, and as chilled, starved, and shelterless as the soldiers, our tents, baggage, rations, and cooks, having all gone to Winchester. Notwithstanding these discomforts, notwithstanding the thought of slain and wounded comrades, it was delightful to talk the whole day over, even of our defeat of the morning, because we could say, "All's well that ends well." It was laughable to think of the fugitives who had fled beyond the hearing of our victory, and who were now on their way to Martinsburg, spreading the news that Sheridan's army had been totally defeated, and that they (of course) were the only survivors. Then every half hour or so somebody galloped in from the advance with such a tale of continuing success that we could hardly grant our credence to it before a fresh messenger arrived, not so much to confirm the story as to exaggerate it.

It was "Hurrah! twenty cannon taken at Strasburg. That makes twenty-six so far."

"Glorious! Don't believe it. Isn't it splendid? Impossible! All our own back again," answered the contradictory chorus.

Then came another plunge of hoofs, reining up with another "Hurrah! forty-six guns! More wagons and ambulances than you can count!"

In truth the amount of material captured in this victory was extraordinary. Two days after the battle I saw near Sheridan's headquarters a row of forty-nine pieces of artillery, of which twenty-four had been lost by us and retaken, while the others were Early's own. In addition, the rebels lost fifty wagons, sixty-five ambulances (some of them marked "Stonewall Brigade"), sixteen hundred small arms, several battle flags, fifteen hundred prisoners, and probably two thousand killed and wounded. Our own losses were: Crook's command, one hundred killed and wounded, and seven hundred prisoners; the Ninteenth Corps, sixteen hundred killed and wounded, and one hundred prisoners; the Sixth Corps, thirteen hundred killed and wounded; total, three thousand eight hundred.

The only reinforcement which the Army of the

Shenandoah received, or needed to recover its lost field of battle, camps, intrenchments, and cannon was one man—SHERIDAN.

REFUSING TO VOLUNTEER IN THE REBEL ARMY.—In the same prison with Parson Brownlow and other Unionists in Tennessee, was a venerable clergyman, named Cate, and his three sons. One of them, James Madison Cate, a most exemplary and worthy member of the Baptist church, was there for having committed no other crime than that of refusing to volunteer in the rebel army. He lay stretched at full length upon the floor, with one thickness of a piece of carpet under him, and an old overcoat doubled up for a pillow—and he in the agonies of death. His wife came to visit him, bringing her youngest child, which was but a babe. They were refused admittance. Parson Brownlow here put his head out of the jail window, and entreated them, for God's sake, to let the poor woman come in, as her husband was dying. The jailer at last consented that she might see him for the limited time of fifteen minutes. As she came in, and looked upon her husband's wan and emaciated face, and saw how rapidly he was sinking, she gave evident signs of fainting, and would have fallen to the floor with the babe in her arms, had not Parson B. rushed up to her and seized the babe. Then she sank down upon the breast of her dying husband, unable to speak. When the fifteen minutes had expired, the officer came in, and in an insulting and peremptory manner notified her that the interview was to close.

NARRATIVE OF CAPTAIN JOHN F. PORTER, JR.,

FOURTEENTH NEW YORK CAVALRY—PARTICULARS OF HIS ESCAPE.

Captain John F. Porter, of the Fourteenth New York Cavalry, arrived in New York on Monday night, February 15th, 1864, from Washington, having escaped from Richmond, where he was a prisoner of war. Captain Porter was taken prisoner on the 15th of June, 1863, in the attack on Port Hudson. He was carried to Jackson, and thence conducted to the rebel capital, which he reached on the 29th of June. In Richmond, he was incarcerated in the now famous Libby prison.

Some two months previous to his escape, Captain Porter determined upon making such an attempt. He then tried to purchase a rebel uniform, but could not get it. At a later date, however, he succeeded in procuring rebel clothing, several brother officers in prison providing him with each article suitable for his purpose, which they possessed. Captain Porter was so emaciated from want of food and the sufferings while in prison, as well as a severe wound which he received at the second Bull Run, that he found much difficulty in walking; but after taking a little exercise daily, and gradually increasing the same, he soon found his strength increasing, and nerved himself to the task of an effort to escape.

On the morning of the 29th of last January, accompanied by Major E. L. Bates of the Eighteenth Illinois Volunteers, Captain Porter made his first attempt. He went down to the main entry of the prison and entered the surgeon's room. Here he informed the surgeon that he was attacked with chills, and so deceived this excellent medical gentleman that he gave him medicine for the disease. He next passed down into the room occupied by the commissary, shaved his beard and darkened his eyebrows and hair, thus disguising himself perfectly. Captain Porter did not then endeavor to pass out of the gate, but waited until three o'clock in the afternoon, which was the hour designated for roll-call. At this time he went into the middle room of the prison, and, roll-call being over, went down with the guard. Captain Porter then waited until the guard went into the building, and while a new one was being placed on duty, passed Post No. 1, down Carey street, in which Libby Prison is situated. Having got outside of the city limits, he suddenly stumbled against a battery, and, seeing a negro in the vicinity, asked the name of the battery, and was told it was No. 4. Passed out along the Nine Mile road, and, coming to a wood, stayed there over night, and returned to Richmond next morning, in order to await a more favorable opportunity for reaching the Union lines. In Richmond, Captain Porter now remained nine days without suspicion, during which time he passed around the entire fortifications of the city. At the end of that time he procured a passport from a rebel officer, and, in company with a family of Irish refugees, started for the Army of the Potomac. Arriving at Cat Tail Church, in Hanover county, the party were suddenly surrounded by rebel cavalry. Captain Porter's passport was rigorously examined, and his person robbed of one hundred dollars Confederate money, the rebels leaving him fifty in his possession. Two days after, having reached the Rappahannock, the river was crossed into Richmond county, and the party reached the banks of the Potomac on Thursday. They were secreted in the house of a Union gentleman until Friday night, who, for twenty dollars in gold, chartered a boat to carry them to Maryland. They were then landed at Clement's bay, St. Mary's county, Maryland. Captain Porter here fell in with a detachment of the Second, Fifth, and Sixth Regular Cavalry, and was by them escorted to Leonardtown. Here the escaped officer was provided with transportation to Point Lookout, where, on reporting to General Manton, he was sent on to Washington.

Major Bates, who escaped a few hours previous to Captain Porter, was subsequently recaptured.

Captain Porter says that the tunnel by which the last batch of officers made their escape from Libby Prison, was commenced on last New Year's Night. It extended from one of the lower rooms of the prison some two hundred yards into the street, opening on a vacant lot.

The Youngest Soldier in the Army of the Cumberland.—At the Caledonian supper in Cincinnati, Ohio, during December, 1863, General Rosecrans exhibited the photograph of a boy who he said was the youngest soldier in the Army of the Cumberland. His name is Johnny Clem, twelve years of age, a member of Company C, 22d Michigan Infantry. His home was at Newark, Ohio. He first attracted the attention of General Rosecrans during a review at Nashville, where he was acting as marker for his regiment. His extreme youth (he is quite small for his age) and intelligent appearance interested the general, and calling him to him he questioned him as to his name, age, regiment, etc. General Rosecrans spoke encouragingly to the young soldier, and told him to come and see him whenever he came where he was. He saw no more of the boy until the end of 1863, when he went to his place of residence—the Burnet House—and found Johnny Clem sitting on his sofa, waiting to see him. Johnny had experienced some of the vicissitudes of war since last they met. He had been captured by Wheeler's cavalry near Bridgeport. His captors took him to Wheeler, who saluted him with—

"What are you doing here, you d——d little Yankee scoundrel?"

Said Johnny Clem, stoutly: "General Wheeler, I am no more a d——d scoundrel than you are, sir."

Johnny said that the rebels stole about all that he had, including his pocket-book, which contained only twenty-five cents.

"But I wouldn't have cared for the rest," he added, "if they hadn't stolen my hat, which had three bullet holes it received at Chickamauga."

He was finally paroled and sent north. On Saturday he was on his way from Camp Chase to his regiment, having been exchanged. General Rosecrans observed that the young soldier had chevrons on his arm, and asked the meaning of it. He said he was promoted to a corporal for shooting a rebel colonel at Chickamauga. The colonel was mounted, and stopped Johnny at some point on the field, crying, "Stop, you little Yankee devil." Johnny halted, bringing his Australian rifle to an "order," thus throwing the colonel off his guard, cocked his piece (which he could easily do, being so short), and suddenly bringing his piece to his shoulder, fired, the colonel falling dead with a bullet through his breast.

The little fellow told his story simply and modestly, and the general determined to honor his bravery. He gave him the badge of the "Roll of Honor," which Mrs. Saunders, wife of the host of the Burnet House, sewed upon Johnny's coat. His eyes glistened with pride as he looked upon the badge, and little Johnny seemed suddenly to have grown an inch or two taller, he stood so erect. He left his photograph with General Rosecrans, who exhibits it with pride. We may hear again of Johnny Clem, the youngest soldier in the Army of the Cumberland.

"God's Flag:"—As one of the brigades of the reserve corps which came up to the rescue of General Thomas at Chickamauga was marching through the town of Athens, a bright-eyed girl of four summers was looking intently at the sturdy fellows as they tramped by. When she saw the sun glancing through the stripes of dazzling red and on the golden stars of the flag, she exclaimed, clapping her hands: "Oh, pa! pa! God made that flag! —see the stars!—it's God's flag!" A shout, deep and loud, went up from that column, and many a bronzed veteran lifted his hat as he passed the sunny-haired child of bright and happy thoughts, resolving, if his good right arm availed any thing, God's flag should conquer. What a sweet and happy christening the glorious ensign received from those artless lips—"God's flag!" and so it is.

HOW THE PRISONERS ESCAPED

FROM THE RICHMOND JAIL—INCREDIBLE UNDERGROUND WORK—FRIENDSHIP OF VIRGINIA NEGROES.

About the beginning of the year 1864 the officers confined in Libby Prison conceived the idea of effecting their own exchange, and after the matter had been seriously discussed by some seven or eight of them, they undertook to dig for a distance toward a sewer running into a basin. This they proposed doing by commencing at a point in the cellar near to the chimney. This cellar was immediately under the hospital, and was the receptacle for refuse straw, thrown from the beds when they were changed, and for other refuse matter. Above the hospital was a room for officers, and above that yet another room. The chimney ran through all these rooms, and prisoners who were in the secret, improvised a rope, and night after night let working parties down, who successfully prosecuted their excavating operations.

The dirt was hid under the straw and other refuse matter in the cellar, and it was trampled down to prevent too great a bulk. When the working party had got to a considerable distance underground, it was found difficult to haul the dirt back by hand, and a spittoon, which had been furnished the officers in one of the rooms, was made to serve the purpose of a cart. A string was attached to it, and it was run in the tunnel, and as soon as filled was drawn out and deposited under the straw. But after hard work, and digging with finger nails, knives, and chisels, a number of feet, the working party found themselves stopped by piles driven in the ground. These were at least a foot in diameter. But they were not discouraged. Penknives, or any other articles that would cut, were called for, and after chipping, chipping, chipping, for a long time, the piles were severed, and the tunnelers commenced again, after a time reaching the sewer.

But here an unexpected obstacle met their further progress. The stench from the sewer and the flow of filthy water was so great that one of the party fainted, and was dragged out more dead than alive, and the project in that direction had to be abandoned. The failure was communicated to a few others beside those who had first thought of escape, and then a party of seventeen, after viewing the premises and surroundings, concluded to tunnel under Carey street. On the opposite side of this street from the prison was a sort of carriage house or outhouse, and the project was to dig under the street, and emerge from under or near the house. There was a high fence around it, and the guard was outside of this fence. The prisoners then commenced to dig at the other side of the chimney, and after a few handfuls of dirt had been removed they found themselves stopped by a stone wall, which proved afterward to be three feet thick. The party were by no means daunted, and with pocket-knives and penknives they commenced operations upon the stone and mortar.

After nineteen days and nights at hard work they again struck the earth beyond the wall, and pushed their work forward. Here, too (after they got some distance under ground) the friendly spittoon was brought into requisition, and the dirt was hauled out in small quantities. After digging for some days the question arose whether they had not reached the point aimed at; and in order if possible to test the matter, Captain Gallagher, of the Second Ohio Regiment, pretended that he had a box in the carriage house over the way, and desired to search it out. This carriage house, it is proper to state, was used as a receptacle for boxes and goods sent to the prisoners from the North, and the recipients were often allowed to go, under guard, across the street to secure their property. Captain Gallagher was allowed permission to go there, and as he walked across under guard, he, as well as he could, paced off the distance, and concluded that the street was about fifty feet wide.

On the 6th or 7th of February the working party supposed they had gone a sufficient distance, and commenced to dig upward. When near the surface they heard the rebel guards talking above them, and discovered they were two or three feet yet outside the fence.

The displacing of a stone made considerable noise, and one of the sentinels called to his comrade and asked him what the noise meant. The guards, after listening a few minutes, concluded that nothing was wrong, and returned to their beats. The hole was stopped up by inserting into the crevice a pair of old pantaloons filled with straw, and bolstering the whole up with boards, which they secured from the floors, etc., of the prison. The tunnel was then continued some six or seven feet more, and when the working party supposed they were about ready to emerge to daylight, others in the prison were informed that there was a way now open for escape.

One hundred and nine of the prisoners decided to make the attempt to get away. Others refused, fearing the consequences if they were recaptured.

At half-past eight o'clock on the evening of the 9th the prisoners started out, Colonel Rose, of New York, leading the van. Before starting, the prisoners had divided themselves into squads of two, three, and four, and each squad was to take a different route, and after they were out were to push for the Union lines as fast as possible. It was the understanding that the working party were to have an hour's start of the other prisoners, and, consequently, the rope-ladder in the cellar was drawn out. Before the expiration of the hour, however, the other prisoners became impatient, and were let down through the chimney successfully into the cellar.

The aperture was so narrow that but one man could get through at a time, and each squad carried with them provisions in a haversack. At midnight a false alarm was created, and the prisoners made considerable noise in their quarters. Providentially, however, the guard suspected nothing wrong, and in a few moments the exodus was again commenced. Colonel Kendrick and his companions looked with some trepidation upon the movements of the fugitives, as some of them, exercising but little discretion, moved boldly out of the enclosure into the glare of the gaslight. Many of them were, however, in citizen's dress, and as all the rebel guards wore the United States uniform, but little suspicion could be excited, even if the fugitives had been accosted by a guard.

Between one and two o'clock the lamps were extinguished in the streets, and then the exit was more safely accomplished. There were many officers who desired to leave, who were so weak and feeble that they were dragged through the tunnel by mere force, and carried to places of security, until such time as they would be able to move on their journey. At half-past two o'clock, Captain Joyce, Colonel Kendrick, and Lieutenant Bradford passed out in the order in which they are named, and as Colonel Kendrick emerged from the hole he heard the guard within a few feet of him sing out: "Post No. 7, half-past two in the morning and all is well." Lieutenant Bradford was intrusted with the provisions for this squad, and in getting through was obliged to leave his haversack behind him, as he could not get through with it upon him.

Once out they proceeded up the street, keeping in the shade of the buildings, and passed eastwardly through the city.

A description of the route pursued by this party, and of the tribulations through which they passed, will give some idea of the rough time they all had of it. Colonel Kendrick had, before leaving the prison, mapped out his course, and concluded that the best route to take was the one toward Norfolk or Fortress Monroe, as there were fewer rebel pickets in that direction. They therefore kept the York River railroad to the left, and moved toward the Chickahominy river. They passed through Boar Swamp, and crossed the road leading to Bottom Bridge. Sometimes they waded through mud and water almost up to their necks, and kept the Bottom Bridge road to their left, although at times they could see and hear the cars travelling over the York River road.

While passing through the swamp near the Chickahominy, Colonel Kendrick sprained his ankle and fell. Fortunate, too, was that fall for him and his party, for while he was lying there one of them chanced to look up, and saw in a direct line with them a swamp bridge, and in the dim outline they could perceive that parties with muskets were passing over the bridge. They therefore moved some distance to the south, and after passing through more of the swamp, reached the Chickahominy about four miles below Bottom Bridge. Here now was a difficulty. The river was only twenty feet wide, but it was very deep, and the refugees were worn out and fatigued. Chancing, however, to look up, Lieutenant Bradford saw that two trees had fallen on either side of the river, and that their branches were interlocked. By crawling up one tree and down the other, the fugitives reached the east bank of the Chickahominy.

They subsequently learned from a friendly negro that, had they crossed the bridge they had seen, they would assuredly have been recaptured, for Captain Turner, the keeper of Libby Prison, had been out and posted guards there, and in fact had alarmed the whole country, and got the people up as a vigilant committee to capture the escaped prisoners.

After crossing over this natural bridge they laid down on the ground and slept until sunrise on the morning of the 11th, when they continued on their way, keeping eastwardly as near as they could. Up to this time they had had nothing to eat, and were almost famished.

About noon of the 11th they met several negroes, who gave them information as to the whereabouts of the rebel pickets, and furnished them with food.

Acting under the advice of these friendly negroes, they remained quietly in the woods until darkness had set in, when they were furnished with a comfortable supper by the negroes, and after dark proceeded on their way, the negroes (who everywhere showed their friendship to the fugitives) having first directed them how to avoid the rebel pickets. That night they passed a camp of rebels, and could plainly see the smoke and camp fires. But their wearied feet gave out, and they were compelled to stop and rest, having only marched five miles that day.

They started again at daylight on the 13th, and after moving awhile through the woods they saw a negro woman working in a field and called her to them. From her they received directions and were told that the rebel pickets had been about there looking for the fugitives from Libby. Here they laid down again, and resumed their journey when darkness set in, and marched five miles, but halted till the morning of the 14th, when the journey was resumed.

At one point they met a negress in a field, and she told them that her mistress was a secesh woman, and that she had a son in the rebel army. The party, however, were exceedingly hungry, and they determined to secure some food. This they did by boldly approaching the house and, informing the mistress that they were fugitives from Norfolk, who had been driven out by Butler; and the secesh sympathies of the woman were at once aroused, and she gave them of her substance, and started them on their way, with directions how to avoid the Yankee soldiers, who occasionally scouted in that vicinity. This information was exceedingly valuable to the refugees, for by it they discovered the whereabouts of the Federal forces.

When about fifteen miles from Williamsburg the party came upon the main road and found the tracks of a large body of cavalry. A piece of paper found by Captain Jones satisfied him that they were Union cavalry; but his companions were suspicious, and avoided the road and moved forward. At the "Burnt Ordinary" (about ten miles from Williamsburg) they awaited the return of the cavalry that had moved up the road, and from behind a fence corner, where they were secreted, the fugitives saw the flag of the Union, supported by a squadron of cavalry, which proved to be a detachment of Colonel Spear's 11th Pennsylvania Regiment, sent out for the purpose of picking up escaped prioners. Colonel Kendrick says his feelings at seeing the old flag are indescribable.

At all points along the route the fugitives describe their reception by the negroes as most enthusiastic, and there was no lack of white people who sympathized with them and helped them on their way.

In their escape the officers were aided by citizens of Richmond; not foreigners or the poor class only, but by natives and persons of wealth. They know their friends there, but very properly withhold any mention of their names. Of those who got out of Libby Prison there were a number of sick ones, who were cared for by Union people, and will eventually reach the Union lines through their aid.

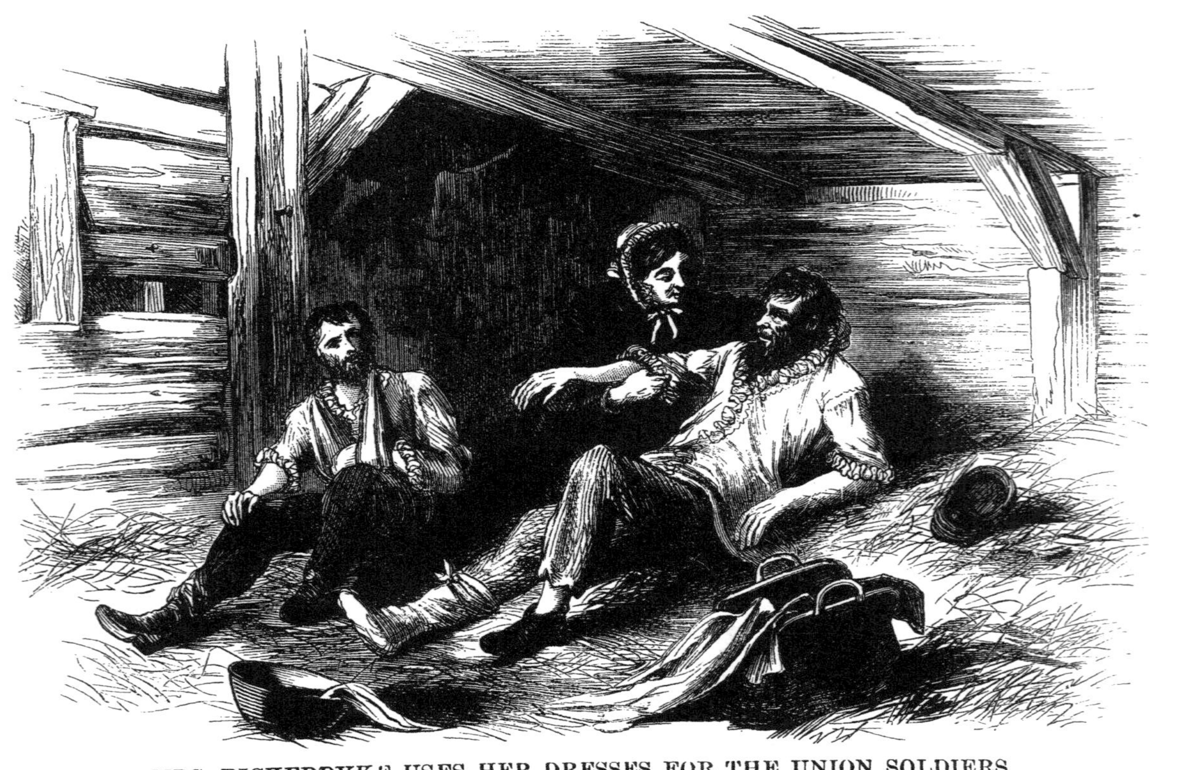

MRS. BICKERDYKE USES HER DRESSES FOR THE UNION SOLDIERS.

PART III.

INCIDENTS
OF
ARMY LIFE IN CAMP, FIELD, AND HOSPITAL.

MOTHER BICKERDYKE, "THE SOLDIERS' FRIEND."

AMONG the many noble women who have contributed so largely to the comfort of our sick, wounded, and exhausted soldiers in the Western armies, there is none more deserving the title of the "Soldier's Friend" than Mrs. Bickerdyke. She is of humble origin, and of but moderate education, a widow, with two noble and beautiful little boys, somewhat more than forty years of age, we should judge, with a robust frame and great powers of endurance, and possesses a rough, stirring eloquence, and earnestness of manner which has proved very effective in carrying measures on which she has set her heart.

At the commencement of the war, she was, we have heard, housekeeper in a gentleman's family in Cleveland, but she commenced very early her labors of love and kindness among the sick and wounded men of the army, and continued them with ever increasing success till the close of the conflict. It has been one of her peculiarities that she devoted her attention exclusively or nearly so to the private soldiers. The officers, she said, had enough to look after them; but it was the men, poor fellows, with but a private's pay, a private's fare, and a private's dangers, to whom she was particularly called. They were dear to somebody, and she would be a mother to them. And throughout the war, she has contended stoutly and almost always successfully for their rights and comfort. The soldiers all over the Western armies knew her and fairly idolized her, as well they might. But woe to the surgeon or assistant surgeon, the commissary or quartermaster, whose neglect of his men and selfish disregard for their interests and needs came under her cognizance. For such a one she had no mercy, and in more instances than one, by the fierce torrent of her invective, or the more effective method of appealing to the commander of the army, with whom she always had great influence, she procured their dismissal from the service. Her will was strong, and when she had determined to do a thing it would be carried through, whatever obstacles might present themselves; yet while officers even of high rank stood appalled and yielded to her commands, urged as they often were in a tone and manner which brooked no denial, she was gentle and tender as a mother to the common soldiers. The contrabands regarded her as almost a divinity, and would fly with unwonted alacrity to obey her commands. Her authority, however, great as it was, was used most beneficently; and with every day her influence was greater with the commanding generals, who saw, in her, an instrument of great good to the army. At Perryville she set the negro women to gathering the blankets and clothing left upon that bloody field, and such of the clothing of the slain and desperately wounded as could be spared, and having had it carefully washed and repaired, distributed it to the wounded, who were in great need of additional clothing. The arms left on the field were also picked up by her corps of contrabands and delivered over to the Union quartermaster. Not long after she was put in charge of the Gayoso Hospital, in what was formerly the Gayoso Hotel, one of the largest hotels in Memphis. Here she was in all her glory. It was her ambition to make her hospital the best regulated, neatest, and most comfortable in Memphis or its vicinity, and this, in such a building, was not easy. She accomplished it, however. It was usual in the hospitals there as elsewhere to employ convalescent soldiers as nurses, ward masters, etc., for the drudgery of the hospital; and as these were often weak, and occasionally peevish and ill-tempered from their own past or present sufferings, it may be imagined that they did not always make the best of nurses. Mrs. Bickerdyke substituted negro women for these duties, and the improvement was speedily manifest. Herself a skilful and admirable cook, she superintended the preparation of all the food for the sick or wounded, and often administered it in person. Nothing displeased her so much as any neglect of the men on the part of the surgeon or assistant surgeons. On one occasion, visiting one of the wards at nearly eleven o'clock A. M., where the men were very badly wounded, she found that the assistant surgeon-in-charge, who had been out "on a spree" the night before and had slept very late, had not yet made out the special diet list for the ward, and the men, faint and hungry, had had no breakfast. She at once denounced him in the strongest terms.

He came in meanwhile, and on his inquiry, "Hoity toity, what's the matter?" she turned upon him with, "Matter enough, you miserable scoundrel! Here these men, any one of them worth a thousand of you, are suffered to starve and die, because you want to be off upon a drunk! Pull off your shoulder-straps," she continued, as he tried feebly to laugh off her reproaches, "pull off your shoulder-straps, for you shall not stay in the army a week longer." The surgeon still laughed, but he turned pale, for he knew her power. She was as good as her word. Within three days, she had caused his discharge. He went to headquarters, and asked to be reinstated. General Sherman, who was then in command, listened patiently, and then inquired who had caused his discharge. "I was discharged in consequence of misrepresentations," answered the surgeon, evasively. "But who caused your discharge?" persisted the general. "Why," said the surgeon, hesitatingly, "I suppose it was that woman, that Mrs. Bickerdyke." "Oh," said Sherman. "Well, if it was her, I can do nothing for you. She ranks me."

Some months later, the chief surgeon of the hospital, a martinet in discipline, was dissatisfied at Mrs. Bickerdyke's innovations, though he acknowledged the admirable order and neatness of the hospital; he knew that she valued highly her well trained corps of negro women employed as nurses, etc., in the hospital, and he, therefore, procured from the medical director an order that none but convalescent soldiers should be employed as nurses in the Memphis hospitals. The order was to take effect at nine o'clock the following morning. Mrs. Bickerdyke heard of it just at night. The Gayoso Hospital

MRS. BICKERDYKE AND THE UNFAITHFUL SURGEON.

was three fourths of a mile from headquarters; it was raining heavily, and the mud was deep; but nothing daunted, she sallied out, having first had the form of an order drawn up permitting the employment of contrabands as nurses at the Gayoso Hospital. Arrived at the headquarters, she was told that the commanding general, Sherman's successor, was ill, and could not be seen. She understood very well that his illness was only intoxication, and insisted that she must and would see him, and, in spite of the objections of the staff officers, she forced her way to his room, and, finding him in bed, roused him partially, propped him up, put a pen in his hand, and made him sign the order she had brought. This done, she returned to her hospital, and the next morning, when the surgeon and the medical director came round to enforce the order of the latter, she flourished in their faces the order of the commanding general, permitting her to retain her contrabands.

While in charge of this hospital, she made several journeys to Chicago, and other cities of the northwest, to procure aid for the suffering soldiers. The first of these was characteristic of her energy and resolution. She had found great difficulty in procuring, in the vicinity of Memphis, the milk and butter needed for her hospital, and the other hospitals had also been but scantily supplied. She resolved to have a dairy for the hospitals, and going among the farmers of central Illinois she begged two hundred cows, and as eggs were required in large quantities she obtained also, by her solicitations, a thousand hens, and returned in triumph with her drove of cows and her flock of hens. On reaching Memphis her cattle and fowls made such a lowing and cackling that the rebel sympathizing inhabitants of the city entered their complaints, and the commanding general assigned her an island in the Mississippi opposite the city, where her dairy and hennery were comfortably accommodated.

We are not certain whether it was on this journey or the next that, at the request of Mrs. Hage and Mrs. Lovemore, of the Northwestern Sanitary Commission, she visited Milwaukee. The Ladies' Aid Society of that city had memorialized the Chamber of Commerce of the city to make an appropriation to aid them in their efforts for helping the soldiers, and were that day to receive the reply of the Chamber. Mrs. Bickerdyke went with the ladies, and the President of the Chamber, in his blandest tones, informed them that the Chamber of Commerce had considered their request, but that they had expended so much in the fitting out of a regiment, that they thought they must be excused from making any contributions to the Ladies' Aid Society. Mrs. Bickerdyke asked the privilege of replying. For half an hour she held them enchained, while she described, in simple but eloquent language, the life of the soldier, his privations and sufferings, the patriotism which animated him, and led him to endure, without murmuring, hardships, sickness, wounds, and even death itself, for his country. She contrasted this with the sordid love of gain which not only shrunk from these sacrifices in person, but grudged the pittance necessary to alleviate them, and made the trifling amount which it had already contributed an excuse for making no further contributions, and closed with this forcible denunciation: "And you, merchants and rich men of Milwaukee, living at your ease, dressed in your broadcloth, knowing little and caring less for the sufferings of the soldiers, from hunger and thirst, from cold and nakedness, from sickness and wounds, from pain and death, all incurred that you may roll in wealth, and your homes and your little ones be safe. You will refuse to give aid to these poor soldiers, because, forsooth, you gave a few dollars some time ago to fit out a regiment. Shame on you—you are not men—you are cowards—go over to Canada—this country has no place for such creatures!" The Chamber of Commerce was not prepared for such a rebuke, and they reconsidered their action, and made an appropriation at once to the Ladies' Aid Society.

When Rosecrans moved forward from Murfreesboro in June, 1863, Mrs. Bickerdyke, tired of the confinement of the hospital, joined the army in the field again, and amid all the hardships and exposures of the field, ministered to the sick and wounded. Cooking for them in the open air, under the burning sun and the heavy dews, she was exposed to disease, but her admirable constitution enabled her to endure fatigue and exposure, better even than most of the soldiers. Though neat and cleanly in person, she was wholly indifferent to the attractions of dress, and amid the flying sparks from her fires in the open air, her calico dresses would often take fire, and as she expressed it, "the soldiers would put her out;" *i. e.*, extinguish the sparks which were burning her dresses, till they became completely riddled.

It was with her clothing in this plight that she again visited Chicago, in the summer of 1863, and the ladies of the Sanitary Commission replenished her wardrobe, and soon after sent her a box of excellent clothing for her own use. Of this, some articles, the gift of those who admired her earnest devotion to the interests of the soldier, were richly wrought and trimmed. Among them were two beautiful night-dresses, trimmed with ruffles and lace. On receiving the box, Mrs. Bickerdyke, who was again for the time in charge of a hospital, reserving for herself only three or four of the plainest and cheapest articles, traded off the remainder, except the two night-dresses, with the rebel women of the vicinity, for butter, eggs, and other delicacies for her sick soldiers; and as she purposed going to Cairo soon, and thought that the night-dresses would bring more for the same purpose in Kentucky, she reserved them to be traded on her journey. On her way, however, at one of the towns on the Mobile and Ohio railroad (Jackson, we believe), she found two poor fellows who had been discharged from some of our hospitals with their wounds not yet fully healed, and their exertions had caused them to break out afresh. Here they were, then, in a miserable shanty, sick, bleeding, hungry, penniless, and with only their soiled clothing. Mrs. Bickerdyke at once took them in hand. Washing their wounds and stanching the blood, she tore off the lower portions of the night-dresses for bandages, and as the men had no shirts, she arrayed them in the remainder of these dresses, ruffles, lace, and all. The soldiers modestly demurred a little at the ruffles and lace, but Mrs. Bickerdyke suggested to them that if any inquiries were made, they could say that they had been plundering the secessionists.

Visiting Chicago at this time, she was again invited to go to Milwaukee, and went with the ladies to the Chamber of Commerce. Here she was very politely received, and the President informed her that the Chamber, feeling deeply impressed with the good work she and the other ladies were doing in behalf of the soldiers, had voted a contribution of twelve hundred dollars a month to the "Ladies' Aid Society." Mrs. Bickerdyke was not, however, disposed to tender them the congratulations to which perhaps they believed themselves entitled for their liberality. "You believe yourselves very generous, no doubt, gentlemen," she said, "and think that because you have given this pretty sum, you are doing all that is required of you. But I have in my hospital a hundred poor soldiers, who have done more than any of you. Who of you would contribute a leg, an arm, or an eye, instead of what you have done? How many hundred or thousand dollars would you consider an equivalent for either? Don't deceive yourselves, gentlemen. The poor soldier who has given an arm, a leg, or an eye to his country (and many of them have given more than one), has given more than you have, or can. How much more, then, he who has given his life? No! gentlemen, you must set your standard higher yet, or you will not come up to the full measure of liberality in giving."

Mrs. Bickerdyke was on the field in the battles of November, 1863, around Chattanooga, and in the hospitals of Chattanooga during the winter. In May, 1864, she and Mrs. Porter, of Chicago, both in the service of the Northwestern Sanitary Commission, followed Sherman's Army in the march to Atlanta; being present at every battle, and ministering to the wounded and the exhausted soldiers. Her great executive ability had fair play here, and with few or none of the ordinary apparatus for cooking, or preparing needed dishes for the sick, she would manage to make barrels of delicious coffee, manufacture panada and gruel out of hard tack, and other food for the sick from the most unpromising materials.

It is said that soon after General Grant took command at Chattanooga, in the autumn of 1863, she visited his headquarters, and in her rough, blunt way, said to him, "Now, General, don't be a fool. You want your men to do a great deal of hard fighting, but the surgeons here, in the hospitals, are neglecting them shamefully, and you will lose hundreds of men who would do you good service unless you see to it yourself. Disguise yourself so that the surgeons or men won't know you, and go around to the hospitals and see for yourself how the men are neglected."

"But, Mrs. Bickerdyke," said the general, "that is the business of my medical director, he must attend to that. I can't see to every thing in person."

"Well," was her reply, "leave it to him if you think best; but if you do, you will lose your men."

The general made no promises, but a night or two later the hospitals were visited by a stranger, who made very particular inquiries, and within a week nearly half a dozen surgeons were dismissed, and more efficient men put in their places.

After the capture of Atlanta, Mrs. Bickerdyke returned northward, stopping for a time, we believe, at Nashville. In January, 1865, she went to Savannah to superintend one of the hospitals there.

Generous to a fault, Mrs. Bickerdyke has never been influenced, even in the slightest degree, by mercenary motives. Much of her service has been rendered without fee or reward, and when the necessity of providing for the care and education of her boys has compelled her to receive compensation, it has been only in such amount as would suffice for that purpose. Yet her eminent services, many of them such as none but herself could have rendered, richly deserve a noble testimonial.

THE ROMANCE OF WAR.—The following order is said to have originated at the headquarters of that correct disciplinarian, Major-General Rosecrans:—

"HEADQUARTERS DEPARTMENT OF THE CUMBERLAND, *April* 17, 1863.

"GENERAL:—The general commanding directs me to call your attention to a flagrant outrage committed in your command—a person having been admitted inside your lines without a pass and in violation of orders. The case is one which calls for your personal attention, and the general commanding directs that you deal with the offending party or parties according to law.

"The medical director reports that an orderly sergeant in Brigadier-General ——'s division *was to-day delivered of a baby*—which is in violation of all military law and of the army regulations. No such case has been known since the days of Jupiter.

"You will apply the proper punishment in this case, and a remedy to prevent a repetition of the act."

THE DEATH OF JOHN,

THE WEST VIRGINIA BLACKSMITH.

MISS L. M. ALCOTT, the accomplished daughter of A. B. Alcott, the Concord philosopher, and the bosom friend of Ralph Waldo Emerson, was for a time a nurse in one of the hospitals for the wounded in the vicinity of Washington, D. C. She subsequently published a little volume, entitled "Hospital Sketches," in which the life, heroism, and death of some of our brave fellows, wounded in the struggle for the nation's life, are portrayed with a graphic power which has never been surpassed. Among these descriptions of life and death in the hospital, none surpasses, in beauty and pathos, the story of John, the West Virginia Blacksmith. Miss Alcott is in one of the wards of the hospital, ministering to the sick, when a messenger from another ward comes in with the expected yet dreaded message:

"John is going, ma'am, and wants to see you if you can come."

"The moment this boy is asleep; tell him so, and let me know if I am in danger of being too late."

The messenger departed, and while I quieted poor Shaw, I thought of John. He came in a day or two after the others; and one evening, when I entered my "pathetic room," I found a lately emptied bed occupied by a large, fair man, with a fine face, and the serenest eyes I ever met. One of the earlier comers had often spoken of a friend who had remained behind that those apparently worse wounded than himself might reach a shelter first. It seemed a David and Jonathan sort of friendship. The man fretted for his mate, and was never tired of praising John—his courage, sobriety, self-denial, and unfailing kindliness of heart; always winding up with: "He's an out an' out fine feller, ma'am; you see if he aint."

I had some curiosity to behold this piece of excellence, and when he came, watched him for a night or two, before I made friends with him; for, to tell the truth, I was a little afraid of the stately looking man, whose bed had to be lengthened to accommodate his commanding stature; who seldom spoke, uttered no complaint, asked no sympathy, but tranquilly observed what went on about him; and, as he lay high upon his pillows, no picture of dying statesman or warrior was ever fuller of real dignity than this Virginia blacksmith. A most attractive face he had, framed in brown hair and beard, comely featured and full of vigor, as yet unsubdued by pain; thoughtful and often beautifully mild while watching the afflictions of others, as if entirely forgetful of his own. His mouth was grave and firm, with plenty of will and courage in its lines, but a smile could make it as sweet as any woman's; and his eyes were child's eyes, looking one fairly in the face with a clear, straightforward glance, which promised well for such as placed their faith in him. He seemed to cling to life as if it were rich in duties and delights, and he had learned the secret of content. The only time I saw his composure disturbed, was when my surgeon brought another to examine John, who scrutinized their faces with an anxious look, asking of the elder: "Do you think I shall pull through, sir?" "I hope so, my man." And, as the two passed on, John's eye still followed them, with an intentness which would have won a clearer answer from them, had they seen it. A momentary shadow flitted over his face; then came the usual serenity, as if, in that brief eclipse, he had acknowledged the existence of some hard possibility, and, asking nothing yet hoping all things, left the issue in God's hands, with that submission which is true piety.

The next night, as I went my rounds with Dr. P., I happened to ask which man in the room probably suffered most; and, to my great surprise, he glanced at John:

"Every breath he draws is like a stab; for the ball pierced the left lung, broke a rib, and did no end of damage here and there; so the poor lad can find neither forgetfulness nor ease, because he must lie on his wounded back or suffocate. It will be a hard struggle, and a long one, for he possesses great vitality; but even his temperate life can't save him; I wish it could."

"You don't mean he must die, doctor?"

"Bless you, there's not the slightest hope for him; and you'd better tell him so before long; women have a way of doing such things comfortably, so I leave it to you. He wont last more than a day or two, at furthest."

I could have sat down on the spot and cried heartily, if I had not learned the wisdom of bottling up one's tears for leisure moments. Such an end seemed very hard for such a man, when half a dozen worn-out, worthless bodies round him, were gathering up the remnants of wasted lives, to linger on for years, perhaps, burdens to others, daily reproaches to themselves. The army needed men like John, earnest, brave, and faithful; fighting for liberty and justice with both heart and hand, true soldiers of the Lord. I could not give him up so soon, or think with any patience of so excellent a nature robbed of its fulfilment, and blundered into eternity by the rashness or stupidity of those at whose hands so many lives may be required. It was an easy thing for Dr. P. to say: "Tell him he must die," but a cruelly hard thing to do, and by no means as "comfortable" as he politely suggested. I had not the heart to do it then, and privately indulged the hope that some change for the better might take place, in spite of gloomy prophecies, so rendering my task unnecessary. A few minutes later, as I came in again, with fresh rollers, I saw John sitting erect, with no one to support him, while the surgeon dressed his back. I had never hitherto seen it done; for, having simpler wounds to attend to, and knowing the fidelity of the attendant, I had left John to him, thinking it might be more agreeable and safe; for both strength and experience were needed in his case. I had forgotten that the strong man might long for the gentler tendance of a woman's hands, the sympathetic magnetism of a woman's presence, as well as the feebler souls about him. The doctor's words caused me to reproach myself with neglect, not of any real duty, perhaps, but of those little cares and kindnesses that solace homesick spirits, and make the heavy hours pass easier. John looked lonely and forsaken just then, as he sat with bent head, hands folded on his knee, and no outward sign of suffering, till, looking nearer, I saw great tears roll down and drop upon the floor. It was a new sight there; for, though I had seen many suffer, some swore, some groaned, most endured silently, but none wept. Yet it did not seem weak, only very touching, and straightway my fear vanished, my heart opened wide and took him in, as gathering the bent head in my arms, as freely as if he had been a little child, I said, "Let me help you bear it, John."

Never, on any human countenance, have I seen so swift and beautiful a look of gratitude, surprise, and comfort, as that which answered me more eloquently than the whispered—

"Thank you, ma'am; this is right good! this is what I wanted!"

"Then why not ask for it before?"

"I didn't like to be a trouble; you seemed so busy, and I could manage to get on alone."

"You shall not want it any more, John."

Nor did he; for now I understood the wistful look that sometimes followed me, as I went out, after a brief pause beside his bed, or merely a passing nod, while busied with those who seemed to need me more than he, because more urgent in their demands; now I knew that to him, as to so many, I was the poor substitute for mother, wife, or sister, and in his eyes no stranger, but a friend who hitherto had seemed neglectful; for, in his modesty he had never guessed the truth. This was changed now; and, through the tedious operation of probing, bathing, and dressing his wounds, he leaned against me, holding my hand fast, and, if pain wrung further tears from him, no one saw them fall but me. When he was laid down again, I hovered about him, in a remorseful state of mind that would not let me rest, till I had bathed his face, brushed his "bonny brown hair," set all things smooth about him, and laid a knot of heath and heliotrope on his clean pillow. While doing this, he watched me with the satisfied expression I so liked to see; and when I offered the little nosegay held it carefully in his great hand, smoothed a ruffled leaf or two, surveyed and smelt it with an air of genuine delight, and lay contentedly regarding the glimmer of the sunshine on the green. Although the manliest man among my forty, he said, "Yes, ma'am," like a little boy; received suggestions for his comfort with the quick smile that brightened his whole face; and now and then, as I stood tidying the table by his bed, I felt him softly touch my gown, as if to assure himself that I was there. Any thing more natural and frank I never saw, and found this brave John as bashful as brave, yet full of excellencies and fine aspirations, which, having no power to express themselves in words, seemed to have bloomed into his character and made him what he was.

After that night, an hour of each evening that remained to him was devoted to his ease or pleasure. He could not talk much, for breath was precious, and he spoke in whispers; but from occasional conversations, I gleaned scraps of private history which only added to the affection and respect I felt for him. Once he asked me to write a letter, and as I settled pen and paper, I said, with an irrepressible glimmer of feminine curiosity, "Shall it be addressed to wife or mother, John?"

"Neither, ma'am; I've got no wife, and will write to

mother myself when I get better. Did you think I was married because of this?" he asked, touching a plain ring he wore, and often turned thoughtfully on his finger when he lay alone.

"Partly that, but more from a settled sort of look you have, a look which young men seldom get until they marry."

"I don't know that; but I'm not so very young, ma'am, thirty in May, and have been what you might call settled this ten years; for mother's a widow, I'm the oldest child she has, and it wouldn't do for me to marry until Lizzy has a home of her own, and Laurie's learned his trade; for we're not rich, and I must be father to the children and husband to the dear old woman, if I can."

"No doubt but you are both, John; yet how came you to go to war, if you felt so? Wasn't enlisting as bad as marrying?"

"No, ma'am, not as I see it, for one is helping my neighbor, the other pleasing myself. I went because I couldn't help it. I didn't want the glory or the pay; I wanted the right thing done, and people kept saying the men who were in earnest ought to fight. I was in earnest, the Lord knows! but I held off as long as I could, not knowing which was my duty; mother saw the case, gave me her ring to keep me steady, and said 'Go:' so I went."

A short story and a simple one, but the man and the mother were portrayed better than pages of fine writing could have done it.

"Do you ever regret that you came, when you lie here suffering so much?"

"Never, ma'am; I haven't helped a great deal, but I've shown I was willing to give my life, and perhaps I've got to; but I don't blame anybody, and if it was to do over again, I'd do it. I'm a little sorry I wasn't wounded in front; it looks cowardly to be hit in the back, but I obeyed orders, and it don't matter in the end, I know."

Poor John! it did not matter now, except that a shot in front might have spared the long agony in store for him. He seemed to read the thoughts that troubled me, as he spoke so hopefully when there was no hope, for he suddenly added:

"This is my first battle; do they think it's going to be my last?"

"I'm afraid they do, John."

It was the hardest question I had ever been called upon to answer; doubly hard with those clear eyes fixed on mine, forcing a truthful answer by their own truth. He seemed a little startled at first, pondered over the fateful fact a moment, then shook his head, with a glance at the broad chest and muscular limbs stretched out before him:

"I'm not afraid, but it's difficult to believe all at once. I am so strong it don't seem possible for such a little wound to kill me."

Merry Mercutio's dying words glanced through my memory as he spoke: "'Tis not so deep as a well, nor so wide as a church door, but 'tis enough." And John would have said the same could he have seen the ominous black holes between his shoulders: he never had; and, seeing the ghastly sights about him, could not believe his own wound more fatal than these, for all the suffering it caused him.

"Shall I write to your mother, now?" I asked, thinking that these sudden tidings might change all plans and purposes; but they did not; for the man received the order of the Divine Commander to march with the same unquestioning obedience with which the soldier had received that of the human one, doubtless remembering that the first led him to life and the last to death.

"No, ma'am; to Laurie just the same; he'll break it to her best, and I'll add a line to her myself when you get done."

So I wrote the letter which he dictated, finding it better than any I had sent; for, though here and there a little ungrammatical or inelegant, each sentence came to me briefly worded, but most expressive; full of excellent counsel to the boy, tenderly bequeathing "mother and Lizzie" to his care, and bidding him good-by in words the sadder for their simplicity. He added a few lines, with steady hand, and, as I sealed it, said, with a patient sort of sigh, "I hope the answer will come in time for me to see it;" then, turning away his face, laid the flowers against his lips, as if to hide some quiver of emotion at the thought of such a sudden sundering of all the dear home ties.

These things had happened two days before; now John was dying, and the letter had not come. I had been summoned to many death-beds in my life, but to none that made my heart ache as it did then, since my mother called me to watch the departure of a spirit akin to this in its gentleness and patient strength. As I went in, John stretched out both hands:

"I knew you'd come! I guess I'm moving on, ma'am."

He was; and so rapidly that, even while he spoke, over his face I saw the gray vail falling that no human hand can lift. I sat down by him, wiped the drops from his forehead, stirred the air about him with the slow wave of a fan, and waited to help him die. He stood in sore need of help—and I could do so little; for, as the doctor had foretold, the strong body rebelled against death, and fought every inch of the way, forcing him to draw each breath with a spasm, and clench his hands with an imploring look, as if he asked, "How long must I endure this and be still!" For hours he suffered dumbly, without a moment's respite, or a moment's murmuring; his limbs grew cold, his face damp, his lips white, and again and again he tore the covering off his breast, as if the lightest weight added to his agony; yet through it all his eyes never lost their perfect serenity, and the man's soul seemed to sit therein, undaunted by the ills that vexed his flesh.

One by one the men woke, and round the room appeared a circle of pale faces and watchful eyes, full of awe and pity; for, though a stranger, John was beloved by all. Each man there had wondered at his patience, respected his piety, admired his fortitude, and now lamented his hard death; for the influence of an upright nature had made itself deeply felt, even in one little week. Presently, the Jonathan who so loved this comely David came creeping from his bed for a last look and word. The kind soul was full of trouble, as the choke in his voice, the grasp of his hand, betrayed;

but there were no tears, and the farewell of the friends was the more touching for its brevity.

"Old boy, how are you?" faltered the one

"Most through, thank heaven!" whispered the other.

"Can I say or do any thing for you anywheres?"

"Take my things home, and tell them that I did my best."

"I will! I will!"

"Good-by, Ned."

"Good-by, John, good-by!"

They kissed each other, tenderly as women, and so parted, for poor Ned could not stay to see his comrade die. For a little while, there was no sound in the room but the drip of water from a stump or two and John's distressful gasps, as he slowly breathed his life away. I thought him nearly gone, and had just laid down the fan, believing its help to be no longer neded, when suddenly he rose up in his bed, and cried out with a bitter cry that broke the silence, sharply startling every one with its agonized appeal:

"For God's sake, give me air!"

It was the only cry pain or death had wrung from him, the only boon he had asked; and none of us could grant it, for all the airs that blew were useless now. Dan flung up the window. The first red streak of dawn was warming the gray east, a herald of the coming sun; John saw it, and with the love of light which lingers in us to the end, seemed to read in it a sign of hope of help, for over his whole face there broke that mysterious expression, brighter than any smile, which often comes to eyes that look their last. He laid himself gently down, and stretching out his strong right arm, as if to grasp and bring the blessed air to his lips in a fuller flow, lapsed into a merciful unconsciousness, which assured us that for him suffering was forever past. He died then; for, though the heavy breaths still tore their way up for a little longer, they were but the waves of an ebbing tide that beat unfelt against the wreck, which an immortal voyager had deserted with a smile. He never spoke again, but to the end held my hand close, so close that when he was asleep at last, I could not draw it away Dan helped me, warning me, as he did so, that it was unsafe for dead and living flesh to lie so long together; but though my hand was strangely cold and stiff, and four white marks remained across its back, even when warmth and color had returned elsewhere, I could not but be glad that through its touch, the presence of human sympathy, perhaps, had lightened that hard hour.

When they had made him ready for the grave, John lay in state for half an hour, a thing which seldom happened in that busy place; but a universal sentiment of reverence and affection seemed to fill the hearts of all who had known or heard of him; and when the rumor of his death went through the house, always astir, many came to see him, and I felt a tender sort of pride in my lost patient; for he looked a most heroic figure, lying there stately and still as the statue of some young knight asleep upon his tomb. The lovely expression which so often beautifies dead faces, soon replaced the marks of pain, and I longed for those who loved him best to see him when half an hour's acquaintance with Death had made them friends. As we stood looking at him, the ward master handed me a letter, saying it had been forgotten the night before. It was John's letter, come just an hour too late to gladden the eyes that had longed and looked for it so eagerly: yet he had it; for, after I had cut some brown locks for his mother, and taken off the ring to send her, telling how well the talisman had done its work, I kissed this good son for her sake, and laid the letter in his hand, still folded as when I drew my own away, feeling that its place was there, and making myself happy with the thought, that even in his solitary place in the "Government Lot," he would not be without some token of the love which makes life beautiful and outlives death. Then I left him, glad to have known so genuine a man, and carrying with me an enduring memory of the brave Viginia blacksmith, as he lay serenely waiting for the dawn of that long day which knows no night.

ROBINSON, THE WOUNDED SOLDIER.

Miss Dunlap, a Philadelphia lady, who devoted herself with great assiduity to the care of the wounded soldiers in the hospitals, which were so numerous around that city, has related some incidents of her experience in the hospitals in a most charming volume, entitled "Notes of Hospital Life," a work deserving of much wider circulation than it received.

Among these incidents there is perhaps none more touching than those she relates concerning Robinson, a soldier of the Army of the Potomac, wounded at Fair Oaks, May 31, 1862, and whom soon after that battle she found in one of the wards of the hospital she was most accustomed to visit, with his arm bandaged from shoulder to finger-tip, and who was whistling a bright, cheerful tune in a voice of uncommon sweetness. Coming up to him, she said, "I am glad you can whistle: it shows you are not suffering so much as I feared when I saw your bandages."

He smiled, but said nothing; and she noticed, as she came closer, that large drops of perspiration were standing in beads upon his brow; his one free hand was tightly clenched, and a nervous tremor ran over his whole frame.

One of the patients in a neighboring bed, who had become somewhat acquainted with Miss Dunlap, now spoke:

"Ah, miss, you don't know Robinson yet; he's a new fellow, and we all laugh at him here; he says when the pain's just so bad he can't bear it nohow, he tries to whistle with all his might, and he finds it does him good."

"Whether," says Miss Dunlap, "from the suspension of this novel remedy for acute suffering, or a sudden increase of pain, I cannot tell; but, as I turn to Robinson for a confirmation of this singular statement, the large tears are in his eyes, and roll slowly down his cheeks. He tries to smile, however, and says:

"'Oh, yes; it does help me wonderfully; it kind of makes me forget the pain, and think I'm at home again, where I'm always whistling. Nothing like keeping up a good heart. It don't always ache like this—only in spells—it'll stop after a bit. Never mind me, ma'am, I'm not half so bad as poor Darlington there.'"

The gentle, unselfish, and patient sufferer who could

thus attempt to subdue and control the anguish of his wounds, by whistling up the bright memories of home, soon became a prime favorite in the hospital, where he was long detained by the severity of his wounds. "His left arm," says Miss Dunlap, "was terribly shattered, just below the shoulder, and injuring the shoulder blade; and for a long time his case was a very critical one, requiring the most close and constant watching. He was entirely confined to his bed for many tedious weeks, and yet I know not why I should apply that term to the time so passed; for they were certainly never 'tedious' to us, although we felt great anxiety for him, and we never had any proof that they were so to him. Patient and uncomplaining, the only sign he gave of suffering, save the contraction of his brow, was the constant effort to whistle away the pain, and his moans in his sleep. There was always something inexpressibly sad to me in these moans; it seemed as though the body were compensating itself, during sleep, for the powerful restraint imposed upon it during waking hours.

"I have rarely seen greater unselfishness in any one. During his illness, it was all-important to keep up his strength, for as the wound began to heal, one abscess followed another, and kept him much prostrated; we, therefore, tried to tempt his appetite in every way; and often, when I have brought him some delicacy, he has pointed me to some one near him, with the words: 'Please give it to him; he cares for such things more than I do.'

"His love for his mother, and anxiety to spare her all unnecessary suffering on his account, was very beautiful, and attracted me to him from the first. His weakness was so great that he was utterly unable, for a long time, even to feed himself, and, of course, could not write. When I offered to do so for him, he declined, saying, that she knew, through a friend, that he was here; and that the sight of a strange hand, with the conviction that it would bring that he was too ill to write for himself, would be worse for her than to wait for a little while.

"One day, some time afterward, I came to his bedside, and found a paper lying there with a few unmeaning scratches, as I thought, upon it; he held them up to me.

"'The best I could do.'

"'What were you trying to do?' said I; 'did you mean that for drawing?'

"A look of intense disappointment passed over his face.

"'I was afraid so,' said he; 'then it would frighten her, as I thought. I meant it for my signature, and I've looked at it, and looked at it, and hoped it didn't look as bad as I thought, at first; but if you ask what I'm trying to do, when you see it, the game's up, and it's no use.'

"I assured him that such a signature would be stronger proof of the real state of the case than any letter I could send telling the facts, and giving the reasonable ground for hope which we now felt. But he still preferred to wait; and ere very long we found, by pinning the paper to the table, to keep it firm, he could execute a tolerably legible epistle. The weeks rolled on, and, by slow degrees, he regained his strength; his bright, hopeful disposition, even temper, and uniform cheerfulness, were great aids to his recovery; and we watched his improvement with great satisfaction, and at last had the pleasure of seeing him able to be up, and even out, for a short time.

"He came to me, one morning, in our ladies' room, saying, 'Miss ——, would it be troubling you too much to ask you to write to mother?'

"'Brought to it at last!' said I. 'Why do you ask me now, Robinson, when you have refused so often before, and can write for yourself?'

"'That's just it; she wont believe what I say; thinks I'm fooling her, and pretending to be better than I really am; and has an idea they're going to take my arm off, and I'm keeping it from her; and I thought if you'd just write, and tell her it wasn't coming off, she'd be sure to believe you.'

"'Sure to believe a stranger in preference to her own son, Robinson? Does that tell well for the son.'

"'Yes, ma'am, I think so; she knows you could have no object in deceiving her; while the thing I care most for in the world is to keep her from fretting, and she knows it.'

"There was no combating this reasoning, and in a short time I received a beautiful answer to my letter, well written and well expressed, confirming all that Robinson had told us: that he was the youngest son, and had always been carefully and tenderly brought up; that he had two brothers, the only other children—one had gone to Texas, before the breaking out of the rebellion, and never having heard from him since, they feared he had been pressed into the rebel service; fortunately she had never heard, and I trust, now, never may hear what Robinson had told us—that while pressing on at the Battle of Fair Oaks, over heaps of the enemy's dead, he saw an upturned face on the field—wounded or dead, he knew not which—that face, he said, he never could mistake—it was that of his brother!

"We tried to convince him that this was most improbable—that his imagination was excited at the time, and that the dread that such a thing might happen had been 'father to the thought;' but in vain; we never could persuade him to the contrary; and yet, whether from a doubt in his mind, or the dread of the pain it must cause, he never, as we afterward found, had made any allusion to the subject in his letters home.

"One morning, after he had been able to be about, and even out for some weeks, I was surprised, on going into his ward, to find him in bed again.

"'Why, Robinson, I am sorry to see you there! What have you been doing?'

"He hesitated, twisted the end of his coverlid, but made no answer.

"'Nothing wrong, I'm very sure of that. It wasn't your own fault, was it?' said I, fearing he thought I doubted him, as so many of the relapses here are caused by excess, the moment the men are able to be out, and I well knew there was no such danger here.

"He looked up at me, at once, with his clear, honest eyes, and said, 'Yes, Miss ——, all my own fault; but I thought *she* worried so——'

"'Your mother?' I questioned.

"'Yes, ma'am; and if I could just slip my arm into my coat-sleeve long enough to have my picture taken, she'd see it was better, and it would set her mind at rest more than all the letters I could write.'

"So to satisfy this mother's heart, the poor wounded shoulder had been forced into his sleeve, giving him, as it did, several weeks of added suffering and confinement to his bed. Can any one wonder that such a man should have won his way to our hearts; or at our regret, when we found he was to be transferred to another hospital, at some distance from the city? We thus lost sight of him for many months. Several times when I asked after him at our own hospital, I was told that he had been there but a short time since; sometimes the week before; sometimes only the day before; but it so happened that we never met. His wound they told me was far from well, varying very much; some days giving hope that it would heal, and then bursting out again. I had received many and urgent letters from his mother, before he left us, begging me to use all the influence I could bring to bear, to have him transferred to a hospital near his home (this was of course before the present order on the subject had been given); but on applying to the surgeon, I found that he considered his wound far too serious to attempt the journey, and that Robinson so fully agreed with him, that I wrote the poor disappointed mother to that effect, trying to console her with the hope of restoring him to her, ere very long, perfectly cured. The winter slipped away; the pressure of present hospital duties and interests had almost crowded out all thoughts of Robinson, when I am surprised, one sunny April afternoon, to receive a note from one of our lady visitors, telling me of Robinson's extreme illness, and that it is scarcely supposed he can recover.

"An hour later finds M. and myself driving rapidly out to the hospital where he now is; and here we are at the gates; how shall we enter? Ah! we do not now fear a guard with a bayonet, as we should have done some time since; and fifteen minutes more suffices for all the necessary 'red tape' connected with admittance, and we are at the door of Robinson's ward, listening to the ward-master's answer to our question:

"'Yes, ladies, walk in; but he wont know you; he's too low, and he's flighty all the time.'

"'Wont know us!' Robinson not know us! We cannot believe that; but see! he is leading the way; and we follow to a bed where lies a man tossing restlessly, and talking or rather muttering to himself in an indistinct tone; his bandaged shoulder and arm resting on a pillow, for an operation has been performed—a large piece of bone extracted—and the result still doubtful. Doubtful? No; too certain; that face is enough. Poor mother in your western home, you can never look upon your boy, till you meet at the final Bar, in the presence of your Judge! God in his mercy grant that it may be to spend a happy eternity together!

"And yet, as we stand, we find ourselves almost doubting whether this can really be our merry, laughing, whistling Robinson. Little hope, indeed, that he will recognize us, but let us try.

"'Robinson, do you know me?' He starts, and in a moment the vacant gaze changes into one of his old bright smiles of recognition.

"'Know you! Why shouldn't I know you? How long it is, Miss ——, since I have seen you—and you too,' added he, stretching out his hand to M.; but even as he spoke, his expression changed, and his mind wandered again.

"And this was the end of all our care—this the result of so many weary months of suffering. He seemed pleased at our coming, and would answer any direct question, but could not sustain a conversation of even a few moments. We found our old friend, 'handsome Harry,' of concert memory, who had been transferred at the same time, established here as Robinson's devoted nurse, although entirely unable to move without crutches. He told us that the surgeon had told him that morning, that if his family wished to see him he had better telegraph for them at once. Robinson heard us, and catching the word 'telegraph,' said quickly, 'Don't telegraph; father's poor, and he might come on; I'll be better soon, and get a furlough, and go out to them.'

"'But, Robinson,' said I, 'you are very ill; perhaps you may not be better, and you would like to see your father.'

"'I don't think I am very ill—they said so to-day; but I think I'll come round soon.'

"The next moment he was on the field, and evidently going over the fatal 'Fair Oaks' fight.

"His friend Harry told us that it had been his most earnest desire and longing to see his father; and that he had urged him some days ago, if he should be worse, to let them know at home. I therefore wrote the telegram on his table, and we drove to the office on our return to the city, that no time might be lost.

"I was detained at home for the two succeeding days; but some of our ladies went out to see him each day, as he was a general favorite; one lady going in a pouring rain, although she knew that she would have nearly a mile to walk after leaving the cars; their report of the case was most unfavorable. On the third day, the Rev. Mr. ——, who had been a most constant and faithful friend to Robinson, in our hospital, went out with me. When we arrived, we found him in a terrible state of excitement; he had been talking, and was now almost shrieking, and dashing himself from side to side.

"'It's no use speaking to him to-day,' said the ward master; 'he don't know anybody.'

"But once again I tried it, and once again he extended his hand, and repeated my name, and then said, 'And Mr. ——, how very kind in him to come!'

"I sat down by him, and tried to soothe and calm that dreadful restlessness; his mind was too much gone for words, I only gently stroked his brow, and fanned him. 'I am out on the water; out on the water!' was his one cry, from a low tone ascending till it amounted almost to a scream. Truly he was 'out on the water,' and where was compass or chart for the final voyage? Those words, with the constant repetition of his brother's name, were the last I ever heard him utter. The only moment of calmness I noticed, was when Mr. —— knelt at his bedside, and repeated those soul-soothing prayers, from the 'Visitation of the Sick.' He attempted no conversation, for we well knew Robinson was in no state to bear it. We had felt, from the first, that prayer *for* him was all that we could offer; not *with* him, as his intervals of consciousness were merely momentary. His father had not yet arrived, and there appeared little hope that he could now do so in time, as he was very much lower than on my last visit, and evidently sinking

As our presence could give him no comfort, we left him with heavy hearts.

"When I reached there the next day, I found that an order had been given prohibiting all admittance for visitors to his ward, as the surgeon thought that Robinson had been excited by those he had seen the day before, but that his father had come, and that we could see him; he had arrived that morning.

"There are few things connected with this hospital work which I recall with more pleasure than the simple, earnest gratitude of this bronzed and weather-beaten old man, for the trifling kindnesses which we had been able to offer to his boy. There was something about him altogether so real, so honest, genuine, and sincere, that one could not help feeling drawn to him at once. He was a rough, plain Western man, primitive in the extreme; but no one could listen to him without the consciousness that a warm, true, noble heart, beat beneath that uncouth exterior.

"Had the telegram been a day later he could not have reached here for nearly a week longer. The train, which only runs on certain days, left the morning after he received the news; he had travelled night and day, making every connection, and performing the journey as rapidly as it could be done.

His boy, he said, had recognized him, and he was pleased to find him better than he had hoped for. He thought with care he would get well now, and he was going at once to telegraph the good news to his wife.

"We were thunderstruck; how could he be so deceived? For although we had not seen Robinson that day, we well knew he was in a condition from which he could not rally. It seemed, therefore, no kindness to allow his mother to be tortured with false hope, and we earnestly represented (hard as it seemed to do so) that the surgeons did not look for any improvement; but all in vain—he had seen sickness—he had seen doctors mistaken before now—his boy was going to get well; so he accompanied us to the telegraph station, and sent his message. That evening I was told some one wanted to see me, from the —— hospital, and on going out, was met by the words, 'Miss ——, my boy's gone, my boy's gone!' and a burst of sobs, which seemed as though it must shake that poor old frame to pieces.

"He had scarcely left, in the morning, to send his hopeful telegram, when the change took place, and Robinson breathed his last just as his father reached his bedside. The blow fell heavier, as we had feared, from the strong hope he had persisted in entertaining, and even then it seemed as though he were too much bewildered and stunned to realize fully what had occurred. There was something inexpressibly touching in the grief of that poor, bowed-down old man, shattered as he was, too, by hard travel and loss of rest; and yet I hardly knew how to comfort him, or to answer that sad appeal, 'How can I go back to his mother without him?' Deep grief must ever bear with it a reverence of its own, and this seemed something one scarcely dared meddle with.

"He said the funeral was to take place the next afternoon, and begged that the ladies who had been so kind to him would be present for his mother's sake; he thought it would comfort her to know it. I readily consented, and promised to inform the others.

"He rose to go, and drawing a little paper from his pocket, said: 'I thought maybe you might care for this; it is a lock of my boy's hair, which I cut off for you, and I thought his mother would be glad to know you had it.'

"I expressed my feelings in a few words, which seemed to soothe and gratify him.

"That poor mother seemed never out of his thoughts; and again and again would he repeat that piteous question, 'How can I go back to her without him?'

"But he need not have feared; that mother's heart was anchored on the Rock which alone can withstand the storms of earth. Listen to but one sentence from her first letter (to one of the ladies, who had been a kind and constant correspondent), after that sad return.

"'At first it seemed I could not bear it. My bright-faced, joyous boy—my sunbeam! But soon came the thought, how short the journey would be for me to go to him, and that my sunbeam would now shed its ray upon me from the sky, to light my path onward and upward.'

"It would be of little avail to go into the dreary details of that dreariest afternoon. Touching in the extreme did it seem to see the little band (for the ladies willingly agreed to the request to be present) take their places as mourners with the father; mourners in reality, though so lately strangers; mourners, for we claimed a right to grieve; for was it not, as I have said, a young life given for our country as well as his?—for the one common cause which forms so strong a bond between all loyal hearts?

"A heavy, pouring rain added to the general gloom; the only comfort came from the words of our Burial Service, which must always fall with blessed balm upon the sorrowful soul. It was performed at his father's request, and with the permission of the surgeon in charge, by Robinson's kind and true friend, the Rev. Mr. ——, to whom I have alluded before.

"It was a long, long time ere I could forget the face of that broken-hearted old father, as—every thing over—he stood at the door, as we drove off, leaving him lonely and desolate among strangers. He was to start that night alone, in the rain, on his sad, homeward journey, and seemed to long to keep us with him to the last; and how we longed to stay to comfort him! But we must say good-by, and with a long, warm grasp of that rough hand, we parted, and one more hospital sorrow was over.

"Brave, gentle, heroic heart! The aching limb, the suffering frame, the strained, excited nerves are stilled forever. Robinson sleeps in a land of strangers; but the turf that covers that 'soldier's grave' will be moistened and kept green by the tears of those who can never forget that bright example of noble unselfishness and beautiful patience under severest suffering and trial."

CHALLENGING THE SENTINEL.—It was the custom of the colonel of the Eighty-fifth Pennsylvania Volunteers to make the rounds every night in person, and satisfy himself that every sentinel was at his post and doing his duty. On one occasion, while in the discharge of that self-imposed duty, he approached a post, and received the challenge as usual, "Who comes there?"

"Friend with the countersign," was the colonel's reply.

Here the poor sentinel was at a loss. The rest of his instructions had been forgotten. The colonel was a very particular man, and insisted that every thing should be done exactly right. So, after spending considerable time in the endeavor to impress the "role" upon the mind of the sentinel, he suggested that *he* would act as sentinel while the other should personate the colonel. "Blinky"—for such was this soldier's surname in the regiment—moved back a few paces and then turned to approach the colonel. "Who comes there?" challenged the colonel.

"*Why, Blinky; don't you know me, colonel?*"

This was too much for even so patient and forbearing a man as Colonel Howell. "As green as verdigris," thought he. The gun was handed over, and the colonel passed on to the next post, meditating upon the vanity of all earthly things in general, and of things military in particular.

RACHEL SOMERS, THE NOBLE MOTHER.

MR. J. R. GILMORE (Edmund Kirke) relates an incident which occured under his own observation in East Tennessee, which proves that the Spartan mother who gave her sons the charge, as she handed them their shields, "Come back with these, or upon them!" has been far surpassed in lofty heroism by an American, Christian mother. A chaplain of one of the regiments of the Army of the Cumberland, whom he was visiting, invited him to accompany him to the regimental hospital. "One of my boys is dying," he said—"a Tennessee boy, wounded at Stone river. He has lingered long, but now is going." Mr. Gilmore continues:

Walking rapidly across the open fields, we entered, at the end of a short half hour, a dingy warehouse in the very heart of the city. About fifty low cots were ranged along the two sides of a narrow, cheerless apartment on the ground floor of this building, and on one of them the wounded soldier was lying. His face was pallid, his eyes were fixed, a cold, clammy sweat was on his forehead—he was dying. Sitting at his feet was a lad of sixteen; and kneeling at his side, her hand in his, was a middle-aged woman, with worn garments, and a thin, sorrow-marked face.

"You are too late! He is almost gone," said the colonel of the regiment, as we paused before the group.

The chaplain made no reply, but slowly uncovered his head, for the dying man was speaking.

"Mother," he said, "good-by. And you, Tom, good-by. Be of good heart, mother. GOD will take care of you, and save—save the——." A low sound then rattled in his throat, and he passed away, with the name of his country on his lips.

The mother bent down and closed the eyelids of her dead son; and then, kissing again and again his pale face, turned to go away. As she did so, the chaplain, taking her hand in his, said to her:

"The LORD gave: the LORD hath taken away."

Looking up to him with tranquil face and tearless eyes, the woman answered:

"'Blessed be the name of the Lord.' They have murdered my husband, Mr. Chapl'in, my oldest boy, and now John, too, is gone." Then, laying her hand on the shoulder of her living son, she turned to the colonel, and while her voice trembled a very little, she added: "He's all I've got now, Mr. Cunnel—give him John's place in the rigiment."

A tear rolled down the colonel's weather-beaten cheek, and he turned his face away, but said nothing. There was a convulsive twitching about the chaplain's firm-set mouth, as *he* said:

"The Spartan mother gave only *two* sons to her country: would you give *three?*"

"I'd give all—all I've got, Mr. Chapl'in," was the low answer.

And this was a "poor white" woman! Her words should be heard all over the land. They should go down in history, and make her name—RACHEL SOMERS—immortal.

Prison Camp at Andersonville.

THE SOLDIERS' GUARDIAN ANGEL.

Among those who have sacrificed all the comforts of life, the pleasures of society, and the delights of intellectual culture and association for the still higher and holier joy of ministering to those, who, on our great battle fields, have fallen in defence of their country, there is none more deserving of a nation's gratitude and enduring remembrance than Miss Clara H. Barton.

Of an excellent family in Massachusetts, a family numbering among its connections some of the most eminent citizens of the Old Bay State, highly educated, and though modest and diffident in manner, possessing extraordinary executive ability, and an active and self-reliant disposition, this young and gifted woman, from the time of the wounding of our soldiers in Baltimore, gave herself wholly to the work of ministering to the sick and wounded soldiers of the Army of the Potomac. At first, owing to the obstacles which were in the way of the personal ministrations of women unconnected with the Sanitary Commission in the field, she confined her labors to the hospitals, and to the sending of supplies by trustworthy distributers to the army in the field, from Washington. Soon, however, this ceased to satisfy her patriotic heart, which longed to give to the wounded heroes, on the battle field or in the field hospitals, those gentle ministries which woman only can bestow. After a severe mental struggle with those conventional ideas which declared it altogether improper for a young lady, unprotected, to go even on an errand of mercy into the army, she went first with a car load of supplies to Culpepper Court House, just after the disastrous battle of Cedar Mountain, on the 9th of August, 1862. Returning to Washington, she obtained the assistance of other ladies and one or two gentlemen as companions in her labors of love, and with another car load of supplies reached the battle field of Bull Run at the close of the second struggle of that name, on the 30th of August, 1862. Her coming here was almost like an angel's visit. The surgeons, overworked by the sad necessities of that bloody fray, which had come upon a succession of previous battles, were just ready to give out and abandon their work in despair. They were without bandages, without cordials, without lights, without food for themselves or the wounded, when just at the moment of despair, Miss Barton, who, finding that locomotives could not be made to work, had impressed into her service some mules, who dragged the car along the rickety track, drove up herself, greatly exhausted with her exertions, but with every thing that was needed, bandages, cordials, lights, and food, and by her own ministrations of gentleness and tenderness, recalled to life and hope many who were already far on their way into the land of shadows. She remained on the field, amid great personal peril, during the next two days, ministering to the wounded from the battle of Chantilly, even when surgeons fled from the field. By the 3d of September, the army with its wounded were safe under the shelter of the fortifications around Washington, and her vocation for the moment had ceased. Three days later they were marching in long columns northward to meet the foe in Maryland, and a great battle was evidently impending near the Pennsylvania border. Miss Barton promptly sought the opportunity of carrying aid and succor to those who were destined to suffer in the impending battle. But the place where the battle would be fought was unknown, and transportation almost wholly unattainable. With great difficulty, her friend, General Rucker, superintendent of transportation, managed to spare her a single army wagon and one teamster. Loading this with such supplies as her experience had taught her would be needed, and accompanied only by Mr. C. M. Welles, a missionary of the Free Mission Society, she started, on the morning of Sunday, September 14th, 1862, to follow the route of the army, riding in the army wagon, and sleeping in it at night. On her route she purchased all the bread she could find at the farm-houses. After three days of travel over the dusty roads of Maryland, she reached Burnside's corps after dark on the night of the 16th, and found the two armies lying face to face along the opposing ridges of hills that bound the valley of the Antietam. There had already been heavy skirmishing, far away on the right, where Hooker had forded the creek, and taken position on the opposite hills; and the air was dark and thick with fog and exhalations, with the smoke of camp-fires, and the preparations for the fierce struggle of the morrow.

There was little sleep that night, and as the morning sun rose bright and beautiful over the Blue Ridge, and its rays lit up what was soon to become the valley of death, the firing on the right was resumed. Reinforcements soon began to move along the rear to Hooker's support. Believing that the place of danger was the place of duty, Miss Barton ordered her mules to be harnessed, and took her place in the swift moving train of artillery that was passing. On reaching the scene of action, they turned into a field of tall corn and drove through it to a large barn. They were close upon the line of battle; the rebel shot and shell flew thickly around and over them, and in the barnyard and among the corn, lay wounded and bleeding men—the worst cases—just brought from the places where they had-fallen. The army medical supplies had not yet arrived, nor the Sanitary Commission stores, which indeed did not come till one or two days later; the small stock of dressings brought by the surgeons was exhausted, and the surgeons, in their desperate necessity, were endeavoring to make bandages out of corn husks. Miss Barton opened to them her stock of bandages and dressings, and with her companion in travel proceeded to procure soft bread dipped in wine for the wounded and fainting. In the course of the day she picked up twenty-five men who had come to the rear with the wounded, and set them to work administering restoratives, bringing and applying water, lifting men into easier positions, checking hemorrhages by extemporized tourniquets, and the use of styptics, etc., etc. At length her supply of bread was exhausted, but fortunately a part of the liquors she had brought was found to have been packed in meal, and she at once determined to prepare gruel for the men. The farm-house to which the barn belonged was discovered at a little distance, and on searching its cellar she found three barrels of flour and a bag of salt which had been hidden there by the rebels the day before. Kettles were collected from the house, and the preparation of gruel commenced on a large scale, and as fast as cooked it was carried in buckets and distributed along the line for miles. On the ample piazza of the house were ranged the operating tables, where the surgeons with terrible rapidity performed their fearful work; and on that piazza Miss Barton kept her place from before noon till nightfall, preparing gruel, ministering to the wounded, and directing her assistants, the whole time directly under the fire of one of the fiercest battles of the war. Before night her face was as black as a negro's, and her lips and throat parched with the sulphurous smoke of battle. But night came at last, and with it a cessation of the deadly conflict. The dead and wounded lay everywhere. Amid the rows of corn, in the barn, in the yard, and on the piazza, and in the rooms of the house, they were laid so thickly that it was difficult to move between the rows.

As the night closed in, the surgeon in charge looked despairingly at a bit of candle, and said it was the only one on the place, and no one could stir till morning A thousand men dangerously wounded and suffering fearfully with thirst lay around that building, and if not succored many must die before the morning's light. It was a fearful thing to die alone and in the dark, but for aught he could see, it must come to that. Miss Barton replied, that profiting by her experience at Chantilly, she had brought with her thirty lanterns and an abundance of candles. It was worth a journey to Antietam to see the joy and hope that beamed from the faces of the wounded, when they learned that they were not to be left in darkness through that long, sad night, and found that it was due to her careful forethought which had provided for their needs. On the morrow the fighting had ceased, but the work of caring for the wounded was resumed and continued all day. On the third day the regular supplies arrived, and Miss Barton having exhausted her small stores, and finding that her protracted fatigue and watching was bringing on a fever, turned her course toward Washington. It was with difficulty that she was able to reach home, where she was confined to her bed for some time.

About the 23d of October, 1862, another great battle being expected in the vicinity of Harper's Ferry, she left Washington with a well appointed and heavily laden train of six wagons and an ambulance, with seven teamsters and thirty-eight mules. The government furnished transportation and the support of its teamsters, but the supplies were mostly procured from her own means or the contributions of friends. Her teamsters were rough and ruffianly fellows, who had no disposition to be commanded by a woman, and who mutinied when they had gone but a few miles. Perfectly self-possessed and dignified in her manner, Miss Barton directed them to proceed, and stated to them the course she should pursue if they continued insubordinate, and they sulkily returned to their duty, venting their oaths and imprecations, however, on every thing in their way. She overtook the army as it was crossing the Potomac below Harper's Ferry. Her teamsters refused to cross. She summoned them to her ambulance, and gave them the alternative of crossing peaceably and behaving themselves as they should, or of being instantly dismissed and replaced by soldiers. They knew very well that their dismission under such circumstances would be followed by their arrest and punishment, and having become convinced by this time that this gentle and winning woman possessed sufficient resolution and determination to act promptly and vigorously, they yielded, and from that day forward gave her no further trouble, obeying readily her every request.

The expected battle did not come off, but in its place there was a race for Richmond between the opposing armies. The Army of the Potomac had the advantage of interior lines, keeping for some time along the eastern base of the Blue Ridge, while the rebel army followed the course of the Shenandoah. There was a struggle at every gap in the Blue Ridge, the rebels usually gaining possession of the pass first, and endeavoring to surprise some portion of the Union army as it passed, or to capture a part of the supply trains. Thus every day brought its battle or skirmish, and its additions to the list of the sick and wounded; and for a period of about three weeks, until Warrenton Junction was reached, the national army had no base of operations, nor any reinforcements or supplies. The sick were carried all this time over the rough roads in ambulances or the hard, jolting army wagons. Miss Barton with her wagon train accompanied the Ninth Army Corps, as general purveyor for the sick. Her original supply of comforts was very considerable, and her men contrived to add to it every day such fresh provisions as could be gathered from the country. At each night's encampment, they lighted their fires and prepared fresh food and necessary articles of diet for the moving hospitals. Through all that long and painful march from Harper's Ferry to Fredericksburg, those wagons constituted the hospital, larder, and kitchen for all the sick within reach. At Warrenton Junction she left her train in charge of a friend like-minded with herself, and hastened to Washington for fresh supplies, with which she soon rejoined the army at Falmouth. The great and disastrous battle of Fredericksburg was approaching, and she felt that there was ample work for her to do. The Lacy House, at Falmouth, where she had her quarters at first, was a mark for the enemy's fire, and more than one shell crashed through the house, and passed her as she was engaged in her work of mercy, but she was too calm and fearless to be disturbed by them. At the time of the attack of the 11th of December, she was at the bank of the river, and received the wounded Union men, as well as the Rebel wounded who were brought over as prisoners. An incident which occurred at this time may serve to show the spirit of the woman. Among those who were brought to the hither shore of the Rappahannock was a rebel lieutenant, mortally wounded, a man of culture and intelligence. Her sympathies and ministrations were bestowed alike upon friend and foe; that a man was wounded and suffering was ever a sufficient passport to her kindly offices. Thus it happened that this young rebel officer was tenderly cared for, and though it was evident that his life could not be prolonged, his pains were assuaged, his suffering alleviated, and the passage into the dark valley smoothed by her care and attention. He was deeply grateful for these kindnesses received from the hands of those whom he had regarded as enemies, and, seeing that she was about to cross the river to Fredericksburg, where her services were needed to organize the temporary hospitals there, he beckoned to her, and, in a voice broken by the pangs of dissolution, implored her not to go over. He unfolded to her, in gratitude for her kindness, the plan of the rebel commander to draw the Union army into a trap, by withholding his fire till they had all crossed the Rappahannock, and then opening upon them from all his batteries, which covered every point of their progress. He assured her that to cross over was to go to certain death, and begged, that for his sake and that of the thousands of wounded sure to need her services, she would remain on that side of the Rappahannock. Of course she could not reason with him, but her mind was made up that she must cross the river; the soldiers of the Ninth Army Corps, to whom she had so often ministered, were there, and she could not let them fall in the fierce battle that was impending, without being near them to minister relief and comfort to soul and body. Accordingly she went over, and was received with the most cordial of welcomes by the Ninth Corps, who regarded her as almost their guardian angel. She at once organized hospital kitchens, provided supplies for the wounded, and when the wounded men were brought in, sought to alleviate their sufferings. While thus engaged, one day, some soldiers came to her quarters, bringing an elegant Axminster carpet, whose great weight almost crushed them to the ground. "What is this?" asked Miss Barton. "A carpet we have brought for your quarters," answered the soldiers. "Where did you get it?" asked Miss Barton. "Oh! we confiscated it!" the soldiers replied promptly. "No! No!" said Miss Barton, "that will never do. Government confiscates, but soldiers, when they take such things, steal! I thank you for the kind spirit which prompted you to bring it to me, and am very sorry, but you must carry it back to the house from which you took it." The soldiers scratched their heads, looked sheepishly at each other, but finally gathered up the carpet, and with infinite pains tugged it back to the house from which they had taken it.

In the skilfully managed retreat from Fredericksburg, she remained till the wounded were mostly across, and then tripped across the pontoon bridge just before its removal. On the Falmouth side she established a private kitchen and hospital for the wounded, and occupied an old tent, while her train was encamped round her, performing the cooking in the open air, though it was midwinter. When the wounded from the attack on the rebel batteries were recovered by flag of truce, fifty of them were brought to her camp at night. They had lain for several days in the cold, and were badly wounded, famished, and almost frozen. She had the snow cleared away promptly, large fires built, and the men wrapped in blankets. An old chimney was torn down, the bricks heated in the fire, and placed around them. She prepared warm and palatable food and hot toddy for them, and they were allowed to partake of both freely enough to insure them a comfortable night's sleep, and in the morning the medical officers took them in charge. Soon after General Hooker superseded General Burnside, Miss Barton went to Hilton Head, South Carolina, to be present at the combined military and naval attack to be made on Charleston on the 7th of April. That attack, it will be remembered, was a failure, though not accompanied with much loss of life. Miss Barton remained at Hilton Head for several weeks, visiting the hospitals, and caring for the welfare of a dear brother, who was an officer in the army there; but when General Gillmore moved on his expedition against Morris Island, she could no longer remain away from her work, and accompanied the expedition. Pitching her tent on the sand of Morris Island, and herself engaging in the drudgeries of the kitchen, she ministered to the soldiers, who, amid the burning heat of the Southern sun, were besieging simultaneously Fort Sumter and Fort Wagner, and awaited the fierce and bloody assaults which she knew were coming. When Wagner was stormed and the assault repulsed, she went to the relief of the wounded, wading through the deep sand, and putting the cool water and the refreshing restoratives to their parched lips, while she staunched their bleeding wounds, and brought life and healing to those that were ready to perish. Throughout that long, hot summer, when all who could fled to cooler climes, she toiled on. "Some one," she said, "must see to these poor wounded and fever-stricken men, and, as others could not or would not, it seemed to be her duty to do it." More than once her health seemed about to give way, but she held out, and did not leave the island till winter, when, she said, she had become so accustomed to the shriek of the shells from Gillmore's monster guns, that she could not sleep at first, when no longer lulled to slumber by their music. In January, 1864, she returned to the North, and after a brief visit to her friends in Massachusetts and New York, returned to Washington, and employed herself in preparation for the great campaign of the summer of 1864. Her great services were recognized by the Government, and she was assigned to a position of usefulness and responsibility in connection with the Army of the James, in which, with the liberal supplies at her command, she was able to accomplish perhaps as much for the soldiers' comfort during this protracted campaign as in all her previous history. In January, 1865, she was recalled to Washington by the sickness and death of a brother and nephew, and did not again join the army in the field. She could not rest, however, while the soldiers were suffering, and after spending some time at Annapolis in the care of the poor fellows who had suffered so cruelly in the rebel prisons, she returned to Washington, and, with the sanction of President Lincoln, commenced the work of making a systematic record of the missing soldiers of the Union armies, and ascertaining their whereabouts, condition, and fate. The organization of this bureau of correspondence in relation to the missing soldiers required records, and the employment of six or eight clerks, beside an infinity of labor on her part. At the request of the Secretary of War, she visited Andersonville with Captain James M. Moore and Dorrence Atwater, a soldier who had been a prisoner there, and superintended the establishment of a cemetery there, and the erection of headboards for the thirteen thousand Union dead there, the greater part of them murdered by the inhumanities of rebel officers and guards. In this bureau of correspondence and her previous labors in behalf of the soldier, Miss Barton had exhausted her own patrimony and resources, and partly in payment for these expenditures, and partly to enable her to keep up her organization, which was of very great value to Government, especially in regard to pensions, Congress made an appropriation to her, in January, 1866, of fifteen thousand dollars.

To few persons, however heartily disposed they may

have been to undertake the work, has been vouchsafed so firm a constitution, and such rare executive ability as have been granted to Miss Barton; and these gifts, added to a sound judgment, a clear head, and a zeal which never flags, have enabled her to accomplish a vast amount of good for the army.

History will record few examples of higher, more earnest, and more continuous patriotic endeavor, than those which have graced the name of this young and gifted woman. To her belongs pre-eminently, the noble title, often bestowed upon her, of "THE SOLDIER'S GUARDIAN ANGEL."

MILITARY ETIQUETTE.—Lieutenant ——, of the Third Rhode Island Heavy Artillery, at one of the posts in the Department of the South, while on duty in a carriage, had the kindness to favor a staff officer with a ride. On meeting a private of a colored regiment, who paid the required salute, which was properly returned by the lieutenant, the following dialogue, in substance, ensued:

Staff Officer.—"Do you salute niggers?"

Lieutenant.—"He is a soldier; and he saluted me."

Staff Officer.—"I swear that I wont salute a nigger."

Lieutenant.—"The regulations require you to return a salute."

Staff Officer.—"Curse such regulations; I'll never salute a nigger; and I don't think much of a man that will."

Lieutenant—(coolly reining in his horse.)—"You can get out and walk, sir."

The official was consigned to shoe leather and the sand, with the reflection, we could hope, that he was less of a man than a soldier.

A HEROINE AND MARTYR.

From the anti-revolutionary period of our country's history few families have wielded a more potent influence than the Breckinridges. Intellectually and physically vigorous, they had never been wanting in patriotism until the outbreak of the late Rebellion, when a scion of the house on whom the nation had showered its honors far beyond his deserts, a man who for four years had presided over its Senate and occupied the highest position but one in the Republic, took the fearful leap into treason, and, after doing what injury he could to the nation to which he owed so much in the Senate chamber, completed his infamy by entering the army of the rebels, where he soon became a major-general, though without achieving any considerable success. Like Lucifer of old he drew downward with him the third part of his family, and led them with him into the mire of rebellion; but the old Spartan spirit yet remained in the family, bred by a mother who, in the time of the Revolution, sent her sons forth to fight for their country with the injunction, "Come back to me living or dead, as God may will it, but never with a wound in your backs!"

There were a considerable number of clergymen in the different generations of the family, and for the most part they belonged to the church militant; men of great logical power, and loving dearly to fight a giant wrong. Among these was the present patriarch of the family, Rev. Robert J. Breckinridge, who, during the war, with all the energy and ability of his great intel lect, has fought against secession and rebellion. Such a spirit, too, were many of his kinsmen—such would have been his brother, Rev. John Breckinridge, had he lived to see the day of trial, and such was the spirit of the children of that eminent departed minister. One of these, Judge Samuel Breckinridge, of St. Louis, has been one of the most earnest Union men of that region ; a man who has striven earnestly to undo, so far as lay in his power, the wrongs which his cousin, John C. Breckinridge, has done to his country.

But among all the members of the family there was none who combined more perfectly the characteristics of the heroine, the saint, and the martyr, than the sister of the judge, Miss Margaret E. Breckinridge. She was highly educated, and gifted beyond most of her sex with intellectual ability, of fragile form, but attractive in person and manner, and possessing a soul all aflame with the holiest patriotism, and at the same time of the most angelic purity. Her love of her country and of its cause knew no limits, for it she was willing to sacrifice her property, her health, her life itself; and she counted no sacrifice dear which should enable her to fulfil the duty which she felt she owed to its gallant defenders. From the first she had wielded her eloquent pen in its behalf, and early in the spring of 1862, she determined to consecrate herself to the work of caring specially for the sick and wounded soldiers. Her first experiences of hospital life were in the Baltimore hospitals, where she contracted the measles, and was sick for some time. Thence she went to Lexington, Ky., when it was in the possession of the rebel General E. Kirby

Smith. Her loyalty blazed out even while under the sway of the rebels. Thence she went to St. Louis, where, after some time spent in the hospitals, she proceeded down the river in a hospital steamer to bring up the sick and wounded soldiers from Vicksburg and other points. After two of these trips, in which she went beyond her strength in her zeal for the poor suffering soldiers, she returned to St. Louis, to endeavor to recover her health, sadly impaired by her labors, and would visit the hospitals every day. In March, 1864, she went eastward to her friends, in hope of recovering so far as possible, that she might again serve her country, or as she expressed it, in her communication to the Sanitary Commission, "Do a little to atone for the great evils which some of her kinsmen had inflicted upon her beloved country." Here, after some rest, she went into the Episcopal Hospital, Philadelphia, and took lessons from the surgeons in the dressing of wounds and the medical care of the wounded, lessons which she hoped to be able to make serviceable on the field, but it was not so to be. Her brother-in-law, Colonel Peter A. Porter, of Niagara Falls, N. Y., had fallen in one of the fierce battles of that terrible campaign from the Rapidan to the James, and frail and ill as she was, her friends feared to communicate the sad event to her. At last they were obliged to let her know it, and she went at once to meet the family, who had come on to receive the body of the dead hero. She returned with them to Niagara, where, after an illness of five weeks, she fell asleep, whispering to a friend in her last conscious moments, "Underneath are the everlasting arms."

No memoir can do justice to the noble and patriotic spirit which so vivified and glorified every act of this young and gifted woman, but a few incidents, gathered by friends or culled from her letters, of her experiences in hospital life, may be of interest to our readers. Of her zeal for her country's cause and defenders, even when surrounded by its enemies, some idea can be formed from the following incident related in a letter to a friend:

"At that very time, a train of ambulances, bringing our sick and wounded from Richmond, was leaving town on its way to Cincinnati. It was a sight to stir every loyal heart; and so the Union people thronged round them to cheer them up with pleasant, hopeful words, to bid them God speed, and last, but not least, to fill their haversacks and canteens. We went, thinking it possible we might be ordered off by the guard, but they only stood off, scowling and wondering.

"'Good-by,' said the poor fellows from the ambulances. 'We're coming back as soon as ever we get well.'

"'Yes, yes,' we whispered, for there were spies all around us, 'and every one of you bring a regiment with you.'"

When she first began to visit the hospitals in and around St. Louis, she wrote: "I shall never be satisfied until I get right into a hospital, to live till the war is over. If you are constantly with the men, you have hundreds of opportunities and moments of influence in which you can get their attention and their hearts, and do more good than in any missionary field."

Once, on board a steamer, near Vicksburg, during

the fearful winter siege of that city, some one said to her: "You must hold back, you are going beyond your strength, you will die if you are not more prudent."

"Well," said she, with thrilling emphasis, "what if I do? Shall men come here by tens of thousands and fight, and suffer, and die, and shall not some women be willing to die to sustain and succor them?"

A friend, who had been associated with her in her work of love, speaks of her thus: "With her slight form, her bright face, and her musical voice, she seemed a ministering angel to the sick and suffering soldiers, while her sweet, womanly purity, and her tender devotion to their wants, made her almost an object of worship among them. 'Aint she an angel?' said a grayheaded soldier, as he watched her one morning, while busily getting breakfast for the boys on the steamer 'City of Alton.' 'She never seems to tire, she is always smiling, and don't seem to walk. She flies all but—God bless her!' Another, a soldier boy of seventeen, said to her, as she was smoothing his hair, and saying cheering words about mother and home to him, 'Ma'am, where do you come from? How could such a lady as you are come down here to take care of us poor, sick, dirty boys?' She answered: 'I consider it an honor to wait on you, and wash off the mud you've waded through for me.' Another asked this favor of her: 'Lady, please write down your name, and let me look at it, and take it home to show my wife who wrote my letters, and combed my hair, and fed me. I don't believe you are like other people.'"

In one of her letters, she says: "I am often touched with their anxiety not to give trouble, not to *bother*, as they say. That same evening I found a poor, exhausted fellow lying on a stretcher, on which he had just been brought in. There was no bed for him just then, and he looked uncomfortable enough, with his knapsack for a pillow. 'I know some hot tea will do you good,' I said. 'Yes, ma'am,' he answered, 'but I am too weak to sit up with nothing to lean against; it's no matter—don't bother about me;' but his eyes were fixed longingly on the smoking tea. Everybody was busy, not even a nurse in sight, but the poor man must have his tea. I pushed away the knapsack, raised his head, and seated myself on the end of the stretcher, and, as I drew his poor tired head back upon my shoulder, half holding him, he seemed, with all his pleasure and eager enjoyment of the tea, to be troubled at my being so bothered with him. He forgot I had come so many hundred miles on purpose to be 'bothered.'"

Early in January of '63, Miss Breckinridge descended the Mississippi to Vicksburg, for the purpose of attending to the sick and wounded there, and rendering aid in bringing them up to St. Louis. It was a trip attended with great peril, because of the guerillas lying in ambush, and the bands of rebels ever on the watch for the steamers and transports as they passed, but her mission was too important to allow herself to dwell upon danger. She reached her destination in safety, and returned to St. Louis on a small hospital boat, on which there were one hundred and sixty patients in care of herself and one other lady. A few extracts from one of her letters will show what brave work it gave her to do: "It was on Sunday morning, 25th of January, that Mrs. C. and I went on board the hospital boat which had received its sad freight the day before, and was to leave at once for St. Louis, and it would be impossible to describe the scene which presented itself to me as I stood in the door of the cabin. Lying on the floor, with nothing under them but a tarpaulin and their blankets, were crowded fifty men, many of them with death written on their faces; and looking through the half open doors of the state-rooms, we saw that they contained as many more. Young, boyish faces, old and thin from suffering, great, restless eyes that were fixed on nothing, incoherent ravings of those who were wild with fever, and hollow coughs on every side; this, and much more that I do not want to recall, was our welcome to our new work; but, as we passed between the two long rows, back to our cabin, pleasant smiles came to the lips of some, others looked after us wonderingly, and one poor boy whispered, 'Oh, but it is good to see the ladies come in!' I took one long look into Mrs. C.'s eyes, to see how much strength and courage was hidden in them. We asked each other, not in words, but in those fine electric thrills by which one soul questions another, 'Can we bring strength and hope and comfort to these poor, suffering men?' and the answer was, 'Yes, by God's help, we will.' The first thing was to give them something like a comfortable bed, and, Sunday though it was, we went to work to run up our sheets into bed sacks. Every man that had strength enough to stagger was pressed into the service, and by night most of them had something softer than a tarpaulin to sleep on. 'Oh, I am so comfortable now!' some of them said; 'I think I can sleep to-night,' exclaimed one little fellow, half laughing with pleasure. The next thing was to provide something that sick people could eat, for coffee and bread was poor food for most of them. We had two little stoves, one in the cabin and one in the chambermaid's room, and here, the whole time we were on board, we had to do the cooking for a hundred men. Twenty times that day I fully made up my mind to cry with vexation, and twenty times that day I laughed instead; and surely, a kettle of tea was never made under so many difficulties as the one I made that morning. The kettle lid was not be found, the water simmered and sang at its leisure, and when I asked for the poker, I could get nothing but an old bayonet, and, all the time through the half open door behind me, I heard the poor, hungry fellows asking the nurses, 'Where is that tea the lady promised me?' or 'When will my toast come?' But there must be an end to all things, and when I carried them their tea and toast, and heard them pronounce it 'plaguey good,' and 'awful nice,' it was more than a recompense for all the worry.

"One great trouble was the intense cold. We could not keep life in some of the poor, emaciated frames. 'Oh, dear! I shall freeze to death!' one poor little fellow groaned, as I passed him. Blankets seemed to have no effect upon them, and at last we had to keep canteens filled with boiling water at their feet.

"There was one poor boy about whom from the first I had been very anxious. He drooped and faded from day to day before my eyes. Nothing but constant stimulants seemed to keep him alive, and at last I summoned courage to tell him—oh, how hard it was!—that he could not live many hours. 'Are you willing to die?' I asked him. He closed his eyes and was silent a moment; then came that passionate exclamation which I have heard so often—'My mother! Oh, my mother!' And to the last, though I believe God gave him strength to trust in Christ, and willingness to die, he longed for his mother. I had to leave him, and, not long after, he sent for me to come, that he was dying, and wanted me to sing to him. He prayed for himself in the most touching words; he confessed that he had been a wicked boy, and then, with one last message for that dear mother, turned his face to the pillow, and died. And so, one by one, we saw them pass away, and all the little keepsakes and treasures they had loved and kept about them, laid away to be sent home to those they should never see again. Oh, it was heart-breaking to see that!"

After the "sad freight" had reached its destination, and the care and responsibility are over, true woman that she is, she breaks down, and cries over it all, but brightens up, and looking back upon it, declares: "I certainly never had so much comfort and satisfaction in any thing in all my life, and the tearful thanks of those who thought in their gratitude that they owed a great deal more to us than they did, the blessings breathed from dying lips, and the comfort it has been to friends at home to hear all about the last sad hours of those they love, and know their dying messages, all this is a rich and full and overflowing reward for any labor and for any sacrifice." And again, she says, "There is a soldier's song of which they are very fond, one verse of which often comes back to me:

"'So I've had a sight of drilling,
And I've roughed it many days;
Yes, and death has nearly had me,
Yet I think the service pays.'

"Indeed it does—richly, abundantly, blessedly, and I thank God that he has honored me by letting me do a little and suffer a little for this grand old Union, and the dear, brave fellows who are fighting for it."

Early in June, 1864, Miss Breckinridge reached Niagara on her way to the East, where she remained for a month. For a year she had struggled against disease and weakness, longing all the time to be at work again, making vain plans for the time when she should "be well and strong, and able to go back to the hospitals." With this cherished scheme in view, she went, in the early part of May, 1864, into the Episcopal Hospital, Philadelphia, that she might acquire experience in nursing, especially in surgical cases, so that in the autumn she could begin the labor of love among the soldiers more efficiently and confidently than before. She went to work with her usual energy and promptness, following the surgical nurses every day through the wards, learning the best methods of bandaging and treating the various wounds. She was not satisfied with merely seeing this done, but often washed and dressed the wounds with her own hands, saying, "I shall be able to do this for the soldiers when I get back to the army." The patients could not understand this, and would often expostulate, saying, "Oh, no, miss, that is not for the like of you to do!" but she would playfully insist, and have her way. Nor was she satisfied to gain so much without giving something in return. She went from bed to bed, encouraging the despondent, cheering the weak and miserable, reading to them from her little testament, and singing sweet hymns at twilight—a ministering angel here as well as on the hospital boats of the Mississippi.

THE FARMER'S CONTRIBUTION

TO THE CHICAGO SANITARY FAIR.

THE Sanitary Fair at Chicago, in October and November, 1863, was the first of the series of great outpourings of the sympathy of the nation for its brave defenders, which were held successively at Boston, Cincinnati, Brooklyn, New York, Pittsburg, Philadelphia, and St. Louis, and which yielded such abundant resources for the Sanitary Commissions, in the prosecution of their work of mercy. Rev. Frederick N. Knapp, one of the secretaries of the U. S. Sanitary Commission, was present at Chicago, when, on the first day of the fair, the long procession of teams, extending many miles, came in from the country laden with provisions and other articles for the fair, and thus describes an incident which came under his notice:

Among these wagons which had drawn up near the rooms of the Sanitary Commission to unload their stores, was one peculiar for its exceeding look of poverty. It was worn and mended, and was originally made merely of poles. It was drawn by three horses which had seen much of life, but little grain. The driver was a man past middle age, with the clothes and look of one who had toiled hard, but he had a thoughtful and kindly face. He sat there quietly waiting his turn to unload. By his side, with feet over the front of the wagon, for it was filled very full, was his wife, a silent, worn-looking woman (many of these men had their wives with them on the loads); near the rear of the wagon was a girl of fifteen, perhaps, and her sister, dressed in black, carrying in her arms a little child.

Some one said to this man (after asking the woman with the child if she would not go into the Commission rooms and get warm): "My friend, you seem to have quite a load here of vegetables; now I am curious to know what good things you are bringing to the soldiers; will you tell me what you have?" "Yes," said he; "here are potatoes, and here are three bags of onions, and there are some ruta-bagas, and there are a few turnips, and that is a small bag of meal, and you will see the cabbages fill in; and that box with slats has some ducks in it, which one of them brought in." "Oh! then this isn't all your load, alone, is it?" "Why, no! our region just where I live is rather a hard soil, and we haven't any of us much to spare any way, yet for this business we could have raked up as much again as this is, if we had had time; but we didn't get the notice that the wagons were going in till last night about eight o'clock, and it was dark and raining at that, so I and my wife and the girls could only go around to five or six of the neighbors within a mile or so, but we did the best we could; we worked pretty much all the night, and loaded, so as to be ready to get out to the main road and start with the rest of them this morning; but I can't help it if it is little, it's *something* for those soldiers." "Have you a son in the army?" "No," he answered, slowly, after turning around and looking at his wife. "No, I haven't *now*, but we had one there once; he's buried down by Stone River; he was shot there—and that isn't just so either—we called him our boy, but he was only our adopted son; we took him when he was little, so he was just the same as our own boy, and (pointing over his shoulder without looking back) that's his wife there with the baby! But I shouldn't bring these things any quicker if he were alive now and in the army; I don't know that I should think so much as I do now about the boys away off there." It was in turn for his wagon to unload, so with his rough freight of produce, and his rich freight of human hearts with their deep and treasured griefs, he drove on—one wagon of a hundred in the train.

A Romantic Incident of the War.—Governor Curtin, of Pennsylvania, was called upon at the Continental Hotel at Philadelphia, by a young lady. When she was introduced into the parlor she expressed her great joy at seeing the governor, at the same time imprinting a kiss upon his forehead.

"Madam," said he, "to what am I indebted for this unexpected salutation?"

"Sir, do you not know me?"

"Take a chair," said the governor, at the same time extending one of the handsomest in the parlor.

"Shortly after the battle of Antietam you were upon that bloody field," said she to the governor.

"I was," replied the governor.

"You administered to the wants of the wounded and the dying."

"It was my duty as a feeling man."

"You did your duty well. Heaven alone will reward you, sir, for in this life there is no reward adequately expressive of the merit due you. You, sir, imparted consolation and revived the hopes of a dying soldier of the Twenty-eighth Ohio. He was badly wounded in the arm; you lifted him into an ambulance, and, the blood dripping from him, stained your hands and your clothing. That soldier was as dear to me as life itself."

"A husband?" said the governor.

"No, sir."

"A father?"

"No, sir."

"A lover?"

"No, sir."

"If not a husband, father, brother, son, or lover, who, then, could it be?" said the governor, at length breaking the silence, "this is an enigma to me. Please explain more about the gallant soldier of Ohio."

"Well, sir, that soldier gave you a ring—C. E. D. were the letters engraved upon the interior. That is the ring now upon your little finger. He told you to wear it, and carefully have you done so."

The governor pulled the ring off, and sure enough the letters were there.

"The finger that used to wear that ring will never

wear it any more. The hand is dead, but the soldier still lives."

The governor was now more interested than ever.

"Well, madam," said he, "tell me all about it. Is this ring yours? Was it given to you by a soldier whom you loved?"

"I loved him as I love my life; but he never returned that love. He had more love for his country than for me; I honor him for it. The soldier who placed that little ring upon your finger stands before you."

So saying, the strange lady rose from her chair, and stood before the governor.

The scene that now ensued we leave to the imagination of the reader. A happy hour passed. The girl who had thus introduced herself was Catherine E. Davidson, of Sheffield, Ohio. She was engaged to be married, but her future husband responded to the call of the President, and she followed him by joining another regiment. He was killed in the same battle where she fell wounded. She is alone in the world, her father and mother having departed this life years ago. She was the soldier of the Twenty-eighth Ohio who had placed the ring upon the finger of Governor Curtin, for the kind attention given her upon the bloody field of Antietam.

UNACCEPTABLE GRATITUDE.—Lieutenant J——n, late of the Sixteenth Regiment, was a few days ago walking down Main street, when he was accosted by a fellow, half soldier, half beggar, with a most reverential military salute:

"God bless your honor," said the man, whose accent betrayed him to be Irish, "and long life to you."

"How do you know me?" said the lieutenant.

"Is it how do I know your honor?" responded Pat. "Good right, sure, I have to know the man that saved my life in battle."

The lieutenant, highly gratified at this tribute to his valor, slid a fifty cent piece into his hand, and asked him, when?

"God bless your honor and long life to you," said the grateful veteran. "Sure it was Antietam, when seeing your honor run away as fast as your legs would carry you from the rebels, I followed your lead, and ran after you out of the way; whereby, under God, I saved my life. Oh! good luck to your honor, I never will forget it to you."

A CORRESPONDENT with the Army of the Cumberland, narrates the following incident:

A certain wealthy old planter, who used to govern a precinct in Alabama, in a recent skirmish was taken prisoner, and at a late hour brought into camp, where a guard was placed over him. The aristocratic rebel supposing every thing was all right—that he was secure enough any way as a prisoner of war—as a committee of the whole, resolved himself into "sleep's dead slumber." Awaking about midnight, to find the moon shining full into his face, he chanced to "inspect the guard," when, horror of horrors, that soldier was a negro! And, worse than all, he recognized in that towering form, slowly and steadily walking a beat, *one of his own slaves!*

Human nature could not stand that; the prisoner was enraged, furious, and swore he would not. Addressing the guard, through clenched teeth, foaming at the mouth, he yelled out:

"Sambo!"

"Well, massa."

"Send for the colonel to come here immediately. My own slave can never stand guard over me. It's a d—d outrage; no gentleman would submit to it."

Laughing in his sleeve, the dark-faced soldier promptly called out, "Corp'l de guard!"

That dignity appeared, and presently the colonel followed.

After listening to the Southerner's impassioned harangue, which was full of invectives, the colonel turned to the negro with:

"Sam!"

"Yes, colonel."

"You know this gentleman, do you?"

"Ob course; he's Massa B., and has a big plantation in' Alabam'."

"Well, Sam, just take care of him to-night," and the officer walked away.

As the sentinel again paced his beat, the gentleman from Alabama appealed to him in an argument.

"Listen, Sambo!"

"You hush dar; I's done gone talkin' to you now. Hush, rebel!" was the negro's emphatic command, bringing down his musket to a charge bayonet position, by way of enforcing silence.

THE VICKSBURG SCOW.

A BALLAD.

BRAVE Porter deals in hard, dry pokes,
He's also good at a clever hoax;
Of all his deeds, in fight or fun,
That queer old scow is "Number One."

Abandoned by the river's marge,
She had served her time as coaling barge;
Of refuse planks he shaped her roof
Like iron-clads, quite cannon-proof.

Pork barrels old, with ne'er a head,
As twin stacks rose, in chimnies' stead;
These vomited, to aid the joke,
From hearths of mud, a dreadful smoke.

In place of turret, on this raft,
(Oh, was not she the drollest craft!)
He rigged, from some plantation stript,
A small outbuilding, nondescript.

Two guns of log, of frightful size,
Frowned from her ports in grisly guise;
To fit this monster of the stream
To scare the rebels' guilty dream.

The moon was neither bright nor dim,
When Porter loosed this flat boat trim,
And let her drift, her course to steer,
With pilot none, nor engineer.

On Mississippi's eastern side,
The sentries soon her coming spied,
They raised alarm at dead of night—
All Vicksburg waked in deadly fright.

Drummers and generals, boy and man,
And gunners too, to quarters ran;
Oh, how they feared the awful ark
That loomed so large through midnight dark!

As fast as she in range drew near,
Their batteries roared with rage and fear;
Brimful when she began to float,
No balls could sink this mystic boat.

They marvelled much she did not sink;
"She's shot-proof, sure!" the rebels think;
Who ever heard of Yankee trick
That worked than this more 'cute and slick?

The Butternuts waste shell and shot,
Their cannonade gets loud and hot,
They burn their powder, burst their guns,
And shake the shores with deafening stuns.

Louder than powder, on our side,
Our soldiers laughed until they cried;
Some held their ribs, some rolled on grass,
To think Secesh was such an ass.

Nor was this din of laugh and gun,
The choicest part of Porter's fun.
The Queen of the West, that captive ram,
Escaped by flight a dreaded jam.

Away she went, we know not where!
But *hers* was not the biggest scare,—
For down the stream, their valued prey,
The captured Indianola lay.

They thought to fit this costly prize,
To run and "blast the Yankees' eyes;"
But blew her up, as the scow drew near—
Blew her to shivers, in their fear.

And so let all their projects burst,
And blow to atoms Treason curst;
But long live all our jolly tars,
The UNION too, with the Stripes and Stars!

MISS MELVINA STEVENS,

THE EAST TENNESSEE HEROINE.

THE position of East Tennessee during the Rebellion was different from that of any other portion of the Southern States except Western Texas. A majority of its inhabitants were loyal, but the rebels controlled the country by their troops, and had a sufficient number of sympathizers among the inhabitants to make the position of the Union-loving citizens perilous. But so thoroughly outspoken and defiant was the loyalty of the people that it constantly found expression in their acts. The men capable of bearing arms were almost universally enlisted in the Union army or acting as scouts for it, and the women, with a heroism above all praise, let slip no opportunity of benefiting the Union cause. For the Union men who were "lying out," as it was termed, *i. e.*, concealing themselves by day to avoid the ruthless conscription, or the murderous violence of the rebels, they had always words of cheer and acts of kindness, feeding them from their own scanty supplies, and sheltering them whenever it was safe to do so. When, as was the case in the later years of the war, the Union prisoners who had escaped from Richmond, Salisbury, Wilmington, Charleston, Millen, and Andersonville, began to find their way over the Black and Cumberland mountain ranges, these faithful Unionists, both men and women, guided and escorted them, concealed them by day or night, and led them by secret routes past the rebel troops which were hunting them, till they were safe within the Union lines. A single guide, Dan Ellis, brought through between four and five thousand escaped prisoners in this way.

Among those who assisted actively in this good work was the young and beautiful girl, long known as "the nameless heroine," whose services we here record. She was from a loyal family, and avowed openly her earnest sympathies with the North, but her youthfulness, grace, and intelligence, made her so widely and universally beloved and petted, that the rebel officers, many of whom were much fascinated by her beauty and pleasing manners, never suspected her of giving active aid to the escaped Unionists or to the Union army. Yet she had obtained from them information in regard to their plans and expectations, of which she made most effectual use for the Union cause. Night after night, too, did she escort the escaped prisoners past the most dangerous points of the rebel garrisons and outposts, doing this from the age of about fourteen, at the risk of her liberty and life, from no other motive than her ardent love for her country and its cause, and in spite of the flatteries and persuasions of the secessionists, who would gladly have won a maiden so gifted and so well educated to their cause. The correspondents of the *Tribune* and the Cincinnati *Gazette*—Messrs. Richardson, Browne, and Davis—were indebted tc her guidance for their escape from the rebels.

SOMEBODY'S DARLING.

Into a ward of the whitewashed halls,
  Where the dead and dying lay,
Wounded by bayonets, shells, and balls,
  Somebody's Darling was borne one day—
Somebody's Darling, so young and so brave,
  Wearing yet on his pale, sweet face,
Soon to be hid by the dust of the grave,
  The lingering light of his boyhood's grace.

Matted and damp are the curls of gold,
  Kissing the snow of the fair young brow,
Pale are the lips of delicate mould—
  Somebody's Darling is dying now.
Back from his beautiful blue-veined brow,
  Brush all the wandering waves of gold;
Cross his hands on his bosom now—
  Somebody's Darling is still and cold.

Kiss him once for somebody's sake,
  Murmur a prayer both soft and low;
One bright curl from its fair mates take—
  They were somebody's pride, you know;
Somebody's hand hath rested there—
  Was it a mother's, soft and white?
And have the lips of a sister fair
  Been baptized in the waves of light?

God knows best! he has somebody's love:
  Somebody's heart enshrined him there;
Somebody wafted his name above,
  Night and morn, on the wings of prayer.
Somebody wept when he marched away,
  Looking so handsome, brave, and grand;
Somebody's kiss on his forehead lay,
  Somebody clung to his parting hand.

Somebody's waiting and watching for him—
  Yearning to hold him again to her heart;
And there he lies with his blue eyes dim,
  And the smiling, child-like lips apart.
Tenderly bury the fair young dead,
  Pausing to drop on his grave a tear;
Carve in the wooden slab at his head,
  "Somebody's Darling slumbers here."

RALLYING A FLYING BRIGADE.

WHEN a body of troops are panic-stricken, and break and fly in confusion, military men agree in saying that it is almost an impossibility to rally them so as to make them immediately of service. The next day, or perhaps, if their panic occurred in the morning, on the evening of the same day, they may have so far recovered from its effects, as to be ready again for a fight, and to conduct themselves as well as any troops in the field. But the attempt to rally them when flying almost invariably proves a failure. They may stop for a few moments, but presently they will be edging off in another direction. In the attack of Sherman's troops upon Fort Buckner, in the battle of Chattanooga, however, an exception to this general rule occurred. A flying brigade was stopped in its flight, and turned again and marched instantly upon the enemy. An eye-witness thus relates the incident, which has no parallel save Sheridan's turning back his flying men at Middletown:

It was a partial repulse, but that momentary episode

of the battle will reflect undying honor on the army of which those repulsed troops formed a part. I know not the cause—the rebel artillery may have been concentrated upon it, but one brigade broke—broke in utter confusion, I thought, as I saw it, and the men came rushing down the hill. The others still stood, and the reinforcements continued to move forward. But the retreating troops did not fly to the foot of the hill, for at the moment they were passing the reinforcements an officer sprang forward among them, seized the standard of one of the regiments and stuck it in the ground. I saw him wave his sword once over his head, and point up the hill. I could not hear his voice, but the men did, and as if by magic—which will be forever a mystery to me—that routed column turned, turned instantly, and in a single second was marching up the hill, as firmly and as strongly formed as that of the newly arrived troops, and apparently forming a part of them. Not a man went further than where the reinforcements were met, and there all turned and re-charged as if it were a movement they had been practicing for years.

And then this whole line pushed forward again—certainly the most wonderful display of human nature under thorough discipline I have ever beheld or imagined. Both brigades had broken once; yet now, after half an hour's fight, they again returned to the fight by the side of a third leader. It is to me, writing it, perfectly incomprehensible, and I turn to my notes to see if my memory is not at fault. But no—the wonderful achievement is there in black and white—the very hour marked and roted.

NIGHT SCENE IN A HOSPITAL.

It was past eleven, and my patient was slowly wearying himself into fitful intervals of quietude, when, in one of these pauses, a curious sound arrested my attention. Looking over my shoulder, I saw a one-legged phantom hopping nimbly down the room; and, going to meet it, recognized a certain Pennsylvania gentleman, whose wound-fever had taken a turn for the worse, and, depriving him of the few wits a drunken campaign had left him, set him literally tripping on the light, fantastic toe "toward home," as he blandly informed me, touching the military cap, which formed a striking contrast to the severe simplicity of the rest of his decidedly *undress* uniform. When sane, the least movement produced a roar of pain or a volley of oaths; but the departure of reason seemed to have wrought an agreeable change both in the man and his manners; for, balancing himself on one leg, like a meditative stork, he plunged into an animated discussion of the war, the President, lager beer, and Enfield rifles, regardless of any suggestions of mine as to the propriety of returning to bed, lest he be court-martialed for desertion.

Any thing more supremely ridiculous can hardly be imagined than this figure, scantily draped in white, its one foot covered with a big blue sock, a dingy cap set rakingly askew on its shaven head, and placid satisfaction beaming in its broad, red face, as it flourished a mug in one hand, an old boot in the other, calling them canteen and knapsack, while it skipped and fluttered in the most unearthly fashion. What to do with the creature I didn't know; Dan was absent, and if I went to find him, the perambulator might festoon himself out of the window, set his toga on fire, or do some of his neighbors a mischief. The attendant of the room was sleeping like a near relative of the celebrated Seven, and nothing short of pins would rouse him; for he had been out that day, and whiskey asserted its supremacy in balmy whiffs. Still declaiming, in a fine flow of eloquence, the demented gentleman hopped on, blind and deaf to my graspings and entreaties; and I was about to slam the door in his face, and run for help, when a second saner phantom, "all in white," came to the rescue, in the likeness of a big Prussian, who spoke no English, but divined the crisis, and put an end to it, by bundling the lively monoped into his bed, like a baby, with an authoritative command to "stay put," which received added weight from being delivered in an odd conglomeration of French and German, accompanied by warning wags of a head decorated with a yellow cotton nightcap, rendered most imposing by a tassel like a bell-pull. Rather exhausted by his excursion, the member from Pennsylvania subsided; and, after an irrepressible laugh together, my Prussian ally and myself were returning to our places, when the echo of a sob caused us to glance along the beds. It came from one in the corner—such a little bed!—and such a tearful little face looked up at us, as we stopped beside it! The twelve years old drummer boy was not singing now, but sobbing, with a manly effort all the while to stifle the distressful sounds that would break out.

"What is it, Teddy?" I asked, as he rubbed the tears

away, and checked himself in the middle of a great sob to answer plaintively:

"I've got a chill, ma'am, but I aint cryin' for that, 'cause I'm used to it. I dreamed Kit was here, and when I waked up he wasn't, and I couldn't help it, then."

The boy came in with the rest, and the man who was taken dead from the ambulance was the Kit he mourned. Well he might; for, when the wounded were brought from Fredericksburg, the child lay in one of the camps thereabout, and this good friend, though sorely hurt himself, would not leave him to the exposure and neglect of such a time and place; but, wrapping him in his own blanket, carried him in his arms to the transport, tended him during the passage, and only yielded up his charge when Death met him at the door of the hospital, which promised care and comfort for the boy. For ten days, Teddy had shivered or burned with fever and ague, pining the while for Kit, and refusing to be comforted, because he had not been able to thank him for the generous protection, which, perhaps, had cost the giver's life. The vivid dream had wrung the childish heart with a fresh pang, and when I tried the solace fitted for his years, the remorseful fear that haunted him found vent in a fresh burst of tears, as he looked at the wasted hands I was endeavoring to warm:

"Oh! if I'd only been as thin when Kit carried me as I am now, maybe he wouldn't have died; but I was heavy, he was hurt worser than we knew, and so it killed him; and I didn't see him to say good-by."

This thought had troubled him in secret; and my assurances that his friend would probably have died at all events, hardly assuaged the bitterness of his regretful grief.

At this juncture, the delirious man began to shout; the one-legged rose up in his bed, as if preparing for another dart; Teddy bewailed himself more piteously than before; and if ever a woman was at her wit's end, that distracted female was nurse Periwinkle, during the space of two or three minutes, as she vibrated between the three beds, like an agitated pendulum. Like a most opportune reinforcement, Dan, the handy, appeared, and devoted himself to the lively party, leaving me free to return to my post; for the Prussian, with a nod and a smile, took the lad away to his own bed, and lulled him to sleep with a soothing murmur, like a mammoth bumble-bee. I liked that in Fritz, and if he ever wondered afterward at the dainties which sometimes found their way into his rations, or the extra comforts of his bed, he might have found a solution of the mystery in sundry persons' knowledge of the fatherly action of that night.

HOW THE SOLDIERS "TOOK THEIR EASE IN THEIR INN."

THE mad spirit of destructiveness and the love of mischief, were often displayed in the army, especially in that portion of it under General Sherman's command, when any position was captured which had served as an abiding place or headquarters of the officers of the rebel army. This disposition was very vividly illustrated at "Big Shanty," a station on the route between Chattanooga and Atlanta, in Sherman's Atlanta campaign. A correspondent of the Tribune thus describes the scene:

At Big Shanty, on the Atlanta line of railroad, stands quite a respectable looking two-storied wooden hotel, which in peace times was used as the dinner station for the famished passengers travelling from Chattanooga, Tennessee, to Atlanta, Georgia.

On Friday, while some of our cavalry were out on a reconnoissance, shelling the woods, one of our shells passed through a part of the hotel, entering a large sleeping apartment containing some eight or ten bedsteads, and passing through the bedstead out of the south side of the room, the shell burst in the yard. At this time, several rebel officers were partaking leisurely of a sumptuous dinner, and, without waiting for orders, they changed their base, retiring in the wildest confusion. Several ladies were in the hotel at the time this unruly "Yankee" messenger entered, and one of them was in the room through which the shell whizzed on its deadly errand, but fortunately the fuse was long enough to prevent its explosion for several seconds, thereby saving the terrified woman's life.

Upon the arrival of our advance at Big Shanty, this hotel, which was quite well furnished for this section of the country, was guarded. The owners having abandoned the property the guard was relieved, and in less than half an hour the rooms were filled, yes, the hotel was fairly besieged with soldiers representing every arm of the service, with a sprinkling of negro servants, the rough crowd all intent upon getting "something good to eat," while another portion was bent upon mischief. Such scenes as were there enacted, and such a terrible realization of Pandemonium, no artist's facile pencil, or this feeble pen, can half portray. Up-stairs, down-stairs, inside, outside, kitchen, dining-room, parlor, and bedroom, all shared the general tumult, and not a cobwebbed nook escaped overhauling from these inquisitive "mudsills."

In the parlor was a fine piano, drummed and played upon alternately, with a boisterous crowd of soldiers leaning upon it, each one shouting for some particular tune expressive of their musical tastes. "Give us Glory Hallelujah," shouts one. "No, that's played out," says another. "Play Rally Round the Flag." "Pshaw! give us a jig," and thus it went, a perfect jargon of sound filling the apartment, while in one corner of the room two soldiers were at work winding up and causing an old clock to strike. Look into the entry with me, and see the scrambling of fifty soldiers over a barrel of flour and a barrel of sugar and molasses, while feather beds are torn to pieces. One mischievous fellow has found the dinner bell, and yells out "Fifteen minutes for dinner." Another has discovered a string of cow bells, and at once strives to drown the inharmonious sounds of his rivals.

With the drumming of the piano, the striking clock, the blowing of horns, the rattling of dishes, the ringing of cow and dinner bells, the clatter of a sewing machine, and the wrangling of soldiers over the spoils, the ear was appalled and deafened, furniture, bedding, cooking utensils, books, pictures, china-ware, ladies' wearing apparel, hoop skirts and bonnets, were thrown together in promiscuous heaps with all sorts of dirty rubbish.

INCIDENTS OF GRIERSON'S RAID.

WHILE several of the Union scouts were feeding their horses at the stables of a wealthy planter of secession proclivities, the proprietor looking on, apparently deeply interested in the proceeding, suddenly burst out with: "Well, boys, I can't say I have any thing against you. I don't know but on the whole, I rather like you. You have not taken any thing of mine except a little corn for your horses, and that you are welcome to. I have heard of you all over the country. You are doing the boldest thing ever done. But you'll be trapped, though; you'll be trapped; mark me."

At another place, where the men thought it advisable to represent themselves as Jackson's cavalry, a whole company was very graciously entertained by a strong secession lady, who insisted on whipping a negro because he did not bring the hoe cakes fast enough.

On one occasion, seven of Colonel Grierson's scouts stopped at the house of a wealthy planter, to feed their jaded horses. Upon ascertaining that he had been doing a little guerilla business upon his own account, our men encouraged him to the belief that, as they were the invincible Van Dorn cavalry, they would soon catch the Yankees. The secession gentleman heartily approved of what he supposed to be their intentions, and enjoined upon them the necessity of making as rapid marches as possible. As the men had discovered two splendid carriage horses in the planter's stable, they thought, under the circumstances, they would be justified

ROUSSEAU
KAUTZ
STONEMAN
GRIERSON
PLEASANTON
GREGG
WILSON
VAN INGEN-SNYDER

in making an exchange, which they accordingly proceeded to do.

As they were taking the saddles from their own tired steeds and placing them on the backs of the guerilla's horses, the proprietor discovered them, and at once objected. He was met with the reply that, as he was anxious that the Yankees should be speedily overtaken, those after them should have good horses.

"All right, gentlemen," said the planter; "I will keep your animals until you return; I suppose you'll be back in two or three days at the farthest. When you return you'll find they have been well cared for."

The soldiers were sometimes asked where they got their blue coats. They always replied, if they were travelling under the name of Van Dorn's cavalry, that they took them at Holly Springs of the Yankees. This always excited great laughter among the secessionists. The scouts, however, usually wore the regular "secesh" uniforms.

FORAGING.

NOTHING in the excitement of army life has been the cause of more sport than the liberty given under certain circumstances, and taken under others, for the private soldier to "forage." In civilized warfare, ordinarily, the supplying of the troops with necessary food from the enemy's country is supposed to be a systematic business operation, conducted by the officers of the army of occupation, by requisition, either in money or produce, for which receipts of greater or less value are given. In a civil war, the supplies are to be paid for, according to the tenor of the receipt, on proof of the loyalty of the party furnishing them to the government of the captors. But in actual practice, there is a large amount of private plundering, which army officers, though they may censure, find it convenient to wink at. The men may have been on hard and unpalatable fare for days or weeks, and it is nearly impossible to prevent them from taking pigs, chickens, etc, when they are in a vicinity where they abound. The plunder and destruction of other valuables, such as watches, jewelry, clothing, musical instruments, books, and the burning of houses, etc., as it was practiced by the "bummers" or camp followers of Sherman's army, is an outrage on civilized warfare, and is a just ground of bitter reproach to the administration of that very able commander. Some of the foraging stories are, however, full of humor, and could hardly be otherwise regarded than as excellent jokes, even by the sufferers themselves. We subjoin a few.

Drawing Rations.—There are some episodes in the life of a soldier provocative of laughter, and that serve to disperse, in some manner, the ennui of camp life. A farmer, who did not reside so far from a camp of "the boys" as he wished he did, was accustomed to find every morning that several rows of potatoes had disappeared from the field. He bore it for some time, but when the last of his fine field of kidneys began to disappear, he thought the thing had gone far enough, and determined to stop it. Accordingly, he made a visit to camp early next morning, and amused himself by going round to see whether the soldiers were provided with good and wholesome provisions. He had not proceeded far, when he found a "boy" just serving up a fine dish of kidneys, which looked marvellously like those that the good wife brought to his own table. Halting, the following colloquy ensued:

"Have fine potatoes here, I see."

"Splendid," was the reply.

"Where do you get them?"

"Draw them."

"Does government furnish potatoes for rations?"

"Nary tater."

"I thought you said you drew them?"

"Did. We just do that thing."

"But *how?* if they are not included in your rations."

"Easiest thing in the world—wont you take some with us?" said the soldier, as he seated himself opposite the smoking vegetables.

"Thank you. But will you oblige me by telling how you draw your potatoes, as they are not found by the commissary?"

"Nothing easier. Draw 'em by the tops mostly! Sometimes by a hoe—if there's one left in the field."

"Hum! ha! Yes; I understand. Well, now, see here! If you wont draw any more of mine, I will bring you a basketful every morning, and draw them myself!"

"Bully for you, old fellow!" was the cry, and three cheers and a tiger were given for the farmer.

The covenant was duly observed, and no one but the farmer drew potatoes from that field afterward.

That Pig.—A few nights since, as two of the regiments were at Annapolis Junction, on their way here, a mischievous soldier, who was placed on guard at some distance from the main body, as he was walking his rounds, shot a pig. A member of the other regiment, hearing the report, hastened to the spot, and demanded that the pig should be divided, or he would inform his officers. The prize was accordingly "partitioned," and served up to the friends of each party. The officers, however, observing the bones, soon found out the guilty party; and, on questioning him, he replied that he did it in obedience to the orders he had received, "not to let any one pass without the countersign." He saw the pig coming toward him, and challenged it; but, receiving no answer, he charged bayonet on it, and, the pig still persisting, he shot it. The officers laughed heartily at the explanation, and sent him to find the owner, and pay for the pig, which he states was the hardest job he ever performed.

In the summer of 1861, a regiment of light infantry from the vicinity of Norway, Maine, were encamped in Washington for a few days. Two of the men had become dissatisfied with their fare, and they conceived the sublimely impudent idea of foraging on the President's rations. How they did it is related as follows:

They proceeded directly to the President's house. Without ceremony they wended their way quietly into the broad kitchen—"bowing to a tall man" on their passage—and carefully selecting what they thought would "go round," made the following speech to the cook:

"Look here; we've sworn to support the government;

for three days we've done it on salt junk; now if you *would* spare us a little of this it would *put the thing along amazingly*.

It is needless to say that the boys had an abundance that day.

HOW A YANKEE SOLDIER KEPT A HOTEL IN DIXIE.—When General Banks' army moved on up the Shenandoah valley from New Market, Quartermaster-Sergeant Reuben W. Oliver, of Cochran's New York battery, had to be temporarily left in a barn, on account of injuries he had received. Soon after our departure he made application at the lady's house adjoining for board; but he was informed, in true Virginia style, that she did not board "Yankee barbarians."

"Very well," replied Oliver, "if you wont board me I shall keep a hotel in your barn, but shall probably call upon you occasionally for supplies;" and he hobbled back to the barn.

Oliver was every inch a soldier, and he went to work at once. Taking a revolver, he shot madam's finest young porker, which his assistant immediately dressed. His able assistant next went to the apiary and "took us" a hive of bees, and transferred the honey to the barn. He then went to the lot and milked a pail of milk from her ladyship's cows. Then, going to her servants' house, he made a "requisition" for a quantity of fresh corn-dodgers that had been prepared for supper. The addition of these articles to his ordinary rations placed him far beyond the point of starvation.

True to his Yankee instincts, he invited the lady to take tea with him, at the hotel across the way—at which she became spitefully indignant. But Oliver was as happy as a lark, and for the time almost forgot his injuries.

Soon he had several sick soldiers added to his list of boarders; and in due time a sheep, and another young porker, and a second hive of bees, were gathered under the roof of his "hotel;" and furthermore, not a cock remained to proclaim when the morning dawned. By this time her ladyship thought she could "see it," and sent for Oliver, who, as promptly as the nature of his injuries would permit, reported at the door.

"See here, young man," said she, "I perceive that it would be cheaper for me to board you in my house—and, if you will accept, you can have board and a room free."

"Thank you, madam, thank you," replied Oliver, removing his cap and bowing politely; "but I prefer boarding at a first-class Yankee hotel to stopping at any secession house in Virginia at the same price. You will therefore be so kind as to excuse me for declining your generous offer, as it comes too late!" And back he hobbled to the barn—and actually remained there two weeks—taking in and boarding every sick soldier that came along; making frequent "requisitions" upon her for supplies.

Her ladyship was mightily pleased when Oliver's Yankee hotel was discontinued; but it taught her a valuable lesson, and Yankee soldiers never thereafter applied to her in vain for food and shelter. They always got what they wanted, she evidently not relishing the Yankee hotel system.

FORAGING FOR WHISKEY.—The appetite for strong drink was so fierce among some of the soldiers, that they would resort to all kinds of expedients to obtain it. At the commencement of the war, when the troops were encamped near Washington, in spite of the most stringent orders many would get intoxicated; and it was found that it was smuggled into camp in gun barrels. At Falmouth, before the battle of Fredericksburg, General Burnside ordered several hundred barrels of commissary whiskey to be sent down from Washington to Acquia creek. Lieutenant ———, of the Twenty-ninth New York, acting brigadier commissary in Getty's division, sent repeatedly to the creek for a supply; but every barrel that was furnished here would disappear from the cars before reaching Falmouth, rumor having it that the roguish Hawkins' Zouaves had "gobbled" them. At length, despairing of obtaining any of the stuff by order, he proceeded personally to Acquia creek for a supply. He obtained one barrel, and standing it up in the car, *seated himself upon the top* of the barrel, confident that no one would get that away from him. What was his dismay, on springing down to the platform at Falmouth, to find the barrel *empty!* Some ingenious soldiers had bored a hole up through the bottom of the car while the train halted at Potomac creek or Burke's station, tapped the barrel, and drained it to the dregs!

FORAGING BY VETERAN SOLDIERS.—In March, 1862, in the advance upon Winchester, Brigadier-General Abercrombie commanded the first brigade, having Cochran's battery with it. Abercrombie was very strict, not allowing his men to forage. The next morning after we camped near Berryville, the general rode through the battery. The captain was in his tent. Approaching it, he discovered the quarters of a fine young beef that the men had "foraged" the previous night, lying against a tree. The general's brow contracted as he demanded of Sergeant Leander E. Davis:

"Where the d—l did you get that beef? I gave the commissary no orders to issue fresh beef here."

Davis, who was a very polite soldier, removed his cap, and saluted the general, saying, in a tone evincing perfect coolness and sincerity:

"General, I was sergeant of the guard last night, and about ten o'clock I heard a terrible commotion in the camp of the Twelfth Massachusetts, Colonel Webster's regiment, across the road. I rushed out to see what was going on, and just as I passed the captain's tent I saw a fine steer coming through the camp of the Twelfth Massachusetts, with about a hundred men after it. The animal appeared very much frightened, general, and, true as you live, it jumped clear across the road (about two rods), over both stone fences, and as it alighted in this lot it struck its head against this tree, and being so terribly scared, its head, hide, and legs kept right on running, while the quarters dropped down here, where they have remained ever since. It is very fine, tender beef, general, and I had just come here for the purpose of cutting off and sending you a fine sirloin roast for dinner. Will you be so obliging as to accept of it?"

"How long have you been a soldier?" demanded the old general.

"About six months general."

"Well, sir, I perceive that you thoroughly appreciate the art of war, and have become a *veteran* in half a year. Were you a green soldier I should order you under arrest, and have you court-martialed; but, on account of your *veteran* proclivities, I shall recommend you for promotion!" and putting spurs to his horse he rode away, shaking his sides with laughter.

MAKING A CLEAN SWEEP.—If the practice of plundering the house of an enemy of all its provisions were ever justifiable, it would seem to have been partially so in the following instance, which is related by a veteran of the Army of the Cumberland:

We had had but a scanty allowance of food for several days, and the boys were getting to be pretty wolfish. Not far from our camp—by the way, this was down in Tennessee, in '62—there was a large rebel plantation, with a fine house, which the niggers said was actually overstocked with every thing nice. Some of the boys went there to try and raise something to eat. Several very stylish-looking ladies came out on the portico; but when we asked them for food—gracious!—how they abused us! It was perfectly savage! They presented pistols, and said they'd blow out our brains, and in fact "carried on" as only "reb" women *can*. Well—we retreated.

About an hour after, Major W—— and several others of our officers went to the same house, where the ladies gave them a luncheon, and at the same time provoked and annoyed them as much as possible, by giving an exaggerated account of the manner in which they had, as they said, driven off a band of Federal thieves that morning, and scared them to death with rusty and unloaded old pistols. They didn't spare the major, and insulted him by ridiculing his soldiers, until he was as mad as a hornet.

I don't know how it was, but, soon after the major got back to camp, somebody proposed to shell that house out. Down we went with a rush. The ladies came out in a rage, and flourished their old pistols, and abused us like street-walkers; but it was all of no use. The boys swarmed like bees into the cellar; and I tell you, it was the best filled house I ever foraged on. What they ever intended to do with such supplies of canned fruits and meats, such rows on rows of hams, and barrels of every thing nice, I can't imagine. The boys filled bags, and sheets, and blankets, and wheeled the plunder off, or carried it—"like good fellows."

Of course the ladies sent off post haste to Major W——, to come and stop this business. He was a very long time in coming—very. I think that the messenger must have had a hard time to find him. And when he got there he didn't speak to any of us, and seemed to be rather slow in taking in the whole story from the ladies. When he had heard them out—and it takes a long time for an angry woman to say all that she has to say—he bowed, and said: "Ladies, I will see to it at once." So down he came, and began to rate us in this style:

"Men, what do you mean by such infernal conduct? Stop your pillaging *at once!*" (*Then aside.*) "I hope you've cleaned the place out, d—n it!" (*Aloud.*) "Put down that bag of potatoes, you scoundrel!" (*Aside.*) "And roll off that barrel of sugar, you d—d fool!" (*Aloud.*) "If I catch you foraging again in this fashion, I'll make you repent it." (*Aside.*) "Pitch into the grub, boys!—there's a whole chest of tea in that dark corner!"

As the major went up-stairs, the cellar was empty. The last thing I heard him say to the ladies was, that "*his* men should never forage there again;" and his last aside—"I don't think they've left a single d—d thing to steal."

THE PEN MIGHTIER THAN THE SWORD.—While the Army of the Potomac was making its way into Virginia, a party of soldiers, hungry and fierce, had just reached a rail fence, tied their horses, and pitched their officers' tents, when four pigs incautiously approached the camp. The men, on noticing them, immediately decided on their capture. They stationed two parties, one at each end of a V in the fence, with rails to complete the two sides of a square; two men were then sent to scatter corn before the pigs, and lead them along inside the V, when the square was finished and the pigs penned. A cavalry officer, whose men had attempted their destruction with their sabres, came up, and said to the army correspondent who tells the story, "Ah! the *pen* is still mightier than the *sword!*"

General Payne, of Illinois, commanded a brigade in the Army of the Cumberland, composed of Ohio and Illinois troops. A soldier of the Seventy-ninth sent to the Dayton (Ohio) *Journal*, the following in reference to this officer:

THE REBELLION MUST BE SQUELCHED.—One day a wealthy old lady, whose plantation was in the vicinity of camp, came in and inquired for General Payne. When the commander made his appearance, the old lady in warm language at once acquainted him with the fact that his men had stolen her last coopful of chickens, and demanded their restitution, or their value in currency.

"I am sorry for you, madam," replied the general; "but I can't help it. The fact is, ma'am, we are determined to squelch out this unholy rebellion, if it takes every d—d chicken in Tennessee."

This exhibition of utter recklesness of means for the accomplishment of a purpose which the old lady deemed most foul, temporarily deprived her of the power of speech, and she passed from the presence of the general without asserting her right—the last word.

A DARK SHADOW.—A captain in front of Petersburg writes:

Last March, our regiment (the Twenty-second United States Colored Troops) was on rather a wild raid in King and Queen county, Virginia. As the raid was intended as a punishment for the brutal murder of the gallant young Dahlgren, the men were allowed much more liberty than is common even on such occasions, and great was the havoc inflicted upon the natives, in the way of private excursions among the hen-houses, and many were the remarks created among the "smokes." One enterprising fellow brought in with his supply of poultry an ex-

THE COUNTRY MUST BE SAVED IF IT TAKES EVERY CHICKEN IN THE CONFEDERACY."

ceedingly lean and thin hen. This fact being observed by one of his comrades, gave rise to the following remark:

"Golly! I tho't I's berry good forr'ger, but nebber seen a man afore could cotch de shadder of a hen!"

ADVENTURE OF A SPY.

I HAVE lately returned from the South, but my exact whereabouts in that region, for obvious reasons, it would not be politic to state. Suspected of being a Northerner, it was often my advantage to court obscurity. Known as a spy, "a short shrift" and a ready rope would have prevented the blotting of this paper. Hanging, disguised, on the outskirts of a camp, mixing with its idlers, laughing at their jokes, examining their arms, counting their numbers, endeavoring to discover the plans of their leaders, listening to this party and pursuing that, joining in the chorus of a rebel song, betting on rebel success, cursing abolitionism, despising Northern fighters, laughing at their tactics, and sneering at their weapons; praising the beauty of Southern belles and decrying that of Northern; calling New York a den of cutthroats and New Orleans a paradise of immaculate chivalry, is but a small portion of the practice of my profession as a spy. This may not seem honorable nor desirable. As to the honor, let the country benefited by the investigations and warnings of the spy be judge; and the danger, often incurred, is more serious and personal than that of the battle field, which may, perhaps, detract from its desirability.

It was a dark night. Not a star on the glimmer. I had collected my quotum of intelligence, and was on the move for the Northern lines. I was approaching the banks of a stream whose waters I had to cross, and had then some miles to traverse before I could reach the pickets of our gallant troops. A feeling of uneasiness began to creep over me; I was on the outskirt of a wood fringing the dark waters at my feet, whose presence could scarcely be detected but for their sullen murmurs as they rushed through the gloom. The wind sighed in gentle accordance. I walked forty or fifty yards along the bank. I then crept on all fours along the ground, and groped with my hands. I paused—I groped again —my breath thickened—perspiration oozed from every pore, and I was prostrated with horror. I had missed my landmark, and knew not where I was. Below or above, beneath the shelter of the bank, lay the skiff I had hidden ten days before, when I commenced my operations among the followers of Jeff. Davis.

As I stood gasping for breath, with all the unmistakable proofs of my calling about me, the sudden cry of a bird, or plunging of a fish, would act like magnetism upon my frame, not wont to shudder at a shadow. No matter how pressing the danger may be, if a man sees an opportunity of escape he breathes with freedom. But let him be surrounded by darkness, impenetrable at two yards' distance, within rifle's length of concealed foes, for what knowledge he has to the contrary; knowing toc, with painful certainty, the detection of his presence would reward him with a sudden and violent

THE SCOUT AND THE BLOODHOUND.

death, and if he breathes no faster, he is more fitted for a hero than I am.

In the agony of that moment—in the sudden and utter helplessness I felt to discover my true bearings—I was about to let myself gently into the stream, and breast its current for life or death. There was no alternative. The Northern pickets must be reached in safety before the morning broke, or I should soon swing between heaven and earth, from some green limb in the dark forest in which I stood.

At that moment the low, sullen bay of a bloodhound struck my ear. The sound was reviving—the fearful stillness broken. The uncertain dread flew before the certain danger. I was standing to my middle in the shallow bed of the river, just beneath the jutting banks. After a pause of a few seconds, I began to creep mechanically and stealthily down the stream, followed, as I knew, from the rustling of the grass and frequent breaking of twigs, by the insatiable brute; although, by certain uneasy growls, I felt assured he was at fault. Something struck against my breast. I could not prevent a slight cry from escaping me, as, stretching out my hand, I grasped the gunwale of a boat moored beneath the bank. Between surprise and joy I felt half choked.

In an instant I had scrambled on board, and began to search for the painter in the bow, in order to cast her from her fastenings. Suddenly a bright ray of moonlight—the first gleam of hope in that black night—fell directly on the spot, revealing the silvery stream, my own skiff (hidden there ten days before), lighting the deep shadows of the verging wood, and, on the log half buried in the bank, and fiom which I had that instant cast the line that had bound me to it, the supple form of the crouching bloodhound, his red eyes gleaming in the moonlight, jaws distended, and poising for the spring. With one dart the light skiff was yards out in the stream, and the savage after it. With an oar I aimed a blow at his head, which, however, he eluded with ease. In the effort thus made, the boat careened over toward my antagonist, who made a desperate effort to get his fore paws over the side, at the same time seizing the gunwale with his teeth. Now or never was my time. I drew my revolver, and placed the muzzle between his eyes, but hesitated to fire, for that one report might bring on me a volley from the shore. Meantime the strength of the dog careened the frail craft so much that the water rushed over the side, threatening to swamp her. I changed my tactics, threw my revolver into the bottom of the skiff, and grasping my "Bowie," keen as a Malay creese, and glittering as I released it from the sheath, like a moonbeam on the stream. In an instant I had severed the sinewy throat of the hound, cutting through brawn and muscle to the nape of the neck. The tenacious wretch gave a wild, convulsive leap half out of the water, then sank and was gone. Five minutes' pulling landed me on the other side of the river, and in an hour after I was among friends within the Northern lines.

General Pope and the Assistant Secretary of War.—A correspondent of the *N. Y. Tribune* says:

I heard, while at Pillow, an anecdote of General Pope —an officer of ability, but sometimes a very unpleasant man, with a pompous and hectoring manner—which will bear repetition. While at his headquarters, the general was approached by a rather small, plain-looking, and entirely unassuming man, in citizen's attire, with the question: "Are you General Pope, sir?"

"That is my name," was the answer, in rather a repelling tone.

"I would like to see you, then, on a matter of business."

"Call on my adjutant, sir. He will arrange any business you may have."

"But I wish to have a personal conversation with you."

"See my adjutant," in an authoritative voice.

"But—"

"Did I not tell you to see my adjutant? Trouble me no more, sir;" and Pope was about walking away.

"My name is Scott, general," quietly remarked the small, plain man.

"Confound you! What do I care," thundered Pope, in a rising passion, "if your name is Scott, or Jones, or Jenkins, or Snooks, for the matter of that? See my adjutant, I tell you, fellow! Leave my presence!"

'I am," continued the quiet man, in his quiet way, "the Assistant Secretary of War, and—"

What a revolution those simple words made in the general's appearance and manner!

His angry, haughty, domineering air was dispelled in a moment, ar.d a flush of confusion passed over his altered face

"I beg your pardon, Mr. Scott, I had no idea whom I was addressing. Pray be seated; I shall be happy to grant you an interview at any time."

Possibly a very close observer might have seen a faint, half contemptuous smile on the Secretary's lips; though he said nothing, but began to unfold his business without comment.

After that unique interview, Pope and the Assistant Secretary were very frequently together, and I venture to say the latter had no reason subsequently to complain of the general's rudeness.

THE RELIGIOUS SENTIMENT IN THE ARMY.

It is well known that some of our bravest and most efficient of the Union generals were men of undoubted and pre-eminent piety. General Howard maintained the lustre of his Christian profession amid the most trying scenes which a soldier could be called to encounter. General Burnside was also known as a decided Christian; and many of the division and brigade commanders were remarkable for their deeply religious character. Mr. William Swinton, author of the "History of the Army of the Potomac," relates some incidents in regard to General Couch and General Rosecrans, which demonstrate the power of the religious sentiment in their characters.

"Never," says Mr. Swinton, "shall I forget how General Couch, the commander of the second corps, and successor of General Sumner (that old brave, with the courage of a lion and the tenderness of a child), replied to a question which I put to him as to whether he was ever afraid in battle. It was on that dark December day when the plains of Fredericksburg were lit up with baleful fires, and the placid serenity of the general amid the winged messengers of death prompted the question. I should strive in vain to convey the tender and unaffected grace of his words and manner; but, looking heavenward, he said: "*No; for in battle I always see the figure of Christ in the sky!*"

This recalls a somewhat similar anecdote respecting General Rosecrans, which was told me by the staff officer mentioned below, and which I believe has not before been in print. It is well known that General Rosecrans is a Catholic, and a devout and fervent Christian. At the battle of Stone river, the day for a time went against him. The whole right wing was disrupted, and irretrievable disaster seemed imminent. The commander constantly rushed to the front to animate his men by his presence—and on one occasion, when about to dash forward to a position of peculiar peril, one of his aides, young Captain Thompson, protested against his thus exposing himself. "O, my boy," was Rosecrans' reply, "*make the sign of the true cross, and let us go in!*" Thus, unconsciously, that illustrious soldier, perhaps the greatest strategist of the war, uttered almost the very maxim of Constantine, *In hoc signo vinces*—in that sign shalt thou conquer. I afterward made with him that wondrous campaign from Murfreesboro to Chattanooga. Every move was preceded by religious exercises; and I could well see, in his manifestations of deep and fervent piety, that a higher inspiration than the blazon of martial glory moved him—that it was truly in that *sign* that he sought to conquer.

The same writer says of Captain G. W. Rodgers, of the *Catskill*, U. S. N.:

Of the officers of the fleet to which Captain Rodgers belonged—the North Atlantic blockading squadron, under Admiral Dupont—I scarcely knew one that was not either a sincere Christian or at least a respecter of religion. Rodgers was one of its brightest ornaments. I lived on board his vessel, the Catskill, for several weeks previous to his death, and had sounded the depths of his tender and pious nature. Latterly there was seen in him a strange unworldliness that seemed to withdraw him from life, lifting him above the coils and confusions of this "weary and unintelligible world;" and there was seen that in his mood and manner which struck his friends with the sad premonition that he was not long to move among us. Yet this took away none of his alacrity in the discharge of his duty, and in the iron-clad assault on Fort Sumter that soon followed, he ran his vessel far ahead of his fellows, and laid it almost under the frowning battlements of the fort. The assault failed, and I spent the night with him in his cabin. It was expected that the attack would be renewed in the morning. Our conversation was prolonged till after midnight, and without undressing I lay down. Rodgers never retired; but, when he thought his companion was

PARSON BROWNLOW'S DAUGHTER AND THE REBEL SOLDIERS.

asleep, he took down his Bible, and passed the whole remainder of the night on his knees in prayer. The assault was not renewed; but a short time after, in an act of heroic daring, he ran his vessel under the very guns of Wagner, and was killed by a bolt shot through his pilot-house. To my mind he remains forever in the prayerful attitude in which I saw him on that *triste noche*,

> "A statue solid set,
> And moulded in colossal calm."

PARSON BROWNLOW'S DAUGHTER

AND THE REBEL SOLDIERS.

After the fraudulent vote for secession in Tennessee, in June, 1861, the rebels began to annoy and insult Parson Brownlow and his family. His house, up to midsummer of that year, floated the American flag, though many an attempt was made to drag it down. Early in June a Louisiana regiment, *en route* for Virginia, tarried at Knoxville, awaiting transportation over the railway, then crowded beyond its capacity. The parson says, in his record of the events of that year:

"These mean scoundrels visited the houses of Union men, shouted at them, groaned and hissed. My humble dwelling had the honor to be thus greeted oftener than any other five houses in Knoxville. The Southern papers said they were the flower of their youth. I said to my wife, if this is the flower, God save us from the rabble."

Upon one of these occasions nine members of the Louisiana regiment determined to see the flag humbled. Two men were chosen as a committee to proceed to the parson's house to order the Union ensign down. Mrs. More (the parson's daughter) answered the summons. In answer to her inquiry as to what was their errand, one said, rudely:

"We have come to take down that d—d rag you flaunt from your roof—the Stripes and Stars."

Mrs. More stepped back a pace or two within the door, drew a revolver from her dress pocket, and levelling it, answered:

"Come on, sirs, and take it down!"

The chivalrous Confederates were startled.

"Yes, come on!" she said, as she advanced toward them.

They cleared the piazza, and stood at bay on the walk.

"We'll go and get more men, and then d—d if it don't come down!"

"Yes, go and get more *men*—you are not men!" said the heroic woman, contemptuously, as the two backed from the place and disappeared.

GENERAL BANKS

AND THE MILITARY SPECULATORS.

CORRESPONDENTS universally accord to General Banks the credit of being "faithful among the faithless"—perhaps the only prominent man in his department in Government employ who is not grasping after the spoils. One writer records the following specimen scene at the general's headquarters:

Enter an ex-colonel of a Massachusetts regiment, and after waiting for an interview, a colloquy something like the following occurs:

Ex-colonel.—"Good-morning, general."

General B.—"Good-morning, sir; I am very happy to see you."

Ex-colonel.—"General, I called to ask for a pass to go to New Iberia."

General B.—"Your name is ——"

Ex-colonel.—"Yes, sir."

General B.—"You were colonel of the Massachusetts —— Regiment?"

Ex-colonel.—"Yes, sir."

General B.—"And you resigned your commission to engage in speculation?"

Ex-colonel.—"Why, general, you would not suppose I should continue in the service when I saw a chance to make twenty or thirty thousand dollars in a few months!"

General B.—"Sir, I did not come here to make money by speculation, and it is because men like yourself are willing to see my command broken up, if they can accomplish their own purposes, that this Department is in no better condition to-day. I give no passes to New Iberia, sir, and especially I shall not grant one to you. Good-morning, sir."

Exit ex-colonel evidently considering how he should get to New Iberia *without* General Banks' pass.

A WOMAN'S PLUCK AND PATRIOTISM.

An interesting incident is told concerning the independent and successful stand taken by a Union woman in New Orleans, in 1861. She and her husband, a Mississippi steamboat captain, occupied the middle front room of the lowest range of sleeping apartments in the St. Charles Hotel, at the time when the city was to be illuminated in honor of secession. She refused to allow the illuminating candles to be fixed in the windows of her room, and the proprietors remonstrated in vain, she finally ordering them to leave the room, of which she claimed, while its occupant, to have entire control. The rest of the story is thus told:

Determined not to be outdone in a matter of such grave importance, the captain, who was not in the room during the above proceedings, was next found and appealed to. He heard their case; said his wife had reported him correctly on the Union question, nevertheless, he would go with them to the room, and see if the matter could be amicably arranged. The captain's disposition to yield was not to be seconded by his better half. The proprietors next proposed to vacate the best chamber in her favor in some other part of the house, if that would be satisfactory; but the lady's "No!" was still as peremptory as ever. Her point was gained, and the St. Charles was doomed to have a dark front chamber. Pleased with this triumph, Mrs. —— devised the following manœuvre to make the most of her victory.

Summoning a servant, she sent him out to procure for her an American flag, which at dusk she suspended from her window. When evening came, the streets, animated by a merry throng, were illuminated. But, alas! the St. Charles was disfigured by its sombre chamber, when suddenly, a succession of lamps, suspended on both sides of the flag, were lit up, revealing the stars and stripes, and the ensign of the Union waved from the centre of a hotel illuminated in honor of its overthrow. The effect was to give the impression that the whole house was thus paying homage to the American flag; and what is more significant, is the fact that the flag was greeted by the passing crowd with vociferous applause. So much for the firmness of a true Union woman.

GIVING FOR THE WOUNDED SOLDIERS.

Mrs. D. P. Livermore, one of the acting managers of the Northwestern Sanitary Commission, relates the following instances of liberal and generous giving to that branch of the Sanitary Commission, for the care and welfare of the sick and wounded heroes of the army.

Some two or three months ago, a poor girl, a seamstress, came to the rooms of the Chicago Sanitary Commission. "I do not feel right," she said, "that I am doing nothing for our soldiers in the hospitals, and have resolved to do *something* immediately. Which do you prefer—that I should give money, or buy material and manufacture it into garments?"

"You must be guided by your circumstances," was the answer made her; "we need both money and supplies, and you must do that which is most convenient for you."

"I prefer to give you money, if it will do as much good."

"Very well; then give money, which we need badly, and without which we cannot do what is most necessary for our brave sick men."

"Then I will give you the entire earnings of the next two weeks. I'd give more, but I have to help support my mother, who is an invalid. Generally, I make but one vest a day, but I will work earlier and later these two weeks."

In two weeks she came again, the poor sewing girl, her face radiant with the consciousness of philanthropic intent. Opening her portemonnaie, she counted out—how much do you think, reader?—*nineteen dollars and thirty-seven cents!* Every penny was earned by the slow needle, and she had stitched away into the hours of midnight, on every one of the working days of the week. We call that an instance of patriotism married to generosity.

SOME farmers' wives in the north of Wisconsin, eighteen miles from a railroad, had given to the Commission of their bed and table linen, their husbands' shirts and drawers, their scanty supply of dried and canned fruits, till they had exhausted their ability to do more in this direction. Still they were not satisfied. So they cast about to see what could be done in another way. They were all the wives of small farmers, lately moved to the West, living all in log cabins, where one room sufficed for kitchen, parlor, laundry, nursery, and bedroom, doing their own housework, sewing, baby tending, dairy work, and all. What *could* they do?

They were not long in devising a way to gratify the longings of their motherly and patriotic hearts, and instantly set about carrying it into action. They resolved to beg wheat of the neighboring farmers, and convert it into money. Sometimes on foot, and sometimes with a team, amid the snows and mud of early spring, they canvassed the country for twenty and twenty-five miles around, everywhere eloquently pleading the needs of the blue-coated soldier boys in the hospitals, the eloquence everywhere acting as an *open sesame* to the granaries. Now they obtained a little from a rich man, and then a great deal from a poor man—deeds of benevolence are half the time in an inverse ratio to the ability of the benefactors—till they had accumulated nearly five hundred bushels of wheat. This they sent to market, obtained the highest market price for it, and forwarded the proceeds to the Commission. As we held this hard-earned money in our hands, we felt that it was consecrated—that the holy purpose of these noble women had imparted an almost sacredness to it.

A LITTLE girl not nine years old, with sweet and timid grace, came into the rooms of the Commission, and laying a five dollar gold piece on our desk, half frightened, told us its history. "My uncle gave me that before the war, and I was going to keep it always; but he's got killed in the army, and mother says now I may give it to the soldiers if I want to—and I'd like to do so. I don't suppose it will buy much for them—will it?"

We led the child to the storeroom, and proceeded to show her how valuable her gift was, by pointing out what it would buy—so many cans of condensed milk, or so many bottles of ale, or pounds of tea, or codfish, etc. Her face brightened with pleasure. But when we explained to her that her five dollar gold piece was equal to seven dollars and a half in greenbacks, and told her how much comfort we had been enabled to carry into a hospital with as small an amount of stores as that sum would purchase, she fairly danced for joy. "Oh, it will do lots of good, wont it?" And folding her hands earnestly before her, she begged, in her charmingly modest way, "Please tell me something that you've seen in the hospitals." A narration of a few touching events, not such as would too severely shock the little creature, but which plainly showed the necessity of continued benevolence to the hospitals, filled her sweet eyes with tears, and drew from her the resolution "to save all her money, and to get all the girls to do so, to buy things for the wounded soldiers." And away she flew, revelling in the luxury of doing good, and happy in the formation of a good resolution.

A ragged little urchin, who thrusts his unkempt pate daily into the rooms, with the shrill cry of "Matches! matches!" had stood watching the little girl, and listening to the talk. As she disappeared, he fumbled in his ragged pocket, and drew out a small handful of crumpled and soiled postal currency. "Here," said he, "I'll give you so much for them 'ere sick fellers in the hospi-

"I'LL GIVE YOU SO MUCH FOR THEM 'ERE SICK FELLOWS IN THE HOSPITAL."

tals," and he put fifty-five cents into our hand, all in five cent currency. We hesitated. "No, my boy, don't give it. You're a noble little fellow, but I'm afraid you can't afford to give so much. You keep it, and I'll give the fifty-five cents, or somebody else will."

"Oh, no," he replied, "you keep it. P'raps I ain't so poor as yer think. My father, he saws wood, and my mother, she takes in washin', and I sells matches —and p'raps we've got more money than yer think. Keep it!" And he turned his dirty, but earnest face up to us with a most beseeching look. "Keep it—do!"

We took the crumpled currency—we forgot the dirty face and the tattered cap—we forgot that we had called the little scamp a "nuisance," every day for months, when he had made us fairly jump from our seat with his shrill, unexpected cry of "Matches! matches!" and made a dive at him to kiss him. But he was too quick for us, and darted out of the room as if he had been shot. Ever since, when he meets us, he gives us a wide berth, and walks off the sidewalk into the gutter, eyeing us with a suspicious, sidelong glance, as though he suspected we still meditated kissing intentions toward him. If we speak to him, he looks at us shyly, and offers no reply—but if we pass him without speaking, he challenges us with a hearty "halloo, you!" that brings us to a halt instantly.

THE DISAPPOINTED BUMMER.—In Sherman's march through the Carolinas, during the skirmish in front of

Fayetteville, one of the captains in the Union army, who was in advance of his men, crept, in a citizen's coat, up to a fence, in order to get a better look at the enemy, who were retreating but firing rapidly. Suddenly he was confronted by a ragged and barefooted fellow, whom he instantly recognized as one of the "bummers." The recognition, however, was not reciprocal, for the "bummer" exulted in the thought that he had caught a rebel, and proceeded to salute him thus:

"Halloo! just stop right thar," surveying his extremities. "I say, come up out of them boots."

"I couldn't think of it," was the reply; "they are a fine pair of boots, and they are mine."

"You needn't say another d—d word. Come out of them boots. P'raps you've got a watch about your breeches pocket; just pull her out. No nonsense, now; I'm in a hurry to get arter them rebs."

"Perhaps you would like a horse?"

"A horse?" (the "bummer's" eyes sparkled.) "A horse? Well, now, you jis' come up out of them boots, and we'll discuss that ar' hoss question sudden. Where is the hoss?"

"Oh, he is right near by, in charge of my orderly."

"Thunder! are you an officer of our army? I thought you was a reb."

And then the "bummer" went to the rear under arrest, disgusted beyond measure.

A Sergeant Halts a Whole Regiment.—Among the beauties of the war in Western Virginia was the "mixed up" way in which the combatants manœuvre among the mountains. Here is an incident in which a single loyal soldier halted an entire rebel regiment:

Sergeant Cart, of Tippecanoe, Ohio, was upon the post first attacked by the enemy. The advance-guard of the Second Virginia (rebel), consisting of twelve men, came suddenly upon him and his three companions The bright moonlight revealed the flashing bayonets of the advancing regiment. He was surrounded and separted from his reserve. With great presence of mind he stepped out and challenged, "*Halt!* Who goes there?" The advanced guard, supposing they had come upon a scouting party of their own men, answered, "Friends, with the countersign." At his order, "Advance and give the countersign!" they hesitated. He repeated the order peremptorily, "Advance and give the countersign, or I'll blow you through!" They answered, without advancing, "Mississippi!" "Where do you belong?" he demanded. "To the Second Virginia Regiment." "Where are you going?" "Along the ridge." They in turn, questioned him, "Who are *you?*" "That's my own business," he answered, and, taking deliberate aim. shot down the questioner.

Calling his boys to follow him, he sprung down a ledge of rocks, while a full volley went over his head. He heard his companions summoned to surrender, and the order given to the major to advance with the regiment. Several started in pursuit of him. He had to descend the hill on the side toward the enemy's camp. While thus eluding his pursuers, he found himself in a new danger. He had got within the enemy's pickets!

He had, while running, torn the U. S. from his cartridge box, and covered his belt plate with his cap box, and torn the stripes from his pantaloons. He was challenged by their sentinels, while making his way out, and answered, giving the countersign, "'Mississippi,' Second Virginia Regiment." They asked him what he was doing there. He answered that the boys had gone off on a scout after the Yankees, while he had been detained in camp, and in trying to find them had lost his way.

As he passed through, to prevent further questioning, he said, "Our boys are upon the ridge—which is the best way up?" They answered, "Bear to the left and you'll find it easier to climb." Soon, however, his pursuers were again after him, "breaking brush behind him," this time with a hound on his trail. He made his way to a brook, and running down the shallow stream threw the dog off the scent, and, as the day was dawning, came suddenly upon four pickets, who brought their arms to a ready, and challenged him. He gave the countersign, "Mississippi," and claimed to belong to the Second Virginia Regiment. They asked him where he got that belt (his cap box had slipped from before his belt-plate), to which he replied that he had captured it that night from a Yankee. They told him to advance, and, as he approached, he recognized their accoutrements, and knew that he was among his own men, a picket guard from the First Kentucky.

He was taken before Colonel Enyart, and dismissed to his regiment. He said his plan was to give intimation to the reserves of their advance, that they might open upon them on their left flank, and so, perhaps, arrest their advance.

How Cheatham Deceived the Illinois Cavalry.—The Cairo correspondent of the St. Louis *Republican*, in 1861, visited the rebel camp, at Columbus, under a flag of truce. He relates the following story, told by the rebel General Cheatham, of the manner in which he escaped capture at the battle of Belmont, Missouri:

Just as the opposing armies were approaching one another, General Cheatham discovered a squadron of cavalry coming down a road near his position. Uncertain as to which force it belonged, accompanied only by an orderly, he rode up to within a few yards of it and inquired:

"What cavalry is that?"

"Illinois cavalry, sir," was the reply.

"Oh! Illinois cavalry. All right!—just stay where you are!"

The cavalry obeyed the rebel order, and unmolested by them (who supposed he was a Federal officer) the general rode back safely under the guns of another Federal regiment, which had by that time come up, but who, seeing him coming from the direction of the cavalry, also supposed that he was "one of them." Some of our officers remembered the incident, and agreed with the hero of it, that, if they had known who he was, there would have been one rebel general less that night.

One Man Capturing a Dozen.—During one of the movements made by the Eleventh Ohio, at the battle of South Mountain, to drive the rebels from their position, Colonel Coleman was unfortunately cut off from the regiment, and on emerging from a dense thicket of pine and laurel bushes, found himself confronting some ten or a dozen rebels, having in charge several Union soldiers as prisoners. In an instant he flourished his sword over his head, dashed right at them, and, in a stern, commanding voice, ordered them, in no very complimentary terms, to surrender. Down went every gun, and up went every hand, and, ordering them to fall in, he marched them within the lines—the Union boys and rebels having meanwhile changed positions considerably.

"SOLD AGAIN."—A scouting party of the Eleventh Ohio, under command of Captain Jordan, made a descent on a happy company of the chivalry in a manner which was both adroit and amusing. The captain seeing a bright light in a house marched his party to within a short distance of it, and leaving them in a concealed place, with his instructions to be on the alert, proceeded by himself to reconnoitre the position. On approaching the house, he discovered that the light was from a blazing fire. Walking boldly up to the door, but shielding his face and dress from the glare of the light, he accosted a Confederate soldier, who, at that moment, opened the door and looked out. Ascertaining that the house was full of rebels, he replied to an invitation to come in and warm himself, by saying that he would, as soon as he had hitched his horse. Having done this, he brought up his men, who were concealed within a few rods. Without noise, in a few minutes their bayonets were closed around the house, and Captain Jordan, with revolver in hand, sprang into the centre of the rebels, ordering them to surrender instantly. A rifle or two were raised at him, but he, with great coolness, laughed at their boldness. Seeing a file of blue-coated boys, with guns in hand, crowding in at the door, and several approaching bayonets, the rebels put down their guns, and raised their hands in token of surrender.

"Pretty well done, captain," said the officer in charge of the picket post, as this turned out to be.

"Yes," said Jordan, "we always do things pretty well. Fall in here, and keep pretty quiet if you know what is good for you."

When the rebels, after surrendering their arms, were marched off, and beheld the very inferior force to which they had surrendered, some of them could not help muttering, "Sold again!"

CUTTING OFF THE SUPPLIES.—During the battle of Chancellorsville, just as we were starting out of an oak thicket, a solid shot from the enemy instituted a search into the haversack of one of the boys of Company H, tearing it from him in a very rude manner, and throwing his hard tack in every conceivable direction. At first it felled him to the earth, but finding himself uninjured, he rose to his feet, and, looking around, said: "Hallo! the d—d villains are cutting off my supplies!"

VETERANS OR MILITIA?—At the battle of Gettysburg, when Longstreet made his attack on the Union centre, the Union troops were behind a stone wall. The rebels were told that the men ahead were only militia, and so marched boldly up. When within thirty yards of the Union line they recognized the bronzed features of their old enemy, and the cry was raised: "*The Army of the Potomac!*" when they became at once demoralized, and were cut to pieces. Nearly all the rebels shot in the attack on the centre were struck in the head.

"SET 'EM UP ON T'OTHER ALLEY."—At Antietam our boys (One-hundred-and-seventh New York Volunteers) supported Cothern's battery. The rebels advanced in a solid mass. One of our boys, a sporting character from Elmira, climbed a high rock, where he could view the whole scene. He occupied his place unmindful of the bullets whizzing like bees around him. The rebels came on until we could see their faces, and then Cothern poured the canister into them. The advancing column was literally torn to pieces by the fire. Our friend on the rock grew frantic in his demonstrations of delight, and as one of the battery sections sent a schrapnel which mowed down a long line of Johnnies, he swung his cap, and shouting so that the flying rebels could have heard him, sung out: "Bul—l—l—l—ee! *Set 'em up on t'other alley!*"

A LITTLE HERO.—At the siege of Fort Donelson, a boy of eleven years of age, whose father, a volunteer, had been taken prisoner by the rebels at Belmont, smuggled himself on board one of the transports at Cincinnati, laden with troops for Fort Donelson. On the field, on the morning of the great fight, he joined the Seventy-Eighth Ohio Regiment, and being questioned by one of the officers, he told him of his father having been taken prisoner, and having no mother, he had no one to care for him, and wanted to fight his father's captors. The officer tried to persuade him to turn back; but he was not to be denied. So he succeeded in obtaining a musket and went into the thickest of the battle. He then crept up by degrees within a short distance of the rebel intrenchments, and posted himself behind a tree, from which he kept firing as often as he could see a head to fire at. He was soon discovered by the enemy's sharpshooters, who endeavored to drive him away from his position, as he kept picking them off very frequently. One of the rebels who was outside of the work, got a sight on the boy with his rifle, but before he could discharge his piece the little warrior fired, and down went the rebel. As this rebel had a fine minie rifle, the boy ran out and picked it up; taking time to get pouch and balls, together with his knapsack, while the bullets were flying on all sides of him, and then retreated to his wooden breastwork, where he renewed his fire and with better success than before; and after being in the fight all day, he returned to the Seventy-eighth at night with his prizes. Many of the members of that regiment saw the gallant conduct of the little hero, and vouched for the truth of his story.

A Brave Irishman.—One of the Indiana regiments was fiercely attacked by a whole brigade, in one of the battles in Mississippi. The Indianians, unable to withstand such great odds, were compelled to fall back about thirty or forty yards, losing, to the utter mortification of the officers and men, their flag, which remained in the hands of the enemy. Suddenly a tall Irishman, a private in the color company, rushed from the ranks across the vacant ground, attacked the squad of rebels who had possession of the conquered flag, with his musket felled several to the ground, snatched the flag from them, and returned safely to his regiment. The bold fellow was, of course, immediately surrounded by his jubilant comrades, and greatly praised for his gallantry. His captain made him a sergeant upon the spot; but the hero cut every thing short by the reply:

"Oh! never mind, captain—say no more about it. I dropped my whiskey flask among the rebels, and fetched that back, and I thought I might just as well bring the flag along!"

MORGAN'S MEN

AND THE SECESSIONISTS.

In Morgan's rash but daring raid into Indiana and Ohio, in July, 1863, his band of guerillas, after they entered Indiana, plundered right and left, sparing nothing they could render available. In their forays, however, they were more severe upon Northern men who professed to be secessionists than upon any others, despising them for their meanness and treachery. This was especially exemplified at Salem, Indiana.

After Morgan entered the town, some of his men went to burn the bridges and water-tanks on the railroad. They captured on their way two men, one of whom was a Quaker. The broad-brimmed patriot urged that he as a peaceable citizen attending only to his own business, ought not to be held as a prisoner of war.

"But are you not hostile to the Confederacy?"

"Thee is right. I am."

"Well, you voted for Abraham Lincoln, did you not?"

"Thee is right. I did vote for Abraham."

"Well, what are you?"

"Thee may naturally suppose that I am a Union man. Can thee not let me go to my home?"

"Yes, yes; go and take care of the old woman," said the rebel, releasing the man, whose brave and honest truthfulness won the respect of the foe.

The other captive was not pleased with the speedy release of his comrade in misfortune. Turning to his captors with the ignoble and malicious spirit which has characterized all of his class, he said, hoping to ingratiate himself with the rebels:

"Look here! What did you let that fellow go for? He is a black abolitionist. Now *I* voted for Breckinridge. I have always been opposed to the war. I am opposed to fighting the South *decidedly*."

"You are?" replied the rebel, contemptuously. "You are what they call about here a *Copperhead*, aren't you?"

"Yes, yes," replied the Copperhead, insinuatingly. "That is what all my neighbors call me. They know that I am not with them."

"Come here, Dave!" shouted the rebel to one of his comrades. "There is a Copperhead! Just look at him! Now, old man," continued he, turning to the wretch, "where do you live? We want what horses you have to spare. And if you have any greenbacks just shell them out; that's all!"

MY CAPTURE AND ESCAPE FROM MOSBY.

CAPTAIN W. W. BADGER, Inspector-General of Cavalry in the Army of the Shenandoah, thus relates, in the *United States Service Magazine*, the story of his capture by Mosby's guerillas, and his escape from them:

Belle, my favorite mare, neighed impatiently in front of my tent, just as the bright sunrise of early autumn was gilding the hill. The morning was cold and brilliant, and the first crisp of frost had just sufficiently stiffened the sod to make a brisk gallop agreeable to both rider and horse.

The bold Shenandoah shook the icy wrinkles from its morning face, and rolled smoothly away before me into the gorgeous forest of crimson and gold below Front Royal.

It is the day of the regular train, and a thousand army wagons are already rolling away from Sheridan's headquarters down the famous Valley Pike, to bring food and raiment to a shivering and hungry army. I spring into the saddle, and Belle, in excellent spirits, evidently thinks she can throw dust in the eyes of Mosby or any other guerilla who dares follow her track. It is nine miles to where the train is parked, and before I arrive there, the last wagon has passed out of sight, and the picket gate of the army has been closed for an hour behind it. My orders are imperative to accompany this train, and military law allows of no discretion. With a single orderly and my colored servant, George

Washington, a contraband, commonly called Wash, to constantly remind him of the Christian virtue of cleanliness, I pass out into the guerilla-infested country.

It is but an hour's work to overtake the train, and mounted as I am, I feel great contempt for guerillas, and inwardly defy any of them to catch *me*, as I give Belle the rein and dash on at a sweeping gallop till I come in sight of the train, a mile ahead, winding it way through the little village of Newtown, nine miles south of Winchester.

"Mosby be hanged!" I said to myself, as I slacken speed and pass leisurely through the town, noticing the pretty women, who, for some reason, appear in unusual force at the doors and windows, and one or two of whom wave their handkerchiefs in a significant manner, which, however, I fail to understand, and ride heedlessly forward. Who would suppose a pretty woman waving a handkerchief to be a sign of danger?

Evidently no one but a cynic or a crusty old bachelor, and, as I am neither, I failed to interpret the well-meant warning.

As I had nearly passed the town, I overtook a small party, apparently of the rear-guard of the train, who were lighting their pipes and buying cakes and apples at a small grocery on the right of the pike, and who seemed to be in charge of a non-commissioned officer.

"Good-morning, sergeant," I said, in answer to his salute. "You had better close up at once. The train is getting well ahead, and this is the favorite beat of Mosby."

"All right, sir," he replied, with a smile of peculiar intelligence, and nodding to his men they mounted at once and closed in behind me, while, quite to my surprise, I noticed three more of the party, whom I had not before seen, in front of me.

An instinct of danger at once possessed me. I saw nothing to justify it, but I felt a presence of evil which I could not shake off. The men were in Union blue complete, and wore in their caps the well known Greek cross, which distinguishes the gallant Sixth Corps. They were young, intelligent, cleanly, and good looking soldiers, armed with revolvers and Spencer's repeating carbine.

I noticed the absence of sabres, but the presence of the Spencer, which is a comparatively new arm in our service, re-assured me, as I thought it impossible for the enemy to be, as yet, possessed of them.

We galloped on merrily, and just as I was ready to laugh at my own fears, Wash, who had been riding behind me, and had heard some remark made by the soldiers, brushed up to my side, and whispered through his teeth, chattering with fear, "Massa, secesh sure! Run like de debbel!"

I turned to look back at these words, and saw six carbines levelled at me at twenty paces' distance; and the sergeant, who had watched every motion of the negro, came riding toward me with his revolver drawn, and the sharp command, "Halt—surrender!"

We had reached a low place where the Opequan Creek crosses the pike a mile from Newtown. The train was not a quarter of a mile ahead, but out of sight for the moment over the next ridge. High stone walls lined the pike on either side, and a narrow bridge across the stream in front of me was already occupied by the three rascals who had acted as advance-guard, who now coolly turned round and presented carbines also from their point of view.

I remembered the military maxim, a mounted man should never surrender until his horse is disabled, and hesitated an instant considering what to do, and quite in doubt whether I was myself, or some other fellow whom I had read of as captured and hung by guerillas; but at the repetition of the sharp command "Surrender," with the addition of the polite words, "you d——d Yankee son of a b——h," aided by the somewhat disagreeable presence of the revolver immediately in my face, I concluded I was undoubtedly the other fellow, and surrendered accordingly.

My sword and revolver were taken at once by the sergeant, who proved to be Lieutenant C. F. Whiting, of Clark County, Virginia, in disguise, and who remarked, laughing, as he took them, "We closed up, captain, as you directed; as this is a favorite beat of Mosby's, I hope our drill was satisfactory."

"All right, sergeant," I replied. "Every dog has his day, and yours happens to come now. You have sneaked upon me in a cowardly way, disguised as a spy, and possibly my turn may come to-morrow."

"Your turn to be hung," he replied. And then, as we hurried along a wood path down the Opequan, he told me with great satisfaction, how they had lain in ambush in expectation of catching some stragglers from our train, and seeing me coming, had reached the little grocery from the woods behind it, just in time to appear as belonging to our party; that Mosby was three miles back, with a hundred men, and I should soon have the honor of seeing him in person.

They were a jolly, good-natured set of fellows, who evidently thought they had done a big thing; and as I scanned them more closely, the only distinction in appearance between them and our soldiers which I could discover, was that the Greek cross on their caps was embroidered in yellow worsted.

I was offered no further indignity or insult, and was allowed to ride my own horse for the present, though I was quietly informed on the way that Mosby had threatened to hang the first officer he should catch, in retaliation for his men who had been hung as guerillas at Front Royal, and that I would undoubtedly be the unfortunate individual.

With this consoling information I was ushered into the presence of the great modern highwayman, John S. Mosby, then lieutenant-colonel C. S. A.

He stood a little apart from his men, by the side of a splendid gray horse, with his right hand grasping the bridle-rein, the forearm resting on the pommel of his saddle, his left arm akimbo, and his right foot thrown across the left ankle and resting on its toe. He is a slight, medium-sized man, sharp of feature, quick of sight, lithe of limb, with a bronzed face of the color and tension of whip-cord; his hair a yellow-brown, with full but light beard, and mustache of the same. A straight Grecian nose, firm-set expressive mouth, large ears, deep-gray eyes, high forehead, large well-shaped head, and his whole expression denoting hard services, energy, and love of whiskey.

He wore top-boots, and a civilian's overcoat—black, lined with red—and beneath it the complete gray uniform of a Confederate lieutenant-colonel, with its two stars on the sides of the standing collar, and the whole surmounted by the inevitable slouched hat of the whole Southern race. His men were about half in blue and half in butternut.

He scarcely noticed me as I approached, but fixed his gaze on the noble animal I rode, as evidently the more valuable prize of the two. As I dismounted, he said to his servant, "Dick, take that horse;" and I knew the time had come when I must part with my beautiful Belle, whom I had rode nearly three years, through many a bloody field and hair's-breadth escape, and who loved me with an almost human love. Twice during the last three miles, as I came to a space of open country, had I resolved to dash away and trust to her nimble feet to distance their deadly rifles—and twice the sweet faces of home had appeared to scare me back to propriety.

Ah! what will a man not endure for the sweet faces of home? Beware of tender ties, you who aspire to deeds of desperate daring! For, although ennobling and inspiring to all that is duty, you will be either more or less than man if they fail to compel you to prudence wherever there is a choice of action left. I could not refrain from throwing my arms around Belle's neck, and tenderly caressing her for the last time before she was led away.

The lieutenant ventured to protest against Mosby's appropriating the mare to himself, without an apportionment and division of her value, in accordance with the rules of the gang; but he was promptly silenced, and ordered to content himself with his choice of the other two horses he had captured—which he immediately did by taking both of them. While this colloquy was passing, Mosby was quietly examining my papers, which had been taken from my pocket on my arrival; and presently, looking up with a peculiar gleam of satisfaction on his face, he said:

"Oh, Captain B——! inspection-general of ——'s cavalry? Good morning, captain—glad to see you, sir! Indeed, there is but one man I would prefer to see this morning to yourself, and that is your commander. Were you present, sir, the other day, at the hanging of eight of my men as guerillas at Front Royal?"

This question pierced me like a sword, as I really had been present at the terrible scene he mentioned. And although I had used my full influence, even to incurring the charge of timidity, in attempting to save the lives of the wretched men, believing that retaliation would be the only result, I could not show that fact, and doubted if it would avail me aught if I could.

I therefore answered him firmly: "I was present, sir, and, like you, have only to regret that it was not the commander, instead of his unfortunate men."

This answer seemed to please Mosby, for he apparently expected a denial. He assumed a grim smile, and directed Lieutenant Whiting to search me. My gold hunting watch and chain, several rings, a set of shirt studs and buttons, some coins, a Masonic pin, and about three hundred dollars in greenbacks, with some letters and pictures of the dear ones at home, and a small pocket Bible, were taken.

A board of officers was assembled to appraise their value, also that of my clothing, and to determine the ownership of each of the articles—the rules of the gang requiring that all captures shall be thus disposed of, or sold, and their value distributed proportionately among the captors.

My boots were appraised at six hundred and fifty dollars in Confederate money; my watch at three thousand; and the other articles in the same proportion, including my poor old servant Wash, who was put up and raffled for at two thousand dollars. Wash was very indignant that he should be thought worth only two thousand dollars Confederate money, and informed them that he considered himself quite unappreciable; and that, among other accomplishments, he could make the best milk punch of any man in the Confederacy—and, if they had the materials, he would like to try a little of it now. This hit at the poverty of their resources raised a laugh; and Mosby's man Dick, to show that they had the materials, offered Wash a drink—which, quite to my surprise, and doubtless to that of his own stomach also, he stubbornly refused. On asking him privately why he refused, he replied: "You know, massa, too much freeder breeds despise!"

When all this was concluded, Mosby took me one side, and returned to me the Bible, letters, and pictures, and the Masonic pin, saying quietly, as he did so, alluding to the latter with a significant sign:

"You may as well keep this; it may be of use to you somewhere. Some of my men pay some attention to that sort of thing. Your people greatly err in thinking us merely guerillas. Every man of mine is a duly enlisted soldier, and detailed to my command from various Confederate regiments. They are merely picked men, selected from the whole army for their intelligence and courage. We plunder the enemy, as the rules of war clearly allow. To the victors belong the spoils, has been a maxim of war in all ages. I can hang two for one all the year round, if your men insist upon it; but I hope soon to have a better understanding. I yesterday executed eight of your poor fellows on the valley pike, your highway of travel, in retaliation for my men hung at Front Royal; and I have to-day written to General Sheridan, informing him of it, and proposing a cessation of such horrible work, which every true soldier cannot but abhor. I sincerely hope he will assent to it."

I thanked him warmly for his kindness, as I took his offered hand with a grip known all the world over to the brethren of the mystic tie, and really began to think Mosby almost a gentleman and a soldier, although he had just robbed me in the most approved manner of modern highwaymen.

The sun was now approaching the meridian, and immediate preparations were made for the long road to Richmond and the Libby. A guard of fifteen men, in command of Lieutenant Whiting, was detailed as our escort; and accompanied by Mosby himself, we started directly across the country, regardless of roads, in an easterly direction, toward the Shenandoah and the Blue Ridge. We were now in company of nine more of our men, who had been taken at different times, making eleven of our party in all, besides the indignant contraband, Wash, whom it was also thought prudent to send to the rear for safe keeping.

I used every effort to gain the acquaintance and confidence of these men, and by assuming a jolly and reckless manner, I succeeded in drawing them out and satisfying myself that some of them could be depended on in any emergency. I had determined to escape if even half an opportunity should present itself, and the boys were quick in understanding my purpose and intimating their readiness to risk their lives in the attempt.

Two of them, in particular—George W. McCauley, of Western Virginia, commonly known as Mack, and one Brown, of Blaser's scouts—afterward proved themselves heroes of the truest metal.

We journeyed rapidly, making light of our misfortunes, and cracking many a joke with our rebel guard, until we reached Howittsville, on the Shenandoah, nine miles below Front Royal, where we bivouacked for the night in an old school-house, sole relic left of a former civilization. It is an old, unpainted two story building, with wooden blinds nailed shut, and seems to have been fitted up by Mosby as a kind of way station, in which to camp with his stranger guests. Many a sad heart, more hopeless and broken than our's, has doubtless throbbed restless on its naked floors, with premonitions of the dreary Libby. All of the guard confirmed Mosby's statement as to the organization of his band and the execution of our men the day previous; and his letter to Sheridan in regard to it has since been published, and certainly speaks for itself of the business-like habits of its author.

Our party of eleven were assigned to one side of the lower floor of the school-house, where we lay down side by side, with our heads to the wall, and our feet nearly touching the feet of the guard, who lay in the same manner, opposite to us, with their heads to the other wall, except three who formed a relief guard for the sentry's post at the door. Above the heads of the guard, along the wall, ran a low school desk, on which each man of them stood his carbine and laid his revolver before disposing himself to sleep. A fire before the door dimly lighted the room, and the scene as they dropped gradually to sleep was warlike in the extreme, and made a Rembrandt picture on my memory which will never be effaced.

I had taken care, on lying down, to place myself between McCauley and Brown, and the moment the rebels began to snore and the sentry to nod over his pipe, we were in earnest and deep conversation. McCauley proposed to unite our party and make a simultaneous rush for the carbines, and take our chances of stampeding the guard and making our escape; but on passing the whisper quietly along our line, only three men were found willing to assent to it. As the odds were so largely against us, it was useless to urge the subject.

The intrepid McCauley then proposed to go himself alone in the darkness among the sleeping rebels, and bring over to our party every revolver and every carbine before any alarm should be given, if we would only use the weapons when placed in our hands; but again timidity prevailed, and I must confess that I myself hesitated before this hardy courage, and refused to peril the brave boy's life in so rash a venture, as a single false step or the least alarm, in favor of which the chances were as a thousand to one, would have been to him, and probably to all of us, instant death.

I forbade the attempt, but could not help clasping the brave fellow to my heart, and kissing him like a brother for the noble heroism of which he was evidently made. He was a fair boy of but eighteen summers, with soft black eyes, and a rosy, round face as smooth and delicate as a girl's, with a noble forehead and an unusually intelligent countenance. I had picked him out at first sight as a hero, and every hour was increasing my admiration of him. He slept in my arms at last, as the long night wore away, till the morning broke dull and rainy, finding us exhausted and thoroughly wretched and despondent.

The march began at an early hour, and our route ran directly up the Blue Ridge. We had emerged from the forest and ascended about one third the height of the mountain, when the full valley became visible, spread out like a map before us, showing plainly the lines of our army, its routes of supply, its foraging parties out, and my own camp at Front Royal as distinctly as if we stood in one of its streets. We now struck a wood path running southward and parallel with the ridge of the mountain, along which we travelled for hours, with this wonderful panorama of forest and river, mountain and plain, before us in all the gorgeous beauty of the early autumn.

"This is a favorite promenade of mine," said Mosby. "I love to see your people sending out their almost daily raids after me. There comes one of them now almost toward us. If you please, we will step behind this point and see them pass. It may be the last sight you will have of your old friends for some time."

The coolness of this speech enraged me, and yet I could not help admiring the quiet and unostentatious audacity which seemed to be the prominent characteristic of its author. I could hardly restrain an impulse to rush upon him and

> "Try this quarrel hilt to hilt,"

but the important fact that I had not a hilt even, while he wore two revolvers, restrained me, and looking in the direction he pointed, I distinctly saw a squadron of my own regiment coming directly toward us on a road running under the foot of the mountain, and apparently on some foraging expedition down the valley. They passed within a half mile of us under the mountain, and Mosby stood with folded arms on a rock above them, the very picture of stoical pride and defiance, or, as Mack whispered:

> "Like patience on a monument smiling at grief."

We soon moved on, and before noon reached the road running through Manassas Gap, which place we found held by about one hundred of Mosby's men, who signalled him as he approached; and here, much to my regret, the great chieftain left us, bidding me a kindly good-by, and informing me that my last hope of rescue or escape was now gone.

We were hurried on through the gap and down the eastern slope of the mountain, and turning southward, in a few hours passed Chester Gap, finding it also occupied by Mosby's men in force, and we were only able to approach it after exchanging the proper signals.

This gave me an idea of how Mosby conducts his raids so successfully, by leaving a garrison in each of the gaps behind him before he ventures far into the valley. These garrisons he can concentrate at any desired point by signals almost in an hour, and any of them can communicate with him from the mountain tops to any part of the valley, and either warn him of danger or direct him where to strike. If pursued, he has but to retreat in such a direction as to draw his pursuers on to this reserve force, which he concentrates in some strong position, or in ambush, at his pleasure, and develops with fresh horses just as his pursuers are exhausted with the long chase. He is thus enabled, with about five hundred picked men, to remain, as he has been for two years past, the terror of the valley.

After passing Chester Gap, we descend into the valley and move toward Sperryville, on the direct line to Richmond, the last gate of hope seeming to close behind us as we leave the mountains. Our guard is now reduced, as we are far within the Confederate lines, to Lieutenant Whiting and three men, well mounted and doubly armed, and our party of eleven prisoners have seven horses to distribute among us as we please, so that four of us are constantly dismounted. There is also a pack-horse carrying our forage, rations, and some blankets. To the saddle of this pack-horse are strapped two Spencer carbines, muzzle downward, with their accoutrements complete, including two well filled cartridge boxes.

I called Mack's attention to this fact as soon as the guard was reduced, and he needed no second hint to comprehend its significance at once. He soon after dismounted, and when it came his turn again to mount, he secured, apparently by accident, the poorest and most broken down horse in the party, with which he appeared to find it very difficult to keep up, and which he actually succeeded in some mysterious way in laming.

He then dropped back to the lieutenant in charge, and modestly asked to exchange his lame horse for the pack-horse, and being particularly frank in his address, his request was at once granted, without a suspicion of its object, or a thought of the fatal carbines on the pack-saddle. I used some little skill in diverting the attention of the lieutenant while the pack was readjusted; and as the rain had now begun to fall freely, no one of the guard was particularly alert.

I was presently gratified with the sight of Mack riding ahead on the pack-horse, with the two carbines still strapped to the saddle, but loosened and well concealed by his heavy *poncho*, which he had spread as protection from the rain.

These carbines are seven-shooters, and load from the breech by simply drawing out from the hollow stock a spiral spring and dropping in the seven cartridges, one after the other, and then inserting the spring again behind them, which coils as it is pressed home, and by its elasticity forces the cartridges forward, one at a time, into the barrel, at the successive movements of the lock.

I could see the movement of Mack's right arm by the shape into which it threw the *poncho;* and while guiding his horse with his left, looking the other way and chatting glibly with the other boys, I saw him carefully draw the springs from those carbines with his right hand and hook them into the upper button-hole of his coat to support them, while he dropped in the cartridges one after another, trotting his horse at the time to conceal the noise of their click, and finally forcing down the springs and looking round at me with a look of the fiercest triumph and heroism I have ever beheld.

I nodded approval, and fearing he would precipitate matters, yet knowing that any instant might lead to discovery and be too late, I rode carelessly across the road to Brown, who was on foot, and dismounting, asked him to tighten my girth, during which operation I told him as quietly as possible the position of affairs, and asked him to get up gradually by the side of Mack, communicate with him, and at a signal from me to seize one of the carbines and do his duty as a soldier if he valued his liberty.

Brown, though a plucky fellow, was of quite a different quality from Mack. He was terribly frightened, and trembled like a leaf, yet went immediately to his post, and I did not doubt would do his duty well.

I rode up again to the side of Lieutenant Whiting, and like an echo from the past came back to me my words of yesterday, "Possibly my turn may come tomorrow." I engaged him in conversation, and among other things spoke of the prospect of sudden death as one always present in our army life, and the tendency it had to either harden or ameliorate the character according to the quality of the individual. He expressed the opinion which many hold that a brutal man is made more brutal by it, and a refined and cultivated man is softened and made more refined by it.

I scanned the country closely for the chances of escape if we should succeed in gaining our liberty; I knew that to fail or to be recaptured would be instant death, and the responsibility of risking the lives of the whole party, as well as my own, was oppressing me bitterly. I also had an instinctive horror of the shedding of blood, as it were, with my own hands, and the sweet faces of home were haunting me again, but this time, strange to say, urging me on, and apparently crying aloud for vengeance.

We were on the immediate flank of Early's army. His cavalry was all around us. The road was thickly inhabited. It was almost night. We had passed a rebel picket but a mile back, and knew not how near another of their camps might be. The three rebel guards were riding in front of us and on our left flank, our party of prisoners was in the centre, and I was by the side of Lieutenant Whiting, who acted as rear-guard, when we entered a small copse of willow which for a moment covered the road.

The hour was propitious; Mack looked round impatiently; I wove the fatal signal, "Now's the time, boys," into a story of our charge at Winchester, which I was telling to distract attention, and at the moment of its utterance threw myself upon the lieutenant, grasping him around the arms and dragging him from his horse, in the hope of securing his revolver, capturing him, and compelling him to pilot us outside of the rebel line.

At the word, Mack raised one of the loaded carbines, and in less time than I can write it, shot two of the guard in front of him, killing them instantly; and then coolly turning in his saddle, and seeing me struggling in the road with the lieutenant, and the chances of obtaining the revolver apparently against me, he raised the carbine the third time, and as I strained the now desperate rebel to my breast, with his livid face over my left shoulder, he shot him as directly between the eyes as he could have done if firing at a target at ten paces' distance. The bullet went crashing through his skull,

THE RESCUE.

the hot blood spirted from his mouth and nostrils into my face, his hold relaxed, and his ghastly corpse fell from my arms, leaving an impression of horror and soul-sickness which can never be effaced.

I turned around in alarm at our now desperate situation, and saw Mack quietly smiling at me, with the remark:

"Golly, cap! I could have killed five or six more of them as well as not. This is a bully carbine; I think I will take it home with me."

Brown had not accomplished so much. He had seized the second carbine at the word, and fired at the third guard on our flank; but his aim was shaky, and he had only wounded his man in the side, and allowed him to escape to the front, where he was now seen half a mile away, at full speed, and firing his pistols to alarm the country.

Our position was now perilous in the extreme; not a man of us knew the country, except its most general outlines. The rebel camps could not be far away; darkness was intervening; the whole country would be alarmed in an hour; and I doubted not that before sundown even bloodhounds would be on our track. One half of our party had already scattered, panic-stricken, at the first alarm, and, every man for himself, were scouring the country in every direction.

But five remained, including the faithful Wash, who immediately shows his practical qualities by searching the bodies of the slain, and recovering therefrom, among other things, my gold hunting watch from the person of Lieutenant Whiting, and over eleven hundred dollars in greenbacks, the proceeds, doubtless, of their various robberies of our men.

"Not quite 'nuff," said Wash, showing his ivories from ear to ear. "Dey vally dis nigger at two tousand dollers—I think I ought ter git de money."

We instantly mounted the best horses, and, well armed with carbines and revolvers, struck directly for the mountain on our right; but knowing that would be the first place where we should be sought for, we soon changed our direction to the south, and rode for hours directly into the enemy's country as fast as we could ride, and before complete darkness intervened, we had made thirty miles from the place of our escape; and then, turning sharp up the mountain, we pushed our exhausted horses as far as they could climb; and then abandoning them, we toiled on, on foot, all night, to the very summit of the Blue Ridge, whence we could see the rebel camp fires, and view their entire lines and position just as daylight was breaking over the valley.

We broke down twigs from several trees in line to determine the points of compass and the direction of the rebel forces and pickets after it should be light, and then crawled into a thicket to rest our exhausted frames and await the return of friendly darkness in which to continue our flight.

The length of this weary day, and the terrible pangs of hunger and thirst which we suffered on this barren mountain, pertain to the more common experience of a soldier's life, and I need not describe them here.

Neither will I narrate, in detail, how some of our party who scattered arrived in camp before us, and how one feeble old man was recaptured and killed, nor our hopeless despair as day after day we saw the mountain alive with rebel scouts sent out for our capture, and at night blazing with their picket fires; and how we even ate a poor little dog which had followed our fortunes to his untimely end, and were thinking seriously of eating the negro Wash, when he, to save himself from so unsavory a fate, ventured down in the darkness to a cornfield, and brought us up three ears of corn apiece, which we ate voraciously; and how we had to go still farther south and abandon the mountain altogether, to avoid the scouts and pickets; and how we finally struck the Shenandoah, twenty miles to the rear of Early's army, and there built a raft and floated by night forty miles down that memorable stream, through his crafty pickets, and thereafter passed for rebel scouts, earnestly "looking for Yanks" until we found them, and the glorious old flag once more welcomed us to Union and liberty.

These things the writer expects to tell, by the blessing of God, to the next generation, with his great-grandchildren on his knee.

THE HORSE MARINE'S STORY.

Dr. Charles D. Gardette, for some time a surgeon in the army, and a poet and literary man of marked ability, furnished to the *United States Service Magazine* the following very interesting story, as related by one of his patients:

"Yes, doctor, it's me they call the Horse Marine, sure enough."

"But why do they call you so?" I asked, as I replaced the dressings.

The man had got a sabre-slash across the head—not a dangerous one—and was in my ward of the MacFinnegan Hospital at the time.

"Why, you see, sir, I served a good while in the marines before this war broke out; and so, when I 'listed into the land service, the boys soon found out I'd been a sea-soldier, and dubbed me The Horse Marine at once."

"And what made you choose the cavalry, Spaddon?"

"Why, you see, sir, when I was a sea-soldier, I had a ship to carry me. 'And so,' says I, 'if I go into the land service, I will have a horse to carry me, and that's a ship I can steer myself;' for I was a jockey before I was a marine."

"But why not re-enter the marines?"

"Ah, it was the bounty, doctor! The sea-soldiers didn't get any bounty then; nor the sailors neither, for that matter—more's the shame. And though I was not to say very poor, yet money was not amiss, nor the horse neither, to tell you the truth, for another reason. For between you and I, sir, I didn't go into the service again out of what you call pure patriotism altogether, nor for the love of fighting, though I have not shirked the last, if I say it myself, neither."

"I should think not, Spaddon, from appearances; but," continued I, liking the man, of whom I had known something previously, and having a little spare time at the moment—"what did you enlist for, then?"

"To catch my wife, doctor!"

I looked at the man—a good-looking, muscular, shapely fellow, of six or seven and twenty; rather undersized, but firmly knit, with a bright intelligent face, and a manner and language above his present rank (corporal in the Ninety-ninth Cavalry). I looked at him. He was evidently quite serious, and I ignored his having been a marine; and, "Well, did you catch her, Spaddon?" I asked, simply.

"Yes—that is, I did—and I didn't; if you'd. like to hear about it, doctor, I'll tell——"

"Doctor Smith, the surgeon-in-chief, wishes to see you for a moment in his quarters," said a messenger coming in at the instant.

"Very good. Well, Spaddon, I'll hear your story another time—to-night, perhaps. Nurse, give him this as before; he's doing very well." And I left him.

When I came to Spaddon that night, I found him with a slight fever; which, upon inquiry, I conjectured to have been produced by mental excitement on the subject of his wife-catching story. He had become very anxious to tell it to me at once, and his fear lest I should not find leisure to hear it, had run his pulse up a score of beats or so. Considering this of no special gravity, and finding him earnest to have his tale told, I gave him a slight calmant and bade him go ahead, but to be brief, and to keep to the point.

"You know my name, doctor—Thomas Spaddon," he began; "and that I am an American born and bred, as my father was before me. My father was a farmer, and brought me up——"

"Stop!" interrupted I, "I don't want your family

history. There's no time for a long story. Come at once to the gist of the thing, Spaddon—about your wife-catching, you know."

"Very well, sir; though I'd rather—but no matter. I was married seven years ago, sir, before I went into the marines. I traded in horses then. I was only twenty, and my wife hardly seventeen. Her father kept a livery stable in—never mind the place. She was a beauty, sir. Well, sir, in about a year her father broke all to smash, and cleared out. Then I got into a cursed bad streak of luck, and——. Well, sir, there's no use hiding it; I got into jail for horsestealing. But I swear to you I was——"

"Innocent, no doubt. I'll believe you without proof; only get on."

"No!" said Spaddon, gravely; "I was *not* innocent, but I was the tool of sharper men. No matter. I lay in jail a year, and then got pardoned out. When I went to seek my wife she was gone, and I could not find a trace, sir, not a trace. Well, sir, there I was—money gone, wife gone, character gone! What to do? I got drunk next day, and the next I 'listed into the marines. I served my term there, still hearing nothing of Jane, and came out of it as I went into it, an unhappy man, sir. Then the Rebellion broke out. But I thought no more of enlisting. My father had died and left me a little money without wishing it. That is, he had forgot to make a will, and I was the only child living, and mother long gone. It wasn't much; but I didn't care. But one day I met a friend. He was a soldier, and had been a prisoner in the South, and just got back.

"'Tom,' says he, 'I saw Jane in Richmond.'

"'Saw who?' I cried, hardly understanding him at first.

"'Saw Jane, your wife. She's prettier than ever, but it's my opinion, Tom, she's no better than——

"I stopped him, sir; but he didn't mean to hurt my feelings. Well, sir, how to get to her, or get her to me, was the question. I feared she wouldn't come of her own will, at least not unless I went and fetched her. But how to go? I would not turn rebel, even if I could—even for her. I thought, and thought, and the next day I enlisted in the Ninety-ninth Cavalry. The cry was 'On to Richmond!' then, sir, and the Ninety-ninth was at the front. And in a fortnight so was I."

"But you never got quite there, my poor fellow—into Richmond, I mean."

"Yes, but I did, sir."

"What? Oh, as a prisoner! you mean."

"No, sir, but as a corpse!"

"A—a corpse! Come, Spaddon, tell that to—your old comrades!" said I, with stern irony.

"Well, sir, I'm wrong; I didn't mean exactly a corpse, that's a fact; but I *did* mean as a wounded rebel."

"I thought you said you would not turn rebel even——"

"So I did, and so I do, sir! But stratagem's all fair in war, and this was a stratagem, though it didn't do much good in the end, for when a man once——"

"Well, well!" I exclaimed, impatiently, "let us have the stratagem and its consequences—or rather," I continued, as I felt his pulse, and looked at the time, "we will adjourn the conclusion till to-morrow."

"But, doctor——"

"No buts. Here, take this; drink it all. That will do. I will be here in the morning. Good-night!"

Spaddon was in excellent pulse in the morning, but I had no time to listen to him. In the afternoon, however, he was well enough to be helped out to the piazza for a breath of the summer air (I say "helped," for he had been knocked off his horse by the blow he got, or by something else, and was severely bruised about the body), and there, sitting in a comfortable chair, he finished his story, as follows:

"It was within three miles of Richmond that we fought that day, a long and bloody battle, as you know. At night both parties were out picking up their dead and wounded, according to agreement. I had formed a plan in my head, and now I put it into practice. It was desperate, but so was I. There were a good many of both sides, but chiefly rebels, fallen in a bit of scrubby swamp-wood. They hadn't begun to search in there yet. I crept about there till I found what I wanted. I tied a bloody handkerchief round my head and jaw, stripped off my uniform, put on that of a dead rebel, clapped mine on him somehow, and lay down, waiting. After awhile they came along with torches, and began to search. O, doctor! I can tell you I did not feel——"

"I can fancy your feelings, Spaddon; but be brief. They found you, took you for one of their wounded, and carried you into the city, eh?"

"Yes, sir, in a wagon, with a lot of others. It was dark as pitch by this time. I watched my chance, and when we got into the city, in a dark spot, before we reached the better lit streets, I slipped down without being caught, and hid among the buildings. After awhile I found an empty shed or outhouse, and stayed there'till morning. Then I walked boldly out and into the streets. Nobody took especial notice of me. Two or three soldiers stopped me, and asked where I was hurt. I pointed to my jaw, and made signs I could not speak. A little girl offered me a hoe-cake. After walking about a couple of hours, I began to think that I had come on a fool's errand. How should I find her? How should I ask for her? For the first time I began to think of the mortal danger I was in. I thought even of trying to go back somehow. Just then a woman came out of a house opposite me. It was Jane! I knew her at once, though she was thinner and paler, and still prettier with it all! What should I do? Speak to her? I dared not risk it in the street. She went into a house a little farther on. After awhile I made up my mind. I went over to the house she had come out of, and knocked. No answer. Again—again. No one came. I tried the door. It opened, and I went in and shut it behind me. It was a small, poor house. There was a basket of dirty linen on the table. I saw at a glance that Jane was a laundress. She a washer-woman! I sat down, took off my bandage, and waited. In a few minutes she came in. She looked at me. 'What do you want here?' she said.

"'Don't you know me? I'm your husband, Jane!' said I, rising and making toward her.

"'My God!' she cried, and fell back. I caught her, and in a few minutes she came to.

"'Jane,' says I, 'I've come to take you home.'

"'Never!' says she, 'I'll never see the North again.

I hate it! But you—you're a soldier—one of our soldiers. How came you here? Ah!' she says suddenly, you're a spy! a traitor! First a thief, and now a spy! Good God! Thomas Spaddon! Do you think that I would own a thief and a spy for my husband?'

"'And is all your love dead, Jane?' says I, looking her in the face.

"She shook her head, and began to sob. Then, 'How did you come here?' she says again, sharply. 'Who told you——'

"'Nobody,' says I; 'I saw you go out. Jane! Jane, come home with me.'

"'Home? Here's my home, with these noble, injured people. I hate and despise the Yankees!'

"'You're a Yankee yourself, Jane,' says I.

"'Thomas Spaddon,' says she, 'I loved you once, and I'll not betray you. But go, leave me and this city at once, forever! Forever, I tell you! I will never go with you. I—I have a husband here.

"'I'll kill him!' says I, looking around, as if I thought he might be there, and if he had been, I'd have done it, by ——.'

"'Then go and do it like a man,' says she. 'He's out whipping your Yankees now, outside the city. Go and meet him if you dare! Go;' and, sir, she actually pushed me to the door. I could almost have killed her then, doctor. But I went; I don't know how it was; but I went without another word."

Spaddon was gloomily silent, and sat with his head in his hands for a few moments.

"And how did you get out of Richmond?" I asked, presently.

"I don't know, sir," said Spaddon, still gloomily.

"What? Don't know! What do you mean by that, sir?"

"I mean just what I say, doctor. I was crushed. I just walked on and on, hearing nothing, seeing nothing, answering nothing, if any one spoke to me, which I don't know if they did or not. I just walked on and on, till I found myself in the country, in the fields just outside of the city. Then I woke up and looked around me, and saw some negroes, and called one, and asked him the way to our army. He thought I meant his master's forces, of course, but that didn't matter. He told me I was 'clean done gon' round de udder side ob de city,' and that I 'mus' folly dis yer road till I come to the woods ober yander, when I'd see a paff'—in short, sir, he put me in the way; and making a painful march and a wide detour, and creeping through the swamps that night, I got back to our own camps alive, but used up both in body and mind, doctor, perfectly used up!"

Spaddon had been out long enough, and I ordered him back to the ward. As we went along, I pondered over his story, looking at him the while.

"Spaddon," said I, "you say you were first a horse-jockey, then a marine, then a dragoon, and a wife-hunter?"

"Yes, sir," answered Spaddon.

"Well, Spaddon, I've no doubt about the first three phases of your life, but as to that tale of getting into and out of Richmond——"

"It's true, every word of it, doctor," said Spaddon, earnestly.

"It may be," I replied; "but it sounds marvellously like a story for the horse marines."

THE CONTRABANDS IN THE WAR.

THE army correspondents as well as the soldiers have regarded the contrabands as fair subjects for practical jokes, and when these have been harmless in their character the negroes themselves have enjoyed them sometimes as much as their perpetrators. No doubt many of the stories of the contrabands, retailed by the letter writers from the army, had their origin in the brains of those veracious chroniclers; but the following can generally be vouched for.

Company K, of the First Iowa Cavalry, stationed in Tennessee, received into their camp a middle-aged but vigorous contraband. Innumerable questions were being propounded to him, when a corporal advanced, saying:

"See here, Dixie, before you can enter the service of the United States, you must take the oath,"

"Yes, massa, I do dat," he replied; when the corporal continued:

"Well, then, take hold of the Bible!" holding out a letter envelope, upon which was delineated the Goddess of Liberty standing upon something like a Suffolk pig, wearing the emblem of our country. The negro grasped the envelope cautiously with his thumb and finger, when the corporal proceeded to administer the oath by saying:

"You do solemnly swear that you will support the Constitution of the United States, and see that there are no grounds floating upon the coffee, at all times?"

"Yes, massa, I do dat," he replied; "I allers settle 'um in de coffee-pot."

Here he let go the envelope to gesticulate, by a downward thrust of his forefinger, the direction that would be given to the coffee-grounds for the future.

"Never mind how you do it," gravely exclaimed the corporal; "but hold on to the Bible."

"Lordy, massa, I forgot," said the negro, as he darted forward and grasped the envelope with a firmer clutch, when the corporal continued:

"And you do solemnly swear that you will support the Constitution of all loyal States, and not dirty the plates when cleaning them, or wipe them with your shirt sleeves?"

Here a frown lowered upon the brow of the negro, his eyes expanded to their largest dimensions, while his lips protruded, with a rounded form, as he exclaimed:

"Lordy, massa—I *nebber* do *dat*. I allers washes 'um nice. Ole missus mighty 'tickler 'bout dat."

"Never mind ole missus!" said the corporal, as he resumed: "And you do solemnly swear that you will put milk into the coffee every morning, and see that the ham and eggs are not cooked too much or too little?"

"Yes—I do dat. I'se a good cook."

"And lastly," continued the corporal, "you do solemnly swear that when this war is over, you'll make tracks for Africa mighty fast?"

"Yes, massa, I do dat. I allers wanted to go to Cheecargo."

Here the regimental drum beat up for dress parade, when Tom Benton—that being his name—was declared duly sworn and commissioned as chief cook in Company K, of the First Iowa Cavalry.

One of the Anderson Zouaves relates the following incident as having come under his observation:

We were scouting one day in Alabama, when in a remote field we found a negro man and woman ploughing with a good horse. We paused, and the ploughers gazed at us with the greatest curiosity. I never saw a more thoroughly astonished individual. It was evidently his first sight at Yankee soldiers.

"Well, boy, wont you come along with us?" I said.

"De Lawd bless's—mars's, is you really de Fed'rals?"

"That's it, old fellow."

"De rale Linkum sojers?"

"Exactly."

"De kind as wants counterbans?"

"Identically."

Here he proceeded with great deliberation to unhitch his horse from the plough. Gathering up divers small objects, that nothing might be lost, he slung himself on his steed, and cried, over his shoulder, to his amazed work-fellow:

"Good-by, M'ria. I'se off!"

And off he rode, stared at by "M'ria," whose eyes gazed after him in utter and complete bewilderment—"like the grandmother of all the owls when she first saw sunshine."

The contraband of whom the following story is told

was not, it would seem, as courageous as some of his colored brethren, though decidedly a philosopher:

Upon the hurricane-deck of one of our gunboats, an elderly darkey, with a very philosophical and retrospective cast of countenance, squatted upon his bundle, toasting his shins against the chimney, and apparently plunged into a state of profound meditation. Finding, upon inquiry, that he belonged to the Ninth Illinois, one of the most gallantly behaved and heavy-losing regiments at the Fort Donelson battle, and part of which was aboard, the "war correspondent," began to interrogate him on the subject:

"Were you in the fight?"

"Had a little taste of it, sa'."

"Stood your ground, did you?"

"No, sa', I runs."

"Run at the first fire, did you?"

"Yes, sa', and would hab run soona, had I knowd it war comin'."

"Why, that wasn't very creditable to your courage."

"Dat isn't my line, sa'—cookin's my profeshun."

"Well, but have you no regard for your reputation?"

"Reputation's nuffin to me by de side ob life."

"Do you consider your life worth more than other people's?"

"It's worth more to me, sa'."

"Then you must value it very highly?"

"Yes, sa, I does, more dan all dis wuld, more dan a million of dollars, sa', for what would dat be wuth to a man wid de bref cut ob him? Self-preservation am de fust law wid me."

"But why should you act upon a different rule from other men?"

"Becase different men sot different values upon their lives: mine is not in de market."

"But if you lost it, you would have the satisfaction of knowing that you died for your country."

"What satisfaction would dat be to me when de power ob feelin' was gone?"

"Then patriotism and honor are nothing to you?"

"Nuffin whatever, sa'—I regard dem as among de wanities."

"If our soldiers were like you, traitors might have broken up the Government without resistance."

"Yes, sa,' dar would hab been no help for it. I wouldn't put my life in de scale 'ginst any gobernment dat ever existed, for no gobernment could replace de loss to me."

"Do you think any of your company would have missed you if you had been killed?"

"Maybe not, sa'—a dead white man aint much to dese sojers—let alone a dead nigga—but I'd a missed myself, and dat was de pint wid me."

THAT was an admirable retort of a Union officer, a colonel in the Union army, who having been taken prisoner by a rebel officer of the same rank, was taken by his captor in a railroad car to prison. While seated besides his captive, the rebel, for a long time, insulted him in the most cowardly and contemptible manner; but finding that his abuse produced no effect beyond a contemptuous silence, he went out and returned with a particularly black and ragged slave, whom he compelled to sit beside the colonel; having done which, he left him. Half an hour passed by, when the Confederate officer returned, and inquired, with a grin at his white prisoner, how he liked his new comrade. "He is not such a person as I have been accustomed to associate with," was the calm reply; "but he is a better bred man than the one who last sat beside me."

THE monster shells thrown from the heavy guns of the Western gunboats, excited alarm and terror both in whites and blacks. The account of their effect on the former, given by an old contraband, is somewhat amusing:

We were passing along the wharves, a few days ago, wondering at the amount of business that was there transacted. While standing observing a cargo of horses being transferred from a vessel to the shore, an "old contraband" appeared at our elbow, touching his fur hat, and scraping an enormous foot. He opened his battery upon us with the following:

"Well, boss, how is yer?"

"Pretty well, daddy; how are you?"

"I'se fuss rate, I is. B'long to old Burnemside's boys, does yer?"

"Yes, I belong to that party. Great boys, ain't they?"

"Well, I thought yer b'longed to that party. Great man, he is, dat's sartin. Yes, sir. We waited and waited; we heard yer was comin', but we mos' guv yer up. 'Deed we jest did; but one mornin' we heard de big guns, way down ribber, go bang, bang, bang, and de folks round yere begun to cut dar stick mitey short, and trabble up de rail-track. Den, bress de good Lord, we knowed yer was comin', but we held our jaw. Bymeby de sojers begun to cut dar stick, too, and dey trabble! Goramity, 'pears dey make de dirt fly! Ya, ha!"

"Why, were they scared so bad?"

"De sojers didn't skeer um so much as dem black boats. Kase, yer see, de sojers shot solid balls, and dey not mind dem so much; but when dem boats say b-o-o-m, dey know de *rotten balls* was comin', and dey skeeted quickern a streak of litenin'."

"What rotten balls did the boats throw at them?"

"Don't yer know? Why, *dem balls dat are bad;* dey're rotten, an' fly all to bits—'deed does dey—play de very debbil wid yer. No dodgin' *dem* dere balls; kase yer dunno whare dey fly too—strike yah and fly yandah; dat's what skeered 'em so bad!"

"Well, what are you going to do when the war's over?"

"Dunno; p'raps I goes Noff wid dis crowd. Pretty much so, I guess. 'Pears to me dis chile had better be movin'."

DURING the riot in New York city, in July, 1863, the negroes were in great peril from the rioters, and many of them owed their escape to the "ready wit" of some of their friends and employers. The following was one of numerous instances of this:

While President Acton, at the police headquarters,

Surrender of General Lee.

was giving some final orders to a squad of men who were just leaving to disperse the crowd in First Avenue, a wagon containing a hogshead was driven rapidly up to the Mulberry street door by a lad, who appeared much excited and almost breathless.

"What have you there, my lad?" said President Acton.

"Supplies for your men," was the answer.

"What are they?"

"It's an assorted lot, sir; but the people say it's contraband."

Being exceedingly busy, Acton ordered the wagon to be driven round to the Mott street entrance, where an officer was sent to look after the goods. When the wagon arrived the officers were about to tip the cask out, but were prevented by the boy, who exclaimed:

"Wait a minute—bring me a hatchet." A hatchet was brought, and the little fellow set to work unheading the cask; and as he did so the officers were astonished to see two full-grown negroes snugly packed inside. Upon being assured by the lad that they were safe, they raised their heads, took a long snuff of fresh air, and exclaimed, "Bress de Lord!"

The boy stated that the rioters had chased the poor unfortunates into the rear of some houses on the west side of the town, and that they had escaped by scaling a fence and landing in a grocer's yard; that the grocer was friendly to them, but feared his place might be sacked if they were found there. He accordingly hit upon this novel plan of getting them out, and while he kept watch in front the boy coopered up the negroes. The cask was then rolled out like a hogshead of sugar, placed in the wagon, and driven off to Mulberry street.

Heading up the darkies headed off the mob that time.

We presume the slaveholder whose slaves were disposed of by his friend as related below, hardly contemplated adding recruits to the Union army, but he could not complain of his friend for obeying orders:

A slaveholder from the country approached an old acquaintance, also a slaveholder, residing in Nashville, the other day, and said:

"I have several negro men lurking about here some where. I wish you would look out for them, and when you find them, do with them as if they were your own."

"Certainly I will," replied his friend.

A few days after the parties met again, and the planter asked:

"Have you found my slaves?"

"I have."

"And where are they?"

"Well, you told me to do with them just as if they were my own, and as I made my men enlist in the Union army, I did the same with yours."

The astonished planter "absquatulated."

A very independent darkey was Sam, as the reader will discern:

During the winter of 1863, a contraband came into the Federal lines in North Carolina, and marched up to the officer of the day to report himself, whereupon the following colloquy ensued:

"What's your name?"

"My name's Sam."

"Sam what?"

"No, sah—not Sam Watt. I'se just Sam."

"What's your other name?"

"I hasn't got no oder name, sah! I'se Sam—dat s all."

"What's your master's name?"

"I'se got no massa, now—massa runned away—*yah! yah!* I'se free nigger, now."

"Well, what's your father and mother's name?"

"I'se got none, sah—neber had none. I'se jist Sam—*aint nobody else.*"

"Haven't you any brothers and sisters?"

"No, sah—neber had none. No brudder, no sister, no fader, no mudder, no massa—nothin' but Sam. *When you see Sam, you see all dere is of us.*"

In West Point, Virginia, there was a negro scout, named Clairborne, in the employ of the Union forces, who was a shrewd hand at escaping from the rebels. He was evidently a full-blooded African, with big lips and flat nose, and, having lived in this vicinity all his life, was familiar with the country, which rendered him a very valuable aid.

On Clairborne's last trip inside the enemy's lines, after scouting around as much as he wished, he picked up eight chickens and started for camp. His road led past the house of a secesh doctor named Roberts, who knew him, and who ordered him to stop, which, of course,

Clairborne had no idea of doing, and kept on, when the doctor fired on him and gave chase, shouting at the top of his voice. The negro was making good time toward camp, when, all at once, he was confronted by a whole regiment of soldiers, who ordered him to halt. For a moment the scout was dumbfounded, and thought his hour had come, but the next he sang out:

"The Yankees are coming! the Yankees are coming!"

"Where? where?" inquired the rebels.

"Just up in front of Dr. Roberts' house, in a piece of woods. Dr. Roberts sent me down to tell you to come up quick, or they'll kill the whole of us."

"Come in!—come into camp!" said the soldiers.

"No—no," said the cute African, "I've got to go down and tell the cavalry pickets, and can't wait a second." So off he sprang, with a bound, running for dear life—the rebs, discovering the ruse, chasing him for three miles, and he running six, when he got safely into camp, but minus his chickens, which he had dropped at the first fire.

A GOOD USE OF ROMAN CANDLES.

The construction of the firework called the Roman candle is known to most of our readers, and the fact is familiar that when fired they project, in succession, and at intervals of about three seconds, a number of brilliantly luminous balls. These balls are thrown many feet, and cast a clear light for two or three seconds.

We doubt whether the military use of the candles we instance has ever before been made:

At the siege of Knoxville, the enemy attempted to storm before daylight one of the forts—we have forgotten the name, but it was the one before which the wires which so conveniently tripped up the enemy were arranged. In this fort was stationed Lieutenant Charles Herzog, of the Signal Corps, and as a part of his equipment, he was furnished with twenty or thirty Roman candles, containing about twelve balls each. When used as signals, the candles are fired vertically, and the balls are visible at a great distance.

The lieutenant knew of this use of his candles, but it needed the inspiration of battle to develop the other. He had it. Before dawn, one day, the pickets were driven in, and the enemy were swarming after them. They came on over a crest about eight hundred yards distant, and our great guns opened, but the aim was wild—there was need of light. LIGHT there *must* be, or the heavy masses thronging up to the work would sweep its parapet, and the day was lost. Then came the inspiration. At the first alarm the faithful officer had sent his signal-balls whirling into the air, announcing the alarm to every distant station. With the gleam of its balls an idea gleamed upon him. His action, as it, was instant. Putting his match to another candle, he aimed it fairly over the heads of the enemy, and as they came closing up, the sparkling balls, hanging over them, revealed to Johnny Reb not only that there was to be no surprise of that fort, but that his own dark ways were to be lighted. The experiment was a success. The great crowd of charging rebels stood out in fair relief in the glare—the distance had lessened to about three hundred yards—and our pieces, crammed with canister, opened on a mark perhaps as good as could have been had by daylight—only the light was not continuous. The staunch lieutenant did not fail in expedients. He sent half his candles by one of his assistants to the opposite angle of the fort, and then they opened fire together, crossing fire above and in front of the enemy. Now a ball was in the air all the time. Those who have seen batterries of Roman candles at displays of fireworks, can appreciate the effect. It puzzled the enemy, and it amazed them; many of the wild white trash had never seen a Roman candle; how could they tell but these were some infernal explosions of "Yankee device?" It lighted up all the ground to the very edge of the ditch, and musketry and cannon shot swept into their ranks in storms. That they came on and bravely, we know, and that they left in front of the work, more in dead and wounded, by almost twice, than its garrison. It was useless. They were fairly and thoroughly whipped. In twenty minutes all was over, and the last of Herzog's candles lighted up a completely baffled enemy.

Trying to Persuade Mr. Greeley to Enlist.—One of the New York dailies, in 1861, got off the following very good story, of the efforts of some of the Duryea

Zouaves, to persuade the "philosopher" of the *Tribune* to enlist in their regiment.

While walking up the Bowery, a few days ago, we noticed a small-sized crowd in front of the recruiting office of Duryea's Zouaves, between Hester and Grand streets. Upon coming up to the gathering, we discovered the well-known figure of Horace Greeley, surrounded by some half-dozen red-breeched and turbaned soldiers.

"Come, Mr. Greeley!" exclaimed a strapping fellow, who stood six feet high and was proportionably broad across the chest and shoulders, "now's your time to enlist! We give one hundred and eighty-eight dollars bounty to day. Wont you go to the war with us?"

"Gentlemen!" answered the philosopher, "it's impossible. I am too old; besides, I am doing a great deal more service at home."

"Then you wont go?" asked another Zouave.

"I cannot do it, my friend," replied Horace.

"You aint afraid, are you? You don't know how well you'd look, until you saw yourself dressed up in Zouave uniform," chimed in another.

"I have no doubt I should cut a pretty figure in your dress——"

"Especially if you wore a white coat," interrupted a waggish bystander.

"But that is nothing, my friends. Dress neither makes men nor soldiers. Principle, good character, good habits, and resolution are every thing."

"Oh yes, that's all right—but that aint enlisting," persisted the first speaker. "Uncle Sam wants soldiers, and talking or writing isn't the thing. There's lots of men older than you in the ranks, and any quantity of editors, reporters, and printers. If a few men like you enlisted, our regiments would soon fill up."

"That is true—but it is impossible for me to join you," continued Horace.

"You'd soon get a chance to wear the straps. Maybe you might sport a spread eagle," put in another Zou-zou, persuasively.

"No, no; gentlemen. I must leave you; but,"—turning around in a quiet manner and eyeing the crowd, which by this time was considerable, "perhaps some of these citizens I see gathered about you will volunteer. If any one will do so, I will give an extra bounty. Does any one wish to join?"

At this unexpected offer the crowd began to give way and scatter about, while several proposed three cheers for the white-coated philosopher. We did not hear whether Greeley secured any recruits by his extra bounty; but he soon after moved off, followed by the Zou-zous, who laughed quite heartily at the attempt made to entrap Horace into the Union army.

PART IV.

DEEDS OF HEROIC COURAGE AND SELF-SACRIFICE.

THE FIGHT WITH THE "ALBEMARLE."

One of the most remarkable naval conflicts of this or any other war—a single-handed encounter between a delicate river steamer and a most formidable "iron-clad" —occurred on the 5th of May, 1864, in Albemarle sound, about twenty miles below the mouth of the Roanoke river. On the afternoon of that day, three side-wheel gunboats, the "Mattabesett," "Sassacus," and "Wyalusing," were lying at anchor in the sound, awaiting the appearance of the "Albemarle," a most formidable rebel iron-clad ram, whose recent exploits in sinking two of our gunboats, near Plymouth, rendered the prolonged occupation of the sound by our forces somewhat uncertain and problematical. To the three vessels above named had been especially assigned the duty of encountering and, if possible, destroying this dreaded iron monster; and, on the afternoon in question, an advance-guard of picket boats, comprising four or five of the smaller vessels of the Union fleet, with the "Miami," had been sent up to the mouth of the Roanoke, with the design of decoying the rebel "ram" from under the protection of the batteries at Plymouth into the open waters of the sound. The ruse succeeded, and falling back before the "Albemarle," as she left her moorings to pursue them, they quickly drew her into a favorable position for attack. Shortly after three P. M., in obedience to signals from the "Mattabesett," the three vessels got under way, and forming in line ahead, in the order in which their names are above written, proceeded at ordinary speed up the sound. At four P. M. the "Mattabesett" communicated with the army transport "Massasoit," coming down, and immediately signalled to her consorts the "ram is out." Almost at the same instant they discovered the picket boats falling back slowly before the advancing foe; and beyond them a glistening speck upon the waters, with two other dark objects hovering near, which they knew to be the ram, accompanied by her consorts. The Union vessels were now cleared for action, and every preparation was made for a determined struggle with their formidable antagonist, toward whom they were driving under full steam. The day was charming, the broad expanse of water was undisturbed by a ripple, while the sun's beams were dazzlingly reflected from the inclined sides of the "Albemarle," till she seemed like a mass of silver, while above her waved an unusually large and handsome Confederate flag. The rebels were now seen to be communicating by boats, and one of their vessels, a white, stern-wheel steamer, which was afterward ascertained to be the "Cotton Plant," *cotton-clad*, and manned by two hundred sharpshooters and boarders, put hastily back to Plymouth. The other steamer, which proved to be the "Bombshell," closed up on the "ram's" quarter, in readiness for the coming conflict.

Sweeping gracefully along, under a full head of steam, the Union vessels approached, and while the "Mattabesett" hauled up abreast of the "Albemarle," the "Miami," some distance astern, threw a good but ineffectual shot, to which the "ram" promptly responded from guns that were evidently of the heaviest calibre. Almost at the same moment the "Mattabesett" delivered her full broadside, at three hundred yards' distance, and sweeping round the "ram's" stern, ran by the "Bombshell," close aboard, while the latter lay in the quarter post of the "ram." The "Sassacus" now entered the fight, and the "ram," which had failed to get at the "Mattabesett" as she swept by, turned her bow squarely for the former, whose pilot, quickly measuring the distance, sheered his vessel slightly, and passed some one hundred and fifty yards ahead of the "Albemarle," the "Sassacus" delivering with precision her whole broadside of solid shot, which, however, rebounded from the iron-clad like cork balls. Then, sweeping around the stern of the "Albemarle," the "Sassacus" paid her attentions to the "Bombshell," by whose sharpshooters she had been considerably annoyed, and poured into her hull a full broadside, which brought the rebel ensign down, and sent the white flag up in short order. Directing her to drop out of fire and anchor, which order was promptly executed in good faith, the "Sassacus" turned again to the "Albemarle," whom she found hotly engaged by the "Mattabesett" and "Wyalusing." The latter was particularly attracting the attention of the "ram," which was steaming slowly, though using her guns rapidly and with effect, and whose whole side was just then most opportunely exposed to the "Sassacus," now only some eight hundred yards distant. Comprehending, at a glance, the value of the opportunity thus offered, the gallant captain of the "Sassacus" unhesitatingly gave a preconcerted signal, "four bells," again and again repeated, to the engineer, and the ship was headed straight for what was supposed to be the "ram's" weakest part, where the casemate or house joined the hull. The fires were clear, and with thirty pounds of steam on, and throttle wide open, the "Sassacus" dashed upon her adversary, under a headway of nine or ten knots, striking her a fair, square, right-angled blow, without glance or slide! The iron-clad reeled under the blow, and her black hull was forced under water by the bow of the "Sassacus," till the water flowed over it from side to side, and it seemed as if the monster was sinking. "As we struck her," says one of the participants in the fight, "the 'ram' drove a one hundred pounder Brooke's shot through and through us, from starboard bow to port side. Our stem was forced into her side, and keeping up our headway we careened her down beneath our weight, and pushed her like an inert mass beneath our weight, while, in profound silence, our gunners were training their heavy ordnance to bear upon our astonished enemy. Now a black muzzle protrudes from the 'ram's' open port, and the loaders of our Parrott rifle, standing on the slide, served the gun within fifteen feet of that yawning cannon's mouth. It was a grand reproduction of the *old days* of 'broadside to broadside,' and 'yard-arm locked to yard;' but the immense guns, now grinning defiance across the few feet of space which separated them, each one carrying the weight of metal of a whole tier of the old time carronades, rendered this duel of ponderous ordnance a magnificent and imposing spectacle.

"Still we pushed her broadside-to before us, our engine at full speed, pressing our bow deeper and deeper into her. Still she gave way. * * * It was a grapple for life. A silent but fearful struggle for the mastery, relieved only by the sharp, scattering volleys of musketry, the whizzing of leaden bullets, and the deep, muffled explosion of hand grenades, which the brave fellow in our foretop was flinging in the enemy's hatch, driving back their sharpshooters, and creating consternation and dismay among the closely packed crew of the iron-clad; but not until our pilot house and smoke stack had been spattered all over with the indentation of rifle balls. No one had yet fallen. We had thrown shot and shell square into her ports from our rifle guns on the hurricane deck, and driven volley after volley of musketry through every aperture in her iron shield, and now our heavy one hundred pounder was training for another crushing blow."

At this juncture, the sharp, false stern of the "Sassacus," which had cut deeply into the side of the ram, gave way under the pressure, and the two vessels swung around abreast of each other, their guns thundering away with simultaneous roar. At the same moment a shot from the "Albemarle" pierced the boiler of the "Sassacus," and then was heard the terrible sound of unloosed, unmanageable steam, rushing in tremendous volumes, seething and hissing as it spread, till both combatants were enveloped and hidden in the dense, suffocating vapor. Now the contest deepened in intensity, it was a savage fight for life. The gunners of the

"Sassacus" felt that their only chance of injuring their antagonist was to throw their shots with accuracy into her open ports, and that upon their own frail wooden vessel the enemy's every shot would tell with terrible effect. Muzzle to muzzle, the guns were served and fired, the powder from those of the "Albemarle" blackening the bows and side of the "Sassacus," as they passed within ten feet. A solid shot from the latter's hundred pounder struck the "Albemarle's" port sill, and crumbled into fragments, one piece rebounding to the deck of the "Sassacus," and the rest entering the port hole and silencing the enemy's gun. Through the same opening, followed, in rapid succession, a nine inch solid shot, and a twenty pounder shell, and as the tough-hided "ram" drifted clear, the starboard wheel of the "Sassacus" ground over her quarter, smashing the launches that she was towing into shapeless drift wood, and grating over the sharp iron plates with a raw, dismal sound. Then, as the "ram" passed the wheel of the "Sassacus," the crew of the latter drove solid shot into her ports from their after guns—and her armor was rent by a solid shot from the Parrott rifle gun, which, however, had received such damage to its elevating screw that it could not be depressed so as to fire into the enemy's ports. All this cool gunnery and precise artillery practice transpired while the ship, from fire room to hurricane deck, was shrouded in one dense cloud of fiery steam. The situation was appalling as imagination can conceive. The shrieks of the scalded and dying sufferers, rushing frantically up from below, the shrivelled flesh hanging shred-like from their tortured limbs, the engine without control, surging and revolving without check or guide, abandoned by all save the heroic engineer, who, scalded, blackened, sightless, still stood to his post with an indomitable will which no agony of pain could swerve from his duty, and whose clear voice, sounding out from amidst that mass of unloosed steam and uncontrollable machinery, urged his men to return with him into the fire room, to drag the fires from beneath the uninjured boiler, now in imminent danger of explosion. His marvellous fortitude in that hour of intense agony, aided by the bravery of his assistants, saved the lives of the two hundred persons on board the ship—for, as there was no means of instantly cutting off communication between the two boilers, and all the steam in both rushed out like a flash, the vessel was exposed to the additional horror of *fire*. All this time, in the midst of this thick white cloud of stifling vapor, the "Sassacus" moved on, working slowly ahead on a vacuum alone; but her guns thundering steadily and indomitably against her adversary. At last, the cloud of steam lifted from off the scene of conflict, and the rebel "Albemarle" was seen gladly escaping from the close lock in which she had been held, for nearly a quarter of an hour, by her slight but stubborn antagonist. Her broad ensign trailed, draggled and torn, upon her deck, and she loooked far different from the trim, jaunty, and formidable vessel which an hour before had defied the slender river craft who had vanquished her. The gallant captain of the "Sassacus" could not refrain from giving her "another turn," and turning his vessel around, with helm "hard-a-port," which she answered slowly but steadily, she again passed down by the "Albemarle." The divisions stood at their guns, the captain calmly smoking his cigar, gave his orders with surpassing coolness, and directing the movements of his vessel with wonderful precision and relentless audacity, kept his guns at work, so long as they could be brought to bear upon the retiring foe, till the "Sassacus" was carried, by her disabled engine, slowly, gracefully, and defiantly out of range.

Of course, in this hand-to-hand fight between the "Sassacus" and "Albemarle," little aid could be rendered, at close quarters, by the former's consorts, as such aid would have merely endangered her safety. Yet, the "Wyalusing," the "Mattabesett" and the "Miami" did effective service, as opportunity offered, and the little "Whitehead," during the fiercest of the fight, steamed alongside of the iron monster, and delivered shot after shot from her one hundred pounder Parrott gun. The "Commodore Hull" and "Ceres" were also gallantly handled, and rendered all the assistance in their power.

But the main brunt of this novel and unequal engagement fell upon the "Sassacus," an inland light draught river steamer. The result, so contrary to all preconceived ideas of "iron-clad" invincibility, was eminently gratifying. The rebel gunboat "Bombshell," with four rifled guns and a large supply of ammunition, was captured, with all her officers and crew, and the "Albemarle," which was on her way to Newbern to form a junction with the rebel force then moving upon that place, was beaten with her own weapons, in a fair stand up fight, and driven back with her guns disabled, her hull terribly shaken, and leaking so badly that she was with difficulty kept afloat. Twice, also, had her flag been cut down and trailed in the water which swept over her deck. Her discomfiture proved to be the saving of Newbern, which had already been summoned to surrender by the rebel General Palmer, and undoubtedly it prevented the whole Department of North Carolina from being lost to our Government. The "Sassacus," although disabled in guns, machinery, and hull, and suffering severely in killed, wounded, and scalded, was ready, with two months' repair, to return again to active duty, staunch and strong as ever. Her exploit, on the 5th of May, 1864, justly ranks as one of the most remarkable on record, while the skill and coolness of her officers, and the indomitable bravery of her crew rivals the heroic traditions of the days of DECATUR and Commodore JOHN PAUL JONES.

THE BRAVE WISCONSIN BOY.—An example of almost superhuman endurance and spirit, as related by Dr. Voorhies, of Mississippi, a gentleman far too intelligent and skilful to be engaged in such a cause otherwise than in alleviating its miseries, is as follows:

"When, at the bombardment of Fort Henry, a young Wisconsin boy, who had by some means been made a prisoner, had his arm shattered by a ball from our gunboats, he was taken to one of the huts, where Dr. Voorhies attended to him. He had just bared the bone, when an enormous shell came crashing through the hut. The little fellow, without moving a muscle, talked with firmness during the operation of sawing the bone, when another went plunging close by them. The doctor remarked that it was getting to hot for him, and picked the boy up in his arms, and carried him into one of the bomb-proofs, where the operation was completed. The only answer of the Northerner was: 'if you think this hot, it will be a good deal too hot for you by-and-by.' 'And,' says the doctor, 'I should like to see that boy again. He is the bravest little fellow I ever saw.' "

A GALLANT BOY.—Captain Boggs, of the "Varuna," tells a story of a brave boy who was on board his vessel during the bombardment of the forts on the Mississippi river. The lad, who answers to the name of Oscar, was but thirteen years of age, but he has an old head on his shoulders, and is alert and energetic. During the hottest of the fire he was busily engaged in passing ammunition to the gunners, and narrowly escaped death when one of the terrific broadsides of the "Varuna's" rebel antagonist was poured in. Covered with dirt and begrimed with powder, he was met by Captain Boggs, who asked "where he was going in such a hurry?"

"To get a passing-box, sir; the other one was smashed by a ball!" And so, throughout the fight, the brave lad held his place and did his duty.

When the "Varuna" went down, Captain Boggs missed his boy, and thought he was among the victims of the battle. But a few minutes afterward he saw the lad gallantly swimming toward the wreck. Clambering on board of Captain Boggs' boat, he threw his hand up to his forehead, giving the usual salute, and uttering only the words, "All right, sir! I report myself on board," passed coolly to his station.

THE DESTRUCTION OF THE "ALBEMARLE."

THE rebel iron-clad ram, the "Albemarle," whose contest with and discomfiture by the "Sassacus," in May, 1864, has been previously described in this volume, and which had become a formidable obstruction to the occupation of the North Carolina sounds by the Union forces, finally met her fate in October of the same year. During the previous summer, Lieutenant W. B. Cushing, commanding the "Monticello," one of the sixteen vessels engaged in watching the "ram," conceived the plan of destroying their antagonist by means of a torpedo. Upon submitting the plan to Rear-Admiral Lee and the Navy Department, he was detached from his vessel, and sent to New York to provide the articles necessary for his purpose, and these preparations having been at last completed, he returned again to the scene of action. His plan was to affix his newly-contrived torpedo apparatus to one of the picket launches—little steamers not larger than a seventy-four's launch, but fitted with a compact engine, and designed to relieve the seamen of the fatigue of pulling about at night on the naval picket line—and of which half a dozen had been then recently built under the superintendence of Captain Boggs, of "Varuna" fame. Under Lieutenant Cushing's supervision, picket launch No. 1 was supplied with the torpedo—which was carried in a basket, fixed to a long arm, which could be propelled, at the important moment, from the vessel in such a manner as to reach the side of the vessel to be destroyed, there to be fastened, and exploded at the will of those in the torpedo boat, without serious risk to themselves. Having prepared his boat, he selected thirteen men, six of whom were officers, to assist him in the undertaking. His first attempt to reach the "Albemarle" failed, as his boat got aground, and was only with difficulty released. On the following night, however, he again set out upon his perilous duty, determined and destined, this time, to succeed. Moving cautiously, with muffled oars, up the narrow Roanoke, he skilfully eluded the observation of the numerous forts and pickets with which that river was lined, and passing within twenty yards of a picket vessel, without detection, he soon found himself abreast of the town of Plymouth. The night was very dark and stormy, and having thus cleared the pickets, the launch crossed to the other side of the river opposite the town, and sweeping round, came down upon the "Albemarle" from up the stream. The "ram" was moored near a wharf, and by the light of a large camp fire on the shore, Cushing saw a large force of infantry, and also discerned that the "ram" was protected by a boom of pine logs, which extended about twenty feet from her. The watch on the "Albemarle" knew nothing of his approach till he was close upon them, when they hailed, "What boat is that?" and were answered, "the 'Albemarle's' boat;" and the same instant the launch struck, "bows on," against the boom of logs, crushing them in about ten feet, and running its bows upon them. She was immediately greeted with a heavy and incessant infantry fire from the shore, while the ports of the "Albemarle" were opened, and a gun trained upon the daring party. Cushing promptly replied wit a dose of canister, but the gallant young fellow had enough for one man to manage. He had a line attached to his engineer's leg, to pull in lieu of bell signals; another line to detach the torpedo, and another to explode it, besides this, he managed the boom which was to place the torpedo under the vessel, and fired the howitzer with his own hand. But he coolly placed the torpedo in its place and exploded it. At the same moment he was struck on the right wrist with a musket ball, and a shell from the "Albemarle" went crashing through the launch. The whole affair was but the work of a few minutes. Each man had now to save himself as best he might. Cushing threw off his coat and shoes, and leaping into the water, struck out for the opposite shore, but the cries of one of his drowning men attracting the enemy's fire, he turned down the stream. The water was exceedingly cold, and his heavy clothing rendered it very difficult for him to keep afloat, and after about an hour's swimming he went ashore, and fell exhausted upon the bank. On coming to his senses, he found himself near a sentry and two officers, who were discussing the affair, and heard them say that Cushing was dead. Thinking that he had better increase the distance between the rebels and himself, he managed to shore himself along on his back, by working with his heels against the ground, until he reached a place of concealment.

After dark, he proceeded through the swamp for some distance, lacerating his feet and hands with the briars and oyster shells. He next day met an old negro whom he thought he could trust. The negro was frightened at Cushing's wild appearance, and tremblingly asked who he was. "I am a Yankee," replied Cushing, "and I am one of the men who blew up the 'Albemarle.'" "My golly, massa!" said the negro, "dey kill you if dey catch you. You dead gone sure." Cushing asked him if he could trust him to go into the town and bring him back the news. The negro assented, and Cushing gave him all the money he had, and sent him off. He then climbed up a tree and opened his jack-knife, the only weapon he had, and prepared for any attack which might be made.

After a time the negro came back, and to Cushing's joy, reported the "Albemarle" sunk and the people leaving the town. Cushing then went further down the river, and found a boat on the opposite bank belonging to a picket guard. He once more plunged into the chilly river, and detached the boat, but, not daring to get into it, let it drift down the river, keeping himself concealed. At last, thinking he was far enough away to elude observation, he got into the boat, and paddled for eight hours, until he reached the squadron. After hailing them, he fell into the bottom of the boat, utterly exhausted by hunger, cold, fatigue, and excitement, to the surprise of the people in the squadron, who were somewhat distrustful of him when he first hailed, thinking him a rebel who was trying some trick.

Nothing, indeed, but an overruling Providence and an iron will ever saved Cushing from death. He saw two of his men drown, who were stronger than he, and said of himself, that when he paddled his little boat, his arms and his will were the only living parts of his organization.

One man of the party returned on the "Valley City,"

having been picked up after he had travelled across the country, and been in the swamps nearly two days.

But one or two were wounded, and the larger part were captured by the rebels, being unable to extricate themselves from their perilous position among the logs of the boom, under the guns of the "ram." The "Albemarle" had one of her bows stove in by the explosion of the torpedo, and sank at her moorings within a few moments, without loss of life to her crew. Her fate opened the river to the Union forces, who quickly occupied Plymouth—the North Carolina sounds were again cleared from rebel craft, and the large fleet of vessels, which had been occupied in watching the iron-clad, were released from that arduous duty. Lieutenant Cushing, to whose intrepidity and skill the country is indebted for these results, was engaged in thirty-five fights during the war, and, exhausted as he was after this gallant exploit, made the journey to his home in Western New York, near Dunkirk, to vote, being one of those who believes that ballots are as important as bullets, in the preservation of the National life and liberties.

HETTY McEWEN.

AN INCIDENT OF THE OCCUPATION OF NASHVILLE.

BY LUCY HAMILTON HOOPER.

O Hetty McEwen! Hetty McEwen?
What were the angry rebels doing,
That autumn day, in Nashville town?
They looked aloft with oath and frown,

And saw the Stars and Stripes wave high
Against the blue of the sunny sky;
Deep was the oath, and dark the frown,
And loud the shout of "Tear it down!"

For over Nashville, far and wide,
Rebel banners the breeze defied,
Staining heaven with crimson bars;
Only the one old "Stripes and Stars"
Waved, where autumn leaves were strewing,
Round the home of Hetty McEwen.

Hetty McEwen watched that day
Where her son on his death-bed lay;
She heard the hoarse and angry cry—
The blood of "'76" rose high.
Out-flashed her eye, her cheek grew warm,
Uprose her aged stately form;
From her window, with steadfast brow,
She looked upon the crowd below.

Eyes all aflame with angry fire
Flashed on her in defiant ire,
And once more rose the angry call,
"Tear down that flag, or the house shall fall!"
Never a single inch quailed she,
Her answer rang out firm and free:
"Under the roof where that flag flies,
Now my son on his death-bed lies;
Born where that banner floated high,
'Neath its folds he shall surely die.
Not for threats nor yet for suing
Shall it fall," said Hetty McEwen.

The loyal heart and steadfast hand
Claimed respect from the traitor band;
The fiercest rebel quailed that day
before that woman stern and gray.
They went in silence, one by one—
Left her there with her dying son,

And left the old flag floating free
O'er the bravest heart in Tennessee,
To wave in loyal splendor there
Upon that treason-tainted air,
Until the rebel rule was o'er
And Nashville town was ours once more.

Came the day when Fort Donelson
Fell, and the rebel reign was done;
And into Nashville, Buell, then,
Marched with a hundred thousand men,
With waving flags and rolling drums
Past the heroine's house he comes;
He checked his steed and bared his head,
"Soldiers! salute that flag," he said;
"And cheer, boys, cheer!—give three times three
For the bravest woman in Tennessee!"

ONE OF LOGAN'S MEN.—At Fort Donelson a young man, attached to the Thirty-first Regiment of Illinois Volunteers (Colonel John A. Logan), received a musket-shot wound in the right thigh, the ball passing through the intervening flesh, and lodging in the left thigh. The boy repaired to the rear and applied to the doctor to dress his wound. He, however, manifested a peculiar reserve in the matter, requesting the doctor to keep his misfortune a secret from his comrades and officers. He then asked the surgeon if he would dress his wound at once, in order that he might be enabled to return to the fight. The surgeon told him that he was not in a condition to admit of his return, and that he had better go to the hospital; but the young brave insisted upon going back, offering as an argument in favor of it the fact that he had fired twenty-two rounds after receiving his wound, and he was confident he could fire as many more after his wound should be dressed. The surgeon found he could not prevent his returning to the field, so he attended to his wants, and the young soldier went off to rejoin his comrades in their struggle, and remained, dealing out his ammunition to good account until the day was over, as if nothing had happened to him. Several days after he returned to the doctor to have his wound redressed, and continued to pay him daily visits in his leisure hours, attending to duty in the meantime.

THE ACRE OF FIRE.—At the battle of Iuka, Captain, afterward Lieutenant-Colonel Arthur C. Ducat, then an officer of General Ord's staff, and subsequently Inspector-General of the Army of the Cumberland, seeing a division of rebels about to flank one of the Union regiments, rode up and informed Rosecrans of the danger. "Ride on and warn Stanley at once," said the general. An acre of fire, and showered with bullets, lay between them and the menaced troops. The officer looked at it, and said: "General, I have a wife and children."

"You knew that when you came here," said the general, coolly.

"I'll go, sir," was the only answer.

"Stay a moment. We must make sure of this," and hastily writing some despaches, the general called three of his orderlies. Giving a despatch to each, he said to the officer: "Now go." He started, and at intervals of about fifty yards, bearing a similar message, the orderlies followed. The officer ran the fiery gauntlet, and, his clothes pierced with bullets, and his horse reeling from a mortal wound, reached Stanley—the orderlies found their graves on that acre of fire!

GENERAL SUMNER AT FAIR OAKS.

On the first day of that severe battle, the troops were trembling under a pitiless storm of bullets, when General Sumner galloped up and down the advance line more exposed than any private in the ranks.

"What regiment is this?" he asked, as he reined in his horse in front of one of the regiments which stood firmest in that galling fire.

"The Fifteenth Massachusetts," replied a hundred voices.

"I, too, am from Massachusetts; three cheers for our old Bay State!"

And swinging his hat, the general led off, and every soldier joined in three thundering cheers. The enemy looked on in wonder at the strange episode, but was driven back by the fierce charge which followed.

The courage of the old hero was of the grandest order; it was not the mad excitement which hurries a man into deeds of valor, in the rush of battle, of which he would be incapable at any other time; it was cool, calm, and deliberate, but unfaltering.

On this occasion, as on many others, as soon as the heavy artillery began to pound, his usually mild eyes flashed fire. He removed his artificial teeth, which became troublesome in the excitement of battle, and placed them deliberately in his pocket, raised his spectacles from his eyes and let them rest upon his forehead, that he might see more clearly objects at a distance, gave his orders to his subordinates, and then galloped headlong into the thickest of the fight.

Finding his soldiers, most of whom had not before been under so severe a fire, becoming excited and uneasy, he dashed through the fire and smoke, his tall and commanding form erect, his snowy hair streaming in the wind, and as he rode along the front, where the men were falling like grass before the mower, his clear, ringing voice was heard all along the line, "Steady, men, steady! Don't be excited. When you have been soldiers as long as I, you will learn that this is nothing. Stand firm, and do your duty!"

At the end of the second day of that bloody battle of Fair Oaks, the troops which with great peril had been able to cross the Chickahominy before the bridges were carried away with the flood, were under his command; the fighting had been severe, and only parts of three shattered corps were left to resist the enemy's entire force. The situation was one of great peril, but Sumner was equal to the occasion. After making his disposition to receive an attack, he sent for General Sedgwick, his special friend, and, like himself, a man of the most undaunted courage. When he came, General Sumner said: "Sedgwick, you perceive the situation. The enemy will doubtless open upon us at daylight. Reinforcements are impossible; he can overwhelm and destroy us. But the country cannot afford to have us defeated. There is just one thing for us to do. We must stand here and die like men! Impress it upon your officers, that we must do this to the last man—to the last man! We may not meet again; good-by, Sedgwick."

The two grim soldiers shook hands and parted. Morning came, but the enemy failing to discover our perilous condition, did not renew the attack; new bridges were built, and the sacrifice averted. But Sumner was the man to have carried out his resolution to the letter.

"SUFFER MOST—LOVE MOST."—In a quiet neighborhood, where there was more latent than practical patriotism, one earnest woman succeeded, by her energy, in awakening an interest in behalf of the country and our soldiers. The clergyman of the village opened his house to this patriot woman, and all the people vied with each other in the service of preparing comforts for the soldiers. They started on blackberry brandy and cordial, and succeeded in making seventy-six gallons. One night, after the clergyman and family had retired, they were aroused by some one trying to gain admittance; they found, upon opening the door, a humble man, who was not willing to give his name, but said that his children had picked some berries for the soldiers, and that he had brought them, after his day's work was done, a distance of six miles. It was subsequently ascertained that this man had been drafted while the three hundred-dollar exemption clause was in force. With him there was no alternative. His family must starve if he left them. He therefore sacrificed every thing, save the bare necessities of life, to raise the three hundred dollars. His children were stripped of every article of clothing save one suit each, and when, during this time of rigid economy and trial, another child was born, it had literally "nothing to wear." Still this family grew strong through suffering, and learned that they who for their country's sake suffer most, love her most.

"OLD BRADLEY,"

THE TENNESSEE BLACKSMITH.

The sufferings and sacrifices of the loyal men of East Tennessee were as worthy of record as those of the Covenanters in Scotland in the time of the Primate Sharp, and their courage and daring, and their unselfish devotion to the Union and to those who, like themselves, were persecuted for their adherence to it, give life and interest to some of the most thrilling incidents of the war.

One of these incidents, as related by an East Tennessean, is the following:

Near the crossroads, not far from the Cumberland mountains, stood the village forge. The smith was a sturdy man of fifty. He was respected, wherever known, for his stern integrity. He served God, and did not fear man—and it might be safely added, nor devil either. His courage was proverbial in the neighborhood; and it was a common remark, when wishing to pay any person a high compliment, to say, "He is as brave as Old Bradley." One night, toward the close of September, as he stood alone by the anvil plying his labors, his countenance evinced a peculiar satisfaction as he brought his hammer down with a vigorous stroke on the heated iron While blowing the bellows he would occasionally pause and shake his head, as if communing with himself. He was evidently meditating upon something of a serious nature. It was during one of these pauses that the door

OLD BRADLEY.

was thrown open, and a pale, trembling figure staggered into the shop, and, sinking at the smith's feet, faintly ejaculated:

"In the name of Jesus, protect me!"

As Bradley stooped to raise the prostrate form, three men entered, the foremost one exclaiming:

"We've treed him at last! There he is! Seize him!" and as he spoke he pointed at the crouching figure.

The others advanced to obey the order, but Bradley suddenly arose, seized his sledge-hammer, and brandishing it about his head as if it were a sword, exclaimed:

"Back! Touch him not; or, by the grace of God, I'll brain ye!"

They hesitated, and stepped backward, not wishing to encounter the sturdy smith, for his countenance plainly told them that he meant what he said.

"Do you give shelter to an abolitionist?" fiercely shouted the leader.

"I give shelter to a weak, defenceless man," replied the smith.

"He is an enemy!" vociferated the leader.

"Of the devil!" ejaculated Bradley.

"He is a spy! an abolition hound!" exclaimed the leader, with increased vehemence; "and we must have him. So I tell you, Bradley, you had better not interfere. You know that you are already suspected, and if you insist upon sheltering him it will confirm it."

"*Sus-pect-ed!* Suspected of what?" exclaimed the smith, in a firm tone, riveting his gaze upon the speaker.

"Why, of adhering to the North," was the reply.

"Adhering to the North!" ejaculated Bradley, as he cast his defiant glances at the speaker. "I adhere to no North," he continued; "I adhere to my country—my whole country—and will, so help me God! as long as I have breath!" he added, as he brought the sledge-hammer to the ground with great force.

"You had better let us have him, Bradley, without further trouble. You are only risking your own neck by your interference."

"Not as long as I have life to defend him," was the answer. Then pointing toward the door, he continued: "Leave my shop!" and as he spoke he again raised the sledge-hammer.

They hesitated a moment, but the firm demeanor of the smith awed them into compliance with the order.

"You'll regret this in the morning, Bradley," said the leader, as he retreated.

"Go!" was the reply of the smith, as he pointed toward the door.

Bradley followed them menacingly to the entrance of the shop, and watched them until they disappeared from sight down the road. When he turned to go back in the shop he was met by the fugitive, who, grasping his hand, exclaimed:

"Oh! how shall I ever be able to thank you, Mr. Bradley?"

"This is no time for thanks, Mr. Peters, unless it is to the Lord; you must fly the country, and that at once."

"But my wife and children?"

"Mattie and I will attend to them. But you must go to-night."

"To-night?"

"Yes. In the morning, if not sooner, they will return with a large force and carry you off, and probably hang you on the first tree. You must leave to-night."

"But how?"

"Mattie will conduct you to the rendezvous of our friends. There is a party made up who intend to cross the mountains and join the Union forces in Kentucky. They were to start to-night. They have provisions for the journey, and will gladly share with you."

At this moment a young girl entered the shop, and hurriedly said:

"Father what is the trouble to-night?" Her eye resting upon the fugitive, she approached him, and in a sympathizing tone, continued: "Ah, Mr. Peters, has your turn come so soon?"

This was Mattie. She was a fine, rosy girl, just passed her eighteenth birthday, and the sole daughter of Bradley's house and heart. She was his all—his wife had been dead five years. He turned toward her, and in a mild but firm tone, said:

"Mattie, you must conduct Mr. Peters to the rendezvous immediately; then return, and we will call at the parsonage to cheer his family. Quick! No time is to be lost. The bloodhounds are upon the track. They have scented their prey, and will not rest until they have secured him. They may return much sooner than we expect. So haste, daughter, and God bless ye!"

This was not the first time that Mattie had been called upon to perform such an office. She had safely conducted several Union men, who had been hunted from their homes, and sought shelter with her father, to the place designated, from whence they made their escape across the mountains into Kentucky. Turning to the fugitive, she said:

"Come, Mr. Peters, do not stand upon ceremony, but follow me."

She left the shop, and proceeded but a short distance up the road, and then turned off in a by-path through a strip of woods, closely followed by the fugitive. A brisk walk of half an hour brought them to a small house that stood alone in a secluded spot. Here Mattie was received with a warm welcome by several men, some of whom were engaged in running bullets, while others were cleaning their rifles and fowling-pieces. The lady of the house, a hale woman of forty, was busy stuffing the wallets of the men with biscuits. She greeted Mattie very kindly. The fugitive, who was known to two or three of the party, was received in a bluff, frank spirit of kindness by all, saying that they would make him chaplain of the Tennessee Union regiment, when they got to Kentucky.

When Mattie was about to return home, two of the party prepared to accompany her; but she protested, warning them of the danger, as the enemy were doubtless abroad in search of the minister. But, notwithstanding, they insisted, and accompanied her, until she reached the road, a short distance above her father's shop. Mattie hurried on, but was somewhat surprised on reaching the shop to find it vacant. She hastened into the house, but her father was not there. As she returned to go into the shop, she thought she could hear the noise of horses' hoofs clattering down the road. She listened, but the sound soon died away. Going into the shop she blew the fire into a blaze; then beheld that the things were in great confusion, and that spots of blood were upon the ground. She was now convinced that her father had been seized and carried off, but not without a desperate struggle on his part.

As Mattie stood gazing at the pools of blood, a wagon containing two persons drove up, one of whom, an athletic young man of five-and-twenty years, got out and entered the shop.

"Good-evening, Mattie! Where is your father?" he said. Then observing the strange demeanor of the girl, he continued, "Why, Mattie, what ails you? What has happened?"

The young girl's heart was too full for her tongue to give utterance, and throwing herself upon the shoulder of the young man, she sobbingly exclaimed:

"*They* have carried him off! Don't you see the blood?"

"Have they dared to lay hands upon your father? The infernal wretches!"

Mattie recovered herself sufficiently to narrate the events of the evening. When she had finished, he exclaimed:

"Oh, that I should have lived to see the day that old Tennessee was to be thus disgraced! Here, Joe!"

At this, the other person in the wagon alighted and entered the shop. He was a stalwart negro.

"Joe," continued the young man, "you would like your freedom?"

"Well, Massa John, I wouldn't like much to leave you, but den I'se like to be a free man."

"Joe, the white race have maintained their liberty by their valor. Are you willing to fight for yours! Ay! fight to the death!"

"I'se fight for yous any time, Massa John."

"I believe you, Joe. But I have desperate work on hand to-night, and I do not want you to engage in it without a prospect of reward. If I succeed, I will make you a free man. It is a matter of life and death—will you go?"

"I will, massa."

"Then kneel down, and swear before the everliving God, that, if you falter or shrink the danger, you may hereafter be consigned to everlasting fire!"

"I swear, massa," said the negro, kneeling. "An' I hope that Gor Almighty may strike me dead if I don't go wid you through fire and water, and ebery ting!"

"I am satisfied, Joe," said his master; then turning to the young girl, who had been a mute spectator of this singular scene, he continued: "Now, Mattie, you get in the wagon and I'll drive down to the parsonage, and you remain there with Mrs. Peters and the children until I bring you some intelligence of your father."

While the sturdy old blacksmith was awaiting the return of his daughter, the party that he had repulsed returned with increased numbers and demanded the minister. A fierce quarrel ensued, which resulted in their seizing the smith and carrying him off. They conveyed him to a tavern half a mile distant from the shop, and there he was arraigned before what was termed a vigilance committee. The committee met in a long room on the ground-floor, dim y lighted by a lamp which stood upon a small table in front of the chairman.

THE PRICE OF LOYALTY IN EAST TENNESSEE.

In about half an hour after Bradley's arrival he was placed before the chairman for examination. The old man's arms were pinioned, but nevertheless he cast a defiant look upon those around him.

"Bradley, this is a grave charge against you. What have you to say?" said the chairman.

"What authority have you to ask?" demanded the smith, fiercely eyeing his interrogator.

"The authority of the people of Tennessee," was the reply.

"I deny it."

"Your denials amount to nothing. You are accused of harboring an abolitionist, and the penalty of that act, you know, is death. What have you to say to the charge?"

"I say that it is a lie, and that he who utters such charges against me is a scoundrel."

"Simpson," said the chairman to the leader of the band that had captured Bradley, and who now appeared with a large bandage about his head, to bind up a wound which was the result of a blow from the fist of Bradley. "Simpson," continued the chairman, "what have you to say?"

The leader then stated that he had tracked the preacher to the blacksmith shop, and that Bradley had resisted his arrest, and that upon their return he could not be found, and that the prisoner refused to give any information concerning him.

"Do you hear that, Mr. Bradley?" said the chairman.

"I do. What of it?" was the reply.

"Is it true?'

"Yes."

"Where is the preacher?"

"That is none of your business."

"Mr. Bradley, this tribunal is not to be insulted with impunity. I again demand to know where Mr. Peters is? Will you tell?"

"No."

"Mr. Bradley, it is well known that you are not only a member but an exhorter in Mr. Peters's church, and therefore some little excuse is to be made for your zeal in defending him. He is from the North, and has long been suspected, and is now accused of being an abolitionist and a dangerous man. You do not deny sheltering him, and refusing to give him up. If you persist in this you must take the consequences. I ask you for the last time if you will inform us of his whereabouts?"

"And again I answer no!"

"Mr. Bradley, there is also another serious charge against you, and your conduct in this instance confirms it. You are accused of giving comfort to the enemies of your country. What have you to say to that?"

"I say it is false, and that he who makes it is a villain."

"I accuse him with being a traitor, aiding the cause of the Union," said Simpson.

"If my adherence to the Union merits for me the name of traitor, then I am proud of it. I have been for the Union—I am still for the Union—and will be for the Union as long as life lasts."

At these words the chairman clutched a pistol that lay upon the table before him, and the bright blade of Simpson's Bowie knife glittered near Bradley's breast; but before he could make the fatal plunge, a swift-winged messenger of death laid him dead at the feet of his intended victim; while at the same instant another plunged into the heart of the chairman, and he fell forward over the table, extinguishing the lights, and leaving all in darkness. Confusion reigned. The inmates of the room were panic-stricken. In the midst of the consternation a firm hand rested upon Bradley's shoulder; his bonds were severed, and he hurried out of the open window. He was again a free man, but was hastened forward into the woods at the back of the tavern, and through them to a road a quarter of a mile distant, then into a wagon, and driven rapidly off. In half an hour the smith made one of the party at the rendezvous that was to start at midnight across the mountains.

"John," said the smith, as he grasped the hand of his rescuer, while his eyes glistened, and a tear coursed down his furrowed cheek, "I should like to see Mattie before I go."

"You shall," was the reply.

In another hour the blacksmith clasped his daughter to his bosom.

It was an affecting scene—there, in that lone house in the wilderness, surrounded by men who had been driven from their homes for their attachment to the principles for which their patriot fathers fought and bled —the sturdy old smith, a type of the heroes of other days, pressing his daughter to his breast, while the tears coursed down his furrowed cheek. He felt that perhaps it was to be his last embrace; for his resolute heart had resolved to sacrifice his all upon the altar of his country, and he could no longer watch over the safety of his only child. Was she to be left to the mercy of the parricidal wretches who were attempting to destroy the country that had given them birth, nursed their infancy, and opened a wide field for them to display the abilities with which nature had endowed them?

"Mr. Bradley," said his rescuer, after a short pause, "as you leave the State it will be necessary, in these troublous times, for Mattie to have a protector, and I have thought that our marriage had better take place to-night."

"Well, John," he said, as he relinquished his embrace and gazed with a fond look at her who was so dear to him, "I shall not object, if Mattie is willing."

"Oh! we arranged that as we came along," replied the young man.

Mattie blushed, but said nothing.

In a short time the hunted-down minister was called upon to perform a marriage service in that lone house It was an impressive scene. Yet no diamonds glittered upon the neck of the bride; no pearls looped up her tresses; but a pure love glowed within her heart as she gave utterance to a vow which was registered in heaven.

Bradley, soon after the ceremony, bade his daughter and her husband an affectionate farewell, and set out with his friends to join others who had been driven from their homes, and were now rallying under the old flag to fight for the Union, and, as they said, "Redeem old Tennessee!"

JOHN DAVIS THE HEROIC SAILOR.—When the record of the war comes to be written, not the least interesting feature of it will be the heroic deeds of the humble men who compose the rank and file of the army and navy. Instances of individual heroism and self-sacrifice are already presenting themselves in abundance, and when the conflict is happily ended, will furnish a rich harvest of materials for the annalist and historian. One of the most conspicuous of these in any chronicle of the war, must be the case of the gallant tar, John Davis, whose courage in the attack on Elizabeth City, N. C., was made the subject of special mention by his immediate commander and by Commodore Goldsborough, who thus united to make manifest the bond of true chivalry, which binds together all brave men, however widely seperated their station. The following is the story of this brave sailor :—

"Lieutenant J. C. Chapin, commanding United States steamer "Valley City," off Roanoke Island, writing to Commodore Goldsborough, noticed a magnanimous act of bravery by John Davis, gunner's mate on board his vessel, at the taking of Elizabeth City. He says John Davis was at his station during the action, in the magazine, issuing powder, when a shell from the enemy's battery penetrated into the magazine, and exploded outside of it. He threw himself over a barrel of powder, protecting it with his own body from the fire, while at the same time passing out the powder for the guns.

"Commodore Goldsborough, in transmitting this letter to the Navy Department, says: 'It affords me infinite pleasure to forward this communication to the Navy Department, to whose especial consideration I beg leave to recommend the gallant and noble sailor alluded to;' and he adds, in a postscript, 'Davis actually seated himself on the barrel, the top being out, and in this position he remained until the flames were extinguished.'"

The Navy Department promptly rewarded him. He was a gunner's mate, receiving a salary of twenty-five dollars per month or three hundred dollars per year. The evidence of his bravery was received at the Navy Department, and on the next day Secretary Welles appointed him a gunner, an office which carries with it a salary of one thousand dollars per year, and is a life appointment, the salary increasing by length of service to one thousand four hundred and fifty dollars, and the medal of honor was conferred upon him, by order of Congress.

DRIVING HOME THE COWS.

BY MISS KATE P. OSGOOD.

Out of the clover and blue-eyed grass
He turned them into the river-lane;
One after another he let them pass,
Then fastened the meadow bars again.

Under the willows, and over the hill,
He patiently followed their sober pace;
The merry whistle for once was still,
And something shadowed the sunny face.

Only a boy! and his father had said
He never could let his youngest go:
Two already were lying dead
Under the feet of the trampling foe.

But after the evening work was done,
And the frogs were loud in the meadow-swamp,
Over his shoulder he slung his gun
And stealthily followed the foot-path damp.

DRIVING HOME THE COWS.

Across the clover, and through the wheat,
  with resolute heart and purpose grim,
Though cold was the dew on his hurrying feet,
  And the blind bat's flitting startled him.

Thrice since then had the lanes been white,
  And the orchards sweet with apple-bloom;
And now, when the cows came back at night,
  The feeble father drove them home.

For news had come to the lonely farm
  That three were lying where two had lain;
And the old man's tremulous, palsied arm
  Could never lean on a son's again.

The summer day grew cool and late,
  He went for the cows when the work was done;
But down the lane, as he opened the gate,
  He saw them coming one by one:

Brindle, Ebony, Speckle, and Bess,
  Shaking their horns in the evening wind;
Cropping the butter-cups out of the grass—
  But who was it following close behind?

Loosely swung in the idle air
  The empty sleeve of army blue;
And worn and pale, from the crisping hair,
  Looked out a face that the father knew.

For Southern prisons will sometimes yawn,
  And yield their dead unto life again;
And the day that comes with a cloudy dawn
  In golden glory at last may wane.

The great tears sprang to their meeting eyes;
  For the heart must speak when the lips are dumb;
And under the silent evening skies
  Together they followe. the cattle home.

THE LOYALTY OF A CHARLESTON WOMAN.

WIDE spread as was the heresy of secession, and boastful as the rebels were that the entire population of most of the Southern States were radically and thoroughly secessionists, there was, in fact, no part of the South in which there were not earnest and devoted friends of freedom and Union among the whites. The negroes were almost without exception loyal. Even Charleston, hotbed of treason as it was, had its loyal league of Union men and women, who, at the peril of liberty and life, performed acts of kindness to Union prisoners confined there, aided them in escaping, and gave them shelter, food, and clothing, till they could get away from the city. Captain W. H. Telford, of the Fiftieth Pennsylvania Volunteers, escaped from Roper Hospital Prison, in Charleston, and was for five weeks concealed by these devoted Unionists. He relates an incident which occurred to one of the party who escaped with him, which shows the great peril to which the members of the league sometimes subjected themselves to serve the cause they loved. It should be premised that some of the male members of the league had wives who were very bitter rebels, and some of the ladies who were loyal had husbands who were actively engaged in the rebel cause.

The escaped prisoners had remained for several days closely concealed by a trusty member of the league, in consequence of the excitement in the city over the report that Yankee prisoners were being harbored by some of the inhabitants, a report which rendered it unsafe for them to be seen in the streets, even in disguise. One evening, however, one of the party ventured to call upon one of the loyal ladies who had been so kind to them, but whose husband was a bitter rebel, engaged in blockade running, and was at that time away.

While enjoying the pleasant hours of the evening with his loyal friend steps were heard in the front yard, and soon the voice of the husband was heard in the hall. There was no opportunity of escape, and the only thing that could be done was to hide and trust to luck. But *where?* was another difficult question.

A closet in the lady's bedroom was the only refuge. Mrs. —— hurried him into it, and was just fastening the door when her husband stood at the bedroom door, and trying it *found it locked.* She sprung to open it, and encountered her liege lord in a towering passion, who demanded to know the cause of this strange proceeding.

He at once accused her of infidelity, of receiving visits from gentlemen in his absence, and said, further, that he had heard one in the house when he came in, and he wanted to know the whole truth of the matter.

She could only reply, in tears, that she *was true* to him; that all the visits she had ever received were only friendly ones, and she begged him not to condemn her but to believe what she told him.

He was dissatisfied with this explanation, and demanded what had become of the man who was there when he came in. His wife made no reply, and he began to search the room, when, *oh, horrible!* in the closet he found a MAN full dressed in rebel uniform.

"You villain! what are you here for? Guilty, both

of you; bring me my pistol and I will punish the guilty pair. Police! help!" shouted the husband.

"Don't, my dear husband, kill him, for he is not guilty; let him go."

"Confess all, or I will kill you both," said the enraged husband.

"As God lives, we are innocent of any crime," pleaded the suffering wife.

"Away with such talk, you guilty wretches. I will not hear it," said the now infuriated husband, as he rushed out of the room to get his pistol, while the Unionist leaped out of the first window and made good his escape. How the affair ended Captain Telford never learned, as he left the city shortly after, and none of the escaped prisoners were willing to meet the enraged blockade runner again, or subject his wife to so severe a trial. *Her loyalty cost a price.*

A Wounded Color Bearer.—A touching incident in the great battle of Gettysburg will show how courage manifests itself. The color sergeant of the Sixteenth Vermont fell mortally wounded. At once a dozen men rushed forward. The poor wounded sergeant grasped the staff with both his clenched hands, his eyes were already dimmed with death; he could not see who it was that tried to wrest his charge from him. "Are you friends or enemies?" he cried out. "We are friends," was the reply, "give us the colors." "Then, friends," said he, "I am mortally wounded; let me hold up the flag till I die"—and so saying, he fell back—dead. Surely, a nobler soldier than this poor fellow never lived.

COLONEL INNIS,

OR "WE DON'T SURRENDER MUCH."

LAVERGNE, Tennessee, a mere hamlet, but a position of great strategic importance, between Nashville and Murfreesboro, Tennessee, had been garrisoned by a small Union force early in December, 1862. When General Rosecrans commenced his movement from Nashville to Murfreesboro, in the latter part of that month, the movement which culminated in the battle of Stone river, it was absolutely essential that Lavergne should be held, yet the general could spare but a small force for it, and he knew that the rebel cavalry general, Wheeler, would attack it with one greatly superior. In this emergency he knew of no one in whose bravery and unflinching resolution to hold the position against heavy odds he could so fully rely as Colonel William P. Innis of the First Michigan Engineers. Innis's regiment consisted of but three hundred and eight-nine men, and Wheeler would attack with three thousand cavalry and two field pieces, while Innis had no artillery and only some rudely extemporized breastworks. "Edmund Kirke" (Mr. J. R. Gilmore) tells the story of the battle, as he heard it from both sides, as follows:

"Colonel Innis," said General Rosecrans, "will you hold Lavergne?"

"I'll try, general."

"I ask if you will *do* it!" exclaimed the laconic general.

"I WILL," quietly responded the colonel, and he kept his word.

Just as the New Year's sun was sending its first greeting to the little band that crouched there behind the wagons, the head of the rebel column emerged from the woods which skirt the southern side of the town, and Captain Firman, riding forward to the flimsy breastwork, cried out:

"General Wheeler demands an instant and unconditional surrender."

"Give General Wheeler my compliments, and tell him we don't surrender much," came back to him from behind the brush-heaps.

Mounting then his Kentucky roan, the heroic colonel rode slowly around the rude intrenchment. "Boys," he said, "they are three thousand—have you said your prayers?"

"We are ready, colonel. Let them come on!" answered the brave Michigan men.

And they did come on!

"Six times we swept down on them," said Captain Firman to me, "and six times I rode up with a flag, and summoned them to surrender; but each time Innis sent back the message, varied, now and then, with an adjective, 'We don't surrender much.' He sat his horse during the first charges, as if on dress parade; but at the third fire I saw him go down. I thought we had winged him, but when we charged again, there he sat as cool as if the thermometer had been at zero. One of our men took deliberate aim, and again he went down; but when I rode up the fifth time and shouted, 'We'll not summon you again—surrender at once!' it was Innis who yelled out, 'Pray don't, for *we don't surrender much.*' At the seventh charge I was wounded, and the general sent another officer with the summons. Your people halted him a few hundred yards from the breastwork, and an officer, in a cavalryman's overcoat, came out to meet him. ['They had killed my two horses,' said Colonel Innis to me afterward, 'and I was afraid they would singe my uniform—the fire was *rather* hot—so I covered it.']

"'What is your rank, sir?' demanded the Union officer.

"'Major, sir.'

"'Go back and tell General Wheeler that he insults me by sending one of your rank to treat with one of mine. Tell him, too, I have not come here to surrender. I shall fire on the next flag.'

"It was Innis, and by that ruse he made us believe he had received reinforcements. Thinking it was so, we drew off, and the next day Innis sent Wheeler word by a prisoner, that he had whipped us with three hundred and eighty-nine men!"

THE BALLAD OF ISHMAEL DAY.

ONE summer morning a daring band
Of rebels rode into Maryland—
 Over the prosperous, peaceful farms
 Sending terror and strange alarms,
 The clatter of hoofs and the clarg of arms.

Fresh from the South, where the hungry pine,
They ate like Pharaoh's starving kine;
They swept the land like devouring surge,
And left their path, to its furthest verge,
Bare as the track of the locust-scourge.

"The rebels are coming!" far and near
Rang the tidings of dread and fear;
Some paled, and cowered, and sought to hide—
Some stood erect in their fearless pride—
And women shuddered and children cried.

But others—vipers in human form,
Stinging the bosom that kept them warm—
Welcomed with triumph the thievish band,
Hurried to offer the friendly hand,
As the rebels rode into Maryland:

Made them merry with food and wine,
Clad them in garments rich and fine,
For rags and hunger to make amends;
Flattered them, praised them, with selfish ends;
"Leave *us* scathless, for we are friends!"

Could traitors trust to a traitor? No!
Little they favored friend or foe,
But gathered the cattle the farms across,
Flinging back, with a scornful toss—
"If ye are *friends* ye can bear the loss!"

Flushed with triumph, and wine, and prey,
They neared the dwelling of Ishmael Day;
A sturdy veteran, gray and old,
With heart of a patriot, firm and bold,
Strong and steadfast—unbribed, unsold.

And Ishmael Day, his brave head bare,
His white locks tossed by the morning air,
Fearless of danger, or death, or scare,
Went out to raise, by the farm yard bars,
The dear old flag of the Stripes and Stars.

OLD BURNS, THE HERO OF GETTYSBURG.

Proudly, steadily up it flew,
Gorgeous with crimson and white and blue!
His withered hand, as he shook it freer,
May have trembled, but not with fear,
While, shouting, the rebels drew more near

"*Halt!*"—They had seen the hated sign
Floating free from old Ishmael's line—
"Lower that rag!" was their wrathful cry.
"Never!" rung Ishmael Day's reply;
"Fire, if it please you—I can but die!"

One, with a loud, defiant laugh,
Left his comrades and neared the staff.
"*Down!*"—came the fearless patriot's cry—
"Dare to lower that flag, and die!
One must bleed for it—you or I!"

But caring not for the stern command,
He drew the halliards with daring hand;
Ping! went the rifle-ball—down he came
Under the flag he had tried to shame—
Old Ishmael Day took careful aim!

Seventy winters and three had shed
Their snowy glories on Ishmael's head;
But though cheeks may wither and locks grow gray
His fame shall be fresh and young alway—
Honor be to old Ishmael Day!

OLD BURNS, THE HERO OF GETTYSBURG.

In the town of Gettysburg lives an old couple by the name of Burns. The old man was in the war of 1812, and is now nearly seventy years of age, yet the frosts of many winter have not chilled his patriotism or diminished his love for the old flag under which he fought in his early days. When the rebels invaded the beautiful Cumberland valley, and were marching on Gettysburg, Old Burns concluded that it was time for every loyal man, young or old, to be up and doing all in his power to beat back the rebel foe, and if possible, give them a quiet resting-place beneath the sod they were polluting with their unhallowed feet. Taking down an old state musket he had in his house, he commenced running bullets. The old lady, seeing him engaged in this work, inquired what in the world he was going to do? "Ah!" was the reply, "I thought some of the boys might want the old gun, and I am getting it ready for them." The rebels came on. The old man kept on the lookout until he saw the stars and stripes coming in, carried by our brave boys. This was more than he could stand; his patriotism got the better of his age and infirmity, seizing his musket, he started out, the old lady called after him: "Burns, where are you going?" "Oh!" was the reply, "I am going out to see what is going on." He immediately went to a Wisconsin regiment and asked if they would take him in. They told him they would, and gave him three rousing cheers. The old musket was soon thrown aside and a first-rate rifle given him, and twenty-five rounds of cartridges.

The engagement between the two armies soon came on, and the old man fired eighteen of his twenty-five rounds, and says he killed three rebs to his certain knowledge. Our forces were compelled to fall back, leaving the dead and wounded on the field, and our hero, having three wounds, was left among the rest.

Battle of Gettysburg.

There he lay in citizen's clothing, and knowing that if the enemy found him in that condition death would be his portion, so he concluded to try strategy as his only hope. Soon the rebels came up, and approached him, saying: "Old man, what are you doing here?" "I am lying here wounded, as you see," he replied. "Well, but what business have you to be here? and who wounded you, our troops or yours?" "I don't know who wounded me, I only know that I am wounded and in a bad fix." "Well, what was you doing here—what was your business?" "If you will hear my story, I will tell you. My old woman's health is very poor, and I was over across the country to get a girl to help her, and coming back, before I knew where I was I had got right into this fix and here I am." "Where do you live?" inquired the rebels. "Over in town, in such a small house." They then picked him up, and carried him home and left him. But they soon returned, as if suspecting he had been lying to them, and made him answer a great many questions; but he stuck to his old story, and failing to learn any thing more they left him for good. He says he shall always feel indebted to some of his copperhead neighbors for the last call, for he believes some one had informed them of him. Soon after they left a bullet came into his room and struck into the wall six inches above where he lay on the sofa. His wounds proved to be only flesh wounds, from which he recovered with his patriotism not a whit abated.

COOLNESS AND FORTITUDE OF A UNION SOLDIER.—An instance of endurance and patience occurred at the hospital on the right wing, during the fighting at Fort Donelson, Tennessee. The Union columns having been forced back, the hospital, which was a little up from the road, had come within range of the rebels' fire, and was fast becoming an unpleasant position, but no damage was done to it. Just about this time a poor fellow came sauntering leisurely along, with the lower part of his arm dangling from the part above the elbow, it having been struck with a grape-shot. Meeting the surgeon in the house, who was busily attending to other wounded, he inquired how long it would be before he could attend to him, and was told in a few minutes. "All right," said the wounded man, and then walked outside and watched the progress of the battle for a short time, and then returned and waited the surgeon's opportunity to attend to him. The arm was amputated without a murmur from the unfortunate man. After the stump was bound up, the young man put his good hand into his pocket, and took out a piece of tobacco, from which he took a chew, then walking over to the fire, he leaned his well arm against the mantle-piece, and rested his head against his arm, and kept squirting tobacco juice into the fire, whilst his eyes were cast into the flames, all with the most astonishing composure, as though he was indulging in some pleasant reverie. He remained in this position for some time, and then walked off and went out of sight near where the fighting was going on.

CONDUCT OF THE COLORED TROOPS.

THERE has been much dispute and many exaggerations and misstatements in relation to the efficiency of the colored troops in the war. While one party have contended that they were all and always heroes, another have insisted that "Niggers wouldn't fight—they couldn't be made to—they had seen too much of them to believe that they wouldn't run at the very first sight of a hostile white man," etc.

Both were in the wrong. Secretary Stanton, in a review of the whole course of the war, asserts that there has been no perceptible difference between the conduct of the colored and the white troops; both have often displayed extraordinary bravery at some times, and at others, under incompetent leaders, have been affected by panic, and retreated, and in proportion to their numbers, one race have acted thus as much as the other.

This testimony is remarkably creditable to the negroes. When we reflect that the greater part of the colored troops had been field hands, slaves, subject to the irresponsible will of their masters, till within a few weeks, and, in many instances, a few days of their entering the service, that they were almost entirely uneducated, and had no previous military drill or knowledge, it is astonishing that they should have done so well. There was, indeed, a material difference between the intelligent free negro regiments of the North, and those composed of freedmen recently emancipated in the South, just as there was a difference between some of the crack New England or New York regiments, composed of highly intelligent men, men whose bayonets could think, and the more stolid and less intellectual regiments of some of the rural districts, in which one third or one half were compelled to sign their names to the roll with a cross.

There were not wanting, however, instances where individual companies and regiments of the colored troops covered themselves with glory. It is the testimony of officers, not specially friendly to the negro, that no finer regiments went into battle in any part of the Union than the Fifty-fourth and Fifty-fifth Massachusetts; and their charge at Fort Wagner will be reckoned among the finest passages at arms in history. Of the former of these regiments, in this terrible and bloody assault, an eye-witness (R. S. Davis, Esq.) says: "Who fight more valiantly than the Fifty-fourth Massachusetts, as they struggle in the midst of this darkness and death to vindicate their race? They lead the advance, and follow without faltering the brave Shaw, as he ascends the wall of the fort. The parapet is reached, and their lines melt away before the terrible fire of the enemy; but they fight on, though the voice of their colonel is heard no more, and their officers have fallen in the death struggle. Their color sergeant is severely wounded in the thigh, but falling upon his knees, he plants the flag upon the parapet, and lying down holds the staff firmly in his hands. Noble Carney! Half an hour the conflict has been raging, yet the storming column has been unable to capture the fort. The supporting column (of which the Fifty-fifth

Massachusetts formed a part) comes up, and the battle rages more fiercely. What a work of death is here! The eastern angle of the fort is gained, and held by three hundred brave souls against the onsets of a superior enemy for over two hours. Who shall tell the history of these hours, with their deeds of valor more heroic than the thought of man can compass? It will never be written; for the brave and good perished unseen, and the gathering darkness of death and night covered the wounds of heroes. In the stronghold of the enemy the patriot died, God his companion, the storm of battle his death-knell. * * * * * The assault is repulsed. The small band of heroes who have fought so long and so earnestly to drive the rebels from the fort, retire from Wagner, and pass out of range over the heaps of their dead comrades. For nearly three long hours they have fought and fought in vain; Wagner cannot be carried by assault. As our forces retire, Sergeant Carney, who has kept the colors of his regiment flying upon the parapet of Wagner during the entire conflict, is seen creeping along on one knee, still holding up the flag, and only yielding his sacred trust upon finding an officer of his regiment. As he enters the field hospital, where his wounded comrades are being brought in, they cheer him and the colors. Though nearly exhausted with the loss of blood, he says, 'Boys, the old flag never touched the ground.'"

In the disastrous fight near Guntown, Mississippi, when the irresolution and mismanagement of the Union commander, a mismanagement generally attributed to intoxication, resulted in one of the most disgraceful defeats and retreats in the annals of the war, it was the half drilled colored troops, most of them under fire for the first time, who, when the white troops were completely demoralized and panic-stricken by the failure of their commander, fought with the utmost desperation, and kept back the rebels until their white comrades and a portion of the train could make good their escape. One of the ammunition wagons was near them, and the brave fellows, with the intention of maintaining their resistance to the last, filled the breasts of their shirts with cartridges, and fired away till the cartridges had become so moist with perspiration that they could not be fired. But they accomplished their object, and having held the rebels at bay for some hours they finally retreated, bringing up the rear of the Union forces.

In the Virginia campaign of 1864, "Burnside's Smoked Yankees," as they were called in the Army of the Potomac, fought with a stubbornness and tenacity which was surpassed by no troops in the army. Knowing that their doom was sealed if they were captured (for murder, or a slavery worse than death, was the fate reserved by the rebels for the colored troops), they fought to the death, and often accomplished more than their white comrades. In the capture of the outer line of forts around Petersburg they were particularly active and efficient. It is related, in regard to their assault on one of these, that having carried it, and being with some difficulty restrained from avenging the massacre of Fort Pillow on the rebel garrison, a colored lieutenant, who was just then the senior officer in command, demanded the surrender of the fort from the rebel commander. The latter, a pompous Virginian, replied, that "he would be d—d if he would surrender as a prisoner to a nigger;" the colored lieutenant remonstrated, and urged his surrender, but the Virginian, probably hoping that a white officer would be summoned to receive his surrender, refused still more peremptorily. "Very well," said the negro officer, "I have offered you your life, and you wont have it; you may stay here;" and seizing a musket from the hands of one of his men he pinned the rebel officer to the earth with the bayonet.

The most remarkable acts of heroism related of the colored troops, however, were those which occured at Port Hudson. At the time of the siege of that stronghold, there were but few colored troops in the army. Two or three regiments had been raised in New Orleans, and had joined General Banks' army before Port Hudson. Twice, it will be recollected, General Banks attempted to carry the rebel fortress by assault. On the second occasion, June 14, 1863, General H. E. Paine, leading his troops, was severely wounded in the leg, while far in advance, and left upon the ground, while his troops were driven back several hundred yards by the constant and deadly fire of the enemy, who swept the whole field with their artillery. It was of course of great importance to bring the general off the field, or if this should prove impossible, to furnish him with water and food, and to stanch the bleeding from his wound. His adjutant-general called for volunteers to go to his relief and bring him off, if possible; but the men looked upon the wide plain, swept with a constant artillery fire under which nothing could live, and though the adjutant-general offered large rewards not a man could be found willing to risk the almost ine itabl3 death which would follow the attempt. In vain the officer plead and urged; the men could not be induced to take the risk.

But now stepped forward a little squad of colored men from the "Corps d'Afrique," as General Banks had named them, and one of them acting as spokesman for the rest said to the adjutant: "We'se been thinking, sar, dat dere's got to be a good many killed in this war, 'fore our people can get deir freedom, and p'raps it may as well be we as anybody else; so if you please, sar, we'll go after the general." The adjutant-general, as may be supposed, readily accepted their offer, and there being sixteen of the volunteers, they formed into fours, and the first squad, with a stretcher and supplies of water, etc., moved off steadily across that fire-swept plain. The first fifty yards were hardly passed when one of the four was struck down; his companions did not stop, but pressed forward, when another and another, and finally the fourth fell. Without uttering a word or hesitating a moment, the second squad of four stepped out, similarly equipped, to traverse the field of death. They, too, were all smitten down, though they had approached nearer to the general than the first. Instantly and without a moment's delay, a third squad of four went forward on the perilous journey. Two of these fell wounded, but the other two reached the general, and though unable to bring him off, allayed his thrist, and remained near him amid the fiery hail till evening, when he was carried to the bivouac of the troops. These last two had also been wounded, but not severely. We think it is no impeachment of the courage of the white troops to say that in no battle of the war have they ever exhibited a cool and deliberate courage surpassing this

GENERAL RANSOM,

IN THE ASSAULT ON VICKSBURG.

THE army has lost no braver or nobler officer, in all that constitutes soldierly character and ability, than General T. E. G. Ransom. Like the French Chevalier Bayard, he was alike "*sans peur et sans reproche*," without fear and without reproach. Numerous instances are recorded of his calm and magnificent courage; one of the most remarkable is an incident appertaining to the assault on Vicksburg, on the 22d of May, 1863. His brigade formed a part of the charging column that day, and as it advanced toward the rebel breastworks a storm of grape and canister swept through it from an enfilading battery, killing or wounding many officers, and for an instant checking the whole movement. Perceiving that the men wavered, General Ransom seized the colors of a regiment, and rushing to the front, waved them over his head, and shouted, "Forward, men! We must and will go into that fort. Who will follow me?" Inspirited by this action, the column rallied about its intrepid leader, and gained the ditch in front of the fort. But the strength of the position and the commanding fire of the enemy satisfied him that the assault would prove only a useless sacrifice of life. Then, placing himself at a conspicuous point, he addressed his men in a loud, clear voice, as follows: "Men of the second brigade! we cannot maintain this position. You must retire to the cover of that ravine, one regiment at a time." He then announced the order of retiring, regiment by regiment, and added: "The first man who runs or goes beyond that ravine, shall be shot. *I will stand here,* and see how you do it." And there, in full range of the enemy's fire, he mounted a stump, from which he could see his entire command, folded his arms, and watched the movement, himself the most exposed man of the whole brigade. A captain of the Seventy-second Illinois, who had been intimate with Ransom before the war, crawled on his hands and knees to the foot of the stump, and begged the general to leave a position of so much danger. Turning his flashing eyes upon the captain for an instant, Ransom said, with an emphasis that commanded obedience, "*Silence!*" and remained where he was until the movement was accomplished.

At the battle of Sabine crossroads, where, as usual, he was always in the thickest of the fight, inspiriting his men by his presence, he was severely wounded in the left knee. On the day following the battle four surgeons examined the wound at Pleasant Hill, and were divided in their opinion—two being in favor of amputation while the other two deemed it unnecessary. The general, who was an interested listener to the conversation, raised himself on his couch and said: "Well, gentlemen, as the house is equally divided on this subject, I will, as chairman of the meeting, decide the question. I shall retain the wounded leg, loss included."

THE END.

www.ingramcontent.com/pod-product-compliance
Lightning Source LLC
LaVergne TN
LVHW021228110826
845150LV00002B/272

* 9 7 8 1 4 2 5 5 6 3 5 6 1 *